Human Capital Formation for the Fourth Industrial Revolution

Sulaiman Olusegun Atiku
Namibia University of Science and Technology, Namibia

A volume in the Advances in Human and Social Aspects of Technology (AHSAT) Book Series

IGI Global
DISSEMINATOR OF KNOWLEDGE

Published in the United States of America by
IGI Global
Business Science Reference (an imprint of IGI Global)
701 E. Chocolate Avenue
Hershey PA, USA 17033
Tel: 717-533-8845
Fax: 717-533-8661
E-mail: cust@igi-global.com
Web site: http://www.igi-global.com

Library of Congress Cataloging-in-Publication Data

Names: Atiku, Sulaiman Olusegun, 1980- editor.
Title: Human capital formation for the fourth industrial revolution / Sulaiman Olusegun Atiku, editor.
Description: Hershey, PA : Business Science Reference, [2020]
Identifiers: LCCN 2019010638| ISBN 9781522598107 (hardcover) | ISBN 9781522598121 (ebook) | ISBN 9781522598114 (softcover)
Subjects: LCSH: Human capital. | Manpower planning. | Labor supply--Effect of automation on. | Labor supply--Effect of technological innovations on.
Classification: LCC HD4904.7 .H858475 2020 | DDC 331.11--dc23 LC record available at https://lccn.loc.gov/2019010638

This book is published in the IGI Global book series Advances in Human and Social Aspects of Technology (AHSAT) (ISSN: 2328-1316; eISSN: 2328-1324)

British Cataloguing in Publication Data
A Cataloguing in Publication record for this book is available from the British Library.

Advances in Human and Social Aspects of Technology (AHSAT) Book Series

ISSN:2328-1316
EISSN:2328-1324

Editor-in-Chief: Ashish Dwivedil, The University of Hull, UK

MISSION

In recent years, the societal impact of technology has been noted as we become increasingly more connected and are presented with more digital tools and devices. With the popularity of digital devices such as cell phones and tablets, it is crucial to consider the implications of our digital dependence and the presence of technology in our everyday lives.

The **Advances in Human and Social Aspects of Technology (AHSAT) Book Series** seeks to explore the ways in which society and human beings have been affected by technology and how the technological revolution has changed the way we conduct our lives as well as our behavior. The AHSAT book series aims to publish the most cutting-edge research on human behavior and interaction with technology and the ways in which the digital age is changing society.

COVERAGE

- Human Rights and Digitization
- Technoself
- ICTs and social change
- Technology Adoption
- Human Development and Technology
- Philosophy of technology
- Cyber Behavior
- Human-Computer Interaction
- End-User Computing
- ICTs and human empowerment

The Advances in Human and Social Aspects of Technology (AHSAT) Book Series (ISSN 2328-1316) is published by IGI Global, 701 E. Chocolate Avenue, Hershey, PA 17033-1240, USA, www.igi-global.com. This series is composed of titles available for purchase individually; each title is edited to be contextually exclusive from any other title within the series. For pricing and ordering information please visit http://www.igi-global.com/book-series/advances-human-social-aspects-technology/37145. Postmaster: Send all address changes to above address.

Titles in this Series

For a list of additional titles in this series, please visit:
https://www.igi-global.com/book-series/advances-human-social-aspects-technology/37145

Human Behavior and Another Kind in Consciousness Emerging Research and Opportunities
Shigeki Sugiyama (Independent Researcher, Japan)
Information Science Reference • copyright 2019 • 102pp • H/C (ISBN: 9781522582175) • US $135.00 (our price)

Impacts of Mobile Use and Experience on Contemporary Society
Xiaoge Xu (Mobile Studies International, Singapore)
Information Science Reference • copyright 2019 • 354pp • H/C (ISBN: 9781522578857) • US $185.00 (our price)

Managing Screen Time in an Online Society
Lídia Oliveira (University of Aveiro, Portugal)
Information Science Reference • copyright 2019 • 393pp • H/C (ISBN: 9781522581635) • US $185.00 (our price)

Critical Issues Impacting Science, Technology, Society (STS), and Our Future
Heather Christina Lum (Pennsylvania State University, USA)
Information Science Reference • copyright 2019 • 345pp • H/C (ISBN: 9781522579496) • US $185.00 (our price)

Digital Humanities and Scholarly Research Trends in the Asia-Pacific
Shun-han Rebekah Wong (Hong Kong Baptist University, Hong Kong) Haipeng Li (University of California – Merced, USA) and Min Chou (New Jersey City University, USA)
Information Science Reference • copyright 2019 • 310pp • H/C (ISBN: 9781522571957) • US $195.00 (our price)

Handbook of Research on Industrial Advancement in Scientific Knowledge
Vicente González-Prida Diaz (Universidad de Sevilla, Spain & Universidad Nacional de Educación a Distancia (UNED), Spain) and Jesus Pedro Zamora Bonilla (Universidad Nacional de Educación a Distancia (UNED), Spain)

For an entire list of titles in this series, please visit:
https://www.igi-global.com/book-series/advances-human-social-aspects-technology/37145

IGI Global
DISSEMINATOR OF KNOWLEDGE

701 East Chocolate Avenue, Hershey, PA 17033, USA
Tel: 717-533-8845 x100 • Fax: 717-533-8661
E-Mail: cust@igi-global.com • www.igi-global.com

Editorial Advisory Board

Table of Contents

Detailed Table of Contents

Today's business environment is described with volatility, uncertainty, complexity, and ambiguity. In order for organizations to survive in the fourth industrial revolution characterized by continuously changing resulted from digital transformation and technological development, it is critical to identify a vision, to attract qualified human resources, to motivate them, to allocate resources to complete the mission, and to speed activities up to achieve the desired end state. It is of great significance to analyze the organization and create a competency framework to harbor all relevant steps to move the organization further. Therefore, this study aims at drawing attention to competency framework for the Industry 4.0 environment. There is no doubt that a standard competency framework for the fourth revolution may not be proposed. However, as a starting point, a generalized competency framework is proposed as a sample for further conceptual and empirical studies.

Industry 4.0 and its effect on processes and people becomes reality with all organizational and technological complex implications for the future. States around the world including Slovakia face the challenge of defining strategy on how to convert the challenges of Industry 4.0 into competitive advantage. This chapter focuses on Work 4.0 competences development, analyzed in the level of enrichment of the human capital content as well as in the level of labor market polarization. The aim of this chapter is to present opportunities and threats in competence development regarding the concept of Intelligent Industry and discuss sustainable solutions in the context of National Action Plan of Intelligent Industry of Slovak Republic, looking for win-win strategy. The authors analyze differences in competences achieved via education system in Slovakia and expectations of industry. Special attention is given the situation in Slovakia, country-oriented on automotive and with strong cooperation with Germany as innovation leader in European countries, to find strategy within this no zero game.

This chapter explores the trends in human capital formation towards building sustainable organisations. A literature review approach was adopted to investigate

HR practices which contribute to human capital formation, the contribution of human capital, as well as the barriers to human capital formation and theories of human capital formation. Human capital has been conceptualized as the collective knowledge that is embedded in the personnel, organisational routines, and network relationships of an organisation. It was found that many countries such as China, Russia, India, and Brazil are experiencing economic growth because of the investment in their human capital formation. The review of empirical studies showed that human capital has been considered as a firm's strategic resource for sustainable competitive advantage. This chapter submits that to prevent loss of human capital, it is important for organisations to create an environment and culture that will foster or encourage individual and organisational learning.

Chapter 5
Human Capital Management in the Fourth Industrial Revolution....................100
Vivence Kalitanyi, University of Johannesburg, South Africa
Geoff A. Goldman, University of Johannesburg, South Africa

This chapter identifies the drivers and challenges of the fourth industrial revolution. The fourth industrial revolution consists of artificial intelligence, big data, robotics, and many others technological innovations. The recent transformation in the global environment is affecting the way businesses are conducted, managed, and the way governments and societies are run. Today, business analysts are faced with the challenge of managing both human and digital workforce effectively without making any stakeholder in the business environment worse off. Hence, human capital management in the fourth industrial revolution involves effective development and deployment of human resources, artificial intelligence, and robotics to achieve organisational goals and objectives. It is expected that the principles underlying human capital management—planning, staffing, development, compensation, and investment in digital workforce—will become more intense and complex.

Chapter 6
The Future of Workforce Planning 127
Ayansola Olatunji Ayandibu, University of Zululand, South Africa
Irrshad Kaseeram, University of Zululand, South Africa

This chapter examines the future of workforce planning in contemporary work organisations. Workforce planning is regarded as one of the essential human resource management (HRM) activities in recent times. The reason is that it gives indication on areas of needs and serves as the pillar for all HRM activities such as job analysis, recruitment and selection, training and development, remuneration/rewards, and promotion. A review of empirical literature reveals that workforce planning has a strong relationship with organisational performance as well as productivity. This chapter submits that HR metrics and workforce analytics can be used as a tool to

Human capital development is important for organizations and most industries in the United States of America (USA). In the healthcare industry, human capital development is a priority due to the variety of skilled and unique positions within one of the most regulated industries within the USA. Integration of work processes, operational efficiencies, and assimilating regulatory changes are a pre-requisite for human resource professionals to remain competitive as well as remain operationally relevant. Information technology adoption in healthcare must continue to improve to address some of the industry's largest challenges: turnover, retention, and education. The intent of this chapter is to outline the existing challenges of human capital development in healthcare and how information technology provides significant value to closing the gaps of the alarming trends that exist in the industry.

The importance of technology in advancing experiential learning and building entrepreneurs that can withstand the challenges and explore the opportunities in the fourth industrial revolution are enormous. The chapter adopted a literature review approach to establish the link between technology incubator and entrepreneurship development. The concepts of technology incubator and entrepreneurship development as well as other related concepts were extensively discussed. It identifies the need for adequate investments toward tech entrepreneurship development and tech-savvy for the future through technology incubation programmes. Such programmes set to aid innovativeness, creating jobs, fast-tracking research to industry linkages, building wealth by fostering the formation of new ventures, among others. The chapter concludes that institutions for entrepreneurship development need to shift their tents to cover major areas of technological revolution, particularly technological incubation to promote entrepreneurship development in Industry 4.0.

This chapter examines disclosure practices of intellectual capital in the Sri Lankan context. The chapter provides an empirical analysis to showcase the relationship between intellectual capital reporting and the management perception. The three capital components identified in the intellectual capital are human capital, organizational capital, and social capital. Those capitals give a considerable contribution on the wealth of the organization and the main problem is the subjectivity and complexity of the disclosure practices of the listed companies in Colombo Stock Exchange from

Foreword

One of the fundamental necessities of continuing globalization of modern work has been the primary linkage of education and organized training to the probability of success of work organizational systems, particularly in the long term. Apparently, this is more-so with the amazing compounding effects of the increasing ascendancy and popular embrace of seemingly revolutionary agents of contemporary workplace management, such as artificial intelligence, big data, robot technology, related innovations and their general applications to industry and strategic organization. The underlying logic is that purposive organizations should continuously leverage on such pivotal managerial functions like education and training to robustly develop and positively harness (utilize) critical human capital for purposes of the longitudinal pursuit and fulfilment of their founding objectives. It is against the foregoing backdrop that the underlying salience of this book output can be generally appreciated. More specifically, the book acknowledges as well as reinforces the nexus of the educational system within the framework of the fourth industrial revolution. The book also basically underscores the importance of the continuous development of industrial competencies, definable in terms of the possession of knowledge, tool skills, associated positive attitudes to work, and other individualized but work-centered traits (or "KSAOs", in human resource management parlance) – which are often absolutely required for the achievement of aggregate productivity and performance, while the latter outcome also tends to constitute the bottom line of rational business and organizational management.

The book also provides case illustrations of the contextual problems and prospects of human capital formation and competency development in specific multinational circumstances. In the same vein, multinational patterns and trends of practices in human capital formation are documented and appreciably interrogated. In the process, the book further buttresses the role and importance of organizational environment and culture as special catalysts of successful human capital formation and promoters of positive organizational learning. Next is the additional and necessary projection of the enabling role of strategic management (itself) in the process and practice of human capital formation and/or development – the fact that favorable policies and action protocols (including adequate judicious funding) must be devised and holistically embraced to determine and drive trajectories of human capital formation/development – without which any embedded asymmetries in organizational processes and practices will summarily result in tragedies of aggregate human capital deficits, mismatches, outright costly wastages, but which are all managerially and practically avoidable. A further segment of the book is devoted to pondering the futures of human capital (or workforce) planning – in general recognition of the multifaceted dimensions of human capital formation and/or development, but also especially in affirming logical relevance of the planning function, aided by the adoption of valid metrics and measurement battery, as precursor to the achievement of well-rounded development of requisite organizational human capital.

In addition, the issue of perceived connectivity of education (and training) function to labor market participation and system functioning, particularly as applicable to employment scenarios in Sub-Sahara Africa, is further addressed in this book. This focal attention is also significant because general technological education and enhanced computer usage proficiency will continue to serve well the needs of the emerging labor markets and ideally increasingly technological-savvy workforces of the future in that part of the world. Related sundry mentions about the desirable (and indeed necessary) integration of technology and human capital development, the embrace of technology incubation culture and practices for the delivery of wider entrepreneurship education and development, the need for enduring workforce reskilling programs and practices, and acculturation of continuous or lifelong education/learning, etc, provide supplementary support and attribution in this book for the step-up of leadership role and the adoption of an integrated approach to human capital formation – again, generally in favour of the optimization and sustainability of organizational performance and productivity.

Moreover, this book output has definitely not lost sight of the equally contingent variable of workforce diversity and inclusion in the elaboration of the subject-matter. Thus, it is further noteworthy that the nexus of gender and the specific role of women workers in the human capital formation process are also duly accounted in the book – by fulfilling the necessary demand of balance in this textual information presentation. Added to the foregoing coverage of the book is the special information presentation on the concept of intellectual property and its encompassing but separable variants of human capital, organizational capital, and social capital – which are composite indicators in the reckoning of the wealth of an organization or a nation, but in this case with particular reference to organizational practices in Sri Lanka, Asia. By and large, all of the above mentions and foci in the book – which represent cross-cutting issues and definitely explicate the subject-matter of human capital formation – are very appealing and quite commendable. They particularly serve to project the central importance of this subject-matter – in ways that the success factors in the enterprise of contemporary organization and management are easily defined and identifiable in practical terms and for purposes of sustainable organizational management. This book is cosmopolitan in structure, scope and coverage. Thus, the book is highly recommended to students, scholars, social and organizational researchers, and general practitioners and professionals in the multidisciplinary and interdisciplinary fields of human resourcing, human resource planning, human resource management, human capital development, organization studies, international management, and political economy.

Olusegun Matanmi
Lagos State University, Nigeria

Preface

Advances in technological innovations, automation and latest development in artificial intelligence (AI) have revolutionised the nature of work and created a demand for new set of skills to navigate the fourth industrial revolution (industry 4.0). The Fourth Industrial Revolution is occasioned by developments in the fields such as artificial intelligence and machine-learning, robotics, nanotechnology, 3-D printing, and genetics and biotechnology, which have caused widespread disruption in business models and labour markets (World Economic Forum, 2016). Accordingly, with enormous change in the skills requirement to thrive in the new landscape. The use of AI as a form of business process improvement in recent times to attain high levels of efficiency and customers' satisfaction has taken over routine tasks from workers across the globe. To engage displaced workers, there is need to identify the new set of skills or competencies that are required in the industry 4.0. Therefore, it is necessary to equip the displaced workers with new set of skills that are essential for conversion into technical or other functional areas in the world of work. With this intervention, the fourth industrial revolution will result in significant human capital improvements (Franck & Galor, 2015). Hence, the interest of workers and the need to create more jobs should be the major concern of governments and other regulatory bodies across the globe.

The World Economic Forum (2017) submits that education and training systems have remained stagnant due to low investments in education for decades, leading to production of skills that are inadequate for the new labour markets. The higher education institutions and corporate universities world-wide need to review of their curricula in line with the new skills or competencies that are essential in the fourth industrial revolution. Such consideration and development by the higher education institutions will enhance graduate employability in the industry 4.0. The concerted efforts of the corporate universities in developing workers that are about to be displaced by AI for conversion into technical or other functional areas of the business will promote job security in the industry 4.0 (Atiku, 2018). The proposed book is intended to serve as a reference material to conventional and corporate universities on training needs assessment at individual, group and organisational or national levels, and provide a perspective shift in human capital formation based on the challenges of the industry 4.0.

OBJECTIVE OF THE BOOK

The scholarly value of the proposed publication is based on the need to revitalised human capital formation for graduate employability in the industry 4.0. Also, there is need to showcase an elaborate discussion on the new set of skills and competencies that are essential to cope with the challenges of the industry 4.0. The book seeks to provide a basis for curriculum design in line with the advances in technological innovations, automation and AI to enhance current and future employment generation. Due to the vast technological innovations, knowledge is becoming more perishable, which suggests the need for regular update of skills and poses higher demands for technical skills. The proposed publication is a qualified Reference book to its proposed target market/constituents, which will expand the knowledge in human resource development and management discipline. The proposed topic for publication will not only facilitate in bench marking human capital formation but help the conventional universities to meet skills requirements of the industry 4.0. It will also aid the institutions of management education to focus on developmental programmes essential for employment generation, exceptional performance and business sustainability in the fourth industrial revolution. The proposed publication in tends to provide a guideline for policy makers in designing and implementing effective human capital development strategies based on wide range of global issues in human capital improvements for the fourth industrial revolution.

TARGET AUDIENCE

The primary intended audience of the book is scholar-practitioners who have the need for qualified Reference material regarding the subject matter of the proposed publication as outlined. The secondary intended audience is managers, organization development specialists, consultants, educationalist, policy makers and undergraduate/ graduate business students who require the same Reference material.

TOPICS DISCUSSED IN THE BOOK

The chapters of the book address key topics human capital formation for the fourth industrial revolution such as:

- Closing the Gender Gap in Human Capital Formation
- Competency Framework for the Fourth Industrial Revolution
- Effective Integration of Technology and Human Capital Development
- Emerging Trends in Human Capital Formation
- Future of Workforce Planning
- Human Capital Formation
- Human Capital Management in the Fourth Industrial Revolution
- Intellectual Capital
- Principles of Strategic Human Capital Formation
- Reshaping Education for the New Labour Market
- Technology-Based Entrepreneurship Development
- Workforce Reskilling

ORGANISATION OF THE BOOK

This book is structured into thirteen chapters. A brief description of each of the chapters featured in the book is presented below:

Chapter 1, "Rethinking Education System for the Fourth Industrial Revolution," establishes the need for a critical review of education system with the ongoing transformation process in the fourth industrial revolution across the globe. The objective is to enhance human capital development to address the challenges and explore the opportunities of the fourth industrial revolution. The stakeholders' involvement in curricula review and adoption of innovative teaching and learning approaches is effective in meeting labour market requirements in the fourth industrial revolution. The chapter submits that teaching contents and techniques is continuously evolving, and should be structured in line with the learning objectives, students' needs and skills in high demand by employers in the fourth industrial revolution.

Chapter 2, "Competency Framework for the Fourth Industrial Revolution," discusses the set of skills or competencies essential for day-to-day activities by employees and corporations in the modern business environment; which is full of volatility, uncertainty, complexity, and ambiguity. The chapter adopted a critical literation review on human capacity building in various industries to advance competency framework for the future of work. Following the current and emerging trends in the fourth industrial revolution, the author proposes a competency framework in building human capital for the Industry 4.0. The proposed competency framework is a starting point for conceptual and operational scrutiny towards effective human capital development in the digital age.

Chapter 3, "Identification of Challenges and Opportunities for Work 4.0 Competences Developing in Slovakia," assesses the challenges and opportunities in workforce reskilling in the digital age. The chapter examines Industry 4.0 work competencies in the context of automation and polarization of labour market. The key competencies examined are grouped into fundamental and transversal competencies. In the context of job polarization and substitution for human work, it is necessary to support the formation of those skills that enable part of workers to switch to types of work activities that can be sustainable such as care, nursing, creativity and interpersonal skills. The authors submit that it is possible to promote inclusive development and citizen participation through acquisition of digital skills.

Chapter 4, "Current Trends in Human Capital Formation," explores the emerging trends in human capital formation towards building sustainable organisation. Through a literature review, the chapter examines the contributions of human capital as well as the barriers to human capital formation and theories of human capital formation. The authors emphasised that human capital has been conceptualized as the collective knowledge that is embedded in the personnel, organisational routines and network relationships of an organisation. The study revealed that many countries such as China, Russia, India and Brazil are experiencing economic growth because of their level of investment in human capital formation. The review of empirical studies also showed that human capital has been considered as a firm's strategic resource for sustainable competitive advantage. This chapter recommends that to prevent loss of human capital, it is important for organisations to create an environment and culture that will foster or encourage individual and organisational learning.

Chapter 5, "Human Capital Management in the Fourth Industrial Revolution," discusses how artificial intelligence, big data, robotics and automation process is affecting the way businesses are conducted, managed and the way human resources are utilised. The chapter presented the background of industrial revolution from the first to the fourth. The chapter identifies the drivers and challenges of the fourth industrial revolution. To promote sustainable development, the authors provide some guidelines for HR managers in order to attain high level of employees' satisfaction and talent retention culminating into customers' satisfaction.

Chapter 6, "The Future of Workforce Planning," examines the nature of workforce planning in contemporary work organisations. With the aid of literature review, the factors influencing workforce planning were identified and discussed, as well as the importance of workforce planning in contemporary work organisations across the globe; citing realistic examples. The chapter elaborated on the stages involved in workforce planning and the forecasting techniques to meet the labour market requirements in the fourth industrial revolution. This chapter holds that HR metrics and workforce analytics can be used as a tool to improve organisational outcomes.

Chapter 7, "Reshaping Education for the New Labour Market in Sub-Saharan African Countries," examines the vital role of education and training in the new labour markets. The authors emphasise the relative importance of technical education and computer literacy for all able working citizens in Sub-Saharan African countries. The chapter found that heavy investment in education and training has a great return on productivity and has the potential to change societies for all citizens. The literature on new labour market documents that Sub-Saharan African countries that have changed their educational system to reflect technical competency have been able to developed their workforce productivity and national economic development. The chapter asserts that government policies on education and training should be of utmost priority to governance in order to enhance the labour market in the 21st century.

Chapter 8, "Closing the Gender Gap in Human Capital Formation for the Fourth Industrial Revolution," scrutinizes the gender gap in human capital formation and provides a set of plausible recommendations toward closing the gender gap in human capital formation for the fourth industrial revolution. An insight was drawn from the United Nations Sustainable Development Goals, which list gender equality and women empowerment as the fifth of the eight goals. It demonstrated the economic cost of gender inequality in human capital formation (losses in human capital attributable to gender inequality are estimated at $160.2 trillion) and considered some clear-cut involvements that can ease the realization of greater equality. To boost women's human capital formation, investments throughout the life cycle are obligatory. The author suggests that successful involvements can be effected to tackle time use restrictions, support access to productive assets, and resolve market and institutional disappointments that reprimand women. Adding that spending on girls and women is indispensable not only to boosting gender equality and the changing wealth of nations but also allowing nations to grow in maintainable manners.

Chapter 9, "Human Capital Formation for The Fourth Industrial Revolution: The Role of Women," focuses on the drivers of human capital development for the Fourth Industrial Revolution. It discusses the role of women in economic development since 570BC. Women were ignored in most important areas in society, whereas men were found at the frontline. However, available empirical analyses suggest when women are empowered, they are able to turn the tables in their favour. The chapter outlines development role played by selected women across time, and uses data from studies to show poor representation of women on international bodies and parliamentary seats. Selected women that have led and continue to lead various countries all over the world are presented. It argues that women are important stakeholders in economic freedom. The chapter submits that encouraging society and men in particular to help women become front line participants in enhancing human capital development for the Fourth Industrial Revolution.

Chapter 10, "Leadership for Enhancing Organisational Performance Through Workforce Reskilling," emphasises the place of leadership in enhancing organisational outcomes through workforce reskilling. The chapter analysed leadership for enhancing organizational performance through workforce reskilling in the context of a local authority namely municipality. The study adopted a quantitative approach with the used of primary data collected through self-administered questionnaires. A sample size of 100 was drawn out of 346 employees through convenience sampling technique. However out of 100 questionnaires distributed only 96 were completed and returned. Analysis is done by STATISTICA Software. The findings reflect that the styles adopted are both democratic and autocratic leadership styles and there was insufficient workforce reskilling as required to meet the current needs of the organization.

Chapter 11, "Effective Integration of Technology and Human Capital Development in Healthcare," discusses the significance of technology in advancing human capital formation in the health sciences. Human capital development is important for organizations and most industries in the United States of America (USA). In the healthcare industry, human capital development is a priority due to the variety of skilled and unique positions within one of the most regulated industries within the U.S.A. Integration of work processes, operational efficiencies, and assimilating regulatory changes are a pre-requisite for human resource professionals to remain competitive, as well as remain operationally relevant. The authors' affirm that adoption of information technology in healthcare will continue to improve to address some of the industry's largest challenges such as turnover, retention, and education. The chapter outlined the existing challenges of human capital development in healthcare and how information technology provides significant value to closing the gaps of the alarming trends that exist in the industry.

Chapter 12, "Technology Incubator and Entrepreneurship Development," explains the importance of technology in advancing experiential learning in building entrepreneurs that can withstand the challenges and explore the opportunities in the fourth industrial revolution. The chapter adopted a literature review approach to establish the link between technology incubator and entrepreneurship development. The concepts of technology incubator and entrepreneurship development as well as other related concepts were extensively discussed. It identifies the need for adequate investments toward tech entrepreneurship development and tech-savvy for the future through technology incubation programmes. Technology incubation programmes set to aiding innovativeness, creating jobs, fast-tracking research to industry linkages, building wealth by fostering the formation of new ventures, and among others. The objectives of incubator centres in entrepreneurship development in developing and developed countries were highlighted and discussed. The chapter concludes that institutions for entrepreneurship development need to shift their tents to cover major areas of technological revolution, particularly technological incubation to promote entrepreneurship development in Industry 4.0.

Chapter 13, "Intellectual Capital Reporting and Disclosure Practices in Sri Lanka," examines the disclosure practices of intellectual capital in Sri Lankan context.

The chapter provides an empirical analysis to showcase the relationship between intellectual capital reporting and the management perception. The three capital components identified in the Intellectual Capital are Human Capital, Organizational Capital and Social Capital. Those capitals give a considerable contribution on the wealth of the organization and the main problem is the subjectivity and complexity of the disclosure practices of the listed companies in Colombo Stock Exchange from 2013 – 2016. This study is based on the intellectual capital disclosure practiced published in annual reports for the period of 3 years. Managerial perception and company characteristics were linked with the intellectual capital disclosure practices. The study found that no common procedure for disclosure among the annual reports while the details of intellectual capital disclosures vary considerably from one annual report to another.

Concretely, the collection of chapters in this book aimed to provide insights on the paradigm shift in the structure and operations of industrial organisations, competence framework for digital workforce, future of work and human capital formation to meet the current and future labour market requirements. This book can be referred to as a valuable reference source in the field of Human capital Development, change and organisational development, as well as the educational management.

Sulaiman Olusegun Atiku
Naimbia University of Science and Technology, Namibia

REFERENCES

Atiku, S. O. (2018). Reshaping human capital formation through digitalization. In *Radical Reorganization of Existing Work Structures through Digitalization* (pp. 52–73). Hershey, PA: IGI Global. doi:10.4018/978-1-5225-3191-3.ch004

Franck, R., & Galor, O. (2015). *The Complementarity between Technology and Human Capital in the Early Phase of Industrialization*. Retrieved August 27, 2018 from http://d.repec.org/n?u=RePEc:bro:econwp:2015-3&r=his

World Economic Forum. (2016). *The Future of Jobs: Employment, Skills and Workforce Strategy for the Fourth Industrial Revolution*. Retrieved August 27, 2018 from https://www.weforum.org/reports/the-future-of-jobs

World Economic Forum. (2017). *System Innovative on Shaping the Future of Education Gender and Work*. Retrieved August 27, 2018 from https://www.weforum.org/systeminitiatives/shaping-the-future-of-educatio

Acknowledgment

My sincere gratitude goes to IGI team for their support via e-Editorial Discovery, which makes the publishing process less stressful and interesting.

I would like to acknowledge the efforts of all editorial board members, reviewers and all authors for their excellent contributions to this project. Specifically, I am grateful to the authors and reviewers that took part in the review process and gave constructive comments. Without their support, this book would not have become a reality. My sincere gratitude also goes to the chapter's authors who contributed their time and expertise to this book.

Sulaiman Olusegun Atiku
Namibia University of Science and Technology, Namibia

Chapter 1
Rethinking Education System for the Fourth Industrial Revolution

Sulaiman Olusegun Atiku
https://orcid.org/0000-0001-9364-3774
Namibia University of Science and Technology, Namibia

Frank Boateng
University of Mines and Technology, Ghana

ABSTRACT

The use of automation and artificial intelligence in recent times has created two options for stakeholders in the global business environment. The stakeholders are capable of becoming the agents or victims of inevitable transformation. This chapter explores a review of education system across the globe in building human capital to address the challenges and take advantage of the opportunities in the fourth industrial revolution. This chapter combines a literature review approach and personal observation in higher education institutions in advancing education system for the fourth industrial revolution. The use of chatbot as a training needs assessment technique is effective in collecting variety of information about needs, problems, potential problems, perceptions, attitudes, and opinions in the digital age. This chapter holds that teaching contents and techniques should be structured in line with the learners' objectives, students' needs, and skills in high demand by employers in the fourth industrial revolution.

DOI: 10.4018/978-1-5225-9810-7.ch001

INTRODUCTION

Advances in technological innovations, automation and latest development in artificial intelligence (AI) have revolutionised the nature of work and created a demand for new set of skills to navigate the fourth industrial revolution (Industry 4.0). The Industry 4.0 is occasioned by developments in the fields such as artificial intelligence and machine-learning, robotics, nanotechnology, 3-D printing, and genetics and biotechnology, which have caused widespread disruption in business models and labour markets (World Economic Forum, 2016). Accordingly, with enormous change in the skills requirement to thrive in the new landscape. The World Economic Forum (2017) submits that education and training systems have remained stagnant due to low investments in education for decades, leading to production of skills that are inadequate for the new labour markets. The higher education institutions (HEIs) world-wide need to review their curricula in line with the new skills or competencies that are essential in the fourth industrial revolution. Such considerations and developments by the HEIs will enhance graduate employability and entrepreneurial activities in the Industry 4.0.

The Conventional Universities, Corporate Universities and Massive Open Online Courses (MOOCs) should be geared towards developing students or workers that can face the challenges of the Industry 4.0, in terms of knowledge, skills and abilities. Preparing students and workers for the next industrial revolution could be used to reduce the adverse effects of AI on the future workforce. For example, by upskilling workers into technical or other functional areas of the business as a way of promoting job security in the Industry 4.0. This chapter seeks to sensitize HEIs on curricula review through partnership with the Industry in meeting labour markets' requirements in the digital age. The chapter also provide insights on training needs assessment at individual, group, organisational, national and global levels. The chapter explores a perspective shift in human capital formation as technology advances and based on the future challenges of the Industry 4.0.

BACKGROUND

The first industrial revolution occurred in the 18th century, which started with the mechanisation of production starting with water and steam pressure (Noble, 2017; Tann, 2015). This was characterised as the after war economic roar, it consisted of technological advancement in the production and manufacturing sectors. Troxler (2013) puts it that mechanization, centralized factories and industrial capitalists were introduced in the first industrial revolution. Accordingly, the flagship machine was the steam engine, which created a division between labour and capital. The factory working conditions were inhuman and deplorable. There were no laws that protected labour in the early days of the first industrial revolution in the UK. In Africa for example, the Dutch and English colonised South Africa (SA); technology was brought into the country to enhance production in the mines asbestos, gold, and other metals, as well as cotton plants (Fennimore, 2013). Also exploiting the Africans into performing cheap labour and taking away their lands, as well as some atrocities committed by the colonial masters in Africa (Fennimore, 2013).

The second industrial revolution brought automation, scientific management and management consultants (Troxler, 2013). Its flagship machine was the conveyor belt, its social effect was the division between white-collar and blue-collar work. The second industrial revolution consisted of an electrification boom which occurred towards the end of the 19th Century. The term Industry 2.0 was characterised by separate steps being executed by workers specialised in respective areas (Wisskirchen et al., 2017). Serial production was born. At the same time, automatically manufactured goods were transported to different continents for the first time. That was the beginning of aviation. Later was the introduction of a PC/Computer, then later an introduction of electronic appliances. Computer hardware and software became much cheaper and accessible, and became a tool that solved problems and would identify and correct solutions faster than human beings would in mathematics, logical conclusions, data capturing, and storing files. There was no longer the need for basic human calculation. Replacement of manufacturing jobs occurred, however low-wage employment as well as high paid jobs continued.

The third industrial revolution consisted of the digitalisation of things (Wisskirchen et al., 2017). Accordingly, the third industrial revolution began in the 1970s and was characterised by the continued automation of electronic equipment such as personal computers, as well as the internet took over in the workplace. The labour was being replaced by machines in a serial production level. The fourth industrial revolution essentially means "the technical integration of cyber physical systems (CPS) into production, logistics and the use of the 'internet of things' (connection between everyday objects) and services in (industrial) processes – including the consequences for a new creation of value, business models as well as downstream services and work organisation." (Wisskirchen, 2017, p. 12). Industrial production, and automatization as a term is categorised by four components:

1. The production level is controlled my machines. Technical skills for repair and maintenance of machines is essential;
2. "Real-time production" is one of the keys aspects of the Industry 4.0. This is whereby a machine calculates the ideal utilisation of production capability. The value creation aspect makes goods or services available on the basis of

customers' demands to ensure customers satisfaction and retention. This reduces storage costs, and makes the organisation more efficient;

3. "Decentralisation of production" this is the capabilities of the machine to organise itself. This is inclusive of networks of manufacturing components, as well as material planning, control of orders will all be fully automated;
4. "Individualisation of production" is the introduction of robotics and artificial intelligence in the production systems to meet customers' specific needs and wants. This will reduce company costs with regards to planning staff, and companies will have a better competitive advantage internationally.

In the areas of automation, technology was created as a means to speed up a process that would take days and months to handle by labour, which also reduced human error in the production process. For confinements of automation, Frey and Osbourne (2013) in Marsh (2017) put it that computerised technology is unable to replicate human feelings, emotions, and perceptions, as well as to be able to manipulate a factor. Computers are only able to complete tasks in which they are programmed to do. Computers also do not possess creative intellect or innovations whereas human beings have innate processes to think out of the box. The human capital on the other hand, can create new ways of thinking new outlooks on things.

The global economy is at the beginning of an uprising that is known as the Industry 4.0. Hence, "contextual, emotional, inspired, and physical intelligence" are essential in the Industry 4.0 (Oosthuizen, 2016, p. 370). Workforce reskilling becomes eminent in the sense that employees will have to change the way they work, and adapt to changing nature of work. This becomes challenging for those who are older, and challenging on micro and macro level. The Industry 4.0 is an era of automation and innovative technology, which is transforming production systems and posing demands for new set of skills across the globe. (Ooosthuizen, 2016; Schwab, 2016).

According to the World Economic Forum (2015, p.5) in Oosthuizen (2016, p. 372) there are six types of different "software and service megatrends which are shaping society, namely (1) people and the internet, (2) computing, communications and storage everywhere, (3) the Internet of Things, (4) AI and big data, (5) the sharing economy and distributed trust, and (6) the digitisation of matter". With regards to the workplace, Lorenz *et al* (2015, p. 5) in Oosthuizen (2016) categorises "top ten effects of Industry 4.0 on the workforce as being (1) big-data driven quality control, (2) robot-assisted production, (3) self-driving logistic vehicles, (4) production line stimulation, (5) smart supply network, (6) predictive maintenance, (7) machines as a service, (8) self-organising production, (9) additive manufacturing of complex parts, and (10) augmented work, maintenance, and service". Therefore, education system across the global need to start upgrading the teaching and learning approaches in line with the labour market requirements in Industry 4.0. Otherwise, institutions of higher education in particular will keep producing half-baked graduates. Identification of the skill sets that will be in high demands, reskilling and making adequate supply of those skills could be regarded as an effort in the right direction. AI as one of the main drivers of Industry 4.0 is presented below.

ARTIFICIAL INTELLIGENCE

John McCarthy began research on AI in 1955, with the mind-set that other phases of learning and factors of intelligence can be mechanised through a machine (Wisskirchen et al., 2017). AI is the simulation of human intelligence processes by machines, especially computer systems. It is a method of creating and completing tasks that ordinarily humans would do. Artificial intelligence can be grouped into four categories.

- Machines that consider deep learning.
- Robots replacing labour in the production and manufacturing industries for operational reliability and efficiency.
- Work or jobs via apps and 'crowd working' (Wisskirchen, 2017, p. 11) is considered to be a platform that is more organised e.g. Amazon.
- Autonomous vehicles are powered through sensors and navigation. In a world where more of this technology is created there will be no need for car or truck drivers, as well as delivery services.

According to Callaghan (2017), defining technology is somewhat difficult nowadays. Technology is rapidly changing and there are so many innovative technologies in recent times. The definition technology is not considered as important as the impact of technology on workplace. Currently, the focus is on mechanisation and computerisation adopted to manage and control how products are manufactured and services delivered.

Global Automation, AI, and Rethinking Educational System

Some countries are ready to encompass and institute AI into their education systems as well as robotics. The corporate universities of most international companies such as Coke, Unilever, Nestles, KPMG, and Deloitte to mention a few, are able to invest in AI and reskilling their workplaces in Industry 4.0. For example, wearable gadgets (for augmented and virtual reality) and Chabot (AI) are transforming the learning experience in recent times. The conventional universities across the globe on the other hand, are confronted with issues of adequate funding to adopt innovative teaching and learning approaches for human capital formation in the Industry 4.0. The countries such as Hong Kong, Singapore, South Korea, United States of America, and Germany are undertaking research and development to provide solutions to issues in the Industry 4.0, judging from their assets, resources, and manpower aiding the process (Wisskirchen *et al*, 2017).

The major propellers driving Industry 4.0 are automation and proliferation of AI (KPMG, 2019). Automation is not a new concept in the 21st century, in fact automation is one of the major trends in the 20th century (Endsley, 1996). Accordingly, automation is the use of electronics and computer-controlled devices to assume control of processes with the purpose of boosting efficiency and reliability. For example, the use of automated teller machines in the banking industry globally has revolutionised the banking operations. Therefore, the use of traditional banking operations is no longer fashionable, whilst the electronic banking applications, processes and platforms are more efficient and reliable.

The use of software have automated some of the tasks being performed traditionally by white-collar workers in retail, wholesale, and other business services across the globe (Acemoglu & Restrepo, 2018; Inagaki & Sheridan, 2018). The software and AI-powered technologies can now retrieve information, coordinate logistics, handle inventories, prepare taxes, provide financial services, translate complex documents, write business reports, prepare legal briefs, and diagnose diseases. With the proliferation AI in the production processes of many manufacturing and service rendering organisations across the globe (KPMG, 2019), therefore, rethinking educational system become imperative for workforce reskilling to cope with the challenges of Industry 4.0. For example, rethinking education system may involve the use of innovative teaching and learning approaches for workforce reskilling or to meet labour market requirements in Industry 4.0. Acemoglu and Restrepo (2018) put it that applications of AI may enable the education system to become more customized, and in the process create more jobs for education professionals to monitor, design and implement individualized education programmes. For example, chatbots (AI) are effective for design and implementation of individualised education programmes in recent times. The instructors should keep abreast of the shifts in the pedagogical techniques essential to meet educational needs of the Industry 4.0 (Allen, 2019). The author suggests that the following considerations are essential in rethinking the education system in order to equip the next generation of leaders with the knowledge, skills and competencies required to navigate the Industry 4.0.

- The first stage is to ensure regular update of teachers, instructors, lecturers and professors in education system with the shifts in the pedagogical skills essential to meet educational needs of the Industry 4.0. The instructors should keep abreast of the latest innovative teaching and learning technology. The ability to engage learners with AI-based education system (Allen, 2019) will go a long way in preparing them for employment opportunities in the era of innovative technology (Acemoglu & Restrepo, 2018).

- The next consideration in rethinking education system in recent times is conceptualisation and design of AI-based education system (Allen, 2019). This has to do with the outlook of AI-based classroom, which is essential in advancing experiential learning using the network of augmented or virtual reality. This approach could be easily adopted by the developed countries across the globe. The developing countries, specifically in Africa are still confronted with inadequate funding to migrate into e-learning platforms. This implies that adoption of AI-based education system may not be feasible for developing countries in Africa. For example, stable power supply as a product of the second industrial revolution is not yet met in some African countries (e.g. Nigeria and Zimbabwe). Since these countries are having issues catching up with the developments in the second industrial revolution, therefore moving along with the pace of developments in the Industry 4.0 is a big challenge. To meet the increasing interest in machine learning research across Africa, AI research centre has recently been opened by Google in Accra, Ghana in the Month of April 2019 to facilitate local AI development (Business News, 2019, April 10).
- Promoting inclusive education system to reduce inequalities in the society with the use of free Wi-Fi and the internet to access web-based learning and other AI-based education system. This usually extends teaching and learning environments beyond the traditional face-to-face classroom approach. With free Wi-Fi and internet access provided by government, HEIs should be able to implement an inclusive education system to reduce inequalities in the society.
- Establishing the need for substantial changes to science and technology curriculum is necessary to allow students to develop capacity in the rapidly emerging areas of genomics, data science, AI, robotics and nanomaterials (Penprase, 2018). There is need for regular update of universities curricula in line with the changing nature of labour market requirements in the Industry 4.0. For example, in the area of technical education, new frameworks must be developed to respond to the vast innovative technology and increasing complexity and volatility (Penprase, 2018).
- HEIs should consider embracing data mining in order to gain better understanding of student performance, produce graduates to meet labour markets demands, and considering the students' needs (World Economic Forum, 2016). For example, education policy and curriculum reform world-

wide should establish the importance of learning to code, programming and computer science as the focus areas of human capital formation for the Industry 4.0. The benefits of rethinking education system in the digital age are discussed in the next section.

The Benefits of Rethinking Education System

The benefits of realigning the current curricula in the education system from primary to tertiary education levels, as well as technical institutions with the current and future labour markets requirements, student needs, and social demands cannot be overemphasised in the digital age. Winthrop and McGivney (2016) identified the following as the benefits of rethinking education system in a changing world.

- The major benefit of rethinking education in a digital age is to ensure that all learners across the globe are adequately equipped with the essential skills to operate successfully in a virtual environment and technologically advanced world.
- Rethinking education system will result into better academic outcomes in various institutions and prepare learner or future leaders with comprehensive insights to navigate the global business environment.
- It enables the institutions to address the gap between conventional universities and labour market demands. For example, employers' displeasure about the quality of graduates being released into the labour markets can be corrected by equipping the learners with workplace competencies to add value to organisations in various industry.
- It helps in discovering the future skills or future workplace competencies and making adequate preparations to reskill the future workforce. Such competencies should be incorporated at the foundation stages in education system across the globe. The foundation for these skills, such as creativity and learning agility, should be clearly spelled out in the early childhood education globally (Winthrop & McGivney, 2016).
- It helps in redefining basic academic and non-academic skills to meet the challenges of the Industry 4.0. For example, gamification can be useful in inculcating complex academic and non-academic skills into young learners across the globe in an interesting manner. Taking advantage of the innovative technology in the digital age will go a long way in reskilling and upskilling the workforce globally.
- Reskilling education system across the globe is helpful bridging the gap between nations and communities, meeting the social needs of education in the era of AI (Allen, 2019). The skills for social progress (OECD, 2015),

which dwells on the need to strike a balance between cognitive, social and emotional skills for young learners to succeed in the digital age. The nations and communities do not stand in isolation, the support of various stakeholders are essential in rethinking education system for the Industry 4.0. The next section presents the importance of stakeholders support in advancing education system in the era of AI.

Importance of Stakeholders Support in Advancing the Education System

The support from stakeholders in HEIs is crucial in advancing tertiary education across the globe (Atiku, 2018). Therefore, no system can survive without support from its stakeholders. The stakeholders in HEIs include students; alumni; donors; parents; other institutions or providers; accrediting agencies; vendors and suppliers; employers; taxpayers; non-government organisations; government; and academic faculty, both individually and collectively in disciplinary groups and as members of other organisations such as unions and advocacy bodies (Marshall, 2018). The stakeholders can be grouped into internal and external stakeholders (Marshall, 2018; Ulewicz, 2017). Hence, the place of stakeholders in advancing education system cannot be underrated in the digital age. For example, in terms of provision of adequate funding to migrate into AI-based education system (Allen, 2019), an institution requires maximum support from the university management, government (department of education), donors, vendors and employers. Whilst, the acceptance and usage of innovative teaching and learning facilities rest on the shoulders of students, instructors, parents, accrediting agencies and other academic faculty (Atiku, 2018). This shows that each stakeholder needs to support the initiative, and has a role to play in advancing education system in recent times. To ensure maximum support from the other stakeholders, management and the regulatory bodies or agencies must create necessary awareness before the implementation stage for effective institutionalisation of the change process.

The importance of external stakeholders support in advancing education system centres on quality assurance either nationally, regionally or globally (Ulewicz, 2017). This refers to the role of government and other regulatory agencies in shaping the standards of education within a country or internationally. For example, the accreditation bodies either locally or globally regulate each programme being run by universities. Locally, the Department of Higher Education (Ministry of Education in some countries), or National Accreditation Board regulates the standards of education in each country and enforce compliance from the Educational Institutions. According to the European Network of Education Councils (2011), responsibilities of the Ministry of Education include the following.

- Administration of education
- Enforcement of educational laws
- Preparation of educational bills
- Public education is mainly financed by the Government
- Prescription of syllabi, curricula and textbooks
- Regulation and supervision of educational institutions
- Construction of school buildings for the public institutions
- Maintenance and equipment: shared responsibility with local school boards.

The International Network for Quality Assurance Agencies in Higher Education (INQAAHE) is a world-wide association of organisations that is active in the theory and practice of quality assurance in HEIs (INQAAHE, n.d). This network for quality assurance agencies was established in 1991 with 8 members, and has more than 300 members from national or regional quality assurance agencies around the World. The objectives INQAAHE include the following.

- To create, collect and disseminate information on current and developing theory and practice in the assessment, improvement and maintenance of quality in higher education.
- To undertake or commission research in areas relevant to quality in higher education.
- To express the collective views of its members on matters relevant to quality in higher education through contacts with international bodies and by other means.
- To promote the theory and practice of the improvement of quality in higher education.
- To provide advice and expertise to assist existing and emerging quality assurance agencies.
- To facilitate links between quality assurance agencies and support networks of quality assurance agencies.
- To assist members to determine the standards of institutions operating across national borders and facilitate better-informed international recognition of qualifications.
- To assist in the development and use of credit transfer and credit accumulation schemes to enhance the mobility of students between institutions (within and across national borders).
- To enable members to be alert to improper quality assurance practices and organisations.
- To organise, on request, reviews of the operation of members.

Judging from the objectives of INQAAHE, there is no doubt that it plays a significant role in coordinating the activities of its members with aim of improving the quality of HEIs across the globe. Therefore, INQAAHE plays significant roles in advancing higher education system for the Industry 4.0 as a stakeholder. Furthermore, other stakeholders such as students, workers, parents, conventional and corporate universities, government (policy review/reforms, investments and sensitisation for stakeholders' awareness and buy-in) in developed and developing countries also have roles to play in advancing education system in the era of automation and AI. The next section explains the imperatives for curricula review in partnership with the practitioners in various industries.

Curriculum Review and the Fourth Industrial Revolution

The stakeholders in various educational institutions world-wide should be championing regular update of curricula in line with the labour market requirements. This points to the fact that curriculum review is active and ongoing process in HEIs, which requires active participation of the practitioners in industry and faculty members in various disciplines for effective learning outcomes (Aytac & Deniz, 2005; Eberhard, et al. 2017). The active involvement of practitioners in specific industries in curriculum review will go a long way in bridging the gap between the industry and HEIs (McKernan, 2013). Rethinking education system for the Industry 4.0 through curriculum review will encourage the stakeholders in universities to prepare future graduates for a new labour market reality (Eberhard et al. 2017). Accordingly, regular update of curriculum could be used as a yardstick to enhance students' or graduates employability in the Industry 4.0. This chapter subscribes to the view that teaching or learning contents and techniques is continuously evolving, rather than being rigorously static and must be tailored in accordance with the learning objectives, students' needs and labour markets requirements in the digital age.

In corporate universities, training needs assessment is the process of determining the gap between the expected level of outcomes and actual outcomes of employees (Erasmus & Van Dyk, 2003). Training needs assessment could be performed at various levels such as individual, group, organisational, national and global levels in the education system. The types of needs assessment to have a rethink about learning and development for the Industry 4.0 taking insights from Erasmus and Van Dyk, (2003) are listed below.

- Organisation needs assessment (needs unique to the enterprise or enterprise development in the era of automation and artificial intelligence)
- Group needs assessment (number of employees doing the same kind of job and who lack certain skills at a specific level in the digital age)

- Job needs assessment (analysis of individual jobs and tasks in the digital age)
- Individual needs assessment (specific personal needs for the fourth industrial revolution)

It is imperative to note that effective training needs assessment for workforce reskilling in recent times, demands appropriate techniques of needs assessment. These techniques involve the use of questionnaires, individual interviews, observation, group discussion, records and reports, job description and analysis (Erasmus & Van Dyk, 2003). The decision about any of the techniques and participants rests on learning and development practitioners in corporate universities or quality assurance practitioners in conventional universities across the globe. For example, questionnaires are probably the most widely used information gathering technique for training needs assessment. If properly designed, it will provide variety of information about needs, problems, potential problems, perceptions, attitudes and opinions. Hence, student's needs and labour market requirements can be identified with the aid of questionnaire and attended to through active curriculum review. Therefore, meeting the labour market requirements in the digital age involves active curriculum review.

SOLUTIONS AND RECOMMENDATIONS

Rethinking education system to meet future labour market demands require the efforts of all stakeholders in HEIs. In terms of curriculum review for future labour market demands, the university management, employers, and national or international quality assurance agencies or networks have roles to play in advancing education system in the digital age. The development of policies to reform the system rest on these stakeholders. Investments in state-of-the-art teaching and learning technology also rest on the shoulders university management, employers, and national or international quality assurance agencies. The government in developing countries must provide infrastructure facilities to support innovative teaching and learning. There is no doubt that students must be acquainted with the essential technology to render their services in the future labour market through experiential learning approaches. Such exposure is crucial in bridging the gap between the industry and HEIs. For example, investments in wearable technology is valuable in promoting experiential learning through augmented and virtual reality.

Students with the support of their parents or guidance should be able to adopt innovative learning applications or gadgets for enhanced learning experience in the digital age. The adoption involves making funds available for procurement of such gadgets in making learning accessible to students in their comfort zones provided HEIs have been able to extend teaching and learning beyond the classroom. For example, smartphones for mobile learning (m-learning), and social learning (s-learning). Interestingly, Chatbot is also adding value to learning and development in era of automation and AI. Therefore, the use of Chatbot should be encouraged as teaching assistance in conventional universities.

The other stakeholders in HEIs such as alumni, donors, other institutions or services providers, vendors and suppliers, as well as non-government organisations in developed and developing countries should be encouraged to provide the financial resources in advancing education system. This could be considered as part of their social responsibility, considering the social needs of education. The reason is that HEIs across the globe require adequate funding to migrate from traditional learning approaches into innovative teaching and learning approaches to meet labour market demands in the digital age. Above all, this chapter holds that teaching contents and techniques is continuously evolving, and should be structured in line with the learning objectives, students' needs and current/future skills in high demand by the employers in Industry 4.0.

FUTURE AREAS OF RESEARCH

The idea presented in this chapter was based on the literature and personal observations of the authors, suggesting the need to advance education system in accordance with the labour market requirements in the era of automation and AI. Future research direction should be based on the need for empirical studies concerning the relationship between education system and the fourth industrial revolution. For example, a qualitative study could be conducted to establish how education system through curriculum review is addressing the challenges of the fourth industrial revolution. This implies that such study will rely on data collection from the participants (university management, students, alumni, donors, parents, other institutions or providers, accrediting agencies, vendors and suppliers, employers, taxpayers, government, and academic faculty, both individually and collectively in disciplinary groups, unions and advocacy bodies) through in-depth interviews. The other studies may go through a quantitative approach in exploring the relationship between the ongoing rethinking education system and the fourth industrial revolution.

CONCLUSION

This chapter dwells on rethinking education system to meet the labour market requirements in the era of automation and AI. The chapter concludes that teaching contents and techniques is continuously evolving, and should be structured in line with the learning objectives, students' needs and future skills demands by employers in Industry 4.0. To meet the labour market requirements in the era of automation and AI, there is need for active curriculum review; taking insights from both internal and external stakeholders in HEIs.

Curriculum review in the digital age should give priority to technical skills, problem solving skills, analytical skills, social skills, emotional intelligence and tech-savvy rather than the traditional academic skills (Eberhard et al., 2017). Therefore, going forward in curriculum review; conventional universities need to step up their games in building excellent critical thinking skills, creativity, tech-savvy and interdisciplinary knowledge. For example, the use of incubation centres should be encouraged in some disciplines where abstract knowledge is a major setback in promoting experiential learning for graduate employability in the industry.

Lastly, curriculum review in recent times should consider incorporating social, mobile, analytics and cloud (SMAC) platforms in meeting future labour market requirements. Learning all of these skills/platforms will make graduates stand out in their future career endeavours. Hence, delivery of course contents in the digital age suggests the use of innovative teaching and learning approaches to extend the learning environment beyond the classroom. For example, analytics and clouds offer the greatest level efficiency for self-service platforms and shared resources (Kavanagh, Thite, & Johnson, 2012).

REFERENCES

Acemoglu, D., & Restrepo, P. (2018). *Artificial intelligence, automation and work (No. w24196)*. National Bureau of Economic Research. doi:10.3386/w24196

Allen, J. R. (2019). *Why we need to rethink education in the artificial intelligence age*. Retrieved May 9, 2019 from https://www.brookings.edu/research/why-we-need-to-rethink-education-in-the-artificial-intelligence-age/

Atiku, S. O. (2018). Reshaping human capital formation through digitalization. In *Radical Reorganization of Existing Work Structures through Digitalization* (pp. 52–73). Hershey, PA: IGI Global. doi:10.4018/978-1-5225-3191-3.ch004

Aytac, A., & Deniz, V. (2005). Quality function deployment in education: A curriculum review. *Quality & Quantity*, *39*(4), 507–514. doi:10.100711135-004-6814-8

Business News. (2019, April 10). *Google opens Africa's first AI Research Centre in Accra*. Retrieved May 9, 2019 from https://www.ghanaweb.com/GhanaHomePage/business/Google-opens-Africa-s-first-AI-Research-Centre-in-Accra-737336

Callaghan, P. (2017). *Exploring the Impact on Global Labour Markets*. Jobs and the Organisation of Work.

Eberhard, B., Podio, M., Alonso, A. P., Radovica, E., Avotina, L., Peiseniece, L., ... Solé-Pla, J. (2017). Smart work: The transformation of the labour market due to the fourth industrial revolution (I4. 0). *International Journal of Business & Economic Sciences Applied Research*, *10*(3), 47–66.

Endsley, M. R. (1996). Automation and situation awareness. In *Automation and human performance* (pp. 183–202). Routledge.

Erasmus, B. J., & Van Dyk, P. S. (2003). *Training management in South Africa*. Cape Town: Oxford University Press.

European Network of Education Councils. (2011). *Participation and stakeholder involvement in education policy making*. Retrieved May 10, 2019 from http://www.eunec.eu/sites/www.eunec.eu/files/event/attachments/report_brussels.pdf

Fennimore, M. (2013). *Introduction to Labour Relations in South Africa* (7th ed.). LexisNexis.

Inagaki, T., & Sheridan, T. B. (2018). A critique of the SAE conditional driving automation definition, and analyses of options for improvement. *Cognition Technology and Work*, 1–10.

INQAAHE. (n.d). *Mission and values*. Retrieved May 10, 2019 from https://www.inqaahe.org/presentation

Kavanagh, M. J., Thite, M., & Johnson, R. D. (2012). *Human Resource Information Systems: Basics, Applications and future Directions* (2nd ed.). Sage Publishers.

KPMG. (2019). *The future of HR 2019: In the Know or in the No*. Retrieved from https://home.kpmg/xx/en/home/insights/2018/11/the-future-of-human-resources.html

Marsh, M. J. (2017). *Automation: Will The Fourth Industrial Revolution Lead to The Downfall of Human Labour?* Department of Finance, Texas Christian University.

Marshall, S. J. (2018). Internal and external stakeholders in higher education. In *Shaping the University of the Future* (pp. 77–102). Singapore: Springer. doi:10.1007/978-981-10-7620-6_4

McKernan, J. (2013). *Curriculum action research: A handbook of methods and resources for the reflective practitioner*. Routledge.

Noble, D. (2017). *Forces of production: A social history of industrial automation*. Routledge.

OECD. (2015). *Skills for social progress: The power of social and emotional skills*. Retrieved May 10, 2019 from http://www.oecd.org/education/skills-for-social-progress-9789264226159-en.htm

Oosthuizen, J. H. (2016). Entrepreneurial Intelligence: Expanding Scwab's Four-Type Intelligence Proposition to Meaningfully Address the Challenges of the Fourth Industrial Revolution. *Proceedings of the 28th Annual Conference of the Southern African Institute of Management Scientists*.

Penprase, B. E. (2018). The fourth industrial revolution and higher education. In *Higher education in the era of the fourth industrial revolution* (pp. 207–229). Palgrave Macmillan.

Schwab, K. & Samans, R. (2016). *The Future of Jobs: Employment, Skills, and Workfprce Strategy for the Fourth Industrial Revolution*. Global Challenge Insight Report.

Tann, J. (2015). Borrowing brilliance: Technology transfer across sectors in the early Industrial Revolution. *The International Journal for the History of Engineering & Technology*, *85*(1), 94–114. doi:10.1179/1758120614Z.00000000056

Troxler, P. (2013). *Making the 3rd industrial revolution. FabLabs: Of machines, makers and inventors*. Bielefeld: Transcript Publishers.

Ulewicz, R. (2017). The role of stakeholders in quality assurance in higher education. *Human Resources Management & Ergonomics*, *11*(1), 93–107.

Winthrop, R., & McGivney, E. (2016). *Rethinking education system in a changing world*. Retrieved May 10, 2019 from https://ssir.org/articles/entry/rethinking_education_in_a_changing_world#

Wisskirchen, G., Biacabe, B. T., Borman, U., Muntz, A., Niehaus, G., Soler, G. J., & von Brauchitsch, B. (2017). *Artificial Intelligence and Robotics and Their Impact on the Workplace*. IBA Global Employment Institute.

World Economic Forum. (2016a). *The Future of Jobs: Employment, Skills and Workforce Strategy for the Fourth Industrial Revolution*. Retrieved August 27, 2018 from https://www.weforum.org/reports/the-future-of-jobs

World Economic Forum. (2016b). *What role will education play in the Fourth Industrial Revolution?* Retrieved May 9, 2019 from https://www.weforum.org/agenda/2016/01/what-role-will-education-play-in-the-fourth-industrial-revolution/

World Economic Forum. (2017). *System Innovative on Shaping the Future of Education Gender and Work*. Retrieved August 27, 2018 from https://www.weforum.org/systeminitiatives/shaping-the-future-of-education-gender-and-work

KEY TERMS AND DEFINITIONS

Artificial Intelligence: The simulation of human intelligence processes by machines, especially computer systems.

Augment Reality: A computer-generated images of real-world environment to expose learners to experiential learning without the fear of real-world repercussion.

Automation: Automatic application systems to improve operational reliability and efficiency in the digital age.

Chabot: An artificial intelligence developed to collect or provide online information to customers or learners interactively.

Virtual Reality: A learning experience via simulation bringing interactive and similar real-world experience in an artificial platform.

Wearable Tech: Adoption audio-visual technology to advance teaching and learning experience through simulation, it makes augmented and virtual reality possible.

Chapter 2
Competency Framework for the Fourth Industrial Revolution

Mustafa Kemal Topcu
ST Strategy and Technology Development LLC, Turkey

ABSTRACT

Today's business environment is described with volatility, uncertainty, complexity, and ambiguity. In order for organizations to survive in the fourth industrial revolution characterized by continuously changing resulted from digital transformation and technological development, it is critical to identify a vision, to attract qualified human resources, to motivate them, to allocate resources to complete the mission, and to speed activities up to achieve the desired end state. It is of great significance to analyze the organization and create a competency framework to harbor all relevant steps to move the organization further. Therefore, this study aims at drawing attention to competency framework for the Industry 4.0 environment. There is no doubt that a standard competency framework for the fourth revolution may not be proposed. However, as a starting point, a generalized competency framework is proposed as a sample for further conceptual and empirical studies.

INTRODUCTION

Competency as a concept was first introduced by White (1959) in the United States of America to describe attributes leading to high performance and motivation of employees. According to the researcher, competency is interaction of an individual with the work environment. By supporting the researcher with empirical studies,

DOI: 10.4018/978-1-5225-9810-7.ch002

McClelland (1973, 1998) developed competency measurement model still in use. Inadequacy of psychometric scales to measure individual performance and that of using job descriptions to manage performance result in employing competency models (PAHRODF, 2017). Nonetheless, as Barrett and Depinet (1991) state, there is not enough evidence that McClelland's model produces useful results. On the other hand, the model became more common by 1990s after the efforts of Boyatzis (Rothwell & Lindholm, 1999; Cardy & Selvarajan, 2006). To this end, competencies are considered untrivial factor for sustainable competitive advantage of the organizations (Campbell & Sommers Luchs, 1997; Nadler & Tushman, 1999). Thus, we may describe competence as a concept introducing a holistic approach to use workforce, knowledge, and technology effectively and interactively. Likewise, job-based learning urges organizations to analyse, plan, and conduct human capital of the organizations with a better understanding of competencies. In short, competency may be defined as everything to achieve better results in efficiency, effectiveness, and productivity. So, competency is the total of the factors that distinguish the best from the rest at a given work environment (Monk, 2001, p. 47). However, there are some studies identifying competency as a skill or an ability (for instance; Boyatzis & Sala, 2004). To this end, we may contend that competency comprises behaviours, attitudes, and knowledge providing reliable high performance. And we may widely describe competency as a guiding tool including knowledge, abilities, personal attributes, and behaviours contributing to achieving strategic goals of the company (Gangani et al., 2006; Dessler, 2007; Petersen et al., 2011).

Accordingly, competency based human resources management is fed by individual differences, industrial psychology, leadership researches, and job analyses. Besides, contemporary work environment is much more different than the past and is ever changing faster than expected. The fourth industrial revolution is organization of life cycle of a product from customer requirements through recycling following delivery to the end user (Prifti et al., 2017). The aim of the fourth industrial revolution is efficient, flexible, and customized production by means of digitally decentralized controls, self-organized supply chains, and fully automated factories by real-time and sensor technologies (Kagermann et al., 2013; Gebhardt et al., 2015). Therefore, the workforce is anticipated to comprehend the processes, connection along the networks, digitalization, and data collection and utilisation (Ras et al., 2017). By digital transformation and technological development, business environment is continuously changing leading to changes in competencies business world would like to employ. As Longo and his colleagues (2017) state, employees are required to be more flexible and to display adaptive capabilities in this dynamic working environment. The tasks they work on are getting less routine and ask for continuous knowledge and skills development (Ras et al., 2017).

Rapid changes in technology, globalization, and environment require business world adapt to changes to sustain in the VUCA environment. Today's business competitive environment is described with the acronym "VUCA", stands for volatility, uncertainty, complex, and ambiguity. The changing environment urges companies to use resources efficiently, become decentralized and less bureaucratic, decide and act rapidly, produce more qualified products, speed up innovations, deliver better service, and make use of employees to adapt to the (Brockbank et al., 2003). To this end, efficient and effective use of organizational resources may result in facilitating the adaptation of the firms to VUCA environment. It is renowned that human resources are one of the factors that provide organizations sustainable competitive advantage. Hence, competencies as well as other factors are to be well described to employ and develop qualified workforce. Therefore, this study aims at drawing attention to competency framework for the Industry 4.0 environment. Literature on competency models regarding the fourth industrial revolution is scarce (Prifti et al., 2017). Although the research on the fourth revolution itself recalls the change in the workplace, no models are recommended regarding human resources management. Similarly studies on competency modelling in the literature lack a universal understanding of competency framework and relation with organizational strategies and policies (Vraniak et al., 2017). Thus, the study contributes to the literature by a methodology proposal for competency framework oriented through the future's workplace. Within this context, the rest of the study is as follows; after defining competency as a concept, types of competencies are given, and competency framework is discussed. Consequently, a methodology is proposed to prepare competency framework for future workplaces in the fourth industrial revolution.

COMPETENCY FRAMEWORK

Competency as a Concept

Boyatsiz (1982) popularized competency concept developed by McClelland (1973, 1998) in order to measure performance rather than to employ IQ tests in the workplace. Although it has been a long time, literature is not definite on the definition of the competency (Deist, 2005; Heinsman, 2008). Unfortunately, competence and competency, two very similar words, are used to describe two very different constructs and they are used interchangeably (Bartram, 2012). Hartle (1995, p. 107) describes competence as "knowledge, skills, and abilities as well as personal attributes and motivational factors for higher performance workers." Burgoyne (1988), Woodruffe (1990, 1991), and Dessler (2007) describe competence as characteristics to meet job demands and highlight the role of attributes to get a job sufficiently done. In a similar vein, Cockerill (1989) lists competence as concrete ones like presentation skills and abstract ones like self-esteem. On the other hand, Mansfield (2004) underlies that competency is a product of tasks, outcomes, and personalities. Gangani and his colleagues (2006) focuses organizational success and stress the role of skills, knowledge, behaviours, attributes, and motivation as competencies to contribute to the desired end state. Leung and his colleagues (2016) define competency as a multifaceted characteristic of performance.

To this end, making a distinction between the two constructs may be helpful to understand the competency concept. Competence is a job-specific term while competency is generic applying across all jobs (Bartram, 2012). While competence refers to minimum job standards to do it efficiently, competency refers to distinguished personal attributes leading to higher performance. So the two words, competence and competency, are not interchangeable; rather, they are complementary. In short, competence is impossible without competency. However, competency doesn't indicate real performance but lays out competencies for a higher performance.

Towards this end, we may conceptualize competency as a concept that fills the gap between formal learning and job demands (Boon & van der Klink, 2002). It is of great significance that organizational culture is the most dominant factor on competencies. Constructivist theory examines competency as a phenomenon within its context (Sandberg, 2000). Dulewicz (1989) advocates that 70% of competency is generalizable whilst the rest is specific to organization. To summarize, competency conceptually covers attributes providing effective results and higher performance at a given organization (Boyatzis, 1982). As a result, this study refers to competency as a group of observable knowledge, skills, and abilities that ensure higher performance (Gürbüz, 2017). To summarize, some significant features of competency are listed as follows:

- Competency is not a job description.
- Competency is in compliance with mission, vision, strategies, and values.
- Competency needs to be easily understood.
- Competency is observable, measurable, and open to development.
- Competency is based on behaviours.
- Competency describes excellent behaviours.
- Competency may differ by sectors, even sometimes within the sector.

Types of Competencies

Competency came to table after the declaration of the target of EU to make Europe more competitive and knowledge-based public in Lisbon in 2005. Multi-factorial structure is accepted in the literature; but, there is no clear-cut definition for the factors (Le Deist & Winterton, 2005). Haddadj & Besson (2000) epistemologically groups competency as individual and collective. Cheetham & Chivers (1996, 1998) propose a 5-component model including cognitive, functional, personal, ethical, and meta-competency.

There are also some methodological differences because of cultural issues. For instance, cognitive and functional competencies as well as behavioural ones are focused in the United States of America. On the other side, cognitive and behavioural competencies are covered by functional ones in the United Kingdom. French approach distinguishes three distinct competencies; knowledge, experience, and behaviours (Le Deist & Winterton, 2005). German type competencies concentrate on learning process rather than results (Straka, 2004). Action competence approach of Germany describes three competencies; domain, personal, and social (Le Deist & Winterton, 2005). Domain competency includes cognitive and functional competencies, personal competency covers cognitive and social competencies, and social competency includes functional and social competencies. Austria adopts a similar categorization with Germany and groups as cognitive, social, and personal competencies (Archan & Tutschek, 2002).

In general, there are four types of competency; cognitive, personal, functional, and ethical (TRACE Project Report, 2015). On the other hand, German system has been output-based and categorized competency as functional, personal, and social (Straka, 2004; Le Deist & Winterton, 2005). While functional competencies focus on cognition and tasks such as problem solving and analytic thinking, personal competencies have individual and social sides such as developmental opportunities and work-life balance. Likewise, social competencies are related to humanitarian and societal cases such as responsibility, collaboration, communication, and cooperation. There is a similar categorization in Austria model: cognitive, personal, and social (Archan & Tutschek, 2002). Cognitive competencies include knowledge, skills, and abilities of a person towards the job. Personal competencies are related to openness to development and motivation while social competencies collaboration, teamwork, and social responsibility.

One may summarize common characteristics of American and European competency models that they are both based on knowledge and experience, and they both include behavioural dimension (Dejoux, 1999). To this end, we adopt a common view and group competencies as organizational or core, managerial, and functional. Core competencies are asked from all people in the organization irrespective of their statute and position, ranging blue-collar workers to top management (Raja & Swapna, 2010). Core competencies direct human capital towards vision of organizations and are related to values, beliefs, intentions, and emotions of the organization (Gangani et al., 2006). Diversity, sustainability, trust, innovativeness and relevancy may be given examples for core competencies. Core competencies are contingent based on organizational culture, management team, regulations, and industry (Tricker & Lee, 1997).

Managerial positions and manager candidates are awaited to have managerial competencies. Managerial competencies cover organization specific processes for organizational success (Raja & Swapna, 2010). Punctuality, documentary, data collection, programming, meeting management, and budgeting are examples for managerial competencies. American Management Society defines 5 managerial competencies as technical knowledge, intellectual capital, entrepreneurship orientation, relation management, and task orientation based on a nationwide research (Hayes, 1979). Russell (2000) categorizes managerial competencies into three groups; conceptual, technical, and relational. Robertson and his colleagues (1999) list managerial competencies as action, motivation, creativeness, flexibility and sensitivity, leadership and communication, autonomy, and analysis. Scullen and his colleagues (2003) add compliance to managerial competencies. No matter what managerial competencies cover, it is obvious that they refer to cognitive and initating skills in an organizational context. Managerial competencies ask us to comprehend human, organizational structure, processes, and policies.

Competencies required for excellence regarding working style are functional ones. Functional competencies include knowledge, skills and processes to make core product/service of the organization in an excellent manner differentiating the organization from the rest (Raja & Swapna, 2010). Product/service know-how, service presentation, research, indigenous design, and technology literacy are some examples for functional competencies.

Competency Framework

Competency framework is the output of competency modelling, the art and science of identifying the success factors for organizations to distinguish it best from the rivals by driving higher performance led by cultivating the competencies of human resources (PAHRODF, 2017). By creating competency modelling, types and levels of competencies may be identified in order to conduct the job in the most efficient manner and to meet the possible gap between current and future needs of the organization (Mansfield, 2000; Vraniak et al., 2017). Management by competency modelling is human-centric and stresses the significance of human resources to achieve organizational success (Wickramasinghe & Zoyza, 2008). In order to conduct mission of an organization and gain a competitive edge, competencies of human capital is expected to comply with and support organizational strategies. It seems impossible that strategies may not be realized unless competencies are not well conceptualized and modelled for the organization (Cardy & Selvarajan, 2006). Competency based management facilitates identification of knowledge, skills and behaviours related to organizational strategies and policies, of which human resources have today and will require in the future (Draganidis & Mentzas, 2006; Stokes & Oiry, 2012). It provides an integrated design for a sustainable and strategic human resources management. Competencies are common language for organizations to manage and retain qualified workforce Competency-based human resources management is depicted on Figure 1.

Retention of qualified personnel, succession plans, backups, developmental plans, training needs identification, performance appraisal, and staffing are some human resources practices based on competency framework (Sparrow, 1995; Markus et al., 2005; PAHRODF, 2017). Competency framework is a gateway for organizations to meet changing demands of the market by developing talent portfolio for a more competitive and volatile environment and align effectiveness of human resources with the changes (Gangani et al., 2006). Competency framework facilitates to benefit from trainings within lifelong learning concept. Training needs are identified in accordance with knowledge, skills, and abilities related to competencies.

Moreover competency framework aligns human resources practices with organizational strategies and policies (Lucia & Lepsinger, 1999; Shipmann et al., 2000; Gangani et al., 2006). Performance appraisal clearly lays out whether employees have the competencies described in the job descriptions. Therefore, behaviorally-based performance standards are detailed in the framework and employed in the organizations (PAHRODF, 2017). Regarding staffing, competency-based practices highlight quality rather than quantity (Lucia & Lepsinger, 1999). Therefore, while return on investment on human capital is maximized, risk taken by employing unqualified person who does not fit the organization is minimized. There are also some personal benefits of competency framework for employees. Job demands are clearly defined, personal and professional development are well organized, organizational

Figure 1. Competency-based human resources practices

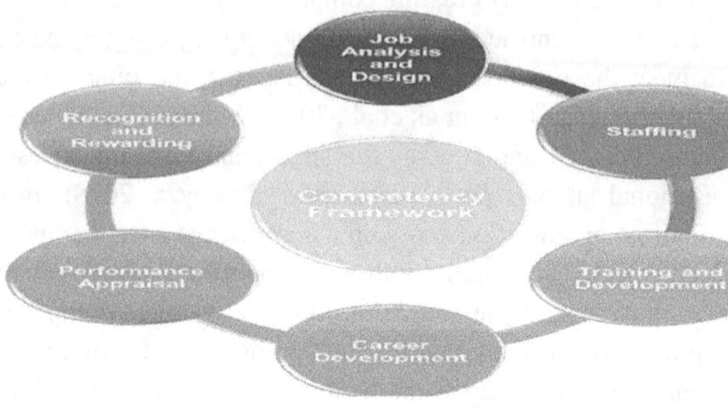

and environmental factors are unambiguously determined, performance appraisal is fairly and objectively made, person-job fit is sought in the beginning. Competencies are used to develop personal growth and career development plans for professionals (Draganidis & Mentzas, 2006: 51-64). In addition, competency framework facilitates managers to assess performance with objectivity and to communicate expectations and obligations effectively with employees (PAHRODF, 2017).

Wright (2005) defines three key performance indicators for competency framework; engagement, empowerment and accountability. Regarding engagement job demands and resources are clearly identified, empowerment refers to testing compliance of criteria with human-centric practices, and accountability urges organizations to create a task- and human-oriented workplace culture for a sustainable success of organization's mission and vision. Areas to benefit from competency framework may be listed as a summary.

- Change management
- Gaining sustainable competitive advantage
- Backup Plans
- Professional development
- Analysis
- Role certainty and job characteristics
- Integrated HR strategies
- Total quality management and standardization
- Recognition and rewarding
- Motivation
- Effectiveness and productivity

Best Practices on Competency Framework

Competency framework of OECD is composed of technical and core competencies. Technical competencies are identified as a prerequisite to perform a specific job; but, they are not documented in the framework. Instead, they are highlighted in job vacancy announcements. On the other hand, OECD defines core competencies and describes key indicators of the competencies in concordance with levels related to the positions. Each level of the core competencies has behavioural indicators that highlights how an individual can demonstrate that competency. Behavioural indicators are designed to show the requirements for successful performance. Levels span 1 through 5 with a bottom-up approach. That's to say, level 1 is typically associated with jobs such as assistants, secretaries and operators whilst level 5 typically associated with jobs such as heads of division, counsellors, deputy directors and directors. OECD competency framework groups competencies into three clusters, i.e. strategic, interpersonal, and delivery-related. The categories are not relevant with the positions and the competency types. OECD lists 15 core competencies under three clusters:

- Interpersonal
    - Client focus
    - Diplomatic sensitivity
    - Influencing
    - Negotiating
    - Organisational knowledge
- Delivery-related
    - Analytical thinking
    - Achievement focus
    - Drafting skills
    - Flexible thinking
    - Managing resources
    - Teamwork and team leadership
- Strategic
    - Developing talent
    - Organisational alignment
    - Strategic networking
    - Strategic thinking

The United Kingdom Civil Service competency framework is well designed and operated one as another best practice. Civil Service Values are at the heart of the framework surrounded by three clusters, i.e. setting direction, delivering results, and engaging people. Worker's Educational Association (WEA) competency framework is prepared according to British context, puts the values at the centre, and is made up of five competencies; achieving results, working collaboratively with others, managing self, delivering excellent service, and behaving student- and organization-focused (WEA, 2018). WEA believes that competencies will support organizational performance and competency framework describes how the organization wants everyone to behave at work. Competency framework is designed to supports recruitment, performance management, and personal and occupational development. WEA details competencies at five levels where level 1 applies to all trainees and apprentices and level 5 applies to strategic and senior leaders.

International Fund for Agricultural Development (IFAD) adopted competency framework in 2004 and reviewed in 2013. IFAD designs four clusters comprising ten competencies at two levels. Level 1 behaviours are relevant with all staff while level 2 ones have wider impacts and are relevant with seniors. Four clusters and relevant competencies are listed below.

- Developing the business
    - Strategic thinking and organizational development
    - Demonstrating leadership
    - Learning, sharing knowledge and innovating
- Achieving results
    - Focusing on clients
    - Problem-solving and decision-making
    - Managing time, resources and information
- Working with others
    - Team working
    - Communicating and negotiating
    - Building relationships and partnerships
- Managing people
    - Managing performance and developing staff

A METHODOLOGY PROPOSAL FOR COMPETENCY FRAMEWORK

A three-component competency framework may be proposed in compliance with global trends, organizational strategy, and human resources policy. The model comprises core, managerial, and functional competencies. While designing a competency framework, labour supply-demand balance is taken into account, developing human capital by job-based learning concept is aimed, organizational culture is complied, performance is easily measured, and innovation and continuous improvement are adopted. As Rothwell and Kazanas (2011) state, organization specific competency framework is more successful in achieving organizational and personal development.

Methodology proposed here is process based, outcome oriented, innovative, task oriented, human centric, and in compliance with global trends. Reminding that one-fit-all recipes are not welcomed, methodology proposed here is a mix of models on hand in use. As Rothwell and Lindlom (1999) suggest, in order to avoid conceptual ambiguity and focusing lessons-learnt, methodology completely ensures future orientation by employing meta-competencies such as open to development and not heavily using terminology. We all know well that the model depends upon scope, context, and autonomy dimensions to determine the level and details. However, a methodology to create a competency framework employed by organizations may comprise the following four steps:

- Creating a competency dictionary
- Collecting data
  - Organizational Analysis
    - Organizational Chart
    - Departmental functions
  - Strategy Analysis
    - Mission, vision, and core values
    - Strategic goals and targets
  - Process Analysis
    - Processes and procedures
    - Work flows
  - Job Analysis
  - Job descriptions
    - Interviews
    - Focus groups
- Creating competency pool
- Creating competency framework

While creating a competency framework, support of top management is critical since vision of the organization makes sense with appropriate talents employed in the organization (Gangani et al., 2006). Thus, competencies are to be aligned with organizational strategies and policies (Cardy and Selvarajan, 2006). Competencies are to be clearly defined and made observable by underlying main behaviours related to the competency (Mansfield, 2000). Basic principles in measuring competency are as follows (McClelland,1973);

- Group competencies in regard with organization size, strategies, policies, and industrial factors,
- Monitor personal development growth,
- Measure observable behaviours,
- Transfer competency not only to job attitudes but extra-role behaviours,
- Measure not reactive behaviours but proactive ones,
- Make results common,
- Standardize desired end states.

Competency framework is detailed regarding observable behaviours and levelled according to positions in the organization because competencies differ by position and reflection on behaviour is diversified. The number of levels span from three to five (PAHRODF, 2017). Nonetheless, at most a four-level structure may be convenient for the organizations. As level increases, it also covers the specifications of the lower. There are some descriptive information on levels in Table 1.

The levels depends upon scope, context, and autonomy dimensions. Scope is about the responsibilities of the position while context describes the environment where the jobs are done. Autonomy is related to the degree of supervision asked and the amount of power to make a decision. Levelling by means of the rubrics mentioned above facilitates the employment of competency framework. First, jobs and roles in the organizations are easily compared. Once behaviour-based performance indicators are clearly defined in accordance with the levels, performance management is easily made.

THE FOURTH INDUSTRIAL REVOLUTION

General Description

1st industrial revolution is caused by mechanization, the cause of the second is the use of electrical energy and 3rd industrial revolution is resulted from electronics and automation (Lasi et al., 2014). The fourth industrial revolution is characterized by technical integration of cyber-physical systems into manufacturing and logistics as well as the use of the Internet of Things and Services in industrial processes (Kagermann et al., 2013). The fourth industrial revolution is organization of life cycle of a product from customer requirements through recycling following delivery to the

Table 1. Levels for competency framework

Level	Remarks
Level 1	• Beginner level • Covers all employees. • Applies to employees who have no managerial responsibility.
Level 2	• Intermediate level • Applies to lower level management. • Applies to few employees whose job requires specialties (e.g. consultant, expert, etc.).
Level 3	• Competent level • Applies to employees who make long-term planning. • Applies to mid-level management. • Applies to few employees whose job requires specialties (e.g. advocate, project coordinator, etc.).
Level 4	• Expert level • Applies to upper-level management.

end user (Prifti et al., 2017). The fourth industrial revolution is differently recalled worldwide even though the context is similar. German-speaking countries call it "Industry 4.0" while France prefers "Industrial Internet" and the United Kingdom uses "Smart Industry" (Grangel-González et al., 2016; Prifti et al., 2017; Ras et al., 2017). And Turkey approaches it as "technological" or "digital transformation". "Smart Factory" is also commonly used for the fourth industrial revolution. The aim of the fourth industrial revolution is efficient, flexible, and customized production by means of digitally decentralized controls, self-organized supply chains, and fully automated factories by real-time and sensor technologies (Kagermann et al., 2013; Gebhardt et al., 2015).

The Needs and the Common Trends of Technological Nature of the Fourth Industrial Revolution

All these industrial revolutions do not influence only the production itself, but also the labour market and the educational system as well (Benešová & Tupa, 2017). It is worth noticing that the concepts addressed by the fourth industrial revolution pertain to different disciplines and key enabling technologies including robotics, big data analysis and, in particular, visual computing and simulation (Longo et al., 2017). The Internet of Things, the Internet of Services and the Internet of People will make connection among the actors in smart factories: machine-machine, human-machine or human-human, and at the same time an enormous amount of data will be obtained (Benešová & Tupa, 2017). To this end, nine technologies are commonly employed by all nations in effort of policy-making supporting the fourth industrial revolution (BCG, 2015):

- Big data and analytics
- Autonomous robots
- Simulation
- Horizontal and vertical system integration
- Internet of things
- Cyber security
- The cloud
- Additive manufacturing
- Augmented reality

The Competency Gaps in the Fourth Industrial Revolution

The fourth industrial revolution will not only change the environment the work is done but also affect the work itself as well as the way the work is performed (Prifti et al.,

2017). As Longo and his colleagues (2017) state, employees are required to be more flexible and to display adaptive capabilities in this dynamic working environment. The tasks they work on are getting less routine and ask for continuous knowledge and skills development (Ras et al., 2017). Since talents are rare, many positions remain unfilled and it seems that they will stay unoccupied due to skills shortage (Ras et al., 2017). On the other hand, competency requirements are changing in concordance with the changes in the workplace. The capabilities of digital solutions have opened up new opportunities and raised ambitious challenges for manufacturing systems (Longo et al., 2017). But only qualified and highly educated employees will be able to control these technologies (Benešová and Tupa, 2017).

Once competency requirements are asked for facilitating effective performance in the workplace, a clear guideline for competencies needed for transformation through the fourth industrial revolution is a must for companies to ease the transformation process (Gebhardt et al., 2015; Prifti et al., 2017). Therefore, European Commission (2016) reviews key competencies required in the workplaces and proposes an action plan as a part of life-long learning. In addition, smart factory concept is developed to support life-long learning to adapt incumbent employees to new work environment. Shallock and his colleagues (2018) advise that smart factory cover technical, transformation, and social skills.

SOLUTIONS AND RECOMMENDATIONS

The fourth industrial revolution transforms the workforce and workplace environment. As design, production, and distribution systems change by Industry 4.0 concept, nature of work changes and job demand and resources diversify through the change. New workplaces are designed as socio-technological places that digitalization is fully employed while providing socialization areas for employees. Advanced technology wants workers equipped with high technological skills as well as creative thinking. It is not wrong to say that competencies change by the changes developed within the Industry 4.0 concept.

There are some competency proposals for new era. For instance; Curtis and McKenzie (2002) stress communication, teamwork, problem-solving, initiative, planning and organizing, self-management, learning, and technology skills. Ananiadou and Claro (2009) research 21st century skills in 16-member countries in OECD. They find out that all countries employ regulations to teach 21st century skills in educational institutions. However, there is no common monitoring and evaluation mechanisms in the countries. The fourth industrial revolution requires identifying basic research, analytical, and entrepreneurial thinking for new solutions, monitoring of practical effects of such implementations and reviewing the potential for future

(Grzybowska and Łupicka, 2017). The timely analysis of the obtained data is important for planning and managing of the flexible production. The obtained data can contain classified information and this leads to increased demands on cyber security to prevent leaks of any data (Benešová and Tupa, 2017).

Grzybowska and Łupicka (2017) review literature on managerial competencies and conclude that future managers and engineers require eight main competencies listed below.

- Creativity
- Entrepreneurial thinking
- Problem solving
- Conflict solving
- Decision making
- Analytical skills
- Research skills
- Efficiency orientation

Prifiti and his colleagues (2017) survey the literature and find out that 68 competencies are mostly mentioned and related with the fourth industrial revolution. The researchers employ SCL universal competency model to develop the framework in order to guide IS, IT, and engineering graduates. SHL universal competency model developed by academicians and practitioners is a behaviour-based competency framework consisting three hierarchical levels as factor level, competency level, and behaviour level (Bartram, 2012). Factor level called "Great Eight" is formed by eight core competencies underpinning organizational and individual performance. According to Bartram (2005), great eight competencies are emerged as a result of factor analyses and multidimensional scaling analyses. At the second level, 20 competencies are described under eight clusters. 112 components are defined as behaviours under the competencies. Factor levels and 20 competencies as well as 68 components found by Prifiti and his colleagues (2017) are displayed on the Table 2 below.

Kantane and her colleagues (2015) ask employers to categorize competencies of employees. Attitudes, motivation, and intellectual properties form a group as well as general skills, appearance and social behaviour form the second group. And third group is formed by professional knowledge and skills. What's interesting is attitudes, motivation, and intellectual properties are attached great significance, more than the rest two groups. And, whatever employee's profession is, the need for soft skills such as communication and collaboration is ever growing. Communication is the most researched competency in the literature, followed by technology literacy, problem-solving, life-long learning, teamwork, and creativity (Prifti et al., 2017).

Table 2. Competencies in the fourth industrial revolution

Big Eight	Competency Dimensions	Competencies
Leading & Deciding	Deciding and Initiating action	Decision Making Taking Responsibility
	Leading and Supervising	Leadership Skills
Supporting & Cooperating	Working with People	Teamwork Collaborating with Others Communicating with People
	Adhering to Principles and Values	Respecting Ethics Environmental Awareness Awareness for Ergonomics
Interacting & Presenting	Relating and Networking	Compromising Creating Business Networks Maintaining Customer Relationships
	Persuading and Influencing	Negotiating Emotional Intelligence
	Presenting and Communicating Information	Presentation and Communication Ability
Analyzing and Interpreting	Writing and Reporting	Targeted/Technical Communication Literacy
	Applying Expertise and Technology	IT and Technology Affinity Economics Extract Business Value from Social Media Big Data/Data Analysis and Interpretation
	Analyzing	Problem Solving Optimization Analytical Skills Cognitive Ability
Creating and Conceptualizing	Learning and Researching	Life-long Learning Knowledge Management
	Creating and Innovating	Innovating Creativity Critical Thinking Change Management
	Formulating Strategies and Concepts	Business Strategy Abstraction Ability Managing Complexity
Organizing and Executing	Planning and Organizing	Project Management Planning and Organizing Work Management Ability
	Delivering Results and Meeting Customer Expectations	Customer Orientation Customer Relationship Management
	Following Instructions and Procedures	Legislation Awareness Safety Awareness Individual Responsibility

Source: Prifti et al., (2017).

Communication skills are attached great significance because workforce for the fourth industrial revolution is asked to excel in general competencies like managerial skills, teamwork, and customer relations as well as strong domain-specific competencies like advanced technology and digital skills (Kusmin et al., 2017). This is true and compliance with EU and UN declarations about the workplace skills as well as ten top competencies business world will be seeking in 2022 mentioned by the World Economic Forum (2018). The World Economic Forum (2018) underlies ten top competencies as analytic and innovative thinking, active learning and learning strategies, creativity, proficiency in new technologies, critical thinking, complex problem solving, leadership and social influence, emotional intelligence, quick comprehension, and system analysis. The EU unveils eight competencies in 2001 that EU citizens would have to move the Union further:

- Native language proficiency;
- Foreign language proficiency;
- Ability to apply basic math and science;
- Ability to learn by digital function;
- Abilities to learn skills such as time-management, problem-solving, information seeking and applying;
- Social commitment;
- Entrepreneurship such as creativity, planning, achievement motivation; and
- Ability to appreciate culture such as art, music and literature.

Likewise, the UN declares 21st century skills as:

- Creativity and innovation
- Critical thinking, problem solving, decision making
- Learning to learn
- Communication
- Collaboration (teamwork)
- Information literacy
- ICT literacy
- Citizenship – local and global
- Life and career
- Personal and social responsibility – including cultural awareness and competence

There is no doubt that a standard competency framework for the fourth revolution may not be proposed. However, as a starting point, a generalized competency framework is formed here to be taken as a sample for further conceptual and empiric studies. But it is critical that competency framework designed here is for general purpose.

Competency framework is not a "will" list; instead, it is a "must" list that carries the organization to the vision (Gangani et al., 2006). Competency framework here presented in Table 3 is a sample for the organizations to survive in the VUCA environment and the fourth industrial revolution.

FUTURE RESEARCH DIRECTIONS

Qin and his colleagues (2016) state that the technology roadmap for accomplishing industrial revolution is still not clear and the gap analysis between current manufacturing systems and the fourth industrial revolution requirements shows that there is still a long way to go (Longo et al., 2017). Therefore, researchers are highly recommended that requirements of contemporary manufacturing systems regarding human resources be researched and modelled.

On the other hand, Cseh (2003) highlights the effect of national culture on competency. It is obvious that nations and industries employ technological transformation at different rates in accordance with their skilled workforce and finance structure. Hence, national and industrial employment policies may be studied and developed to ease the transformation duration.

There is no standard modelling for the companies; however, it is renowned that competencies correlated with higher performance can be measured and developed

Table 3. Competency framework

Core Competencies	Managerial Competencies	Functional Competencies
Stakeholder Focus	Planning and Organizing	Quality Assurance
Analytical Thinking	Future Orientation	Technology Literacy
Communication	Adaptation	Professionalism
Openness to Learning and Development	Leadership	Business Acumen
Social Commitment	Change Management	Knowledge Transfer and Sharing
Teamwork	Holistic Approach	Autonomy
Creativity	Mentorship	Strategic Alignment
Corporate Entrepreneurship		IT security
Proactivity		Risk-based Working
Ethics and Compliance		
Cyber Security		

by training other developmental activities (PAHRODF, 2017). Thus, an integrated human resources management model may be developed to support competency frameworks for future work environment.

Schools have mission to develop human capital for the market. In order to keep up with the changes of the skills required in the industry, schools may change curricula in accordance with future workforce competencies. Towards this end, researchers and practitioners may collaborate and design new curricula covering university-industry collaboration, technology transfer, and apprenticeship models.

CONCLUSION

It is critical for firms to identify a vision, to attract qualified human resources equipped with or ready to equip with competency framework determined, to motivate the qualified workforce, to allocate resources to complete the mission, and to speed activities up to achieve the desired end state. As Gudanowska and his colleagues (2018) recall, organizational success through transformation is based on three milestones; managerial capacity, innovative technology, and competent employees. Therefore, it is of great significance to analyse the organization and create a competency framework to harbour all relevant steps to move the organization further. Because competencies are considered significant factors determining organizational success (Raja & Swapna, 2010), firms are expected to create competency frameworks specific to them by detailing observable behaviours in compliance with organizational culture, strategy, and policies. Unlike general belief in less use of human resources in future's work environment, studies indicate that growth in manufacturing processes results in 6 percent increase in workforce demand. But it is true that required skills at workplace will be changed. Nations and industries are to prepare for competency transformation as well as digital transformation. To this end, this study proposes a generic competency modelling methodology and accordingly a competency framework. Organizations may embrace methodology to prepare competency frameworks specific to themselves and align human resources practices with the framework.

REFERENCES

Ananiadou, K., & Claro, M. (2009). *21st Century Skills and Competences for New Millennium Learners in OECD Countries.* OECD Education Working Papers, No. 41. OECD Publishing.

Archan, S., & Tutschek, E. (2002). *Schlüsselqualifikationen: Wie vermittle ich sie Lehrlingen?* Vienna: Institut für Bildungsforschung der Wirtschaft.

Barrett, G. V., & Depinet, R. L. (1991). A reconsideration of testing for competence rather than for intelligence. *The American Psychologist*, *46*(10), 1012–1024. doi:10.1037/0003-066X.46.10.1012 PMID:1746769

Bartram, D. (2005). The Great Eight competencies: A criterion-centric approach to validation. *The Journal of Applied Psychology*, *90*(6), 1185–1203. doi:10.1037/0021-9010.90.6.1185 PMID:16316273

Bartram, D. (2012). *The SHL universal competency framework*. SHL White Paper. Retrieved from http://assessmentanalytics.com/website/wp-content/uploads/2013/08/White-Paper-SHL-Universal-Competency-Framework.pdf

BCG. (2015). *Embracing Industry 4.0 and Rediscovering Growth*. Retrieved from https://www.bcg.com/capabilities/operations/embracing-industry-4.0-rediscovering-growth.aspx

Boon, J., & van der Klink, M. (2002). Competencies: The triumph of a fuzzy concept. *Academy of Human Resource Development Annual Conference Proceedings*, *1*, 327–334.

Boyatzis, R. E. (1982). *The Competent Manager: A Model for Effective Performance*. New York: Wiley.

Boyatzis, R. E., & Sala, F. (2004). Assessing emotional intelligence competencies. In G. Geher (Ed.), *The Measurement of Emotional Intelligence* (pp. 147–180). Hauppauge, NY: Nova Science Publishers.

Brockbank, W., Ulrich, D., & Yakonich, D. (2003). v. Ann Arbor, MI: University of Michigan Business School.

Burgoyne, J. (1988). *Competency Based Approaches to Management Development*. Lancaster: Centre for the Study of Management Learning.

Campbell, A., & Sommers Luchs, K. S. (1997). *Core Competency-Based Strategy*. London: Thomson.

Cardy, R. L., & Selvarajan, T. T. (2006). Competencies: Alternative Frameworks for Competitive Advantage. *Business Horizons*, *49*(3), 235–245. doi:10.1016/j.bushor.2005.09.004

Cheetham, G., & Chivers, G. (1996). Towards a holistic model of professional competence. *Journal of European Industrial Training*, *20*(5), 20–30. doi:10.1108/03090599610119692

Cheetham, G., & Chivers, G. (1998). The reflective (and competent) practitioner: A model of professional competence which seeks to harmonise the reflective practitioner and competence-based approaches. *Journal of European Industrial Training*, *22*(7), 267–276. doi:10.1108/03090599810230678

Cockerill, T. (1989, September). The kind of competence for rapid change. *Personnel Management*, 52-56.

Cseh, M. (2003). Facilitating learning in multicultural teams. *Advances in Developing Human Resources*, *5*(1), 26–40. doi:10.1177/1523422302239181

Curtis, D., & McKenzie, P. (2002). *Employability skills for Australian industry: literature review and framework development.* Canberra: Australian Chamber of Commerce and Industry.

Deist, F. D., & Winterton, J. (2005). What is Competence? *Human Resource Development International*, *8*(1), 27–46. doi:10.1080/1367886042000338227

Dejoux, C. (1999). *Organisation qualifiante et maturite´en gestion des compe'tences.* Paris: Direction et Gestion des Entreprises.

Dessler, G. (2007). *Human Resource Management*. Pearson Prentice Hall.

Draganidis, F., & Mentzas, G. (2006). Competency Based Management: A Review of Systems and Approaches. *Information Management & Computer Security*, *14*(1), 51–64. doi:10.1108/09685220610648373

Dulewicz, V. (1989). Assessment centres as the route to competence. *Personnel Management*, *21*(11), 56–59.

European Commission. (2016). *A New Skills Agenda for Europe*. Communication from the Commission to the European Parliament, the Council, the European Economic and Social Committee and the Committee of the Regions (COM). Retrieved from https://ec.europa.eu/transparency/regdoc/rep/1/2016/EN/1-2016-381-EN-F1-1.PDF

Foss, N. J., & Knudsen, C. (Eds.). (1996). *Towards a Competence Theory of the Firm*. London: Routledge.

Gangani, N., McLean, G. N., & Braden, R. A. (2006). A Competency-Based Human Resource Development Strategy. *Performance Improvement Quarterly*, *19*(1), 127–140. doi:10.1111/j.1937-8327.2006.tb00361.x

Gebhardt, J., Grimm, A., & Neugebauer, L. M. (2015). Developments 4.0 Prospects on future requirements and impacts on work and vocational education. *Journal of Teacher Education*, *3*(2), 117–133.

Grangel-González, I., Halilaj, L., Coskun, G., Auer, S., Collarana, D., & Hoffmeister, M. (2016, February). Towards a semantic administrative shell for industry 4.0 components. *IEEE Tenth International Conference on Semantic Computing*, 230-237. 10.1109/ICSC.2016.58

Grzybowska, K., & Łupicka, A. (2017). Key competencies for Industry 4.0. *Economics & Management Innovations*, *1*(1), 250–253. doi:10.26480/icemi.01.2017.250.253

Gudanowska, A. E., Alonso, J. P., & Törmänen, A. (2018). What competencies are needed in the production industry? The case of the Podlaskie Region. *Engineering Management in Production and Services*, *10*(1), 65–74. doi:10.1515/emj-2018-0006

Gürbüz, S. (2017). *Human Resources Management: Theory, Research, and Practice*. Ankara: Seçkin Yayınları.

Haddadj, S., & Besson, D. (2000, January). Introduction a` la gestion des compe´tences. *Revue Franc¸ aise de Gestion*, 82-83.

Hartle, F. (1995). *How to Re-engineer your Performance Management Process*. London: Kogan Page.

Hayes, J. L. (1979). A new look at managerial competence: The AMA model of worthy performance. *Management Review*, *68*(11), 2–3.

Heinsman, H. (2008). *The Competency Concept Revealed: Its Nature, Relevance, and Practice* (PhD Dissertation). Vrije Universiteit, Kurt Lewin Institute.

IFAD. (2018). *IFAD competency framework: How we give our best.* International Fund for Agricultural Development. Retrieved from https://newunkampus.unssc.org/pluginfile.php/105615/mod_folder/content/0/Agency%20Leadership%20Frameworks/IFAD/IFAD%20Competency%20Framework.pdf?forcedownload=1

Kagermann, H., Helbig, J., Hellinger, A., & Wahlster, W. (2013). *Recommendations for implementing the strategic initiative INDUSTRIE 4.0: Securing the future of German manufacturing industry; final report of the Industrie 4.0 Working Group*. Forschungsunion.

Kantane, I., Sloka, B., Buligina, I., Tora, G., Busevica, R., Buligina, A., ... Tora, P. (2015). Expectations by employers on skills, knowledge and attitudes of employees. *European Integration Studies*, *9*, 224–234.

Kusmin, K. L., Ley, T., & Normak, P. (2017) Towards a Data Driven Competency Management Platform for Industry 4.0. *Proceedings of the Workshop Papers of i-Know 2017.*

Lasi, H., Fettke, P., Kemper, H. G., Feld, T., & Hoffmann, M. (2014). Industry 4.0. *Business & Information Systems Engineering*, *6*(4), 239–242. doi:10.100712599-014-0334-4

Le Deist, F. D., & Winterton, J. (2005). What is competence? *Human Resource Development International*, *8*(1), 27–46. doi:10.1080/1367886042000338227

Leung, K., Trevena, L., & Waters, D. (2016). Development of a competency framework for evidence-based practice in nursing. *Nurse Education Today*, *4*(39), 189–196. doi:10.1016/j.nedt.2016.01.026 PMID:27006055

Longo, F., Nicoletti, L., & Padovano, A. (2017). Smart operators in industry 4.0: A human-centered approach to enhance operators' capabilities and competencies within the new smart factory context. *Computers & Industrial Engineering*, *113*, 144–159. doi:10.1016/j.cie.2017.09.016

Lucia, A. D., & Lepsinger, R. (1999). *The Art and Science of Competency Models: Pinpointing Critical Success Factors in an Organization*. San Francisco, CA: Jossey-Bass/Pfeiffer.

Mansfield, R. S. (2000). Practical Questions for Building Competency Models. In *Proceedings of Competency-Based Management for the Federal Public Service Conference* (pp. 3-17). Ottawa, Canada: Academic Press.

Markus, L., Thomas, H. C., & Allpress, K. (2005). Confounded by competencies? An evaluation of the evolution and use of competency models. *New Zealand Journal of Psychology*, *34*(2), 117–126.

McClelland, D. (1973). Testing for competence rather than for 'intelligence'. *The American Psychologist*, *28*(1), 1–14. doi:10.1037/h0034092 PMID:4684069

McClelland, D. (1998). Identifying competencies with behavioural-event interviews. *Psychological Science*, *9*(5), 331–339. doi:10.1111/1467-9280.00065

Monk, A. L. (2001). *The development of a competency model for auditors working in a professionalservices environment* (Unpublished master's thesis). University of South Africa, Pretoria, South Africa.

Nadler, D. A., & Tushman, M. (1999). The organisation of the future: Strategic imperatives and core competencies for the 21st century. *Organizational Dynamics*, *27*(1), 45–58. doi:10.1016/S0090-2616(00)80006-6

PAHRODF. (2017). *A Guidebook on Competency Modelling and Profiling*. Manila, Philippines: Author.

Petersen, S. A., Heikurs, T., Cerinŝek, G., & Bedek, M. (2011). *Competence Portfolios*. European Commission.

Prifti, L., Knigge, M., Kienegger, H., & Krcmar, H. (2017). A Competency Model for "Industrie 4.0" Employees. *Proceedings der 13. Internationalen Tagung Wirtschaftsinformatik,* 46-60.

Raja, K. G., & Swapna, R. (2010). Evaluating the differences between Managerial and Executive Level Personal Competencies -A Critical analysis of Select IT Companies. *Bhavan's International. The Journal of Business*, *4*(2), 71–76.

Ras, E., Wild, F., Stahl, C., & Baudet, A. (2017). Bridging the skills gap of workers in Industry 4.0 by Human Performance Augmentation Tools: Challenges and Roadmap. *Proceedings of the 10th International Conference on Pervasive Technologies Related to Assistive Environments*, 428-432. 10.1145/3056540.3076192

Robertson, I., Gibbons, P., Baron, H., MacIver, R., & Nyfield, G. (1999). Understanding Management Performance. *British Journal of Management*, *10*, 5-12.

Rothwell, W. J., & Kazanas, H. C. (2011). *Mastering the instructional design process: A systematic approach*. San Francisco: John Wiley & Sons.

Rothwell, W. J., & Lindholm, J. E. (1999). Competency identification, modelling and assessment in the USA. *International Journal of Training and Development*, *3*(2), 90–105. doi:10.1111/1468-2419.00069

Russell, C. J. (2000). A Longitudinal Study of Top Level Executive Performance. *Journal of Applied Psychology, Vol*, *86*(4), 560–573. doi:10.1037/0021-9010.86.4.560 PMID:11519641

Sandberg, J. (2000). Understanding human competence at work: An interpretative approach. *Academy of Management Journal*, *43*(1), 9–25.

Schallock, B., Rybski, C., Jochem, R., & Kohl, H. (2018). Learning Factory for Industry 4.0 to provide future skills beyond technical training. *Procedia Manufacturing*, *23*, 27–32. doi:10.1016/j.promfg.2018.03.156

Scullen, S. E., Mount, M. K., & Goff, M. (2000). Understanding the latent structure of job performance ratings. *The Journal of Applied Psychology*, *85*(6), 956–970. doi:10.1037/0021-9010.85.6.956 PMID:11125659

Shippmann, J. S., Ash, R. A., Battista, M. A., Carr, L., Eyde, L. D., Hesketh, B., ... Sanchez, J. I. (2000). The Practice of Competency Modelling. *Personnel Psychology*, *53*(3), 703–740. doi:10.1111/j.1744-6570.2000.tb00220.x

Sparrow, P. (1995). Organisational Competencies: A Valid Approach for the Future? *International Journal of Selection and Assessment*, *3*(3), 168–177. doi:10.1111/j.1468-2389.1995.tb00024.x

Stokes, P., & Oiry, E. (2012). An Evaluation of the Use of Competencies in Human Resource Development-a Historical and Contemporary Recontextualisation. *EuroMed Journal of Business*, *7*(1), 4–23. doi:10.1108/14502191211225356

Straka, G. A. (2004). *Measurement and evaluation of competence, in: 3rd European Research Report: Vocational Education and Training*. Thessaloniki: CEDEFOP.

Trace Project Report. (2005). *Overview of European Competency Frameworks*. TRACE Project number: 2005-2028/001 LE2-51OREF.

Vraniak, L., Mazánek, L., & Konečná, Z. (2017). Competence Approaches: Review of Current Concepts and Theories. *Ad Alta: Journal of Interdisciplinary Research*, *7*(2), 134–137.

WEA. (2018). *Competency Framework 2018*. Workers Educational Association. Retrieved from https://www.wea.org.uk/file/5290/download?token=pO4OeKgG

White, R. W. (1959). Motivation reconsidered: The concept of competence. *Psychological Review*, *66*(5), 297–333. doi:10.1037/h0040934 PMID:13844397

Wickramasinghe, V., & Zoyza, N. (2008). Gender, Age and Marital Status as Predictors of Managerial Competency Needs: Empirical Evidence from a Sri Lankan Telecommunication Service Provider. *Gender in Management*, *23*(5), 337–354. doi:10.1108/17542410810887365

Woodruffe, C. (1990). *Assessment Centre: Identifying and developing competences*. London: IPM.

Woodruffe, C. (1991, September). Competent by any other name. *Personnel Management*, 30-33.

World Economic Forum. (2018). *The Future of Jobs Report 2018*. Geneva: Centre for the New Economy and Society, World Economic Forum.

Wright, D. (2005). *The Ultimate Guide to Competency Assessment in Healthcare* (3rd ed.). Minneapolis, MN: Creative Health Care Management.

KEY TERMS AND DEFINITIONS

21st Century Skills: UN declares 21st century skills as: creativity and innovation; critical thinking, problem solving, decision making; learning to learn; communication; collaboration (teamwork); information literacy; ICT literacy; citizenship (local and global); life and career; and personal and social responsibility including cultural awareness and competence.

Competence: Knowledge, skills, and abilities as well as personal attributes and motivational factors for higher performance workers.

Competency: A guiding tool including knowledge, abilities, distinguished personal attributes, and behaviours for higher performance contributing to achieving strategic goals of the company.

Competency Framework: A belief that one's own culture is superior to other cultures.

Competency-Based Human Resources Management: The belief that family is central to well-being and that family members and family issues take precedence over other aspects of life.

Core Competencies: Competencies asked from all people in the organization irrespective of their statute and position, ranging blue-collar workers to top management.

Functional Competencies: Competencies required for excellence regarding working style.

Managerial Competencies: Managerial positions and manager candidates awaited to have managerial competencies covering organization specific processes for organizational success.

VUCA: Acronym stands for volatility, uncertainty, complex, and ambiguity.

Chapter 3
Identification of Challenges and Opportunities for Work 4.0 Competences Developing in Slovakia

Helena Fidlerová
https://orcid.org/0000-0002-3426-5803
Slovak University of Technology, Slovakia

Martina Porubčinová
Slovak Academy of Sciences, Slovakia

Martin Fero
Slovak University of Technology in Bratislava, Slovakia

Ivana Novotná
Slovak University of Technology in Bratislava, Slovakia

ABSTRACT

Industry 4.0 and its effect on processes and people becomes reality with all organizational and technological complex implications for the future. States around the world including Slovakia face the challenge of defining strategy on how to convert the challenges of Industry 4.0 into competitive advantage. This chapter focuses on Work 4.0 competences development, analyzed in the level of enrichment of the human capital content as well as in the level of labor market polarization. The aim of this chapter is to present opportunities and threats in competence development regarding the concept of Intelligent Industry and discuss sustainable solutions in the context of National Action Plan of Intelligent Industry of Slovak Republic, looking for win-win strategy. The authors analyze differences in competences achieved via education system in Slovakia and expectations of industry. Special attention is given the situation in Slovakia, country-oriented on automotive and with strong cooperation with Germany as innovation leader in European countries, to find strategy within this no zero game.

DOI: 10.4018/978-1-5225-9810-7.ch003

INTRODUCTION

Industry 4.0 has attention in manufacturing process all over world, with special focus on technology solution, big data in real time, augmented reality, predictive maintenance as well as Internet of Things.

Main objective of this chapter is as follows: Insight into sustainable strategy focusing not only on digitalization, automation, collaboration with robots and augmented reality from technological point of view, but also on the human as the central point of this revolution.

Authors consider as important not to exclude humans from the production world issue to identify desired Work 4.0 key competences and to invest in boosting those competences of employees, considering their individual skills and knowledge.

The chapter focuses on the development of new job requirements in the field of demand for Work 4.0 competences. The development of demand and supply of Work 4.0 competences is analyzed in both levels as follows: a) in the level of enrichment of the human capital content and b) in the context of the trend of labor market polarization. This means challenge for all countries, but the situation could be different according to political, economic, social, technical and other aspects. This chapter provides closer look on the specific situation in Slovakia. According to OECD Survey (2018), Slovakia has the biggest risk of automation and risk of significant change regarding jobs in comparison with 30 analyzed countries. One of assumed reasons is not enough diversification thus the industry in Slovakia is oriented mainly to automotive industry.

Subsequently an analysis is conducted in the chapter, which comprises the final observations and results of quantitative research-based survey focused on non-formal learning through participation on EU Youth in Action projects in Slovakia. This special study has been developed to explore the learning processes of actors involved in above mentioned projects: how do participants of projects learn and which settings (comparison of school, work, internship etc.), educational approaches, methodologies and methods contribute to the development of their key competences. The findings clearly indicate that participation in non-formal learning (e.g. via Youth in Action projects) contributes to the development of the key competences and skills required by the concept of Intelligent Industry. Special attention is given to competences that respondents would like to learn for future. As the latest, most important challenge in the field of desired Work 4.0 requirements is taking into consideration the need to monitor the impact of changes on the future work requirements that shape Industry 4.0 as the current worldwide innovation.

BACKGROUND

The innovative process of technological change, which is technologically based on the Internet, has formed the basis for Industry 4.0 concept as a new stage of the production process (Lukac, 2015). The concept of "Industry 4.0" was recognized in Germany to refer to the development of "cyber-physical systems" (CPS) and dynamic data processes that use massive amounts of data to drive smart machines (Strange & Zucchella, 2017).

The fourth industrial revolution, as a change within the entire value chain across the product life-cycle in company including a new level of digitalization, automatic data exchange and automation, demands a has significant paradigm shift in management of manufacturing and organization processes (Maslarić, Nikoličić, & Mirčetić, 2016; Saniuk & Saniuk, 2017; Schuh, Gartzen, Rodenhauser, & Marks, 2015; Wolf, Kleindienst, Ramsauer, Zierler, & Winter, n.d.). This cycle is geared to increasingly individualised customer wishes, and extends from the idea, the development and production work, and the delivery of a product to the final customer, to recycling, including the associated services. It is based on the availability of all relevant information in real-time as a result of networking all the parties involved in value creation, and on the ability to infer the optimal value stream from data at any time.

Consequently, Industry 4.0 ideas should be implemented in an interdisciplinary manner and in close cooperation with the other key areas and using different technologies drivers. These are formerly known as the nine pillars of the technological advancement, and they comprise the following technologies: Big Data; Autonomous Robots; Simulation; Universal System Integration; Industrial IoT; Cybersecurity; Cloud Computing; Additive Manufacturing and Augmented Reality (Gattullo et al., 2019; Makris, Karagiannis, Koukas, & Matthaiakis, 2016). The Industry 4.0 is based on four key components: cyber-physical systems, Internet of Things (IoT0, Internet of Services (IoS) and smart factory, that means the interaction and exchange of information not only among human beings and human to machine interfaces and among machines themselves (Roblek, Meško, & Krapež, 2016). This communication between all entities runs in the production system and outside of it in the real world time (Lasi, Fettke, Kemper, Feld, & Hoffmann, 2014). Linking people, objects and systems creates dynamic, real-time optimized, self-organizing and inter-enterprise value creation networks which can be optimized according to various criteria such as costs, availability and resource usage.

The main preconditions required for the successful implementation of Industry 4.0 are new business models, availability of skilled workers, standardization, work organization, availability of products, research, professional development, as well as interaction and collaboration between human and robots in hybrid teams (Schiffeler, Stehling, Haberstroh, & Isenhardt, 2018). Several foreign studies devote considerable attention towards theoretical and empirical analysis of qualification requirements development within the Industry 4.0 concept. In the German environment, the authors are focusing on the analysis of the teamwork competencies as well as the networking of all the elements that are part of the production process. As machines are supposed to be, in addition to human, collaborating team members, the core of the Industry 4.0 concept in this context is being defined as "a digitized and networked production environment within virtual working places or in human-robot-teams" (Richert, Shehadeh, Willicks, & Jeschke, 2016).

Requirements of teamwork and collaborative competencies in hybrid work teams belong to key requirements that transform skill demand and change teaching and training towards Education 4.0. Similarly, as in case of ability to collaborate in hybrid work teams, authors Quint, Sebastian, & Gorecky (2015) place emphasis on competency of working in mixed reality and combining elements of the real world and the virtual information world. The potential offered by a mixed reality to combine sensory experience and experience and information from the digital environment, should be exploited already in the process of education and training,

As already mentioned, Industry 4.0 is reshaping the way how humans and machines divide up work and the decision-making process – calling for new competences from all involved. Ultimately, only companies that are able to identify those competences and make appropriate modifications to the personnel development will be able to make full use of the potential flexibility and productivity of Industry 4.0 affords.

Smart factories, as key feature of Intelligent Industry framework, are capable at managing complexity, less prone to disruption and are able to manufacture goods more efficiently. In the smart factory, human beings, machines and resources communicate with each other as naturally as in a social network. Smart products know the details of how they were manufactured and how they are intended to be used as they actively support the manufacturing process.

The development of Industry 4.0. represents according strategic document *Iniciativa Průmysl 4.0* (Initiative Industry 4.0) one of the most significant technological and structural changes that affect not only industry but also other sectors, science, research, ethics and social order". Issues related to the development of Industry 4.0 go beyond the concept of human capital and cover not only the demand side for work competencies required for the development of a new stage of industrial production, but also the assessment of the future relevance of employment in the context of total self-realization of man. Social systems will face the challenge – differentiated for various types of job positions - of how to support the mechanisms for compensation for relatively simple, physically unpretentious tasks, as well as for tasks requiring analytical, creative and synthetic methods of reasoning.

Creating paradigm for personal self-realization as a complementary activity to work activity, e.g. within a workplace or non-profit environment, can be identified as a challenge for human capital formation in the future, considering different qualification levels degrees and personal preferences. Questions and concerns related to the essence of human competencies uniqueness will become a part of important ethical debate discussing questions as follows: What makes us specific, unique? Is it desirable to strive to imitate specifically human abilities and their possible improvement by artificial intelligence? As the most important current challenge in the field of new work requirements in the context of Industry 4.0, authors stress the need to monitor the impact of changes in the work requirements according to individual's qualification levels.

As a future consequence of the above-mentioned changes, it is expected that the partnerships between businesses/enterprises and higher education institutions will be even more important in the future. It will be important to open access to science and engineering studies and place greater emphasis on transferable skills and skill assessment. There are already several initiatives to bridge this gap of new knowledge and skills between the academic and industrial worlds. Two interesting examples are represented by the "Academy Cube" initiative and the European Commission "eSkills for Jobs 2016" initiative (Motyl, Baronio, Uberti, Speranza, & Filippi, 2017).

INDUSTRY 4.0 WORK COMPETENCIES IN THE CONTEXT OF AUTOMATION AND POLARIZATION OF LABOUR MARKET

Changes in the field of human capital are regarded as one of the key indicators of information society as the entirely new type of social system or, in critical view, as the key indicator of the informatization of established relationships (Webster, 2002). Changes in most required knowledge and skills are supposed to be perceived as one of key indicators of transition to the information society (Bell, 1979, Lévy 2000, Nath 2017). From the early beginning of the information society theory, authors have examined changes toward the new type of the work force with the specific set of competencies in the context of information society development. In the context of employability on the labor market of the information society, the concept of key competencies was defined in 2010.

This capacity may be defined in terms of cognitive factors (e.g. different types of knowledge), intellectual and perceptual motor skills (e.g. dexterity), affective factors (e.g. attitudes, values, motivation etc.), personality traits (e.g. self-confidence) and social skills (e.g. communicative and cooperative skills).

The term competence will be used to refer to the capacity of an individual (or a collective) to successfully (according to certain formal or informal criteria, set by oneself or by somebody else) handle certain situations or complete a certain task or job (Ellström, 1997). Acquired competencies are required to perform the job-related tasks effectively. Additionally, the competencies are characterised by their complex nature that ought to be addressed to meet the market needs (Armstrong & Taylor, 2014).

Key eight competencies cover fundamental competencies of literacy, communication in foreign languages, numeracy and digital competencies identified as essential for learning, as well as transversal competencies of ability learning to learn, social and civic competencies, entrepreneurship and cultural sensitivity (Figure 1). Himanen (2004), Webster (2002), Lévy (2000) and Castells (2004) have emphasized in the area of specific competencies required on the labor market of information society the importance of non-formal (personal) competencies such as:

- creative capacity
- degree of analytic capacities
- ability to process information
- creativity
- enthusiasm
- explicitness
- cooperation
- flexible relation in time in the sphere of work organization ().

The abovementioned specific competences contrast with those ones required in the routine and rigid activities, rigid organization structure, fields with lower need and ability to process information and in working environment where the work

Figure 1. Key competences
Source: Drawn by authors

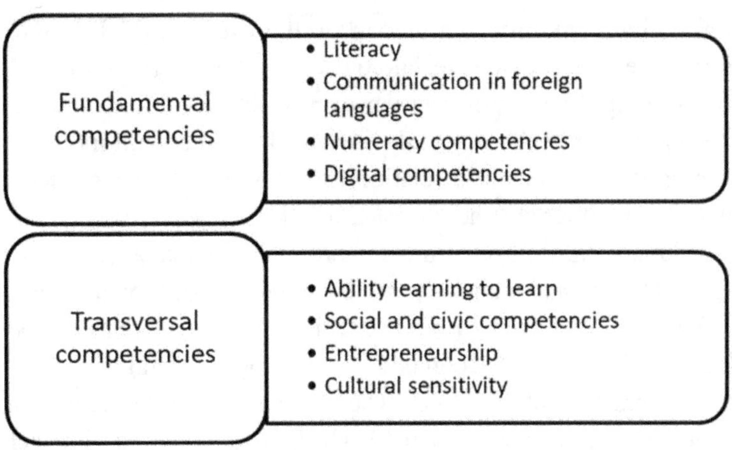

is considered as a duty. The specific competencies relate to the work culture of industrial society (Castells, 2004).

The innovative nature of the Industry 4.0 that can be identified in its core areas of (a) product innovation, (b) technological and process innovation, and (c) knowledge and method innovations calls for the identification of relevant changes in labor market. It is not surprising, due to the innovative character of Industry 4.0 that the character of work is changing towards Work 4.0.

Based on "dynamic and flexible character of work, which is one of key dimensions of labor market flexibility in the information society, demands for professional adaptability and flexibility increase in the information society" in the context of labor market trends (Benner, 2004, p. 179). According to authors (Martinak, 2017; Autor & Dorn, 2013; Berger & Frey, 2016), labor market trends in the context of Industry 4.0 development include the polarization trend in terms of the differentiated impact of technology on employment according skill levels and types of work. Due to the polarization of the labor market, the substitution effect of digital technologies is manifested especially in middle-task and routine work positions, resulting not only in an increase demand for highly qualified workers whose jobs should be at least compromised by the risk of automation, but also in increase demand for lower-level workers in positions that are currently difficult to automate (Berger & Frey, 2016).

Employment decline in middle-skill occupations is related to the prevailing share of routine tasks that machines can replace for part of middle-skill occupations. While some of the work activities as data processing or telecommunication services could become routine, most of the personal services in the area of education, accommodation and meals recently have been demanding for standardization (Berger & Frey, 2016, p. 15). Employment growth that could be expected in the sector of auxiliary and unskilled labor, is related also the employment and income growth in highly skilled jobs that raises demand for services that are currently not replaceable (David H. Autor & Dorn, 2013).

However, digital revolution, dating back to the 1980s in the US, appears to be less transformative than previous technological revolutions (Gordon, 2012), while others point to a significant polarization in productivity due to the introduction of digital technology in technologically advanced and stagnant industries (Autor, 2015). Job polarization occurs in relation to Industry 4.0 development, as "jobs that are intensive in either abstract or manual tasks are generally found at opposite ends of the occupational skill spectrum – in professional, managerial, and technical occupations on the one hand, and in service and laborer occupations on the other" (Autor, 2015, p. 12). As stated by Berger and Frey, "there is no reason to believe that the digital revolution has reduced demand in technologically stagnant sectors such as healthcare, personal or public services. These areas are continuing to create a huge number of jobs" (Berger, Frey, 2016, p. 2). The involvement of digital technologies is related rather with a complementary than a substitution effect, complementing the digital skills rather than replacing the full performance of work. Since digital technologies do not fully replace tacit knowledge, intuitive and creative thinking marked as "abstract – intensive tasks" by Autor (2015) as well as interpersonal skills that allow social interaction, the studies also predict an employment growth in the service sector. This includes employment growth in non-manual manual jobs as personal assistance, gastro and cleaning services, and other areas skilled work positions that are difficult to automate at present.

Areas with the largest range of automated work tasks can be found in the manufacturing, transport, logistics, administrative and services sectors. While the job positions of telemarketers, garment workers, clock technicians, tax accountants, laboratory technicians represent the work with the highest possible future machine substitution currently, the automation affects amount of work in the area of personal and health services such as psychologists, therapists, consultants, surgeons, teachers, human resources managers, and recreational workers to the slightest extent. According to Autor (2015, p. 26) many current middle-skilled jobs will continue to demand a mixture tasks across the skill spectrum, so competencies of flexibility, judgment and common sense remain a comparative advantage of workers in those positions.

In its consequences, the process of de-industrialization as a technological innovation of Industry 4.0 is less job-creating and more work-saving, as the ongoing automation process is involved in changing the technological level of the various production industries. Though, as the boundaries between technologically stagnant and progressive sectors have shifted over time, they can be expected to move forward in the future as well. Increasing productivity in the service sector - as a result of technological advances in sensor activity and increased data capacity (big data) - could help increase the number of non-routine work positions that can be performed by (or in cooperation) digital technologies. Currently, new industrial sectors that emerged in the period 2000-2010 as a result of involvement of digital technologies into work tasks, include 71 new jobs in the field of online auctions, web design, video and audio streaming.

Based on labor market trends, the concept of Work 4.0 reflects specific key requirements of Industry 4.0 as follows:

- Process of work polarization towards human-intensive work tasks and computer-intensive work tasks, due to different amount of automatable tasks
- The acquisition of new work skills related to working with collaborative robots (co-bots) with emphasis on lower qualifications
- Supporting the development of creativity, interpersonal and communication skills that are demanding to automate, in which people (currently) achieve a comparative advantage over robots and artificial intelligence

WORK 4.0: CHANGES IN HUMAN CAPITAL CONTENT

Work 4.0 (in German: Arbeit 4.0) is the conceptual umbrella under which the future of work in context of Industry 4.0. and how the world of work may change until 2030 The concept was introduced in November 2015 by the German Federal Ministry of Labour and Social Affairs (BMAS) when it launched a report entitled Re-Imagining Work: Green Paper Work 4.0.

First it has been discussed in Germany in White Paper. Work 4.0 is characterized by a high degree of integration and cooperation, the use of digital technologies, and a rise in flexible work arrangements. Its drivers include digitalization, globalization, demographic change (ageing, migration), and cultural change. Main challenges of Work 4.0 lie in development of the relationship between the use of human and machine labor (upskilling vs. deskilling, devaluation of experience, individual support vs. behavioral monitoring), profound changes in structure of organizations, flexible work conditions, along with the transformation of economic sectors and activities and its effect on employment, the creation of new markets and new forms of work through digital platforms and the issues associated with Big Data (e.g. data protection).

Thus, beside the field of technological innovations of Industry 4.0, the attention of social theories is heading towards the soft innovations, changes in the work environment, the growths of the flexibility on the labor market and the development, widening and accumulation of the human capital. As Berger and Frey point, "rising skills yields suggest that skill supply is not in line with demand for labor skills created by technological change" (Berger, Frey, 2016, p. 9). Economic advantage, acceleration, and increased reliability of automated business performance also boost the demand for skills that cannot simply be replaced and increases their value. (Martinák, 2017).

Required Skills and Competencies

Industry 4.0 has a significant impact on the change in the required skills in existing professions, as 42% of OECD employees of ICT companies have experienced a change in work or work skills requirements over the last three years (OECD, 2013). Demand for digital competencies has been significantly differentiated according to the International Standard Classification of Occupations level (CEDEFOP, 2015), though, the Industry 4. 0 development could create the opportunity to raise the demand for digital skills not only in highly qualified work positions.

Competencies that can be described as critical for the involvement of digital technologies into production cycle go beyond the area of digital skills. As part of the work becomes more interactive, the authors point to the fact that "work tasks involving communication and interpersonal activities have become important in various occupations and industries" (Michaels at al, in Berger, Frey, p. 23). The growing demand for interpersonal skills results from the fact that part of the high-tech work tasks involves tasks requiring personal contact and physical closeness. Berger and Frey (2016), state that "among workers in positions that have undergone extensive computerization, the range of tasks requiring analytical and interactive significantly increased, due to fact part of routine tasks could be automated" (Berger& Frey, 2016). Work skills in terms of creativity, high-order skills, and social (interpersonal skills) belong thus to critical skills to support Industry 4.0 development.

Skills defined as one`s ability to apply knowledge and use the know-how for the completion of well-defined tasks. Skills may be cognitive (involving the use of logical, intuitive and creative thinking) or practical (involving manual dexterity and the use of methods, materials, and tools).

In the context of a learning process, basic skills are generally: observation and replication of actions task, reproduction from instruction or memory, reliable execution independent of help, adaptation / integration of expertise to meet requirements and automated, unconscious management of activity(Chryssolouris, Mavrikios, & Mourtzis, 2013).

Tasks that can be performed by computers are currently represented by working activities that are easily identifiable (due to Moravec and Polanyi's paradox). The term Polanyi's paradox stresses the importance of tacit knowledge, pointing that there exist many tasks which human beings understand intuitively how to perform but cannot explicitly verbalize and codify. Moravec's paradox reflects the discovery of robotics researchers that high-level reasoning requires very little computation, but low-level sensorimotor skills require enormous computational resources (Autor, 2015, Martinák 2017).Since robots and machines cannot simulate human interaction (Martinák, 2017), these technologies cannot replace human beings in certain jobs: as stated by the authors. Logical thinking, problem solving, creativity and cooperation/ interaction with other belong to work competencies in which people reach a higher level. However, even these competences in digital society will have to be complemented often by digital skills (MGI, 2017), that enable to acquire information, to optimize and plan activities and recognize high-level patterns.

As stated before, it is necessary to support the formation of those skills that enable part of workers to switch to types of work activities that can be sustainable, such as care, nursing, creativity and interpersonal skills. By supporting these competences, universally complemented by digital skills, it is possible to promote inclusive development and citizen participation because without the acquisition of digital skills, the existing divide in the level of key work competencies will intensify.

Competencies that are identified to be essential for the innovativeness (also) in the context of digitalization according to (Kinkel, Schemmann, & Lichtner, 2017) are integrated into four sections:

1. Network competencies, described as a cluster of competencies that refers to the ability to effectively learn, think and act by using personal, social and organizational internal as well as external networks in order to achieve innovation-related advantages or target;
2. Creative problem-solving competence, defined as cluster of competencies that refers to ability to recognize and define problems and to develop novel solutions with the help of knowledge, motivation, systematic problem recognition and creativity;
3. Overview competence, defined as a cluster of competencies that refers to ability to understand different ideas, knowledge, experiences as well as to aware of key people who posse relevant knowledge or experience in order to assess these insights regarding their innovation potential;
4. Integration competence, that is described a cluster of competencies that refers to ability to combine constructively different ideas, knowledge and experience of different people and to integrate both internal and external ideas along the entire innovation process.

Based on the current studies of the authors (Kinkel et al., 2017; Avvisati, Jacotin, & Vincent-Lancrin, 2014; Berger & Frey, 2016), the competencies of complex understanding, interdisciplinarity and ability to rather solve ad-hoc problems than concentrate on routine tasks, along with competency of team-work within hybrid and virtual work-teams and with co-bots represent the core innovative competencies in a context of Industry 4.0 development. The need to understand the roles and requirements of different actors, deeper understanding of production process place emphasize on the importance of overview and integration competencies. Entrepreneurial skills are being involved in a set of key Work 4.0 competencies that, together with business and technological skills, combine "fusion skills" to support the transformation of new technologies into practice.

Competences are classified in different ways and there are many different groups of competences.(Hecklau, Galeitzke, Flachs, & Kohl, 2016). In an extensive study, Hamlin and Stewart (2011) identify "personal development (competencies), team development (collaboration) and organisational development (structure and processes)". The authors divide skills into several groups ((Hecklau et al., 2016; Jerman, Pejić Bach, & Bertoncelj, 2018):

- Technical competencies (Technical skills, Understanding IT security, Process understanding, Media skills);
- Methodological competencies (Creativity, Entrepreneurial thinking, Problem and Conflict solving, Analytical skills, Decision making, Research skills);

- Social competencies (Communication skills, Networking and integration skills, Ability to work in a team, Intercultural skills, Ability to be compromising and cooperative, Leadership skills);
- Personal competencies (Commitment for lifelong learning, Flexibility, Motivation to learn, Ability to work under pressure, Social responsibility).

Summary knowledge required from the manufacturing of Industry 4.0 and impacts on manufacturing workforce are as follows: increased skills and knowledge, higher levels of soft skills and management capabilities as well as software and programming, an increasing need for interdisciplinary skills, especially the combination of programming skills and mechanical engineering knowledge (Haeffner & Panuwatwanich, 2018). Due to increasing complexity and dynamics of products and processes, employees have to be qualified for more than just repetitive operations. The development of problem solving skills to autonomously deal with failures or completely new tasks is getting more and more important (Jerman et al., 2018).

Human Resource Development

One of the most significant opportunities employees seek when they try to find an employer is human resource development. This concept was devised in the 1980s and consisted of a philosophy of theories drawn from the behavioral sciences, strategic management and human capital (Armstrong & Taylor, 2014). Human resource management means the framework for helping person to develop their personal and organizational skills, knowledge, and abilities including training, career development, mentoring, coaching, succession planning etc. (Heathfield, 2018).

Armstrong and Taylor describe human resource development as "all aspects of how people are employed and managed in organizations" (2014, p. 4). It covers the whole range of the activities, such as human capital management, knowledge management, corporate social responsibility, organization development, learning and development, employee relations, employee well-being, etc. The well - known phrase by human resource development founding fathers 'the key resource is people' means that people should be considered as assets rather than variable costs. "The focus of all aspects of Human Resource Development is on developing the most superior workforce so that the organization and individual employees can accomplish their work goals in service to customers." (Heathfield, 2018, p. 1).

Industry development 4.0 is associated with significant challenges in the field of human capital formation within formal and post-formal educational system. Digital competences have become a part of key competences at the different (even lower) qualification level, at least in the level of basic digital work-user competencies. Therefore, support for program-based teaching in the application of the Industry

4.0 principles to the production cycle within formal and post-formal Work based learning (WBL) learning could become a competitive advantage in future. Thus, the key prerequisites for human capital development within Industry 4.0 concept include changing the education system towards the Education 4.0 requirements, incorporating elements of virtual simulation and combined reality into education.

Considering polarization effect of work and expected demand for Work 4.0 competences, the key prerequisites of Industry 4.0 include: work competencies required for working in collaboration with robots; learn new work competencies for highly qualified professions for automation technologies, big data systems development and related issues; supporting creativity, interpersonal and communication in which, for now, human have comparative advantage towards machines (Figure 2).

WORK 4.0 COMPETENCES DEVELOPING IN SLOVAKIA

The following part of this chapter considers specific situation in Slovakia, the country in middle of the Europe, because trends in this country could predict some challenges for future. According to OECD Survey (2018) Slovakia has the biggest

Figure 2. Balance among competences, knowledge and skills
Source: Drawn by authors

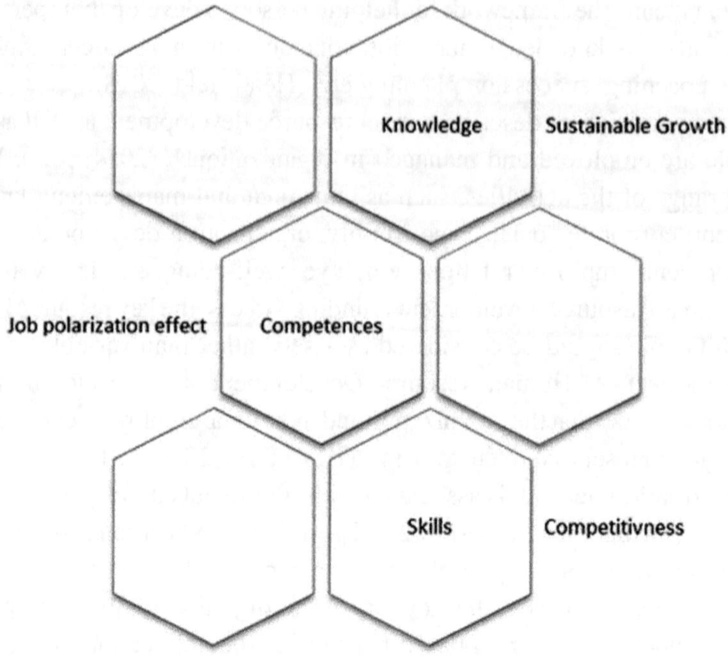

risk of automation and risk of significant change regarding jobs in comparison with 30 analyzed countries. The main reason is that industry in Slovakia is oriented mainly to automotive industry. The share of automotive production in total industrial production in Slovakia reached 44 percent. Slovakia, according to the analysis of Association of Automotive Industry, had production of 189 vehicles per 1000 inhabitants in the year 2017. With no doubt, this fact, along with strong cooperation with German, the innovation leader in Europe, predicts one to seek the win-win strategy for Slovakia within this no zero game.

Work 4.0 Competences Development Analysis of Current State in Slovak Republic

According to the Industry 4.0 Survey conducted in Slovakia in September 2017 on a sample of 47 enterprises, 28% of enterprises started to address the Industry 4.0 problem in the company, 20% said it had created its own strategy for the development of industry 4.0 in the company. According to the data, two-thirds of companies in Slovakia lack important information, more specialized, more specific, or positive examples from practice.

Companies that confirm enough information have acquired them as the know-how of the parent company, which also applies them to our market. It is also desirable in this context to draw up an action plan for the Intelligent Industries Development Strategy for Slovakia, as the European Commission's report lacks the identification of priorities for the development of smart specialization in Slovakia.

Important aspect of competence developing is attitude of employees towards industry 4.0. Current findings of Institute for Public Affairs research provide representative data on employees' attitudes and readiness to meet the requirements of Industry 4.0 in Slovakia. According to empirical findings by Velšic (2018), 11% of respondents, mostly in the automotive and engineering industry, encounter robots in Slovakia. In these sectors, the most significant changes in the content of the work activities related to the abusive formation of Industry 4.0 can be expected. Requirements for the acquisition of new job competencies will be a challenge especially for low-skilled labor, as the "degree of automation of their jobs is higher than in the case of higher-education graduates".

Research findings by Welsh (2018) show an increase in the perceived difficulties of acquiring new skills that can be traced in the context of pressure on their acquisition. Progressive computerization and digitization of Slovakia is reflected in a significant drop in the share of those who are not required to achieve the necessary digital competences from 20% in 2015 to 11% in 2018. According to Arntz et al. (2015), Slovakia belongs to the OECD countries with potentially the highest share of jobs threatened by the automation risk due to the substitution effect, with nearly 11%

Table 1. SWOT analysis of Slovak Republic based in context of strategic objectives of RIS3 SK aiming at improvement of human resources

	Potentials and challenges of human resources competence development in Slovak republic
S	•Good results in selected scientific and technological disciplines, with concentrated research teams and workplaces (materials and nanotechnologies, information and communication technologies, biomedicine and biotechnologies, industrial technologies, energetics and energy, environment and agriculture, social sciences and humanities). •Dynamic growth of ICT usage. •The quality of human resources in the competitive production sectors stemming from the tradition.
W	•Educational system is not linked to the practical needs, especially in the area of technical and natural sciences. •Absence of the system and the support of business education and development of creativity in the educational process. •Low number of efficient Research & Innovation (R&I) employees focused on the practical utilization of the results.
O	•Deepening the trialogue between academic, business and public sectors. •New "EU Industrial Strategy (Industry 2020)". •Insufficiently used HRM potential. •Development of social innovations and creative industry. •Renewal of the tradition of vocational and technical education. •Creation of the suitable environment for the return of the Slovak citizens employed in foreign R&I organizations. •The support for inflow of foreign R&I workers and foreign students to Slovakia. •Involvement of young R&I workers in solving practical business problems. •Dynamic growth of ICT usage in all business processes. •The quality of human resources in the competitive production sectors stemming from the tradition.
T	•Autonomous functioning of sectors of education, R&I and business practice, which results into different understanding of R&I. Changing population structure with increasing share of population with insufficient quality of education and low professional skills. •Persisting educational orientation towards the areas that do not correspond with the needs of the economic practice and knowledge society. •Deteriorating composition and quality of graduates in the educational process. Missing graduates especially in technical and natural sciences. •Persisting brain-drain abroad. •Imbalance of employees' age structure.

Source: RIS3 SK

of jobs being automated and 35% of employees experiencing significant changes in workloads. Analysis SWOT was conducted about potentials and challenges for future in field of human resources for Slovak republic based on strategic objectives of RIS3S. (Table 1)

The increasing pressure to acquire Work 4.0 skills may act as a factor of support for Industry 4.0 in Slovakia context of the structure of the labor market, where the high potential of automation is given by the structure of the economy. In the automotive, mechanical engineering, computer and electronics industries, up to 70% of the total number of computer installations in Slovakia is realized (Martinák, 2017, p.3). On the other hand, companies with the highest expenditures on R & D are from the automotive industry (20.5% share of R & D expenditure), the IT sector (15%), as well as plastics and waste processing (7.6%) and engineering (9.8%).

Collaboration With Robots and Digitalization

The empirical findings in digital competences, along with employee readiness for collaboration in hybrid work teams and for robot acceptance are examined as indicators of adaptation to digitization and provide insight into one of Industry 4.0 key work requirement. As examined by Velšic (2018), respondents in Slovakia consider themselves ready to work with robots, however, this cooperation is mostly based on the use of a robot as a helper mostly in domestic work (62%) or in the field of transport in the case of autonomous transport (48%). When evaluating robots as colleagues at the workplace, 34% of respondents would not mind working with robot colleague. In other areas that require interpersonal interactions, people mostly report that collaboration with robots would interfere with them, as robots working in the administration (e.g. as clerks, barracks, etc.) would bother 60% of the people questioned, 61% of respondents would not accept robots working in the trade and service area as shopkeepers, waiters, hotel receptionists, or postmen. Up to 70% of respondents would be bothered by robots involved in healthcare (eg as doctors and healthcare professionals or facilities for medical operations, etc.). Most respondents in Slovakia does not consider appropriate for robots to possess social skills in which human reach and should reach higher level. Those are abilities to identify the social and emotional state (sadness, joy, surprise), social and emotional thinking and expression (expression of love, compassion, empathy, etc.) where up to 58% of respondents disagree with the robot's ability to understand and express emotions as a person. Similarly, 56% of respondents disagree with the robots physically resembling humans and nearly half (48%) of the respondents even think that the robot should not have the intellectual abilities as a person, such as to learn more quickly, to make quick decisions, etc.

The lack of people's willingness to cooperate in hybrid teams is also reflected in responses to the question of people's attitudes towards communicating with artificial intelligence, according to which 7% of respondents estimated that they would communicate with the robot in a similar way to humans, while 62% would communicate with the robot as with an artificial machine and 31% of respondents reported that they did not know how to communicate with the robot.

The transition to new forms of work including work in hybrid teams brings a challenge in terms of Industry 4.0 development, as this transition is linked to the process of resocialization, adaptation in the human capital, enriching and expanding the content of work competencies. In Slovakia, the barriers of use of digital technologies - in addition to a negative attitude towards digital skills, also includes lacking (missing) access to digital technologies, which remained at almost the same level in 2015 (25% and 26% respectively in 2015) in Slovakia (Velšic, 2018).

Differences in digital literacy are closely related to the demands of the labor market, as the structure of social positions relates to the different set of demands even in digital competencies, that are reflected in different level of digital competencies, in relation to the age and socio-economic factors (type of work) CEDEFOP, 2015). Significant differences in the importance of the digital skills in relation to the work position could be explained in the frame of the overlapping online and offline activities, by the differences in requirements that emerge within a social structure. As the structure of the labor market in Slovakia is typical of its high share of work positions threatened by automation, under the conditions of Industry 4.0, the current innovation development provides a significant opportunity to support the motivation to acquire digital competences as a part of the human capital. At the same time, it is necessary to monitor the conditions for matching supply and demand in the content of human capital through the provision of post-graduate education and retraining opportunities.

Adequate Education and Retraining

According to Baláž, Frank and Ojala (2017), a higher education funding system that is more geared to promoting mass education as highly specialized research can be identified as a risk factor for supporting the innovative industry. Similarly, the risk factor for the development of industry 4.0 can be identified in the inadequate interconnection of the academic research sphere and the industrial sphere.

As the proportion of jobs with a high automation risk affects more than 50% of jobs with basic education, while in higher education positions it is only 1-2% (Arntz, Gregory, & Zierahn, 2004, p. 25). Future challenges in shaping Industry 4.0 thus also include tackling increasing inequality and providing adequate education and retraining (especially) low-skilled workers. In this context, it is necessary to focus on potential inequalities and educational demands generated by technological change that becomes a task not only for the formal but also informal and post-formal education system.

Many countries s as Germany started constantly to retrain their employees to stay competitive on a current market. Many companies already started their campaign to requalify their workforce, but these efforts will need to be expanded and developed. Considering the situation in Slovakia, the initial phase has been started in defining National Strategy of Skills for Slovak republic, at ministry of education, research and sport of Slovak republic, with participation of director of Centre for Education and Skills at the Organization for Economic Cooperation and Development (further OECD) Monserrat Gomendio a OECD Team Leader Andrew Bell in January 2019. Objective of cooperation is to get acquainted with the education system in Slovakia in order to be able to identify the priority objectives and then to propose effective solutions using the experience of other OECD member states.

As above mentioned, future challenges in shaping Industry 4.0 can include tackling increasing inequality and providing better education and retraining (especially) of low-skilled workers. In this context, it is necessary to focus on potential inequalities and educational demands generated by technological change "(Arntz, M. et al., 2016, p. 25, Haeffner & Panuwatwanich, 2018).

Work 4.0 Competences Development in Slovak Republic: Empirical Observation

As Working Group on Education reported in strategic document Digital Skills for Life and Work Broadband of Commission for Sustainable Development in 2017, there has been the widening gap between the knowledge, skills and abilities of young people entering the workforce and the knowledge, skills, and abilities sought by companies. This has been identified as an important deterrent to growth for Sustainable Development.

Taking into consideration human as central point, an analysis of competences was conducted and its observations and results of international quantitative research-based survey non-formal learning through participation on EU Youth in Action projects. Research data based on multilingual online survey were collected in two sequences -first in May and second in November 2012 on national Slovak level (262 participants). This special study has been developed aiming to explore the learning processes of actors involved above mentioned projects: how do participants of projects learn and which settings (comparison of school, work, and internship), educational approaches, methodologies and methods contribute to development of their key competences.

Quantitate analysis of results confirms competencies development via informal learning of survey participants (answers to the question: *„Through my participation in this project I learned better ... ")* focused on common interests and solutions like *to achieve something in the interest of the community or society, to negotiate joint solutions when there are different viewpoints* and to cooperate in a team 63.7%. Authors consider as important that more than 95% of all respondents confirm development of above-mentioned competences (Figure. 3). Similarly, it is to notice a clear prevalence of opinion that participating in projects gave a strong support for the acceptance of multiculturalism, when 58.1% of respondents *agree* with statement that *through the participation in this project, they learned better to get along with people who have*

Figure 3. Competences development focused on conducted analysis of survey participants (N=262)
Source: Created by authors

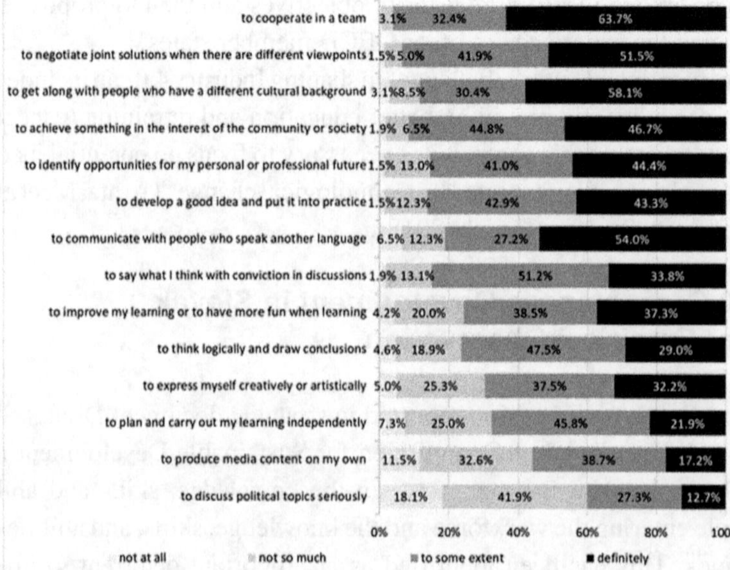

a different cultural background. They are also conformable, but to a lesser extent when around 5/6 respondents, with development of their individual competencies (e.g. *to identify opportunities for my personal or professional future, to develop a good idea and put it into practice* and *to think logically and draw conclusions*).

Focusing attention on the development of social and communication competences in respondents' view clearly states that most of participants learned to collaborate within the team (90.1%), more than three quarters of respondents improved to think logically and to look for solutions (79.2%), or to find solutions compromising different opinions (71.6%) which are skills crucial for such big challenge as Industry 4.0. Comparing the average score of all responses and taking into consideration differences in employment, authors conclude based on the relatively small difference that the currently employed participants admit to the greatest extent (average = 3.17) that, taught or developed some competence, and, to a lesser extent, participants who were unemployed during the project. The greatest difference in mentioned categories was in competence to achieve something in the interest of the community or society (Cramer V = 0.194; p = 0.032), with this statement, the employed respondents agreed significantly more positively than others, that their social competences were significantly improved. Comparing project participants according to their highest level of education, participants with completed basic schooling generally admit the lowest level of competence development (average =3.07). Based on age and gender, there are not any statistically significant differences.

Looking for new form of education and competence improvement is interesting is the view on the development of single competences, depending on the environment in which young people admit that they developed their competences the most (Figure 4). The greatest development of the competence „*to cooperate in a team* "(62.6%) has been noticed in the environment of an association, civil society organizations, doing voluntary work or projects. Also, competence *to negotiate joint solutions when there are different viewpoints* has been also improved the most in the context of *an association, civil society organizations, doing voluntary work or projects* (53.6%) but even more when *they are with their friends or family* (58.1%). The environment *of the family and friends* is also quite clearly the most appropriate for the development of competence *to say what I think with conviction in discussions* (72.5%) and *to discuss political topics seriously* (37.3%). So, role of family and community for learning is essential.

On the other hand, the school environment is the most beneficial for young people to develop their competence to think logically and draw conclusions (57.7%), but it excels also in improving the competence *to plan and carry out their learning independently* (43.6%) and *to produce media content on their own* (38.3%). The greatest development of the ability *to achieve something in the interest of the community or society* (52.7%) is recorded in the context of an association, civil society organizations, doing voluntary work or projects. This environment is also very well suited for the development of a competence *to develop a good idea and put it into practice* (50.5%), but not only, the similar development was observed also in the environment of *the family and friends* (51.4%) or during leisure time/ everyday activities or when pursuing hobbies (46.8%).

It is to consider that traveling, studying, working or living abroad is quite logically the most appropriate way *to develop the competence to communicate with people who speak another language* (66.2%) and *to get along with people who have a different cultural background* (57.7%). Analysis of the benefits of each environment for the development of mentioned competencies considers that the time spent reading (even online), watching TV, listening to the radio (20%) and searching for things on the Internet, in information centres or in libraries (20.4%) are perceived by the project participants to be the least effective way to any competence development (Figure 4).

Focused on competences that young participants declare that to be interested in their improvement/ competence development through participation in future similar non-formal learning projects, are among others mainly for reason to improve their ability to communicate in foreign language (about 3/4 of respondents). They also expressed relatively great interest to improve themselves in future in "soft" competences, which, according to the experts mentioned, are currently relatively

Figure 4. Analysis of competences development according source of learning environment /place of learning
Source: Created by authors

	In an association, civil society organisations, doing voluntary work or projects etc.	At school, college or university	When travelling, studying, working or living abroad	When attending training courses/ seminars, workshops etc.	When I am with my friends or family	During leisure time/ everyday activities or when pursuing hobbies	At work, apprenticeship, work placements, internship etc.	When looking things up, in the library, internet, info centre, etc.	When reading (including online), watching TV, listening to the radio or podcasts etc.	mean
to say what I think with conviction in discussions	53.6%	50.5%	45.9%	49.5%	72.5%	46.4%	33.3%	22.1%	23.9%	44.2%
to think logically and draw conclusions	48.6%	57.7%	39.5%	40.0%	44.1%	40.5%	32.3%	35.9%	33.6%	41.4%
to identify opportunities for my personal or professional future	50.0%	46.8%	49.5%	43.6%	33.6%	43.2%	32.7%	30.5%	32.3%	40.3%
to develop a good idea and put it into practice	50.5%	39.2%	37.4%	39.6%	51.4%	46.8%	26.6%	21.2%	18.0%	36.7%
to negotiate joint solutions when there are different viewpoints	53.6%	39.2%	36.0%	40.5%	58.1%	29.7%	31.1%	15.8%	15.8%	35.5%
to communicate with people who speak another language	44.1%	32.0%	66.2%	33.3%	28.8%	29.3%	21.6%	28.4%	25.2%	34.3%
to cooperate in a team	62.6%	43.2%	40.5%	47.3%	38.7%	30.6%	29.3%	8.1%	7.2%	34.2%
to get along with people who have a different cultural background	46.4%	27.3%	57.7%	38.2%	30.0%	35.5%	22.7%	14.1%	17.3%	32.1%
to achieve something in the interest of the community or society	52.7%	34.7%	31.1%	34.7%	39.6%	36.9%	27.5%	10.4%	10.4%	30.9%
to improve my learning or to have more fun when learning	40.9%	28.2%	33.6%	43.6%	19.1%	35.5%	17.7%	24.1%	25.5%	29.8%
to express myself creatively or artistically	39.5%	30.9%	27.3%	36.8%	30.9%	45.5%	20.9%	13.2%	20.0%	29.4%
to plan and carry out my learning independently	34.5%	43.6%	34.5%	30.0%	21.4%	37.7%	23.2%	21.8%	17.3%	29.3%
to produce media content on my own	34.2%	38.3%	16.7%	25.7%	13.1%	23.0%	20.3%	24.8%	15.3%	23.5%
to discuss political topics seriously	25.5%	27.7%	23.2%	16.8%	37.3%	17.7%	14.5%	15.9%	18.2%	21.9%
mean	45.5%	38.5%	38.5%	37.1%	37.0%	35.6%	25.3%	20.4%	20.0%	

underestimated but highly sought in the future in the context of emerging industry 4.0 trends: Sense of initiative, Intercultural competence, Sense of entrepreneurship, Interpersonal and social competence, Learning to learn (approximately half of respondents). It is to consider in this group of respondents a relatively low extent emphasis in digital competence development, and technology, and mathematical competence (see table 2), which are perceived as an essential part of the competence portfolio's for Industry 4.0.

However, it is important to emphasize some gender differences, whereby men more than women are interested in the development of above-mentioned competencies. The greatest difference is observed in the interest to develop their Science and Technology competencies (Cramer's V = 0.182; $p<0.05$). On the other hand, women, are interested significantly more than men towards the development of cultural awareness and expression (Cramer's V = 0.126; $p <0.05$). In interpersonal and social competence is smaller difference in percentage regarding gender but not statistically significant. However, all other observed gender differences are not statistically significant.

Focusing on age characteristics, it is to consider a significant difference in interest of respondents in the future development of their competence to communicate in a foreign language (Cramer V = 0.199; $p <0.01$), when a notably lower interest is registered in the group of the oldest participants (26+). On the other hand, in the group of the youngest participants (15-17) we found a significant lower interest in the future development of interpersonal and social competences (Cramer V = 0.147; $p < 0.05$). Other percentage differences between age categories were considered, but these are not statistically significant. Differences among respondents from different size of residence were not statistically significant, therefore are not presented in Table 2.

SOLUTIONS AND RECOMMENDATIONS

Several studies have revealed the relationship between educational quality and economic growth, highlighting the fact that human capital is a key to growth (Chryssolouris, Mavrikios, & Mourtzis, 2013). Skills are critical for manufacturing as well. Studies validated skills as one of the drivers for manufacturing competitiveness (Chryssolouris et al., 2013).

Table 2. Analysis of answers about participating in similar project regarding desired competences development by respondents: differences by sex, age and residence

		Sex		Age		
	Total	**Women**	**Men**	**15-17**	**18-25**	**26+**
Communication in a foreign language	73,7%	74,6%	71,7%	82,8%	76,9%	55,3%
Sense of initiative	56,9%	55,0%	59,8%	48,3%	60,2%	48,9%
Intercultural competence	49,6%	52,1%	45,7%	31,0%	52,7%	48,9%
Sense of entrepreneurship	45,4%	41,4%	52,2%	37,9%	45,7%	48,9%
Interpersonal and social competence	44,7%	47,9%	39,1%	24,1%	46,8%	48,9%
Cultural awareness and expression	42,0%	46,7%	33,7%	37,9%	44,6%	34,0%
Learning to learn	41,6%	40,8%	43,5%	37,9%	43,0%	38,3%
Media literacy	30,5%	28,4%	34,8%	37,9%	29,0%	31,9%
Civic competence	30,2%	28,4%	33,7%	31,0%	30,1%	29,8%
Communication in my mother language	23,7%	23,1%	23,9%	37,9%	22,6%	19,1%
Digital competence	22,1%	19,5%	27,2%	13,8%	22,6%	25,5%
For other reasons	22,1%	18,3%	28,3%	20,7%	20,4%	29,8%
Basic competences in science and technology	19,5%	14,2%	29,3%	20,7%	18,8%	21,3%
Mathematical competence	9,5%	7,1%	14,1%	20,7%	8,6%	6,4%

Source: Created by authors

In the coming decade, the 4 A's of technology – Automation, Augmentation, Analytics, and Artificial intelligence– will require new knowledge and work skills to drive business value (Figure 5).

As mentioned in (Autor, Levy, & Murnane, 2003) three engineering bottlenecks were identified that prevent the automation of all jobs – these are creative intelligence, social intelligence and perception and manipulation tasks. It is imperative for companies, society and education system to reassess talent and creativity of human and restructure processes and strategies for evolving requirements towards demands of Work 4.0 competences.

The findings from analysis clearly indicate that participation in non-formal learning such as participating via Youth in Action projects contributes to the development of the key competences and skills required by the concept of Intelligent Industry. Results confirm that most of participants supposed to be absolutely or somewhat better able to cooperate in a team, to achieve something in the interest of the community,

Figure 5. Balance between of Industry 4.0 Requirements and Workforce
Source: Drawn by authors

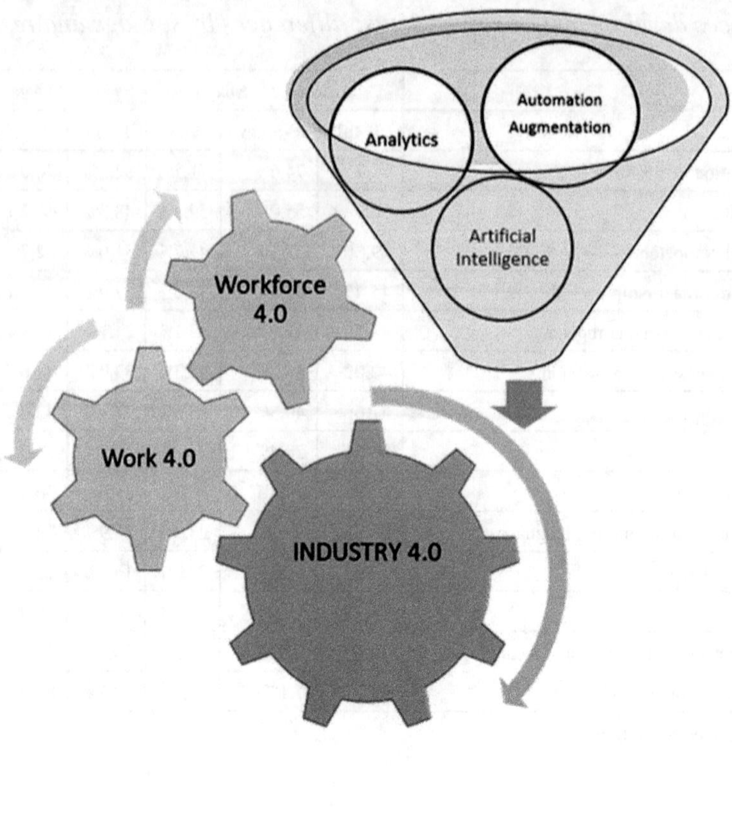

improving in developing and realization of good ideas and improve the ability to think logically and draw conclusions.

On personal level, survey participants have noted thanks to participation non-formal learning to feel significantly more self-confident and better to deal with new situations which can be big advantage in reacting on big changes like Industry 4.0. The support of non-formal learning ought to provide conditions for sustainable growth of society and attention should be paid to prevention and follow a broader approach based on triple helix model (universities- research- companies) as answer to his challenge to bridge the gap between competences and expectations of future to improve desirable competences for Work 4.0.

FUTURE RESEARCH DIRECTIONS

Competences development required by Work 4.0 implementation means that digital technologies do not fully replace tacit knowledge, intuitive and creative thinking as well as interpersonal skills. Hence the future research in Work 4.0 covers complex human capital formation. The research attention focuses on formal and non-formal ways of human capital formation, regarding demand for digital skills as well as abstract-intensive and personal skills and ability to cooperate with robots.

Although there are more as well as less optimistic opinions on future technological unemployment due to computerization according to different methodological approaches of the authors, studying the effective ways for upskilling and retraining of workers according to Work 4.0 requirements can be identified as one the relevant research field within Industry 4.0 concept. The assessment of the risk of automation for specific work tasks ought to be identified in interaction and collaboration of the labor market and ICT researchers focused on win-win strategy.

CONCLUSION

Consolidated view on the literature view along with system analysis of competence development leads to conclusion that content of human work will change and this means that required competences of Workforce 4.0 will change. Based on results it can be assumed, the concept of Work 4.0 reflects specific key requirements of Industry 4.0 as follows:

- Process of work polarization towards human-intensive work tasks and computer-intensive work tasks, due to different number of automatable tasks;

- The acquisition of new work skills related to working with collaborative robots (co-bots) with emphasis on lower qualifications;
- Supporting the development of creativity, interpersonal and communication skills that are demanding to automate, in which people (currently) achieve a comparative advantage over robots and artificial intelligence.

The employment decline in middle-skill occupations related to differentiated impact of technology on employment according skill levels and types of work marked as polarization effect needs to be considered in relation to several obstacles related to task computerization.

In the context of job polarization and substitution for human work, it is necessary to support the formation of those skills that enable part of workers to switch to types of work activities that can be sustainable, such as care, nursing, creativity and interpersonal skills. By supporting these competences, universally complemented by digital skills, it is possible to promote inclusive development and citizen participation because without the acquisition of digital skills, the existing divide in the level of key work competencies will intensify.

As well, examining the effective ways of upskilling and retraining of work force offers the possibility to maintain sustainable human capital developing in the context of Industry 4.0 formation.

On the other hand, the idea of competence development by lifelong learning is also supported by results of conducted analysis focused on competences in Slovakia support importance of long-life learning and non-formal learning will be increased. The main issue is to provide conditions for sustainable competence development and education system enhancement for society based on collaboration within triple helix model (universities- research- companies) as answer to his challenge to bridge the gap between competences and expectations of future to improve desirable competences for Work 4.0.

ACKNOWLEDGMENT

This research was supported by research project VEGA [grant number 2/0077/19] *"Work competencies in the context of Industry 4.0 development."*

REFERENCES

Armstrong, M., & Taylor, S. (2014). *Armstrong's Handbook of Human Resource Management Practice*. London: Kogan Page Publishers.

Arntz, M., Gregory, T., & Zierahn, U. (2004). Benefit Coverage Rates and Household Typologies: Scope and Limitations of Tax-Benefit Indicators (OECD Social, Employment and Migration Working Papers No. 189). Paris: OECD. doi:10.1787/081036000058

Autor, D. (2015). Why Are There Still So Many Jobs? The History and Future of Workplace Automation. *The Journal of Economic Perspectives*, *59*(3), 3–30. doi:10.1257/jep.29.3.3

Autor, D. H., & Dorn, D. (2013). The Growth of Low-Skill Service Jobs and the Polarization of the US Labor Market. *The American Economic Review*, *103*(5), 1553–1597. doi:10.1257/aer.103.5.1553

Autor, D. H., Levy, F., & Murnane, R. J. (2003). The Skill Content of Recent Technological Change: An Empirical Exploration. *The Quarterly Journal of Economics*, *118*(4), 1279–1333. doi:10.1162/003355303322552801

Avvisati, F., Jacotin, G., & Vincent-Lancrin, S. (2014). Educating Higher Education Students for Innovative Economies: What International Data Tell Us. *Tuning Journal for Higher Education*, *1*(1), 223. doi:10.18543/tjhe-1(1)-2013pp223-240

Berger, T., & Frey, C. B. (2016). Structural Transformation in the OECD: Digitalisation, Deindustrialisation and the Future of Work (OECD Social, Employment and Migration Working Papers No. 193). OECD. doi:10.1787/5jlr068802f7-en

Chryssolouris, G., Mavrikios, D., & Mourtzis, D. (2013). Manufacturing Systems: Skills & Competencies for the Future. *Procedia CIRP*, *7*, 17–24. doi:10.1016/j.procir.2013.05.004

Ellström, P. E. (1997). The many meanings of occupational competence and qualification. *Journal of European Industrial Training*, *21*(6/7), 266–274. doi:10.1108/03090599710171567

Gattullo, M., Scurati, G. W., Fiorentino, M., Uva, A. E., Ferrise, F., & Bordegoni, M. (2019). Towards augmented reality manuals for industry 4.0: A methodology. *Robotics and Computer-integrated Manufacturing*, *56*, 276–286. doi:10.1016/j.rcim.2018.10.001

Gordon, R. (2012). *Is U.S. Economic Growth Over? Faltering Innovation Confronts the Six Headwinds (No. w18315)*. Cambridge, MA: National Bureau of Economic Research. doi:10.3386/w18315

Haeffner, M., & Panuwatwanich, K. (2018). Perceived Impacts of Industry 4.0 on Manufacturing Industry and Its Workforce: Case of Germany. In S. Şahin (Ed.), *8th International Conference on Engineering, Project, and Product Management (EPPM 2017)* (pp. 199–208). Cham: Springer International Publishing. 10.1007/978-3-319-74123-9_21

Hecklau, F., Galeitzke, M., Flachs, S., & Kohl, H. (2016). Holistic Approach for Human Resource Management in Industry 4.0. *Procedia CIRP*, *54*, 1–6. doi:10.1016/j.procir.2016.05.102

Jerman, A., Pejić Bach, M., & Bertoncelj, A. (2018). A Bibliometric and Topic Analysis on Future Competences at Smart Factories. *Machines*, *6*(3), 41. doi:10.3390/machines6030041

Kinkel, S., Schemmann, B., & Lichtner, R. (2017). Critical Competencies for the Innovativeness of Value Creation Champions: Identifying Challenges and Work-integrated Solutions. *Procedia Manufacturing*, *9*, 323–330. doi:10.1016/j.promfg.2017.04.021

Lasi, H., Fettke, P., Kemper, H.-G., Feld, T., & Hoffmann, M. (2014). Industrie 4.0. *Wirtschaftsinformatik*, *56*(4), 261–264. doi:10.100711576-014-0424-4

Lukac, D. (2015). The fourth ICT-based industrial revolution "Industry 4.0" — HMI and the case of CAE/CAD innovation with EPLAN P8. In *2015 23rd Telecommunications Forum Telfor (TELFOR)* (pp. 835–838). Belgrade: IEEE. 10.1109/TELFO;R.2015.7377595

Makris, S., Karagiannis, P., Koukas, S., & Matthaiakis, A.-S. (2016). Augmented reality system for operator support in human–robot collaborative assembly. *CIRP Annals*, *65*(1), 61–64. doi:10.1016/j.cirp.2016.04.038

MartinakD. (2017). *Povolanie robot.* Retrieved from https://www.minedu.sk/data/att/11077.pdf

Maslarić, M., Nikoličić, S., & Mirčetić, D. (2016). Logistics Response to the Industry 4.0: The Physical Internet. *Ocean Engineering*, *6*(1), 511–517. doi:10.1515/eng-2016-0073

Motyl, B., Baronio, G., Uberti, S., Speranza, D., & Filippi, S. (2017). How will Change the Future Engineers' Skills in the Industry 4.0 Framework? A Questionnaire Survey. *Procedia Manufacturing*, *11*, 1501–1509. doi:10.1016/j.promfg.2017.07.282

Nath, H. (2017). The Information Society. *Space and Culture, 4*(3), 19-28.

Quint, F., Sebastian, K., & Gorecky, D. (2015). A Mixed-reality Learning Environment. *Procedia Computer Science*, *75*, 43–48. doi:10.1016/j.procs.2015.12.199

Richert, A., Shehadeh, M., Willicks, F., & Jeschke, S. (2016). Digital Transformation of Engineering Education - Empirical Insights from Virtual Worlds and Human-Robot-Collaboration. *International Journal of Engineering Pedagogy*, *6*(4), 23. doi:10.3991/ijep.v6i4.6023

Roblek, V., Meško, M., & Krapež, A. (2016). A Complex View of Industry 4.0. *SAGE Open*, *6*(2), 215824401665398. doi:10.1177/2158244016653987

Saniuk, A., & Saniuk, S. (2017). Analysis of the Situation of Polish Enterprises in Industrial Networks in Industry 4.0. *Nauki O Zarządzaniu*, (31), 12–17. doi:10.15611/noz.2017.2.02

Schiffeler, N., Stehling, V., Haberstroh, M., & Isenhardt, I. (2018). Fostering social construction of knowledge in hybrid teams by augmented reality. In *2018 IEEE Global Engineering Education Conference (EDUCON)* (pp. 1029–1034). Tenerife: IEEE. 10.1109/EDUCON.2018.8363343

Schuh, G., Gartzen, T., Rodenhauser, T., & Marks, A. (2015). Promoting Work-based Learning through INDUSTRY 4.0. *Procedia CIRP*, *32*, 82–87. doi:10.1016/j.procir.2015.02.213

Strange, R., & Zucchella, A. (2017). Industry 4.0, global value chains and international business. *Multinational Business Review*, *25*(3), 174–184. doi:10.1108/MBR-05-2017-0028

Wolf, M., Kleindienst, M., Ramsauer, C., Zierler, C., & Winter, E. (n.d.). Current and future industrial challenges: demographic change and measures for elderly workers in Industry D 4.0. *International Journal of Engineering*, 10.

ADDITIONAL READING

Aringer-Walch, C., & Bengler, K. (2019). *Digitalization in Manufacturing – Employees*. Do You Want to Work There.

Kormanik, M. B., & Shindell, T. J. (2018). Digital Transformation Monitor. Slovakia. Smart Industry. Retrieved from: https://ec.europa.eu/growth/tools-databases/dem/monitor/sites/default/files/DTM_Slovakia_FINAL.pdf

Levy, F., & Murnane, R. J. (2013). *Dancing with Robots. Human Skills for Computerized Work*. Retrieved from: https://www.thirdway.org/report/dancing-with-robots-human-skills-for- computerized-work

KEY TERMS AND DEFINITIONS

Cobot: Collaborative robot designed to interact with humans in a conjoint work flow capable to operate autonomously or with limited guidance.

Job Substitution: Displacement of workers by computers and robots marked especially in work positions with explicit and codifiable tasks.

Non-Formal Learning: Education organized outside formal education provided by different institutions (cultural institutions, enterprises, adult education institutions) in different forms and contents of non-credit education.

Non-Zero Game: Desired situation in which each stakeholder aggregate gains and aim of participation is not competition but the collaboration.

Polanyi's Paradox: The term stresses the importance of tacit knowledge, pointing that there exist many tasks which human beings understand intuitively how to perform but cannot explicitly verbalize and codify.

Win-Win Strategy: Strategy ensuring that both sides are satisfied and there is added value for all stakeholders.

Work 4.0: The term refers to changing human capital content reflecting key signs of work tasks and forms of organization of work in relation to Industry 4.0 requirements.

Work 4.0 Polarization: Trend of development of work towards groupings of human-intensive work tasks and computer-intensive work tasks in relation to different amounts of automatable tasks.

Workforce 4.0: Knowledge, skills and competence development as a result of human resources and Industry 4.0 interaction.

Chapter 4
Current Trends in Human Capital Formation

Ayansola Olatunji Ayandibu
https://orcid.org/0000-0001-5870-2388
University of Zululand, South Africa

Lawrence Abiwu
University of KwaZulu-Natal, South Africa

ABSTRACT

This chapter explores the trends in human capital formation towards building sustainable organisations. A literature review approach was adopted to investigate HR practices which contribute to human capital formation, the contribution of human capital, as well as the barriers to human capital formation and theories of human capital formation. Human capital has been conceptualized as the collective knowledge that is embedded in the personnel, organisational routines, and network relationships of an organisation. It was found that many countries such as China, Russia, India, and Brazil are experiencing economic growth because of the investment in their human capital formation. The review of empirical studies showed that human capital has been considered as a firm's strategic resource for sustainable competitive advantage. This chapter submits that to prevent loss of human capital, it is important for organisations to create an environment and culture that will foster or encourage individual and organisational learning.

DOI: 10.4018/978-1-5225-9810-7.ch004

INTRODUCTION

Many countries such as China, Russia, India and Brazil are experiencing economic growth because of their investment in human capital, the most valuable asset of all resources (Crook, Todd, Combs, Woehr & Ketchen, 2011). The term human capital was originally coined by Adam Smith (1776) who argues that all human beings are similar by birth, but it is education, habits and training that make them different. Human capital is the stock of knowledge, competencies, skills and personality attributes required to produce economic value (Awan, 2012). Theory of human capital focuses mainly on the development of capabilities and skills of human beings, as a major part of economic development. Awan (2012) suggests that human capital formation can be enhanced through education, training and experience. Modern growth theory suggests that the accumulation of human capital is an important driver of economic growth. Scholars argue that China, Russia, India and Brazil have huge human resource bases. Their total population is approximately 41% of the world population, their combined area is 26% percent of the world area and their total Gross Domestic Product (GDP) is 18% of the world GDP. These countries have attracted the interest of scholars and the world at large because of their constant fast economic growth, especially since 2008, when advanced economies have been facing an economic downturn.

Further, Vladikov (2015) expresses a similar view, that, over the last 20 years, developing nations like Bulgaria, Romania and some other former USSR-states, which are successful in their accession to the economy of the European Union, have managed to evolve from command-driven to market-driven economies. According to Vladikov (2015), the transition was coupled with a fundamental change in comprehending how the education of one person affects his/her lifetime decisions and initiates the drive for a better standard of living through successful career advancement.

Esu (2012) points out that the ability of countries or organisations to develop their workforce largely depends on their sustained contribution to human capital formation. Lajili (2012) postulates that certain skills and training are required for growth driven environments. According to Lajili (2012), human capital is the combination of both the skills and knowledge acquired by individuals to increase their worth in the labour market and it remains crucial in developing any sector of the economy. Studies suggest that, while some advanced nations, such as China, Russia, India Brazil, East Asia and the United States, enjoy the benefits of education by promoting and producing the wealth needed to enable continued investments, regrettably, developing nations like Nigeria, Pakistan, Ghana, Kenya, and Zimbabwe are yet to enjoy such benefits (Akhtar, Renyong, Khaskheli & Ali, 2015; Igbokwe-Ibeto, Chukwuemeka & Okechukwu, 2014). Adedeji & Campbell (2013) suggest that, while developed economies are reaping the benefits of investing in education or human capital development, in contrast, developing nations have neither articulated a development strategy linking knowledge to economic growth nor built up their capacity to do so. For instance, in Pakistan, a study shows that the comparatively low investment in human capital has resulted in failure to translate economic growth into a satisfactory level of human development (Akhtar *et al.*, 2015). Pakistan is at the lowest level of human development according to the United Nations Human Development report of 2014.

Research shows that human capital formation is central to institution building competitive advantages. However, the degree of success achieved depends on the institutions' people-embodied knowhow, namely: the knowledge, skills and abilities embedded in their employees (Sultan Qadri & Abdul, 2011). Furthermore, institutions able to meet this challenge are those that acquire and utilise valuable and scarce resources. In addition to the above, seven areas in human capital formation have been identified as needing attention. These include analytics and job assessment, global growth, skilled talent shortage, life balance needs, focus on core competencies, more hire-as-needed and aging workforces. The problem is that there is a paucity of research providing adequate discussion of the ways these emerging trends impact on human capital formation. The review of empirical research further indicates that, although human capital formation has attracted interest from organisational researchers, there are limited studies of the emerging trends in human capital formation. Therefore, the aim of this chapter is to identify the emerging trends in human capital formation, as well as to determine the mechanisms through which human capital can be developed to enable organisations to achieve their desired goals. In addition, the review of empirical works suggests that, although there are diverse theoretical frameworks on human capital formation, existing studies have not established which of the theoretical frameworks is appropriate for human capital formation. The chapter reviews the existing theories of human capital formation and makes appropriate recommendation to organisations regarding which of these theories should be adopted.

The broad aim of the chapter is achieved through the following objectives: to increase knowledge about human capital by conceptualising it, to examine the contribution of human capital formation to organisations and countries, to identify the challenges of human capital formation, to determine the theoretical framework which best supports human capital formation, and to develop a conceptual model linking human capital formation to constructs such as performance and competitive advantage. Further, the chapter emphasises the background, conceptualisation of human capital formation, contribution of human capital, theoretical framework underpinning human capital formation, ways to develop human capital, recommendations arising from of the study, directions for future research and the conclusion.

BACKGROUND

Since the industrial revolution in the early 1800s, the processes of industrialisation have been crucial, with emphasis on mass production. The wide spread of industrialisation in the 1800s marked the beginning of what is called the "capitalist system". This focuses on maximising profit and minimising cost (Wallerstein, 1980). Before the industrial revolution, relations between labour (workers) and owners of capital were founded on exploitation, where the owner of the capital compelled the workers to work long hours with minimal wages and severe working conditions, in return for higher profits. In the 1800s, workers were regarded as mere tools (one of the factors of production) and were exploited by owners of capital to achieve their business goals. This reaffirms the view expressed by Marx, who argues that capitalism is a historical, specific factor of production, where the owners of businesses often exploit the employees (Edwards, 1979).

According to Ronald (1969), the treatment of human beings as a component of capital integral to socio-economic development, is by no means a novel idea as has been demonstrated in research studies by early classical economists. Ronald (1969) states that one can find a repeated reference to the development and utilisation of human resources in various passages of the literature of the era of mercantilism through to contemporary neoclassical writing. During the 1900s, the field of economics failed to integrate adequately the human capital component into the mainstream of economic thought. However, this has been corrected in part, by some prominent writers more concerned about economic development. The concept of human capital remained under-explored until recent times, despite the evidence of publicity by both classical and neoclassical economists. Economists who demonstrated their interest in human capital have adopted one of two procedures for determining the value of human capital: capitalised lifetime earnings or the production cost designing a separate unit of human capital.

The concept of "human capital" in modern neoclassical economic literature dates back to Jacob Mincer's article, "Investment in Human Capital and Personal Income Distribution", in The Journal of Political Economy in 1958. Schultz (1961) further contributed to the development of the subject matter. Gray Becker's application of the idea of "human capital" in economics is best known.. He espouses this in his 's book entitled, "Human Capital", published in 1964 and a standard reference for many years. According to these authors, human capital can be developed by investing in education, training and health care. The human capital theory is based on the premise that education and training transform a raw human being to human capital and the market gives high value to him. The human capital theory is based on the basic idea that a variety of talents are acquired through different activities, such as education or work experience (Mincer, 1993).

Becker (1964) claims that human capital is developed through work experience in specific organisations. Becker (1964) notes that employees become more productive and qualified over time through mechanisms such as 'learning by doing' processes and, as a consequence, their remuneration tends to increase. According to Becker (1964), workers are aware that their competences and skills are firm-specific and therefore, the same wage level will be not be guaranteed if they move to a different organisation. On the other hand, employers also tend to maintain the most productive workers in their firms by keeping wages high and working conditions good. Remuneration and other non-monetary aspects of jobs become, in the current author's view, a powerful tool used by firms to reduce turnover costs. Thus, both workers and organisations have incentives to maintain long term relationships when investment in education and job formation takes place.

The most representative model of human capital in the growth literature was elaborated by Lucas (1988). In his two-sector model, the author points out that human capital and knowledge are synonyms and are a voluntary outcome of the learning process. Based on his theoretical setting, some authors of the new growth literature (Barro and Sala-i-Martin, 1997; Acemoglu & Angris, 1999; Krueger & Lindhal, 2001) have empirically proved that the stock of human capital plays an extremely important role in promoting economic growth and prosperity. Today, the human capital theory has gained momentum among several key authors. This is indicated by the number of publications available.

THE CONCEPT OF HUMAN CAPITAL FORMATION

In today's knowledge economy, human capital is considered the most intangible aspect of human assets. The ability of human capital to accumulate and share knowledge has been found to be a resource which can create sustainable competitive advantage for organisations in the global market (Haas & Hansen, 2007). Kong & Prior (2008) and Schiuma & Lerro (2008) suggest that every organisation needs to develop its human capital base in order to maintain its competitive advantages. Furthermore, Teece (2002) confirms that human capital is the only differentiating factor which delivers sustainable competitive advantages to firms. According to Roos & Jacobsen (1999), human capital has four main attributes differentiating it from other resources. It is rare, valuable, costly to imitate and non-substitutable.

Early writers like Bontis (2002), Kong (2008) and Stewart (1997) claim that human capital represents the collective knowledge that is embedded in the personnel, organisational routines and network relationships of an organisation. Human capital has further been defined as the sum of an organisation's valuable resources, encompassing collective tacit knowledge, human skills, experience and any intellectual resource that contributes to value creation for the organisation (Sullivan, 1998).

The Organisation for Economic Co-operation and Development [OECD] (2001) claims that human capital is the stock of competencies, skills, knowledge and personality attributes embodied in individuals. These attributes facilitate their ability for the creation of personal, economic and social value.

DEVELOPMENT OF HUMAN CAPITAL

Akhtar, Renyong, Khaskheli &Ali (2015) postulate that human capital development has become a notable challenge, particularly in the Pakistan. The authors argue that a lower middle-income country with a huge population and talented labour force lacks the quality of a pool of human capital in a modern economic scenario. However, they suggest that two basic ways to develop human capital are formal education and health spending. This finding underscores the fundamental assumption of the human capital theory, which states that formal education is instrumental, and even necessary, for the improvement of the production capacity of a population. The proponents of human capital theory argue that an educated population is a productive population (ibid).

Metilelu (2016) advocates that human capital can be developed through education and training. However, there is a vast distinction between education and training. The former is concerned with any activity directed at providing the knowledge, skills, moral values and understanding required in the normal course of life, while the latter has to do with a process whereby people acquire capabilities to aid in the achievement of organisational goals (Carrell, Elbert & Hatfield, 2018). According to Metilelu (2016), the knowledge acquired by individuals through education and training is essential for the skills needed in the organisation and society. Mincer & Becker (1964) contend that since human capital is developed through investment in education and training, it is similar to an investment in "physical means of production". Mincer (1962) further affirms that human capital formation is influenced by education and schooling which prepare the existing and prospective workforce for quality performance.

In contrast, Ladkin (2011) argues that employees in Nigeria seem not to attain any form of tertiary education in hospitality and tourism and, even when employees do have some formal education, the industry seems not to expose them to any further training or empowerment to enable them to function effectively and efficiently. McDonald & Hopkin (2003) claim that developing human capital to meet the human resources needs of the future is a major issue. According to McDonald & Hopkin

(2003), the only long term strategic and comprehensive strategy that can sustain human capital growth in the hospitality and tourism industry is education and training.

Becker (1964) developed a conceptual model for human capital development. The model shows that education is central to private and social returns to investment. The author claims that investment in human capital can only be sustained through private sector support and a favourable government framework that supports investment. Alani& Isola (2009) mention that Scultz (1961), as cited in Tariq Khan (2014), examines the extent to which education is linked to economic growth. The findings reveal that formal education impacts on the skills, experience and competence of employers in relation to the organisation's customers. Grant (1996) concurs that a large amount of an organisation's knowledge is a function of its available human capital.

Furthermore, other studies (Ejere, 2011, Eigbiremolen & Anaduaka, 2014; Sankay, Ismail & Shaari, 2010) have found that there are numerous emerging trends in human capital formation, namely: education, resources, health and wellbeing, recruitment and selection, workforce and employment, institution building and remuneration. According to Igbokwe-Ibeto (2014), education is one of the major decisive factors in life chances, equal opportunity and advancement. It is considered the most powerful tool for developing and empowering citizens to master their social and cultural environments and to compete for survival. Igbokwe-Ibeto (2014) posits that the development of human capital means improving the skills and competence of the people by investing in them by providing training, education and by investing in better health of people. It has also been argued that education enhances individuals' chances for employment in the labour market and allows them to reap pecuniary and non-pecuniary returns and gives them the opportunity for job mobility (ibid). Regrettably, some developing countries, particularly in Africa, are yet to reap the full benefits of education.

CONTRIBUTION OF HUMAN CAPITAL

Evidence suggests that human capital contributes significantly to economic growth and to organisational success. Contributions of human capital are discussed below.

Economic Growth

The proponents (Aghion & Howitt, 1992; Lucas, 1988; Romer, 1989, 1990) of the human capital theory argue that human capital contributes to economic growth in at least three ways, namely: it raises productivity of workers due to upgraded skills and better education, it is a source of new ideas and innovations and it facilitates the dissemination and embeddedness of new ideas and practices leading to greater economic growth.

Romer (1990), in his study on human capital, expands on the reason why nations with a large stock of human capital enjoy greater economic benefits than nations with relatively low human capital. Empirical research suggests that Brazil is one of the emerging economic giants of Latin America and the world eighth largest economy. It has been argued that Brazil has experienced a stable and increasing economic growth in the recent years because of its investment in human capital. With a five percent annual growth rate, Brazil is likely to become the world's fifth largest economy to overtake countries like Britain and France (Awan, 2012). Adelakun (2011) investigated human capital development and economic growth in Nigeria. According to him, economists believe that human capital development and utilisation is crucial to countries' economic growth. However, the findings of the study reveal that the illiteracy rate in Nigeria is high and many workers are unskilled, leading to their low productivity. Adelakun's (2011) study shows the relevance of human capital development to the growth of the economy. The overall results of the study show that there as a positive relationship between human capital development and economic growth.

Similarly, Osoba (2017) explored human capital variables and economic growth in Nigeria. The study utilised secondary annual data on education expenditure, health expenditure, real gross domestic product and gross capital formation obtained from the Central Bank Statistical bulletin, 2014. The data were analysed with the help of the Fully Modified Ordinary Least Squares (FMOLS) technique. The study discovered that there was a positive and significant relationship between the interactive effects of human capital components and growth in Nigeria.

Ogunleye, Owolabi, Sanyaolu & Lawal (2017) carried out a study on human capital development and economic growth in Nigeria. The study adopts the ordinary least square regression analysis to explore the link between human capital development and economic growth in Nigeria, using annual time series dates from 1981 to 2015. The results of the study show that human capital development has a significant impact on economic growth, as shown by the gross domestic product. The findings underscore the relevance of human capital theory which states that human capital development indicators, such as secondary school enrolment, tertiary school enrolment, total government expenditure on health and total government expenditure on education, have a positive and statistically significant impact on economic growth.

Oluwatobi & Ogunrinola (2011) explored the link between human capital development efforts of the Government and economic growth in Nigeria. The study sought to discover how government recurrent and capital expenditure on education and health in Nigeria impacts on the country's economic growth. They utilised secondary data sources and the augmented Solow model. The dependent variable in the model was the level of real output while the explanatory variables in the study were government capital and recurrent expenditures on education and health, gross fixed capital formation and the labour force. The overall results of the study suggest that there exists a significant positive correlation between government recurrent expenditure on human capital development and the level of real output, while capital expenditure is negatively related to the level of real output.

Isola & Alani (2012) studied the contribution of different measures of human capital development to economic growth in Nigeria. The study utilised data from Nigeria and adopted the growth account model which specifies the growth of Gross Domestic Products (GDP) as a function of labour and capital. The model also included a measure of policy reforms. Based on the estimated regression and a descriptive statistical analysis of trends of government commitment to human capital development, the study reveals that despite little commitment having been accorded to health compared with education, the empirical analysis showed that both the education and health components of human capital development are crucial to economic growth in Nigeria.

Competitive Advantage

Contemporary management recognises human capital as having the potential to contribute to the sustainable competitive advantage in an organisation. According to Barney (1991), competitive advantage refers to the combination of the concepts of rareness, inimitability, value and non- substitutability. From the resource-based view organisations may utilise resources such as physical, human and organisational resources to gain a sustained competitive advantage in their industry (Barney & Wright, 1998). However, the scholars argue that two significant resources are physical capital and organisational capital because they have been proven to be duplicable by competitors. Hence, they are less likely to be sources of inimitability.

According to Barney (1991) and Chadwick & Dabu (2009) human capital is considered as a prerequisite for competitive advantage. Bartlett & Ghoshal (2002) postulate that human capital is an organisational strategic resource, having the potential to be inimitable since each worker has the ability to contribute in a unique way. The concept of inimitability is connected to the theory of human free will. Reed, Srinivasan & Doty (2009) maintain that the ability of human capital to contribute in a unique way allows it to be associated with the resource-based view. The resource-based view states that when a firm's internal resources are inimitable they contribute to and help to maintain a sustainable competitive advantage (Sariolghalam, Noruzi & Rahimi, 2010).

Other prominent scholars, like Kazlauskaitė & Bučiūnienė (2008) and Downes (2007) believe that the resource-based view theory assumes that human capital should be considered an organisation's most valuable resource with the potential to increase organisational competitiveness, if managed strategically. Moreover, Haas & Hansen (2007) confirm that human capital, with its ability to gather and to share knowledge, is a resource to create a sustainable competitive advantage in a global environment.

Eric (2013) focuses on human capital as a driver of economic growth for developing countries. He argues that this has led to an emphasis on school results' attainment. Developing countries have made considerable progress in closing the gap with developed countries, in terms of school results but recent research has underscored the importance of cognitive skills for economic growth. He claims that attention has been shifted to issues of school quality and, in that area, developing countries have been much less successful in closing the gap with developed countries. Without improving school quality, developing countries will find it difficult to improve their long term economic performance.

Mba, Mba, Ogbuabor & Ikpegbu (2013) examine the impact of human capital development on the growth of the economy, using the ordinary least squares (OLS) technique. In the study, the GDP is as an indicator of economic growth, per capita real Gross Domestic Product, primary school enrolment, public expenditure on education and health, life expectancy and the stock of physical capital as proxy for human capital. The study found that there was a strong positive relationship between human capital development and economic growth.

Mehrara & Musai (2013) investigated the causal relationship between education and GDP in developing countries by using panel unit root tests and panel cointegration analysis for the period 1970-2010. A three-variable model was formulated with capital formation as the third variable. The results show a strong causality from investment and economic growth to education in the developing countries. Yet, education does not have any significant effect on GDP and investment in the short- and long-term. This means that it is the capital formation and GDP that drives education, not vice versa. Thus, the findings of the paper support the view that it is higher economic growth that leads to higher education growth. It seems that as the number of enrolments rises, the quality of education declines. Moreover, the formal education systems are not market oriented in developing countries. This might be the reason that huge educational investments in these developing countries fail to generate greater economic growth. Promoting practice-oriented training for students, particularly in technical disciplines, and matching education systems to the needs of the labour market would help to create long-term jobs and improve the country's future prospects.

Ogujiuba (2013) empirically examines the relationship between economic growth and human capital development. The study uses secondary data and examines the time series characteristics of the variables selected to avoid the problems of spurious correlation often associated with non-stationary time series to concurrently generate long-run equilibrium relationships. In order to achieve linearity, logarithmic calculations were used to examine the variables. Generally, the estimation of the model shows that the variables included in the model provide basic information about the nature of the impact on economic growth. Findings also show that investment in human capital, in the form of education and capacity building at the primary and secondary levels, impacts significantly on economic growth, while capital expenditure on education was insignificant to the growth process. The paper recommends that educational institutions in Nigeria should be re-structured for quality schooling at the primary, secondary and tertiary levels. In a competitive and global economy, this would require strategic planning, an increase in capacity utilisation by the education sector and rebasing of growth fundamentals.

Eigbiremolen & Anaduaka (2014) employed the augmented Solow human-capital-growth model to investigate the impact of human capital development on national output, a proxy for economic growth, using quarterly time- series data from 1999-2012. The study shows that human capital development, in line with theory, exhibits a significant positive impact on output level. This implies that human capital development is indispensable in the achievement of sustainable economic growth in Nigeria, as there is a significant increase in economic performance for every increase in human capital development. Their results further reveal a relatively inelastic relationship between human capital development and output level.

Jaiyeoba (2015) empirically investigated the relationship between investment in education and health in Nigeria, using time series data from 1982 to 2011. The paper employs trend analysis, the Johansen cointegration and ordinary least square technique. The empirical findings indicate that there is a long-term relationship between government expenditure on education, health and economic growth. The variables, health and education expenditure, secondary and tertiary enrolment rate and gross fixed capital formation appear with the expected positive signs and are statistically significant (except for government expenditure on education and primary enrolment rate). These findings have strong implications for education and health policies and suggest that they should be a focus of debate in the country. The study recommends that, in order to accelerate growth and liberate Nigerians from the vicious cycle of poverty, the government should put in place policies geared towards massive investment in education and health

Individual and Organisational Performance

Empirical research suggests that investment in human capital has the potential to increase both individual and organisational performance (Haas & Hansen, 2007). Jamal & Saif (2011) investigated the impact of human capital management on organisational performance. The aim of their study was to explain the relationship between human capital management and organisational performance. Hypotheses were developed to test the impact of human capital on performance of organisations. The data was gathered from 16 firms situated in Peshawar (Pakistan) where it was considered that the source of competitive advantage is human capital, namely higher education institutions and pharmaceutical firms. The results of the study reveal that human capital has a significant positive impact on organisations' performance. Wiesberg (1996) explored the impact of human capital on organisational performance by analysing the performance of 65 workers in 20 groups. The study discovered that a significant positive correlation exists between human capital and organisation performance.

In addition, Seleim, Ashour, & Bontis (2007) examined 38 software development organisations in Egypt and discovered that human capital significantly influences firm performance. Switzer & Huang (2007) contend that variances' performance is attributed to managerial human capital characteristics. Bart (2001) concurs that there is a significant correlation between business missions and human intellectual capital, which ultimately affects the performance of the business.

Alnachef & Alhajjar (2015) carried out a study on the effect of human capital on organisational performance. They found that that the current decline in various economies of the world, with increasing globalisation and saturation of job markets, has resulted in human capital gaining greater importance.. They argue that businesses need to invest in the necessary resources for developing human capital which has an appreciable impact on performance. Costley (2012) finds that the relationship between human capital and organisational performance is positive and further asserts that human capital indicators, such as training and team work practices result in impressive performers where greater productivity could be translated into organisational performance.

BARRIERS TO HUMAN CAPITAL FORMATION

Despite the importance of human capital, however, there are some constraints which hinder its formation and development. The aim of this paper is to identify the challenges which affect human capital in order find a lasting solution to them.

Lack of Finance

Human capital formation is an expensive HRM strategy which requires huge financial commitment and support from top management in organisations. Besides human resources, finance represents the second most important resource in any organisation

(Akhtar, Renyong, Khaskheli & Ali, 2015) . The authors are of the strong view that human capital formation in some organisations fails because top management does not commit or invest part of their financial resources in the training and development of human capital. This assertion underscores the important observation made by Chikwe, Ogidi & Nwachukwu (2015), who believe that human capital formation in the public sector in Nigeria does not attract funding from the government.

In a similar study in China, it was discovered that, given the country's large population, it was very difficult to invest in human capital. According to Jiang (2007), while education and training tend to be the major tools for human capital formation and many economically developed nations invest approximately four to six percent of their total GDP in education, China only invests about three percent of its GDP in education. This demonstrates that the Chinese government is not committed to investment in its human capital. The findings suggest that the investment in human capital in many parts of China is a major concern. For example, a western province, Shanxi, invested only 4.79% of its GDP in education compared with7.59% figure in Beijing (Zhang, 2005).

Low Rating in Human Development Indices

Nwachukwu (2015) suggests that human capital formation in most countries is affected by unfavourable ratings in human development indices. For instance, Nigeria's socio-economic performance and rating in human development indices, which reflects its human capital status, was downgraded by international agencies. This was undeserving in a country of huge natural endowments and human capital potential. According to Nwachukwu (2015), despite Nigeria's richness in biodiversity and vast arable land, in addition to abundant natural and mineral resources, including crude oil and natural gas, the country is still included among poor under-developed countries. The United Nations Development Programme UNDP (2004) Human Development Report ranked Nigeria 151 among the 177 the countries rated. Malaysia is ranked 59, Thailand 76, Tunisia 92, South Africa 119, India 127 and Ghana 131. This implies that Nigeria is only better off than 26 countries in the Measurable Human Development Indices (HDI) and, by implication, this affects the quality of the lives of its citizens.

Brain Drain

Brain drain remains a major challenge to many countries, especially in Sub-Sahara Africa and Asia. Capuano & Marfouk (2013) argue that recent trends suggest that a high percentage of educated Africans migrate from their countries of origin to other countries, in search for greener pastures. According to Capuano & Marfouk

(2013), between 1990 and 2000, the total number of highly educated migrants from African countries living in OECD countries increased by 90%. This phenomenon is likely to exacerbate the already worsening situation in the African continent in terms of human capital. This current trend underscores previous observations made by UNDP (1996) that more than 21,000 Nigerian doctors are practising in the United States whereas, there is a dearth of medical practitioners in the nation's health care system. The brain drain in the Nigeria health sector also manifests itself in other sectors of the economy.

Nwachukwu (2015) concurs that the brain drain in Nigeria is as a result of the increasing rate of unemployment, as well as poor remuneration. The author assumes that the brain drain in Nigeria hugely affects the development of human capital. As in Nigeria, several scholars (Kaplan & Höppli, 2017) have expressed the view that South Africa is experiencing brain drain in most sectors of the economy, especially in the education sector. According to Kaplan & Höppli (2017), although there are no official data on the brain drain in South Africa, however, empirical research suggests that many South Africans migrate to countries such as the United Kingdom, Australia, New Zealand, Canada and the United States. According to Statistics South Africa (2017), the number of emigrants from South Africa in these countries was considerable. The World Bank (2006a, 2006b) highlights the serious implications of brain drain for the growth performance of developing countries, particularly Cape Verde, where the largest fraction of the educated people of its population is living abroad.

In Malaysia, Mahmood (2012) suggests that lack of skills is one of the critical challenges affecting human capital development. Mahmood (2012), in his study at the Islamic Administration Institutes in Malaysia (IAM), found that the staff, especially officers and staff at IAM, often come with religious educational backgrounds. The study reveals that only a small percentage of the staff of this institution possess knowledge and skills in the management and administration field. Mahmood (2012) concludes that the shortage of skills at IAM has affected the effectiveness of human capital development programmes because those who lack sufficient knowledge are in need of more opportunities and time for their training and this is likely to increase the cost of training.

It was also reported that China is facing brain drain in most sectors of its economy. Like many other developing countries, China faces the major challenge of brain drain because it is estimated that every year more than 50, 000 college graduates move to the USA to pursue advanced degrees and that the majority of them remain there (Yang & Wang, 2009).

Underutilisation of Human Capital

Findings suggest that major problems associated with the underutilisation of human capital in Nigeria are the poor human capital development and utilisation policies, encompassing balanced and progressive educational development and the creation of an enabling environment for the full and useful engagement of products of the education system (Nwachukwu, 2015). Evidence shows that most organisations do not fully utilise the potential of their workforce. For example, a study shows that the efficiency of human capital utilisation in China tends to be low (Yang & Wang, 2009).

Aging Workforce

According to Anselmo (2015) and Vasconcelos (2012), the greater proportion of the workforce in most countries falls within the older aged and investing in them becomes very difficult. However, most countries, such as South Africa, Ghana, Nigeria and others, have younger working populations. Anselmo (2015) argues that even though an older workforce may possess more requisite skills, experience and knowledge than a younger and vibrant workforce, however, many organisations prefer to invest in the younger workforce for a number of reasons. Anselmo (2015) believes that human capital development and formation in most countries with an aging workforce is problematic. He, however, cautions organisations and countries to handle the aging workforce and, at the same time, to maintain their competitiveness. He proposes that the challenges confronting an aging workforce could be better managed through initiatives like acknowledgment and sensitivity, workplace diversity, learning, training and development, legislative frameworks, good leadership and HR policies, organisational change, motivation, accommodation of different generations and ethical and moral principles.

Lack of Support From Top Management

Awang & Basir (2016) discovered that lack of support within organisations, particularly from the top management and supervisors, is a major constraint to human capital formation. In most organisations, top management believes that human capital development and formation falls within the functions of the HR department, hence, there is no need for its support. This assertion underscores the findings by Awang & Basir (2016) who, in their interviews with staff at IAM, found that "every time there is a new idea on innovation proposed by the staff and young officers, very often the authorities do not accept their fresh ideas". This phenomenon is likely to result in the demotivation of employees and its consequences may result in the non-achievement of the organisational goals. Some of the participants in the study expressed the opinion that the lack of support among colleagues and top management would result in problems in communication and team work. The study concludes that such developments would inhibit future planning within the organisation.

Human Capital Culture

Sandwell (2011) asserts that the culture of humanitarian organisations is based on certain principles and values of human capital that exist within the firm. According to Sandwell (2011), there is a tendency of culture bringing various organisational changes. It has been noted that some organisations lack the culture of human capital to promote training and development of the workforce. Sandwell (2011), however, proposes that factors such as the educational background of the workforce should be prioritised by organisations when investing in them. He points out that some of the actions developed by the IAM in identifying and developing educated human capital are to provide opportunities for its human capital to further their studies at higher levels, such as master's and PhD degrees. Felício, Couto & Caiado (2014) advocate that it is important to ensure that investment in human capital brings tangible returns to achieve the goals of the organisation.

THEORETICAL FRAMEWORK

According to Francis, Ikemefuna & Ekwoaba (2012, p. 151), "theories are very relevant in providing meanings or understanding of phenomena and problems in the real or practical world". They are also useful in forecasting events or phenomena before they occur. Theories are also important in finding answers to questions such as why, who, where, when and how. (Francis *et al.*, 2012). Chidi & Okpala (2012) express the view that theories are the abstractions of facts which are based on an individual's ideology and cognitive thinking.

Several theories exist regarding human capital formation, namely: talent-based theory, resource-based theory, resource-based view of the firm, knowledge based-view of the firm and human capital theory (Yener, Gurbuz & Acar, 2017; Kimani & Waithaka, 2013). Although these theories are all relevant to human capital formation, the knowledge-based view of the firm is the theory which underpins this study.

Talent-Based Theory

The talent-based theory is credited to prominent scholars like Barney (1991) and Peteraf & Bergen (2003). The theory has gained popularity in recent times and has been applied in many studies (Rabbi, Ahad, Kousar & Ali, 2015), especially with regard to talent management and human capital development. The proponents of the talent-based theory claim that talent is the key organisational asset which assists organisations to gain sustainable competitive advantages over their rivals. The theory suggests that organisations should focus their energy on attracting, developing and maintaining a talented workforce. According to Rabbi *et al.* (2015, p.209), the talent-based theory assumes that the "role of organisations is neither creation nor the acquisition of talent rather, they are regarded as talent integration institutes, since talent resides in the head of individuals and firms only integrates and provides system and structural arrangements for coordination and co-operation between the talented workers".

The talent-based theory is relevant to human capital development because it recognises the importance of developing and enhancing employee competency through a systematic process of talent acquisition, talent transfer and talent sharing. The theory is also important to human capital formation as it encourages organisations to find sustainable means of attracting, developing and retaining potential employees. The theory is also relevant to human capital formation as it describes how talent can be acquired, transferred and shared.

Resource-Based Theory

Barney, Ketchen Jr & Wright (2011) advocate that since the 1991 publication of the first *Journal of Management,* special attention be paid to the resource-based inquiry. According to Barney *et al.* (2011), the resource-based theory (RBT) has evolved from a nascent, upstart perspective to become one of the most prominent and powerful theories for understanding organisations. After 20 years, the RBT appears to have reached maturity stage.

Human Capital Theory

The human capital theory emerged in recent times, focusing on two dominant factors, education and experience (Becker, 1975). Human capital is considered the most relevant resource among all other resources in an organisation, namely: finance, machinery and materials. Human capital has been conceptualised by the author as the knowledge and skills possessed by an individual,. These may be general or specific in nature.

Mincer (1974) points out that the human capital theory has related investments in the development of knowledge and skills to the income distribution of employees. The human capital theory has gained popularity in the field of management and has attracted substantial empirical effort from many organisational research scholars (Unger, Rauch, Frese, & Rosenbusch, 2011). Proponents believe that the human capital theory contributes to an improvement in firms' performance and sustainable competitive advantage. Marvel & Lumpkin, (2007) argue that the human capital theory is important for knowledge-intensive processes such as innovation. They discovered that both general and specific aspects of human capital relate to innovation radicalness. Ucbasaran, Westhead & Wright (2008) recommend that human capital should be able to contribute to higher outcomes in terms of opportunity recognition and creation. Barney (1991) suggests that from the resource-based perspective, human capital theory is regarded as the most valuable in a firm.

Resource-Based View of the Firm (RBV)

The RBV of the firm was developed by Barney (1991) to explain competitive advantage and organisational performance of firms. The RBV of the firm is based on the notion that a firm's competitive advantage and subsequent performance originates in the resources and capabilities controlled by the firm (Barney, 1991).

It has been argued that the RBV of a business focuses specifically on the inside of the business, its resources and capabilities, to explain the profit and value of the organisation (Grant, 1991; Makhija, 2003; Penrose, 1980; Peteraf, 1993; Wernerfelt, 1984). The theory assumes that variation in performance occurs when well established organisations possess more valuable resources than others, allowing them to gain control in a quasi-monopolist form (Wernerfelt, 1984). The existence of capability and resource heterogeneity within a population of firms is one of the principles of the RBV (Helfat & Peteraf, 2003). Organisations are heterogeneous entities characterised by their particular and unique resource bases (Barney, 1991; Nelson & Winter, 1982, Marr, 2004). The RBV of a firm presents an explanation of the heterogeneous competition based on the premise that close competitors differ in important and lasting ways in their resources and capabilities (Helfat & Peteraf, 2003). This perspective recognises that the type, magnitude and nature of resources and capabilities are important determinants of the organisation's capacity to generate profit (Amit & Schoemaker, 1993). By accumulating resources with rent-yielding potential, the organisation may increase the amount of rents generated, and subsequent profits (Szulanski, 2003).

Aldrich (1999) points out that the RBV of the firm stresses the importance of resources such as social, finance and human. Davidson and Honing (2003) maintain that there are three key resources which fall under the RBV of the firm: finance, social and human capital. Clulow, Barry & Gerstman (2007) suggest that the RBV of the firm explores the role of key organisational resources, identified as intangible assets and capabilities, in creating a competitive advantage and superior performance. The scholar, Barney (1991) argues that a sustained competitive advantage can be obtained through the resources and capabilities of the organisation that are valuable, rare, imperfectly imitable and not substitutable. According to Barney (1991), from the perspective of the RBV of the firm, these resources and capabilities can be considered as bundles of tangible and intangible assets, including a firm's management skills, its organisational processes and routines and the information and knowledge it controls.

Knowledge-Based View of the Firm (KBV)

Proponents of the KBV (Barney, 1991, 1986; Foss, 1996; Grant, 1996; Kogut & Zander, 1992; Penrose, 1959) argue that this theory is an extension of the resource-based view (RBV) of organisations. The KBV of an organisation is based on the premise that knowledge is the most important asset of every organisation (Barney, 1991). The KBV of the business assumes that knowledge is an intangible asset which is highly valued in many organisations (Barney, 2001). Hoskisson, Hitt, Wan & Yiu (1999) postulated that the KBV of the firm perceives organisations as heterogeneous entities which are loaded with diverse knowledge. The KBV of the firm is based on the belief that firms exist to develop, share and transform knowledge into competitive advantage (Kogut & Zander, 1992).

CONCEPTUAL MODEL

This chapter develops a conceptual model to establish the link between human capital formation and other organisational constructs such as performance and competitive advantage. As discussed earlier, human capital formation is influenced by a host of factors, including training and development, education, health and wellbeing, recruitment and selection, workforce and employment, institution building and remuneration. From the review of literature, it is evident that human capital leads to greater firm performance and competitive advantage. The firm's performance can be viewed in two ways: financial performance (i.e. increase in productivity, market share and profitability) and non-performance (i.e. customer satisfaction, innovation, workflow improvement and skills development). The information is presented in the Figure 1.

SOLUTION AND RECOMMENDATIONS

In the global competitive market, firms face serious competition from their rivals. However, for firms to gain sustainable competitive advantages, it is important that they use the workforce as a competitive weapon. Against this background, many firms or organisations are searching for strategies that will enable them to increase

Figure 1. Conception model linking human capital formation, human capital effectiveness, performance and competitive advantage
Source: Own compilation

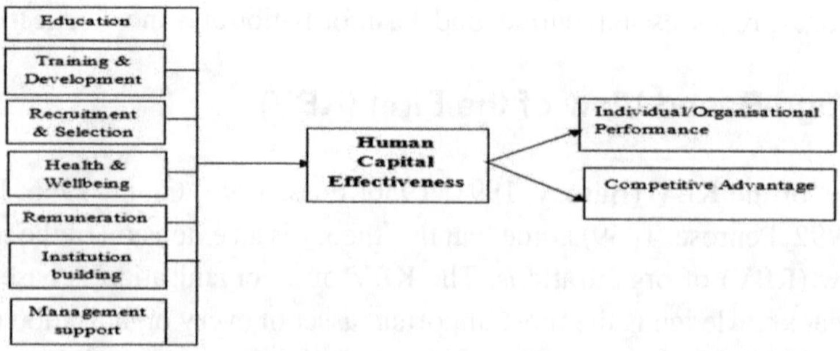

workforce productivity to drive higher value. Because of increasing competition in the labour market, most firms seek to optimise their workforce through comprehensive human capital development programmes, not only to achieve business goals but most importantly, for long-term survival and sustainability. However, to achieve this, firms have to invest a considerable amount of their resources to ensure that their workforce has the skills, knowledge, experience and competence to perform their tasks effectively in the rapidly changing environment. The fundamental objective of any organisation is to maximise or to generate revenue for its shareholders. It is evident that human capital has a significant positive impact on the intellectual capital assets that will yield higher financial results per employee. Human capital formation is influenced by training and the education level of the workforce and their overall satisfaction. Human capital formation is considered a strategic tool which brings returns on investment (ROI).

Moreover, human capital formation tends to create a significant contribution to a firm's competencies which may enhance creativity and innovativeness. Evidence shows that human capital formation paves the way for greater innovativeness and, this in turn, offers positive implications for firm performance. Human capital formation and enhancement results in improved performance. The relevance of human capital formation to firm performance is also observable among technology-based new ventures and it appears that the use of the human capital tool, for instance, in small technology-based new ventures tends to have a great impact on the firms' success.

However, organisations must protect their human capital from eroding. Loss of human capital creates disruption to the firm's operation and may impact negatively on performance. Additionally, the loss of human capital is viewed as problematic as it provides an opportunity through which knowledge and skills may diffuse to competitors, thereby providing a potential risk to the original firm's competitive position. To prevent loss of human capital, it is important for organisations to create an environment and culture that will foster or encourage individual and organisational learning. Additionally, organisations must ensure that both explicit and tacit knowledge are captured and retained at all times through a range of HRM practices.

FUTURE AREAS OF RESEARCH

Human capital formation a complex activity which requires investment in learning, education, training, recruitment and development, as well as other HRM practices. It also requires commitment from top management. However, most empirical research ignores the extent to which top management support or commitment influences human capital formation. Therefore, future research should explore in detail the influence of top management support on human capital formation in an organisation. Moreover, human capital formation can be enhanced through the application of advanced technology. Unfortunately, this area of research has been ignored by many authors. Future studies should examine the extent to which technological advancement influences human capital formation in an organisation.

CONCLUSION

This chapter explores the emerging trends in human capital formation. It examines ways of promoting human capital formation in organisations. Scholarly literature shows that human capital formation in organisations can be promoted through HRM practices such as education, training and development, recruitment and selection, strong commitment from top management and institution building. The chapter further links the conceptualisation of human capital to some fundamentals of economics, competitive advantage and firm performance. The review of empirical research suggests that effective human capital formation contributes to economic growth, innovativeness, competitive advantage and greater firm performance. Further, a conceptual model is developed which shows the link between the human capital formation, competitive advantage and individual/organisational performance. From the discussion, the understanding of firm performance and competitive advantage in relation to human capital formation should not be considered as a phenomenon that only adds value to the organisation. Human capital should rather be regarded as a strategic tool which transforms the entire workforce as the most valuable asset to enable firms to pave ways for greater achievements through innovativeness and creativity. It is therefore important for firms, especially those in the competitive environment, to come up with strategies to invest in their human capital to enable them to remain competitive.

REFERENCES

Adawo, M. A. (2011). Has education (human capital) contributed to the economic growth of Nigeria? *Journal of Economics and International Finance*, *3*(1), 46–58.

Adelakun, O. J. (2011). Human capital development and economic growth in Nigeria. *European Journal of Business and Management*, *3*(9), 29–38.

Adelowokan, O. A. (2012). Growth effect of Education and Health Expenditure in Nigeria (1970-2010). *African Journal of Science and Research*, *1*(1), 510–528.

Aghion, P., & Howitt, P. (1992). Capital, innovation, and growth accounting. *Oxford Review of Economic Policy*, *23*(1), 79–93. doi:10.1093/oxrep/grm007

Akhtar, S. H., Renyong, H., Khaskheli, A., & Ali, A. (2015). Understanding the dynamics of human capital development in Pakistan: A socio economic obstacle framework. *Journal of Poverty, Investment and Development*, *13*(4), 44–53.

Alnachef, T. H., & Alhajjar, A. (2015). Effect of Human Capital on Organizational Performance: A Literature Review. *International Journal of Science and Research*, 1154-1158.

Amit, R., & Schoemaker, P. (1993). Strategic Assets and Organisational Rent. *Strategic Management Journal*, *14*(1), 33–46. doi:10.1002mj.4250140105

Ariely, G. (2003). *Knowledge management as a methodology towards intellectual capital*. Presented at the 3rd European Knowledge Management Summer School, San Sebastian, Spain.

Awan, A. G. (2012). Diverging trends of human capital in BRIC countries. *International Journal of Asian Social Science*, *2*(12), 2195–2219.

Barney, J. (1991). Firm Resources and Sustained Competitive Advantage. *Journal of Management*, *17*(1), 99–120. doi:10.1177/014920639101700108

Barney, J. B., Ketchen, D. J. Jr, & Wright, M. (2011). The future of resource-based theory: Revitalization or decline? *Journal of Management*, *37*(5), 1299–1315. doi:10.1177/0149206310391805

Bart, C. K. (2001). Exploring the application of mission statements on the world wide web. *Internet Research*, *11*(4), 360–369. doi:10.1108/10662240110402812

Bartlett, C. A., & Ghoshal, S. (2002). Building competitive advantage through people: Human, not financial, capital must be the starting point and ongoing foundation of a successful strategy. *MIT Sloan Management Review*, *43*(2), 34–42.

Becker, G. S. (1964). *Human capital: A theoretical and empirical analysis with special reference to education*. New York: Columbia University Press.

Capuano, S., & Marfouk, A. (2013). African brain drain and its impact on source countries: What do we know and what do we need to know? *Journal of Comparative Policy Analysis*, *15*(4), 297–314. doi:10.1080/13876988.2013.813122

Chadwick, C., & Dabu, A. (2009). Human resources, human resource management, and the competitive advantage of firms: Toward a more comprehensive model of causal linkages. *Organization Science*, *20*(1), 253–272. doi:10.1287/orsc.1080.0375

Chidi, C. O., & Okpala, O. P. (2012). Theoretical approaches to employment and industrial relations: a comparison of subsisting orthodoxies. Theoretical and Methodological Approaches to Social Sciences and Knowledge Management, 2(1), 264-277

Chikwe, C. K., Ogidi, R. C., & Nwachukwu, K. (2015). Challenges of Research and Human Capital Development in Nigeria. *Journal of Education and Practice*, *6*(28), 44–47.

Clulow, V., Barry, C., & Gerstman, J. (2007). The resource-based view and value: The customer-based view of the firm. *Journal of European Industrial Training*, *31*(1), 19–35. doi:10.1108/03090590710721718

Costley, K. C. (2012). *Why do we have theories?* Education Resources Information Centre.

Crook, T. R., Todd, S. Y., Combs, J. G., Woehr, D. J., & Ketchen, D. J. J. (2011). Does human capital matter? A meta-analysis of the relationship between human capital and firm performance. *The Journal of Applied Psychology*, *96*(3), 443–456. doi:10.1037/a0022147 PMID:21244126

Davidson, P., & Honing, B. (2003). The role of social and human capital among nascent entrepreneurs. *Journal of Business Venturing*, *18*(3), 301–331. doi:10.1016/S0883-9026(02)00097-6

Downes, S. (2007). Models for sustainable open educational resources. *Interdisciplinary Journal of E-Learning and Learning Objects*, *3*(1), 29–44. doi:10.28945/384

Edwards, R. (1979). *Contested Terrain: The Transformation of the Workplace in the Twentieth Century*. New York: Basic Books.

Eigbiremolen, G. O., & Anaduaka, S. U. (2014). Human capital development and economic growth: The Nigeria experience. *International Journal of Academic Research in Business and Social Sciences*, *4*(4), 25–35. doi:10.6007/IJARBSS/v4-i4/749

Ejere, S. I. (2011). Human capital formation as catalyst for national development: Nigeria in perspective. *International Business and Management*, *2*(2), 98–104.

Esu, B. B. (2012). Linking human capital management with tourism development and management for economic survival: The Nigeria experience. *International Journal of Business and Social Science*, *3*(11), 1–12.

Felício, J. A., Couto, E., & Caiado, J. (2014). Human capital, social capital and organizational performance. *Management Decision*, *52*(2), 350–364. doi:10.1108/MD-04-2013-0260

Foss, N. (1997). *Resources, firms and strategies: A reader in the resource-based perspective*. Oxford, UK: Oxford University Press.

Grant, R. (1996). Towards a knowledge-based view of the firm. *Strategic Management Journal*, *17*(S2), 109–122. doi:10.1002mj.4250171110

Helfat, C., & Peteraf, M. (2003). The dynamic resource-based view: Capability lifecycles. *Strategic Management Journal*, *24*(10), 997–1010. doi:10.1002mj.332

Hoskisson, R., Hitt, M., Wan, W., & Yiu, D. (1999). Theory and research in strategic management: Swings of a pendulum. *Journal of Management*, *25*(3), 417–456. doi:10.1177/014920639902500307

Igbokwe-Ibeto, C., Chukwuemeka, E., & Okechukwu, E. (2014). Enhancing human capital development and service delivery in Nigerian Tertiary institutions through effective academic staff. *Africa's Public Service Delivery & Performance Review*, *2*(3), 125–152. doi:10.4102/apsdpr.v2i3.62

Jaiyeoba, S. V. (2015). Human Capital Investment and Economic Growth in Nigeria, African Research Review. *An International Multidisciplinary Journal, Ethiopia*, *9*(1), 36–44.

Jamal, W., & Saif, M. I. (2011). Impact of human capital management on organizational performance. *European Journal of Economics. Finance and Administrative Sciences*, *5*(34), 13309–13315.

Kaplan, D., & Höppli, T. (2017). The South African brain drain: An empirical assessment. *Development Southern Africa, 34*(5), 497–514. doi:10.1080/0376835X.2017.1351870

Kazlauskaitė, R., & Bučiūnienė, I. (2008). The role of human resources and their management in the establishment of sustainable competitive advantage. *The Engineering Economist, 5*(60), 78–84.

Kimani, S. M., & Waithaka, S. M. (2013). Factors affecting implementation of talent management in state corporations: A case study of Kenya Broadcasting Corporation. *International Journal of Business and Social Research, 3*(4), 42–49.

Kogut, B., & Zander, U. (1992). Knowledge of the firm, combinative capabilities, and the replication of technology. *Organization Science, 3*(3), 383–397. doi:10.1287/orsc.3.3.383

Lajili, K. (2012). Towards building a human-capital based governance framework. *Journal of Management Policy and Practice, 13*(3), 13–30.

Lucas, R. Jr. (1988). On the mechanics of economic development. *Journal of Monetary Economics, 22*(1), 3–42. doi:10.1016/0304-3932(88)90168-7

Mba, I. C., Mba, E. I., Ogbuabor, J. E., & Ikpegbu, C. H. (2013). Human Capital Development and Economic Growth in Nigeria. *Journal of Economics and Sustainable Development, 4*, 18–25.

Mehrara, M., & Musai, M. (2013). The relationship between Economic Growth and Human Capital in Developing Countries. *International Letters of Social and Humanistic Sciences, 5*, 55–62. doi:10.18052/www.scipress.com/ILSHS.5.55

Metilelu, O. O. (2016). Human capital development trends in the hospitality and tourism industry: A case of southwest Nigeria. *African Journal of Hospitality, Tourism and Leisure, 5*(4), 1–9.

Nelson, R., & Winter, S. (1982). *An evolutionary theory of economic change*. Cambridge, MA: Belknap Press.

Oluwatobi, S. O., & Ogunrinola, O. I. (2011). Government expenditure on human capital development: Implications for economic growth in Nigeria. *Journal of Sustainable Development, 4*(3), 72–80. doi:10.5539/jsd.v4n3p72

Osoba, A. M. (2017). Human capital variables and economic growth in Nigeria. *EuroEconomica, 6*(1), 7–18.

Penrose, E. (1959). *The Theory of the Growth of the firm*. Oxford, UK: Basil Blackwell Publisher.

Penrose, E. (1980). *The Theory of the Growth of the firm* (2nd ed.). Oxford, UK: Basil Blackwell Publisher.

Reed, K. K., Srinivasan, N., & Doty, D. H. (2009). Adapting human and social capital to impact performance: Some empirical findings from the US personal banking sector. *Journal of Managerial Issues*, 36–57.

Romer, P. M. (1989). *Human capital and growth: theory and evidence (No. w3173)*. National Bureau of Economic Research. doi:10.3386/w3173

Sandwell, C. (2011). A qualitative study exploring the challenges of humanitarian organisations. *Journal of Humanitarian Logistics and Supply Chain Management*, *1*(2), 132–150. doi:10.1108/20426741111158430

Sankay, O. J., Ismail, R., & Shaari, A. H. (2010). The impact of human capital development on the economic growth of Nigeria. *Prosiding Perkem*, *5*(1), 63–72.

Sariolghalam, N., Noruzi, M. R., & Rahimi, G. R. (2010). The enigma of Howard Gardner's multiple intelligences theory in the area of organizational effectiveness. *International Journal of Business and Management*, *5*(5), 161–173. doi:10.5539/ijbm.v5n5p161

Seleim, A., Ashour, A., & Bontis, N. (2007). Human capital and organizational performance: A study of Egyptian software companies. *Management Decision*, *45*(4), 789–801. doi:10.1108/00251740710746033

Sultan Qadri, F., & Abdul, W. (2011). Human capital and economic growth: Time series evidence from Pakistan. *Pakistan Business ReviK2ew*, *1*, 815-833.

Switzer, L. N., & Huang, Y. (2007). How does human capital affect the performance of small and mid-cap mutual funds? *Journal of Intellectual Capital*, *8*(4), 666–681. doi:10.1108/14691930710830828

Vasconcelos, A. F. (2015). Older workers: Some critical societal and organizational challenges. *Journal of Management Development*, *34*(3), 352–372. doi:10.1108/JMD-02-2013-0034

Vladikov, A. (2015). Human capital formation and use in Bulgaria. *Trakia Journal of Sciences*, *13*(1Suppl.1), 8–15. doi:10.15547/tjs.2015.s.01.003

Wallerstein, I. (1980). *The Modem World System II: mercantilism and the consolidation of the European world-economy 1600-1750*. New York: Academic Press.

Wernerfelt, B. (1984). A resource-based view of the firm. *Strategic Management Journal*, *5*(2), 171–180. doi:10.1002mj.4250050207

World Bank. (2006a). *International migration, remittances and the brain drain.* Washington, DC: World Bank.

World Bank. (2006b). *Global economic prospects. Economic implications of remittances and migration.* Washington, DC: World Bank.

Yang, B., & Wang, X. (2009). Successes and challenges of developing human capital in the People's Republic of China. *Human Resource Development International*, *12*(1), 3–14. doi:10.1080/13678860802638784

Yener, M. I., Gurbuz, F. G., & Acar, P. (2017). Development and validation of a talent management measurement instrument. *Journal of Business Economics and Finance*, *6*(3), 233–245.

KEY TERMS AND DEFINITIONS

Brain Drain: The migration of intelligent, skilled, or capable professionals within a given field or geographic region to another country, economic sector, or field.

Competitive Advantage: An attribute which allows an organisation to outperform its rivals

Economic Growth: The measure of percent rate of increase in real gross domestic product (GDP) or real GDP.

Education: The process of providing the knowledge, skills, moral values and understanding required in the normal course of life.

Human Capital: The collective knowledge that is embedded in the personnel, organisational routines, and network relationships of an organisation.

Performance: The accomplishment of a given task measured against preset known standards of accuracy, completeness, cost, and speed.

Training: The process whereby people acquire capabilities, skills, knowledge, and experiences to aid in the achievement of organisational goals.

Chapter 5
Human Capital Management in the Fourth Industrial Revolution

Vivence Kalitanyi
https://orcid.org/0000-0002-0140-6649
University of Johannesburg, South Africa

Geoff A. Goldman
University of Johannesburg, South Africa

ABSTRACT

This chapter identifies the drivers and challenges of the fourth industrial revolution. The fourth industrial revolution consists of artificial intelligence, big data, robotics, and many others technological innovations. The recent transformation in the global environment is affecting the way businesses are conducted, managed, and the way governments and societies are run. Today, business analysts are faced with the challenge of managing both human and digital workforce effectively without making any stakeholder in the business environment worse off. Hence, human capital management in the fourth industrial revolution involves effective development and deployment of human resources, artificial intelligence, and robotics to achieve organisational goals and objectives. It is expected that the principles underlying human capital management—planning, staffing, development, compensation, and investment in digital workforce—will become more intense and complex.

DOI: 10.4018/978-1-5225-9810-7.ch005

INTRODUCTION

Klaus Schwab, the Founder and Chairman of the World Economic Forum and the International Organization for Public-Private Cooperation, states that throughout history, there have been four industrial revolutions, with the fourth being the present. Schwab (2016) describes the Industrial revolution as the appearance of "new technologies and novel ways of perceiving the world which triggers a profound change in economic and social structures". The First Industrial Revolution was characterized by steam power, while the Second Industrial Revolution is referred to as the age of science and mass production. The Third Industrial Revolution was marked by the digital revolution, and now we are living in the Fourth Industrial Revolution of dramatic technological expansion and social change (Trailhead, 2019).

The objective of this chapter is to create an awareness of new technology revolution and outline the essential practices for managers and Human Resources practitioners about the changes that are brought about by technological advancements, as these changes require constant adaptations and adjustments. Human capital is key to the success of every business, and its effective management is a shared responsibility between the human resources department as well as line management.

Since human capital is a source of competitive advantage, its effective management becomes a crucial function to the organization, and this task seems to be becoming more complex in this 4IR whose technology is having significant consequences on our daily lives. At the work place for instance, the actions and behaviors of human capital (ordinary employees* and managers) is influenced by technology in terms of information exchange and performing daily duties for both sets of human capital for the organizational success, hence its adaptation to new realities becomes imperative.

Human capital is regarded as the job-relevant knowledge, skills, abilities, energy, commitment and capacity to develop and innovate, possessed by people in an organization (Nel, & De Beer, 2014). Barnes (2008) considers human resources as one of the transforming resources that form part of the input resources in the transformation process that constitutes any operation.

Human resources should develop a can-do attitude and provide a company with the much needed competitive advantage if they are properly managed. In his book; *"Competitive advantage through people and the human equation: Building profits by putting people first"*, Professor Jeffrey Pfeffer of Stanford University emphasizes the above argument when he states that the distinction between top-performing companies from their competitors, lies in the way they treat their human resources (Erasmus, Strydom & Rudansky-Kloppers, 2016).

HUMAN CAPITAL MANAGEMENT

Human Capital Management (HCM) is a comprehensive set of practices for recruiting, managing, developing and optimizing the human resources of an organization (Rouse, 2019). By this definition, it is depicted that management has to adopt an approach to human resources management that perceives employees as assets that can be invested in and managed in order to effect maximum profit for the success of the organization.

Swanepoel, Erasmus, Schenk and Tshilongamulenzhe (2014) had a similar perspective in defining Human Capital Management (HCM) from a business-based perspective and pointed out that "*it is a philosophy of people management based on the belief that human capitals are uniquely important to sustained business success. An organization gains competitive advantage by using its people effectively, drawing on their expertise and ingenuity to meet clearly defined objectives. Human Capital Management (HCM) is aimed at recruiting capable, flexible and committed people, managing and rewarding their performance and developing key competencies*".

This task of managing human capital encompasses a number of functions, starting from bringing people into the organization, then train, develop and retain them. Employees need to be fully integrated into the socio-cultural environment of the organization, though these main tasks seem to be costing management's time, they are expected to perform even harder with the 4th Industrial Revolution.

The 4IR is about artificial intelligence, abundant information as well as robotic systems, which implies the use of technology in all spheres of human endeavors (Pribanic, 2018). If Human Capital Management (HCM) function is to be relevant in the 4IR by fulfilling its main role - recruitment and selection, training and development as well as retention - for the company's success, it will also have to embrace technology for example by using available application software in all its activities. In the past, Human Capital Management (HCM) software could be obtained as part of the "Enterprise Resource Planning (ERP) package, and though it is still available, Software as service (SaaS) has superseded it in recent years, and it is most suitable for on premise Human Capital Management (HCM) (Ey Global, 2019). In general, the functions of Human Capital Management (HCM) software are arranged in various categories as described below (ERP, 2018):

- **Core Human Resources**: Including payroll, benefits administration, onboarding, compliance management and maintenance of employee data.
- **Talent Management**: The collective term for the process of recruitment, developing and retaining employees. Talent management suites consists of distinct, yet integrated modules of recruitment, performance management, compensation management, learning and succession planning.

- **Workforce Management**: The set of functions for deploying employees with the necessary skills to particular regions, departments or projects. It includes time and attendance management, workforce planning, labor scheduling and budgeting.
- **Service Delivery**: Which includes the HR help desk, intranet portals, employee self-service and manager self-service.

These Human Capital Management (HCM) suites also have technologies that cut across functional areas, notably analytics, social media, collaboration and employee engagement. A number of them also allow mobile access to Human Resources (HR) data and applications, especially the self-service features. As a reminder, this chapter discusses in more detail, the way these major Human Resources (HR) functions will be performed in the 4IR.

The Critical Role of Properly Managing Human Capital

Authors such as Pribanic (2018) highlighted the critical role of managing human resources. In his view, human capital management is an important task which allows the company to further its goals. He goes on to ascertain that with efficient human capital management system in place, the organization will be able to create and sustain a successful and thriving workforce. Pfeffer as cited by Erasmus, Strydom and Rudansky-Kloppers (2016), argues further that companies that invest in their human capital, are capable of creating a long-lasting competitive advantage that is difficult for their competitors to duplicate. Erasmus, Strydom and Rudansky-Kloppers (2016) highlighted the role of human resources management in the effectiveness of an organization. They state that for an organization to be really effective, top managers need to treat human resources as the key element of that effectiveness. The contribution of human capital management in the organizational effectiveness includes among other aspects:

- Assisting everybody in the organization to achieve stated objectives
- Making efficient use of skills and abilities of the human resources
- Providing the organization with well-trained and motivated employees
- Assisting employees in attainment of job satisfaction and self-actualization
- Developing a quality of work life that makes employment in the organization desirable
- Assisting with the maintenance of ethical policies and socially responsible behavior
- Managing change to the mutual advantage of individuals, groups, organizations and the public

- Executing human resources functional activities in a professional manner, and
- Being involved in strategic decision-making and strategy formulation of the organization.

Human resources management has been performing these activities in a traditional sense and continues to do so at present. Now that the world is changing due to technological advancements, it remains to be seen how the HCM will cope in this new era. And this is what this chapter discusses in more details.

The Nature of Human Capital Management From the First Industrial Revolution to the Fourth

As the work environment changes and becomes more complex, so have the practices and considerations about managing human capital throughout the different industrial revolutions. Any environmental change, affects business management, including human resources management and has to mobilize the workforce to adapt to the new conditions. Industrial revolutions have not only brought new techniques of doing work, but have also caused management to think of how employees should be treated. The sections below describe human capital management practices throughout the history of industrial revolutions (ERP, 2018).

Human Capital Management in the First Industrial Revolution (Age of Mechanical Production)

Before the advent of the steam engine -in around 1760s -, steam power was the source of energy in all sectors of life from agriculture to textile manufacturing. Societies were mainly agrarian, which means life was centered around farming. However, the use of steam power in those agrarian societies, resulted in urbanization, due to the fact that people started to rely on steam power to run machines. Railroads as well as steamships appeared and helped people to move from point A to B. All these events, marked the birth of the factory (The Economist, 2016).

It started with the mechanization of the textile industry, where tasks that were previously done laboriously by hands in hundreds of weavers' cottages, were put together in a single cotton mill, thereby marking the beginning of the factory (Nieuwenhizen & Oosthuizen, 2017). The nature of work, was mainly mechanical production, but sometimes with the use of steam power. Furthermore, the work was also concerned with the drawing of railroads.

The influx of unskilled laborers made labor cheap enough to exploit in difficult conditions, and working hours long (14 hour shifts for both children and adults). On

Figure 1. Steam power use in the first industrial revolution

the other hand, the First Industrial Revolution revolutionized work and affected the human capital of the organizations. In these types of operations, people who headed organizations - currently referred to as managers - came to a conclusion that they greatly depended on their employees in order to achieve their goals of providing products and/or services.

During this period, manufacturing businesses shifted from being home-based businesses to operating from a factory setting, thereby becoming labor incentive operations in organizations. Furthermore, managers started to realize the importance of human capital, and their indispensability for producing the products and achieving organizational goals (Rouse, 2019). They therefore realized that they should treat them better, especially that advancing industrialization created a middle class of skilled workers. Currently, information about the exact way management interacted with employees, and how workers were generally managed, is very superficial.

Human Capital Management in the Second Industrial Revolution (Age of Science and Mass Production)

The Second Industrial Revolution (IR) which started in the mid-1800s, accelerated a number of inventions, such as gasoline engines, airplanes, chemical fertilizers and basically all other inventions that help us go faster and do more. It is important to know that these advancements in the sciences were not limited to the laboratories only. However, some scientific principles were also introduced in factories. Principles such as assembly lines which hugely supported mass production. In terms of work to be performed, it was mainly mass production. This era of the industrial revolution also saw the advent of electrical power as well as the assembly line techniques in production (Author's notes, 2019).

Figure 2. Mass production during the second industrial revolution

The approach to Human Capital Management (HCM) was the application of scientific methods to ensure efficiency, cooperation and motivation. Managers believed that all these results could be achieved through incentives (Swanepoel, Erasmus, Schenk, & Tshilongamulenzhe, 2014). These new methods affected human capital of organizations and the main approach to managing it was to empower the lower-level managers who dealt with employees on a daily basis. Another key focus to Human Capital Management during this period, was on ensuring harmony between management and workers. In this regard, Frederick Winslow Taylor (1856-1915) argued that it is important to seek the one best way to do the job, determine the optimum work pace, train people to do the job properly, and reward successful performance by using an incentive pay system.

It was during this period of the 2nd industrial revolution, that managers started to develop a perception that when workers and managers knew one another's expectations, it would result in a situation characterized by cooperation and conflict avoidance. Furthermore, managers' views on motivating employees, was that money, in terms of a salary is all that was needed. The view that employees needed more than money to be or stay motivated, came in at a later stage in the development of employees' management practices.

Another view on how to manage human capital during the second industrial revolution, came from Frank Bunker Gilbreth (1868-1924). In his view, employee performance could be obtained through reducing unnecessary motions, while limiting fatigue by paying greater attention to total working environment (Ricci, 2012). Though Gilbreth was hugely influenced by his wife's research in industrial psychology, both claim to have departed from Taylor's work on human capital's management theory on motivation. Simply put, the Gilbreths opinion on human capital management, was on work study, a process by which, management conduct a scientific observation and analysis of work, including a study of the nature and contents of a task, with a purpose of developing a more efficient way of doing a piece of work in the shortest possible time, in order to improve productivity.

During this period of Second Industrial revolution, another view that has shaken the world is that of Karl Marx (1818-1883). However, at this point, it would be prudent to reflect upon the contribution of Karl Marx in the broader discussion of HCM, as the Marxist doctrine brought to the fore certain tensions Alvesson & Willmott (2012) that are central to the notion of HCM. However, to fully understand the contribution of Marx, one needs to revert back to a short account of the notion of work itself (Dyer, Humphries, Fitzgibbons & Hurd, 2014). Work, in the form of paid employment, is the path to freedom from a neo-liberal point of view. In this sense, freedom should be seen as the bounties associated with receiving remuneration for work done (Alvesson, Bridgman & Willmott, 2009). This freedom allows people to purchase goods and services to fulfil their needs and wants, its provides the opportunity to invest surplus income for future returns. This freedom also implies the liberty to select a preferred vocation and level of commitment to employment (Dyer, Humphries, Fitzgibbons & Hurd, 2014). This neo-liberal perspective portrays work as a noble act, an emancipation that enables the worker to almost transcend to a different level of existence.

In reaction to this notion, Marx proposed that the idea of western capitalism produced a distinctive class relationship between the owners of capital (who also own factors of production) and workers (Alvesson & Willmott (2012); (Wren &Bedeian, 2009). Marx posits that workers have only their labor to offer in exchange for wages paid to them by the owners of capital (Dyer, Humphries, Fitzgibbons & Hurd, 2014). For Marx, this is an uneven power relationship which inherently becomes exploitative and alienating toward the worker (Alvesson & Willmott (2012). Within the capitalist conception, all factors of production, including labor, are seen as objects that are arranged into systems that are managed by the owners of capital in order to maximize profits. This, in turn, objectifies the worker in a sense that workers sell their time for a wage, and this time becomes a commodity that can be bought, sold and controlled by the owners of capital (Wren &Bedeian, 2009). Marx, therefore, dispels the notion that paid work leads to freedom and emancipation, and rather posits that paid work leads to objectification of the worker, commodification of the act of labor, and exploitation of the working class (Dyer, Humphries, Fitzgibbons & Hurd, 2014); (Alvesson & Willmott (2012); (Wren & Bedeian, 2009). This, in turn, alienates the worker from the organizational institution established by the owners of capital (Alvesson & Willmott, 2012).

The work of Marx, and his colleague, Fredrich Engels, had a marked impact on the First and Second Industrial Revolution, and their views largely influenced the rise of the workers' union movement in (especially) the UK and Europe (Feher, 2009). Most trade unions are to this day still very socialist in their ideology, and to this day the trade union movement sees itself as a watchdog guarding against the exploitative practices of 'owners of capital' (i.e. management) and acting in the best interests of the workers. Thus, the legacy of Marx is that his work highlighted the tension between workers and owners of capital in the pervasive, western capitalist society (Dyer, Humphries, Fitzgibbons & Hurd, 2014); (Alvesson & Willmott (2012). The realization of this tension and the implications it has, not only for the labor force, but also on the business organization, is crucial for HCM, as the modern managerial tendency is to place greater emphasis on not alienating and exploiting the workforce. This can be seen as a strange turn, where management can be seen to agree with the Marxist ideas of objectification and commodification of the workforce and the act of labor.

A further approach of human capital management during the 2nd Industrial Revolution, was proposed by Max Weber (1864-1920), whereby he suggested that there must be a distinction between power (the ability to force human capital to obey) and authority (whereby orders are voluntarily obeyed to, by those receiving them). In such a system, those in the subordinate role (staff) see the issuing of directives and orders by those in the authoritarian role (managers) as legitimate. In simple words, …" this management approach is based on a formal organizational structure with a set of rules and regulations that rely on the specialization of labour, an authority hierarchy, and rigid promotion and selection criteria" (Nieuwenhuizen & Oosthuizen, 2017. The first and second industrial revolutions have made people rich and more urban.

Human Capital Management in the Third Industrial Revolution (The Digital Revolution)

The 3rd Industrial Revolution took its kick off in the mid-1950s, and immediately took momentum, as it was the beginning of automated production including electronics, as well as, the introduction of computers. It brought semiconductors, mainframe computing, personal computing, and the internet, hence the digital revolution. Things that used to be analog, moved to digital technologies, like the old television that was tuned in by antenna (analog) being replaced by Internet-connected tablets that allowed for the streaming of movies (digital) (Florida's solar progress, 2012).

The success of the Third Industrial Revolution was due to the five pillars that set its strong foundation, and each pillar could function in relation to the others (Florida's solar progress, 2012). Those were:

- **Shifting to Renewable Energy**: Develop massive wind farms, new technology etc.

Figure 3. Electronics in the third industrial revolution

- **Transforming the Building Stock of Each Continent Into Micro-Power Plants to Collect Renewable Energies On-Site:** Building account for about half of energy consumption next to cars. Attaching turbines and solar cells to buildings will eliminate this energy demand and instead fed the power back into the electric grid.
- **Deploying Hydrogen and Other Storage Technologies** in every building and throughout the infrastructure to store intermittent energies. NASA has already done extensive research and development.
- **Using Internet Technology to Transform the Power Grid** of every continent into an energy Internet that acts just like the Internet (when millions of buildings are generating a small amount of renewable energy locally, on-site, they can sell surplus green electricity back to the grid and share it with their continental neighbors).
- **Transitioning the Transport Fleet to Electric Plug-In and Fuel Cell Vehicles** that can buy and sell green electricity on a smart, continental, interactive power grid. With the development of smart grid, these vehicles will also be able to sell surplus energy back to the grid.

The Human Capital Management approach that prevailed during the Third Industrial revolution, was "Human Relations approaches". This approach focuses on individuals working in group settings, with a belief that a satisfied employee, will be productive. It is from this perspective that Abraham Maslow (1908-1970), theorized that human needs are ranged in hierarchies, and that management should strive to satisfy them as the appearance of one need actually rests on the prior satisfaction of another, more prominent need. "Man is a perpetually wanting animal" (Maslow, 1943).

This view of human capital management holds that if a person is without job, and therefore has no money for food and shelter, will certainly focus on the lower

Figure 4. Artificial intelligence and robotics in the fourth industrial revolution

two needs (physiological and safety/security). This is to say that; such a person will not be able to focus on status or self-fulfillment. On the other side, a person who is financially stable might be looking to make some contribution to the societal needs, or securing non-financial rewards. It is the responsibility of managers to know and understand where their human capitals are in relation to their hierarchy of needs, so that they can motivate them.

Another approach to management that has marked the Third Industrial Revolution with a focus on human relations, was the Theory X and Theory Y by Douglas McGregor: 1906-1964). It is essential that managers focus on what promotes employees' commitment and performance. Assumptions that managers make about their human capital, have been identified as a starting point. Those assumptions are centered around the dimensions of:

- Attitude,
- Direction,
- Responsibility,
- Motivation as well as
- Creativity.

In brief, McGregor theorizes that managers who make Theory X assumptions believe that workers are naturally lazy, dislike work, side-step responsibility and will do as little as they can in most work situations. On the other side, managers who make Theory Y assumptions believe that workers can enjoy work, desire

Table 1. Theory x and y and their areas of focus

Theory x	Focus areas of assumptions	Theory Y
People dislike work, find it boring and will avoid it, if possible.	Attitude	People need to work, can enjoy their work and want to take an interest in their work.
People must be forced/coerced into compliance.	Direction	People direct themselves towards an acceptable target.
People need to be directed, as they avoid responsibility.	Responsibility	People generally thrive taking responsibility.
People are motivated by fear, lack of money and job security.	Motivation	People want to contribute to the world and are motivated by their desire for self-development .
People show little creativity, except when getting around rules.	Creativity	People are highly creative when given the opportunity and recognition.

Source: McGregor, Lorenzi & Skinner, 1994.

responsibility and want to accept challenges in their work (MacGregor's XY theory of management, 1960).

Merits of the First Three Industrial Revolutions

Each of the first three Industrial Revolutions occasioned enormous changes in the socio-economic lives of the people. Life shifted from being all about the farm to all about the factory, and people moved from rural areas to settle into cities with the introduction of mechanical production. Furthermore, the way people lived and worked fundamentally changed with the discovery of electricity which occasioned mass production, and most recently, the digital revolution affected almost every industry, yet again, transforming how people live, work, managed and communicate (Swanepoel, Ersamus, Schenk & Tshilongamulenzhe, 2014).

The Fourth Industrial Revolution (Artificial Intelligence, Robotics)

Today, many technologies people dreamt about in the 1950s and 60s, have become a reality. What we experience every day, is the generic sequencing and editing,

Figure 5. Maslow's hierarchy of needs

artificial intelligence, miniaturized sensors, and 3D printing, to name just a few. Innovations are unexpected and surprising. This is the beginning of the Fourth Industrial Revolution (The Fourth Industrial Revolution, 2019). The Fourth Industrial Revolution is the core part of this chapter, which therefore begins with a profound exploration of what it is, and its generic effect, before discussing how managers will deal with their human capital in this era.

The Fourth Industrial Revolution is an era which is creating and extending the impact of digitalization in new and unanticipated ways. Therefore, people need to take the time to consider exactly what kind of shifts they are experiencing and how they should collectively or individually benefit from what it has to offer (The Fourth Industrial Revolution, 2019). More importantly, managers at different levels of organizations, public and private, should quickly learn and understand how the Fourth Industrial Revolution is changing the world and understand how better to manage their human resources.

Furthermore, the Fourth Industrial Revolution, is seen as the advent of "cyber-physical systems" which involves new capabilities for human beings and machines. It is said that these capabilities rely on infrastructure and technologies that were brought about by the Third Industrial Revolution, and the Fourth Industrial Revolution represents new ways through which technology becomes embedded within societies and human (The Fourth Industrial Revolution, 2019). New forms of machine intelligence, breakthrough materials, genome editing, and approaches to governance that rely on cryptographic methods such as block chain, are just a few examples.

As pointed out by the United Nations in 2013, more people in the world have access to the mobile phone as opposed to basic sanitation". At the same time, the Fourth Industrial Revolution is spreading across the globe, when aspects of the Third and Second Industrial Revolutions are only reaching and maturing in some parts of the World and organizations now. This is what the novelist William Gibson said "The future is already here – it's just not very evenly distributed."

What managers and business owners need to bear in mind, is the fact that all these technologies and their emergent nature makes many aspects of the Fourth Industrial Revolution feel unfamiliar and to many, threatening. Managers, as well as individuals need to understand that industrial revolutions are driven by people's choices, more importantly the choices of investors, consumers, regulators and citizens who adopt and employ these technologies within their daily lives. To be able to use it to the benefit of the organisations in their process of managing their human resources, managers have to also embrace and adopt technology. Researchers have compared the Fourth Industrial revolution with exogenous forces comparable with the power of a tsunami. However, it is all about people's choices and desires. And at the heart of the debate around emerging technologies, is a critical and central question: what do we want these technologies to deliver for us?

Human Capital in the Fourth Industrial Revolution

During this 4th Industrial Revolution, it is expected that the principles underlying human resources management; planning, staffing, employee development and compensation and governance is going to become more intense and complex. An example to illustrate this is that job seekers around the world have access and the ability to apply for jobs and positions that are open around the world. Management can't resist considering these applicants, and if some of them are successful, they will come into a new environment with different cultural settings. We therefore believe that "diversity" is one of the thorny issues human capital managers will have to face in the Fourth Industrial Revolution (Author's notes, 2019).

Diversity

Kondola and Fullerton (1998) define diversity as "*the basic concept which accepts that the workforce consists of a diverse population of people. The diversity consists of visible and non-visible differences which will include sex, age, background, race, disability, personality and workstyle. It is founded on the premise that harnessing these differences will create a productive environment in which everybody feels valued, where their talents are being fully utilized, and in which organizational goals are met*".

Diversity will play a key role in how businesses run in this fourth industrial Revolution. Due to current technological advancements, there is an increased pool of people available for organizations to choose from. Therefore, organizations will have staff who belong to different cohorts of ages, with a difference of experiences and ambitions. The diversity on age does also imply that human capital managers will have to deal with employees whereby some are more energetic, while others are wiser and self-controlled. Organizations will therefore become multifaceted, and with the recent creation of the Equality and Human Rights Commission, managers will have to efficiently deal with issues of races, religion, ethnic origin, physical disability, age and sexual orientation (Ricci, 2012). According to Mullins and Dossor, rehabilitated offenders are also offered protection discrimination in employment (Mullins & Dossor, 2013).

Conceptual skills are said to be the preferred set of abilities that managers, especially at the higher level of the organization, should have the most. However, in the Fourth Industrial Revolution, interpersonal skills must occupy a crucial role in management day to day operations in order to successfully deal with diversity. The Skills Portal (2019) outlines ten sets of skills that are so essential in the Fourth Industrial Revolution:

- **Complex Problem Solving**: Developed capabilities, essential in solving novel, ill-defined problems in complex and real-world settings. People from diverse background will make the workplace complex and create complicated situations that managers will have to deal with.
- **Critical Thinking:** A reflective and reasonable thinking, focusing essentially on what to believe in or what to do. In the Fourth Industrial Revolution, managers are exposed to a number of options in their day to day activities. It requires them the ability to make a trade off among those available scenarios.
- **Creativity:** Referred to as the inventiveness and the use of imagination or original thought to come up with something new. In this context, managers will have to come up with new methods of dealing and successfully managing diversity.
- **People Management:** Broadly speaking, people management would imply a number of practices including talent management, assessment, evaluate, supervise, processing of staff leaves requests, manage employee relations, hire and fire staff as well as advise upper management.
- **Coordinating With Others:** The human resources department and human capital managers do not operate in isolation. They work hand in hand with all other departments of the organisation, especially in terms of recruiting and developing the employees. This task will be even more complex in the Fourth of Industrial Revolution as diversity occupies a major role in the organisation.
- **Emotional Intelligence:** Diversity in the Fourth Industrial Revolution requires managers to be emotional intelligent. They need to be aware of and

in control of their own emotions, other people's emotions in the organisation, and be able to handle interpersonal relationships with empathy.

- **Judgement and Decision Making:** In the Fourth Industrial Revolution where diversity is unavoidable, judgment and decision making skills are essential as they are concerned with making considered and effective decisions, where some of them will lead to workable conclusions and form objective opinions especially in matters that affect actions.
- **Service Orientation:** Majority of businesses in the Fourth Industrial Revolution are services businesses. In these types of businesses, skills of expert are essential, whether working individually or in teams for the benefits of the customers.
- **Negotiation:** Negotiation is the art of persuasion. In the Fourth Industrial Revolution, managers will have to have this set of skills for a number of reasons including negotiation to bring key employees in the organisation, negotiation to secure big contracts and so forth. Lack of these skills can be detrimental to the organisation.
- **Cognitive Flexibility:** Perhaps not a popular concept, but its meaning and application has been in the business arena for quite some time. In the Fourth Industrial Revolution.

The success of human capital managers in dealing with diversity in this Fourth Industrial Revolution will depend on a number of factors, including the above sets of skills, as well as managers recognize the impact of technology and globalization, and engage staff on how to explore their attitudes, values, beliefs, and prejudices, even if this might be an uncomfortable process. But, this process can lead to many of the people - in the organizations - discovering things about themselves that may cause emotional pain and therefore adjustment of their behaviours.

Abundance of Information: Enhancing Creativity, Flexibility, and Innovation

The World Economic Forum has envisaged that by 2020, creative thinking will be third on the list of the most important skills required to survive and thrive in the Fourth Industrial Revolution. Arts Times (2019) defines a "creative economy" as an "economic system in which value is derived from creative and imaginative qualities, instead of traditional sources such as capital, land and labour" (Howkins, 2013). The Fourth Industrial Revolution is due to transform human capital into creative capital.

"The Fourth Industrial Revolution is fundamentally disrupting the way we think, work and interact with each other, hence creativity can be one of the major currencies", argue Prof Richard Haines and Rosemary Mangope. In this Fourth

Industrial Revolution, Human Capital Managers are faced with a situation where their employees are curious about learning how to adjust to an increasingly complex and automated way of life. Human Capital managers have to play a powerful role in framing, shaping, communicating and influencing the future of their employees.

However, on the other side, every employee has the responsibility to reflect, question, adopt or resist, review and reconstruct when and where it is required. Human Capital Managers have tasks to guide employees towards creative thinking, which is central in todays' thriving economies, and this "currency" is due to become more influential as we progress through the Fourth Industrial Revolution (Shivan, 2019). What we can call to reimagine the future.

Enhancing Customer Relations

In this Fourth Industrial Revolution, customers are more connected than ever: to one another, to products/services, to the brands themselves. As a result, contact centers feel the pinch which sometimes leads to customer crisis. The customer is increasingly taking over some of the responsibilities that were traditionally performed by the business or their call centers. Customers are now capable of deciding how and when to contact businesses for services, and can choose which channel to use for complaints. For example, creating potentially damaging or embarrassing situations for the company, their brands or services on social media. Furthermore, customers understand the level of service expected due to access to technology, and they have no patience for companies that are not responsive or those that are not catching up with evolving standards (Customer Service, 2019).

In today's digitalized environment, customers like to connect and personalize their experiences wherever they are. They are at liberty to connect via text, video or social media, as all these options are open to them. It is also important to remember that old ways of communication; telephone calls, snail mail, and e-mail, are still available to them. All these options at the customers' disposal gives them the ability to see which service provider is advanced with regard to customer service and to compare to ones lagging behind.

Customers can therefore use any channel, and a service provider with more channels will have a competitive edge, as they will be able to meet the demands of the customer wherever they want to be, rather than forcing them to use a particular channel, which they might not want to use. Human Capital Managers have the responsibility to train and drive their employees to these new required standards.

Promoting Sustainable Development

Technological advancements are also allowing customers to more and more ask for personalized products and services. This aspect is putting companies under lot of pressure, hence industries are racing to adjust to this new way of doing business and building new networks of partners and digitalized operations. At the same time, the challenge of climate change is rapidly expanding, while the demand for raw materials and resources are outpacing the Earth's ability to replenish them (The Fourth Industrial Revolution and sustainable development, 2019).

Today, the industry and manufacturing sectors account for 41% of global gross domestic product (GDP). The production sectors are positioned directly at the nexus of economic impact and resource usage so that tomorrow's manufacturers don't run a shortage of the same resources. It is imperative that managers in the Fourth Industrial Revolution bear in mind this fact and manage their employees in a competitive manner while remaining sustainable.

However, there should be no worries for businesses, as the Fourth Industrial Revolution offers a way for manufacturing to increase competitiveness and support regional economies, while assisting in delivering on the United Nations Sustainable Development Goals. This will be enabled by a combination of power of digital, physical and biological technologies (Florida's solar progress, 2012). The attitude of Human Capital Managers in the success of this goal is crucial.

Artificial Intelligence and the Future of Jobs

Academics, executives as well as labour activists and policymakers have contradicting views about the future of jobs with the Fourth Industrial Revolution. Some foresee limitless job opportunities in newly emerging job categories and prospects of improving workers' productivity as well as alleviating their boredom arising from repetitive and routine work. Others, however, foresee massive job losses and displacement of jobs.

The data collected by The World Economic Forum clearly paints a picture of varying situations from industry to industry and from region to region. It is also clear that momentous change is underway, and consequently, our actions today will determine whether that change mainly results in massive displacement of employees or emergence of new job opportunities.

Human Capital Managers need to take urgent action to manage the near-term transition while building a workforce with futureproof skills. If the opposite presents itself, unemployment and inequality will rise, resulting in reduction of customers for businesses. "Chief Human Resources Officers of leading employers who are among those at the frontline of the emerging trends and are key actors in implementing future workforce strategies" (World Economic Forum, 2017).

Team Works

Working in teams has always been an important way of work organization, for the fact that individuals can't work in isolation and hope to achieve organizational goals. It has a purpose of bringing people together, so that they can perform more efficiently than if they acted alone. Moreover, there are tasks that can only be performed by a group of people acting collectively. The philosophy behind teamwork is the belief that when people work together effectively, a significant contribution can be made as opposed to those working individually. Teamwork requires cohesion, complementary skills, but more importantly good leadership (Nel & De Beer, 2014).

Earlier in this chapter, it was mentioned that customers are becoming more demanding, while being aware of the kind of treatment they should get. The Fourth Industrial Revolution allows managers and employees to work together - though they not necessarily physically next to one another – to be able to serve customers in a manner that can satisfy them. Suggestions of how human capital managers can help employees to be more team-players in the Fourth Industrial Revolution include:

- Empowering employees to work in groups so that they can become multi-skilled workers,
- Continuously developing workers' skills.
- Assigning tasks to teams rather than individuals
- Supervisors acting as role-models for workers and as a buffer between managers and workers.

Virtual Teams

One of the merits of the Fourth Industrial Revolution manifesting is the creation of virtual teams. The operation of virtual teams relies on electronic mediation rather than face-to-face communications. People are capable of being connected for meetings despite them being separated by both distance and time. There are various means through which virtual teams can function:

- E-mail,
- Internet message boards,
- Groupware
- Audio or video-conference and more.

Many advantages of virtual teams have been mentioned such as people being able to participate while not being able to physically be there. People on virtual networks have also been characterized as "task oriented". Like many other applications, the use of technology for virtual teams may encounter some hiccups such as the absence of non-verbal signals and lack of opportunity for social interaction, it remains a quick way of conducting meetings in this current industrial revolution (The Fourth Industrial Revolution, 2019). To alleviate some of those problems, it is suggested that virtual team members should meet face-to-face at least once, during the existence of the team, or a bit regular if possible.

Human capital managers must understand the role of virtual teams in the current management setting. They need to be able to bring people together under the same vision and objective. They have to be motivated and be equipped with the required resources in order for them to perform. Workers join the work place with a set of skills from school/university, but these skills need to be supplemented with practical skills of how work needs to be done. The responsibility of the human capital manager is crucial in transferring these skills and providing adequate technology, both of which are essential for work to be adequately done and meetings to be easily conducted.

Drivers and Challenges of the Fourth Industrial Revolution

Schwab contests that the Fourth Industrial Revolution is driven by nine interrelated and interconnected pillars (Bartodziej, 2017; Vaidya, Ambad & Bhosle, 2018):

- **Big Data and Analytics:** To support real time decision making, it will become increasingly more important to collect and evaluate data from many, and varied, sources, such as production systems, customer management systems, and enterprise management systems (Rüßmann; Lorenz; Gerbert; Waldner; Justus; Engel & Harnisch, 2015). According to Witkowski (2017), big data is typified by volume of data, variety of data, speed of generating new data, and the value of the data.
- **Autonomous Robots**: As robots become more autonomous, and it is foreseen that will interact with one another and work side by side with humans and learn from humans to perform tasks freely, more accurately, safer and faster than humans (Rüßmann et al. 2015).
- **Simulation**: A variety of simulations will be used in future in order to mirror the physical world in a virtual one (Rüßmann *et el.* 2015). By so-doing, different scenarios can be enacted in real time to understand the different outcomes associated with complex decisions.
- **System Integration, Horizontal, and Vertical**: It is foreseen that systems will no longer function in isolation in future, but will increasingly communicate,

connect, interact and eventually integrate with each other, not only in terms of the entire production process, but also across the entire value chain (Stock & Seliger, 2016).

- **Internet of Things**: This refers to a worldwide network of interconnected objects communicating independently with each other by using standard protocols (Hozdić, 2015).
- **Cyber Security and Cyber Physical Systems**: Increased connectivity gives rise to a greater need for securing systems and lines of communication from threats. Therefore, secure, reliable communication lines need to be ensured, and at the same time the need arises for more sophisticated identity and access management tools (Rüßmann *et el.* 2015).
- **Cloud computing**: Cloud based IT platforms are seen as the central pillar for the communication and connection of IT based applications (Landherr, Schneider, & Bauernhansl, 2016).
- **Additive Manufacturing**: This implies the use of manufacturing techniques where the part to be manufactured is produced by the addition of raw material, tantamount to 3D printing techniques (Rüßmann *et el.* 2015). This is in contrast to traditional manufacturing that is more subtractive techniques such as milling or lathing. Additive techniques eliminate wastage, enhance quality, eliminate errors, and save time, which implies huge overall cost savings.
- **Augmented Reality**: The use of augmented reality devices will enable people to have access to greater amounts of information at any given time and in any given location, thereby drastically improving the quality and speed of decision making as well as the implementation of decisions (Rüßmann *et el.* 2015).

Against the backdrop of these drivers of the Fourth Industrial Revolution, a couple of issue become apparent. Firstly, although the Fourth Industrial Revolution allows for rapid learning and communication, and allows numerous prospects for expanding knowledge and best practice, it is obvious to see that advanced societies will have the most to gain (Prisecaru, 2016). In less developed and developing societies, the Fourth Industrial Revolution will remain a double-edged sword, with the promise of vast gains to be made from many opportunities if these societies can gear up for it sufficiently on the one hand, but on the other the stark reality that they will be left far behind if they do not manage to gear up sufficiently.

Secondly, although technological progress leads to the reduction of wastage, more efficiently designed production and consumption systems, the innovations brought about by the Fourth Industrial Revolution will place pressure on the job market (Prisecaru, 2016). Many jobs of today will simply become obsolete, others will be taken over by robots, and therefore, the challenge is that of a reduction of the labour force. However, as some authors point out, this, in turn, will bring about new requirements for education. As the nature of work changes, so to the nature of education will have to change as one of the tasks of education – especially tertiary education – is to prepare people for the world of work.

Thirdly, the Fourth Industrial Revolutions challenges our conception about the very nature of work itself. In the Forth Industrial Revolution, being connected is crucial, and so physical location becomes less important (Prisecaru, 2016). Being able to access real time data, anywhere and any-time will be crucial, and the ability to be innovative and inventive on the spot will be more important than to mobilise a management team into a meeting room to solve a problem. Complex problem solving and creativity will become the sought after skills of the future.

RECOMMENDATIONS

Although there has been a deluge of theories guiding human capital management throughout the world, the current technological waves make it imperative that human capital managers learn new ways of doing their jobs. The discussions in this chapter focused on the evolution of those theories as well as the conditions, challenges and opportunities of technology, and it appears that the awareness of those changes can hugely benefit whoever is involved in managing human capital of any organization.

Therefore, human capital managers need to understand that success in their departments will be easier if their operations are guided by technological advancements. Throughout the world, managers as well as employees use technology in many different ways, and they cannot hide their excitement about it. This excitement is pivotal to the success and it needs to be exploited. It is therefore recommended that human capital managers equip themselves with the necessary technological knowledge that is offered by the Fourth Industrial Revolution.

A further recommendation to the organizations, is the investment in technology. In today's competitive environment, organizational success factors are no longer the only employees' knowledge and their management. The way technology is pervaded in the organization, is taking over. Among some achievements that are brought by technology, there are remote access to the companies' information and products/services, responsiveness of businesses to the customers, better interaction with clients, as well as productivity. A significant investment in technology will therefore enable organizations to score positive points towards achieving their overall objectives.

Finally, governments, schools and learning institutions have to teach technology. Technology is changing the people's minds and is empowering them with necessary skills needed by organizations. The involvement of government in technology diffusion is necessary especially in the provision of the required technological infrastructure.

For academics, it remains imperative to develop and teach theoretical and practical technological frameworks, taking into consideration the needs of the organizations that will provide employment for them.

FUTURE AREAS OF RESEARCH

Although the Fourth Industrial Revolution is here, it is still in its embryonic phase, which makes it unclear how it will effectively affect the organizations. Furthermore, the pace with which it moves requires anybody to monitor its changes, especially those who use its different applications in various sections of the organizations. As far as human capital management is concerned, research about value creation through technology is an imperative.

As articulated by (Prosecaru, 2016), the Fourth Industrial Revolution will place more pressure on the job market that already seems to be saturated in some environments. In other environments, labour movements closely monitor the behavior of employers, and warn against replacing humans with robots and other machines of similar kind. In this regard, future researches should focus on how technology adoption, could not drive job losses, but rather drives skills development and innovations.

CONCLUSION

Throughout our existence, human kind has witnessed periods of rapid technological advancement that led to some major changes in almost all areas, and we are presently living in one such period. The Fourth Industrial Revolution which consists of artificial intelligence, big data, robotics and many more to come, is affecting the way businesses are conducted, managed and the way governments and societies run. Today, customers are more connected than ever before, and are exposed to all kinds of practices around the world. The connectivity has also allowed customers to have access to global markets and they can easily interact and buy from any markets.

In this digital age, human capital management has a challenging task of leading workers into this new era. In this fight for coping with technological advancements, managers are faced with a problem of "digital immigrants" employees who have difficulties in understanding technology and be able to use it as their "digital natives" coworkers. However, the onus is on them (human capital managers), to bring those employees up to speed, so that today's customer can remain in touch with the business. This chapter has provided some guidelines human capital managers can make reference to in order to achieve satisfaction of both workers and customers.

REFERENCES

Alvesson, M., Bridgman, T., & Willmott, H. (2009). *The Oxford Handbook of Critical Management Studies*. Oxford, UK: Oxford University Press. doi:10.1093/oxfordhb/9780199237715.001.0001

Alvesson, M., & Willmott, H. (2012). *Making sense of management: A critical introduction*. Los Angeles, CA: Sage.

Arts Times. (n.d.). Available: https://arttimes.co.za/creativity-currency-4th-industrial-revolution/

Barnes, D. (2008). *Operations management, an international perspective*. Thompson Learning.

Bartodziej, C. J. (2017). The concept industry 4.0. In *The Concept Industry 4.0* (pp. 27–50). Wiesbaden: Springer Gabler. doi:10.1007/978-3-658-16502-4_3

Dyer, S., Humphries, M., Fitzgibbons, D., & Hurd, F. (2014). *Understanding management critically*. Los Angeles, CA: Sage.

Erasmus, B., Strydom, J., & Rudansky-Kloppers, S. (2016). *Introduction to Business Management* (10th ed.). Oxford University Press.

Feher, M. (2009). Self-appreciation; or, the aspirations of human capital. *Public Culture*, *21*(1), 21–41. doi:10.1215/08992363-2008-019

Florida's Solar Progress. (2012). Available: https://ournewsynergy.wordpress.com/2012/01/06/the-5-pillars-of-the-third-industrial-revolution/

Global, Ey. (2019). *Four things to know about fourth industrial revolution*. Available: https://www.ey.com/en_gl/digital/four-things-to-know-about-the-fourth-industrial-revolution

HowkinsJ. (2013). Available: http://www.creativeeconomy.com/john.htm

Hozdić, E. (2015). Smart factory for industry 4.0: A review. *International Journal of Modern Manufacturing Technologies*, *7*(1), 28–35.

Kondola, R., & Fullerton, J. (1998). *Diversity in Action: Managing the Mosaic* (2nd ed.). IPD.

Landherr, M., Schneider, U., & Bauernhansl, T. (2016). The Application Center Industrie 4.0-Industry-driven manufacturing, research and development. *Procedia CIRP*, *57*, 26–31. doi:10.1016/j.procir.2016.11.006

MacGregor's XY Theory of Management. (1960). Available: https://www.businessballs.com/improving-workplace-performance/mcgregors-xy-theory-of-management/

Maslow, A. (1943). Theory of human motivation. *Psychological Review*, *80*, Pp3709–Pp396.

Mullins, L. J., & Dossor, P. (2013). *Hospitality management and organizational behavior. Firth Edition*. Pearson.

Nel, J., & De Beer, A. (2014). *Business Management: A contemporary approach* (2nd ed.). Juta.

Nieuwenhuizen, C., & Oosthuizen, T. F. J. (2017). *Business Management, a contemporary compilation* (3rd ed.). Future Vision Business Consultants.

Pribanic, E. (2018). *What role does human capital play in an organisation?* Available: https://www.techfunnel.com/hr-tech/what-role-does-human-capital-management-play-in-an-organization/

Prisecaru, P. (2016). Challenges of the fourth industrial revolution. *Knowledge Horizons. Economics*, *8*(1), 57.

Ricci, T. (2012). *Frank Bunker Gilbreth: Biography*. Available: https://www.asme.org/engineering-topics/articles/construction-and-building/frank-bunker-gilbreth

Rouse, M. (n.d.). Available: https://searchhrsoftware.techtarget.com/definition/human-capital-management-HCM

Rüßmann, M., Lorenz, M., Gerbert, P., Waldner, M., Justus, J., Engel, P., & Harnisch, M. (2015). Industry 4.0: The future of productivity and growth in manufacturing industries. *Boston Consulting Group, 9*(1), 54-89.

Schwab, S. (2016). *The Fourth Industrial Revolution by Klaus Schwab*. Available: https://www.weforum.org/about/the-fourth-industrial-revolution-by-klaus-schwab

Shivam, N. (2019). *Work study: definition, role and objectives*. Available: http://www.economicsdiscussion.net/engineering-economics/work-study-definition-role-and-objectives/21681

Stock, T., & Seliger, G. (2016). Opportunities of sustainable manufacturing in industry 4.0. *Procedia Cirp*, *40*, 536–541. doi:10.1016/j.procir.2016.01.129

Swanepoel, B. J., Erasmus, B. J., Schenk, H. W., & Tshilongamulenzhe, M. C. (2014). *South African Human Resources Management: Theory and Practice* (5th ed.). Juta.

The Economist. The Third Industrial Revolution. (n.d.). Available: https://www.economist.com/leaders/2012/04/21/the-third-industrial-revolution

The Fourth Industrial Revolution. (n.d.). Available: https://www.weforum.org/agenda/2016/01/what-is-the-fourth-industrial-revolution/

The Fourth Industrial Revolution and sustainable development. (n.d.). Available: https://www.weforum.org/whitepapers/shaping-the-sustainability-of-production-systems-fourth-industrial-revolution-technologies-for-competitiveness-and-sustainable-growth

The skills portal: skills for success. (2019). Available: https://www.skillsportal.co.za/content/10-essential-skills-4th-industrial-revolution

Trailhead: The four industrial revolutions. (n.d.). Available: https://trailhead.salesforce.com/en/content/learn/modules/learn-about-the-fourth-industrial-revolution/meet-the-three-industrial-revolutions

Understanding how customer service is changing. (n.d.). Available: https://trailhead.salesforce.com/en/content/learn/modules/customer-service-in-the-fourth-industrial-revolution/understand-how-customer-service-is-changing

Vaidya, S., Ambad, P., & Bhosle, S. (2018). Industry 4.0–a glimpse. *Procedia Manufacturing*, *20*, 233–238. doi:10.1016/j.promfg.2018.02.034

What is ERP? Oracle South Africa. (2019). Available: https://www.oracle.com/za/applications/erp/what-is-erp.html

Witkowski, K. (2017). Internet of things, big data, industry 4.0–innovative solutions in logistics and supply chains management. *Procedia Engineering*, *182*, 763–769. doi:10.1016/j.proeng.2017.03.197

World Economic Forum. (2017). Available: http://www3.weforum.org/docs/WEF_Future_of_Jobs.pdf

Wren, D. A., & Bedeian, A. G. (2009). *The evolution of management thought*. Hoboken, NJ: John Wiley & Sons.

KEY TERMS AND DEFINITIONS

First Industrial Revolution: The first period of major changes that started in late 1700s. It was characterized by mechanical production, railroads invention and steam power.

Fourth Industrial Revolution: This period marks the proliferation artificial intelligence in various industry, which took place since the beginning of 21st century. It is affecting human lives in many different ways through its aspects of artificial intelligence, big data, robotics and many more to come.

Human Capital: A set of knowledge, skills, abilities, or capabilities and experience possessed by an individual or a group of people, considered in relation to the value to the organization or a country.

Human Capital Management: A set of practices concerned with managing people as a resource of an organization. The core of these practices is summarized in employee acquisition, employee development as well their development.

Industrial Revolution: Major changes in manufacturing, technology, transportation, and other domains that cause major transformation and adaption of human kind.

Second Industrial Revolution: The second period of major changes in human kind that started in late 1800s. The major characteristics of this period are mass production, electrical power, and the beginning of assembly line system of production.

Third Industrial Revolution: This period started in late 1900s, and was marked by automated production, electronics as well as the beginning of computers' use.

Chapter 6
The Future of Workforce Planning

Ayansola Olatunji Ayandibu
https://orcid.org/0000-0001-5870-2388
University of Zululand, South Africa

Irrshad Kaseeram
University of Zululand, South Africa

ABSTRACT

This chapter examines the future of workforce planning in contemporary work organisations. Workforce planning is regarded as one of the essential human resource management (HRM) activities in recent times. The reason is that it gives indication on areas of needs and serves as the pillar for all HRM activities such as job analysis, recruitment and selection, training and development, remuneration/rewards, and promotion. A review of empirical literature reveals that workforce planning has a strong relationship with organisational performance as well as productivity. This chapter submits that HR metrics and workforce analytics can be used as a tool to improve organisational outcomes. To boost human activity, intelligence apps and analytics or cognitive analytics robotics could be adopted to improve HR's value to the business.

INTRODUCTION

Workforce planning is considered as the most critical activity of every organisation because it gives indication on areas of needs and serves as the pillar for all human resource management activities such as job analysis, recruitment and selection,

DOI: 10.4018/978-1-5225-9810-7.ch006

training and development, remuneration/rewards, and promotion (Karia, Omari, Mwanaongoro & Ondieki, 2016). According to Aslam, Aslam, Ali, Habib and Jabeen (2014), serious organisations are those that consider human resource as the most valuable asset. Scholars such as Choudhury (2007), Lunenburg (2012), and Werner, Jackson and Schuler (2012) argue that organisational objectives can only be achieved through effective workforce planning. According to Choudhury (2007), effective workforce planning serves as the mechanism for building long-term capacity to meet the workforce challenges. Werner et al. (2012) postulate that workforce planning plays a critical role in HRM due to the fact that it translates the overall objectives of the organisation into a number of workers needed by determining the human resource required by the organisation to achieve its strategic goals. The scholars further suggested that for any organisation to manage human resource, it must ensure effective workforce planning. Jacobson (2010) in his study recommends that workforce planning is the core HRM activity which seeks to prepare organisations for their current and future human resource needs by ensuring that only the right people are recruited into the right place at the right time. Colley and Price (2010) also advocated that workforce planning is an effective tool for organisations to achieve their objectives understanding and planning for people needs in the short, medium and long-term.

However, Akhigbe (2013) in his study, on the "human resource planning: a key factor in ensuring the effectiveness and efficiency of organisation" argues that in spite of the efforts made by most organisations to ensure that there are right persons, in the right place, at the right time, yet they encounter a number of challenges in the effective implementation of workforce planning. According to Akhigbe (2013), the failure of most employers to plan for their workforce or human resources has forced them to become reactive, rather than proactive. The scholar is of the view that the tendency of reactiveness causes problems of rush recruitment which sometimes results in wrong recruitments. Lunenburg (2012), and Robbins and Judge (2011) also supported the view that proactive workforce planning is required for the full realisation of the HR management objectives of the organisation. The scholars are of the view that workforce planning has not been beneficially successful in attaining most of its predetermined objectives as most organisations are still struggling with diverse issues. It has also been argued most HR practitioners still gamble with workforce planning by bringing on board individuals that lack the requisite qualification(s), knowledge, talents, abilities, and skills without actually having a blueprint to develop and enhance these HR for the task and duties ahead (Lunenburg, 2012). Also, most organisations are not able to meet their desired objectives because at the time of stiff competition, their employee's moral becomes very low as compared to their rivals (Karia et al., 2016). According to Buradum (2017), the future of workforce planning is uncertain because of challenges such as labour turnover, absenteeism, seasonal unemployment, market instabilities, and modifications in technology. Buradum (2017) suggests that these critical issues must be well thought-out in the course of workforce planning. There is no doubt that these uncertainties pose a major challenge to the future of workforce planning that is likely to affect managers' ability to forecast human resource needs in particular as it hinders the organisation's much needed strategic actions, with the resultant effect of ineffectiveness, unproductiveness, and unsuccessful goal attainment.

The aim of this chapter is to determine future or working force planning in contemporary organisations. However, to achieve the broad of the chapter, the literature review will be based on the following objectives, namely: to explore internal and external forces which influence workforce planning; to examine the approaches to workforce planning; to identify the strategies for addressing labour shortage and surplus, to determine the contribution of workforce planning in an organisation; to investigate the challenges of workforce planning; and to identify the most appropriate techniques which support workforce planning. The chapter will begin with the background to the study by tracing the historical development of workforce planning. The chapter will proceed with the conceptualisation of the term workforce planning. It will also review empirical works on workforce planning which will focus on the objectives of workforce planning, factors influencing workforce planning in organisations, importance of workforce planning, steps in workforce planning, and hard versus soft workforce planning. The chapter will also cover the solution and recommendations, directions for future book chapters, conclusion and definition of key terms.

BACKGROUND

The concept workforce planning appears during the 1960s and early 1970s in a period of relative economic stability when unemployment was low and organisations were faced with supply shortages and the need to improve labour utilisation (Reilly, 1996). At that time, workforce planning remains a useful strategic approach in most large HR departments right up until the economic downturn of the 1980s when the failure to prove the economic value of workforce plans resulted in many efforts being eliminated (Sullivan, 2002). Several factors contributed to the rejection of workforce planning over this period. The traditional approach had been highly mechanistic and concerned with 'head count' rather than 'head content', which prevented it from being flexible enough to meet the changing conditions (Castley, 1996). A number of shifts in organisational structures and attitudes during the 1980s were opposed to the practice of workforce planning (Reilly, 1996). There was a reaction against a centralised corporate power and organisations began devolving power to the local units. This, in turn, made workforce planning more difficult and led to the loss of some workforce planning skills. In addition, the HR agenda switched from a quantitative approach and a concern for numbers to a more qualitative approach looking at the skills employees bring to the workplace. Furthermore, the fluctuating economy led some to regard planning as a futile activity (Reilly, 1996). The mood at the time.

In the latter part of the 1990s workforce planning started to creep back onto the HR agenda. Today it represents a high priority for an increasing number of organisations as they realise that the need for planning is greater than ever (Sullivan, 2002b). There is an awareness of the importance of skill development in an environment that requires adaptability rather than stability. There is recognition that employee contribution must be maximised through better utilisation and deployment. Finally, there is an understanding of the need to frame employee tasks in the context of business plans and to make them more challenging in the drive for continuous business improvement.

Nowadays organisations need to plan for their own survival as they grapple to deal with: intensified competition from home and abroad; labour market factors, recruitment and retention; the speed of information acquisition and dissemination; the globalisation of economic activities; consumerism and the drive for quality at an acceptable price (Reilly, 1996). In today's business world, there is no time for catch up if an organisation makes mistakes – others will be straight in there to grab the market share (Sullivan, 2002b).

Far from undermining workforce planning, the unpredictable nature of business necessitates thinking about the future. Organisations need to be able to deal effectively with any upturns or downturns they may face. The last couple of years has seen a period of instability in the economy, which has led to downsizing and lay-offs in many industrialised nations. Organisations that were unprepared for the cutbacks are now planning for how they will regenerate the business when the economy brightens up again. There is increasing concern of a failure to protect core competencies (Melymuka, 2002).

Although we cannot predict some of the changes in the business world, we can be certain of others, some of which relate to the workforce itself. The future is expected to bring a shift to higher skilled 'knowledge-worker' jobs, increased competition for talent as well as greater worker diversification, changes in worker values and expectations and an increasing number of workers retiring. An examination of organisation workforce planning guidelines suggests that it is this latter problem which has spurred a number of organisations into creating workforce plans. As the first wave of baby-boomers' edges towards retirement age, organisations that do not prepare for their replacement are expected to face a sudden loss of skills, or 'brain drain'.

Given the changing context over the years, organisations that have resumed workforce planning have typically not returned to older methods of manpower planning, which by now are regarded as too deterministic (Reilly, 1996). Rather, they have accepted the imperatives of the modern world and adapted workforce planning accordingly.

CONCEPTUALISATION OF WORKFORCE PLANNING

Workforce planning also known as "human resources planning or manpower planning" (HRP) has been conceptualised differently by many scholars. Bulla and Scott (1994) conceptualised the term workforce planning as the process of ensuring that the human resource requirements of the organisation are identified and plans are made for satisfying those requirements. Conversely, Milkovich and Boudreau (1993) considered workforce planning as the process of gathering and ustiling information on the base of which it can be discussed as the number of resources spent on personnel activities.

According to Pradeesh (2011), workforce planning is an approach which deals with identifying the number of people to be selected, for specific job within a particular period. However, Ismail and Velnampy (2012) has provided much elaborated definition of workforce planning which is far different from that of Pradeesh (2011). Ismail and Velnampy (2012) argued that workforce planning is a process used by organisations to analyse their business plans to determine the future human resource requirements, to forecast the future supply of labour/human resource, to reconcile the human resource requirements and future supply of labour and to formulate actions to address the gap with the general objective that leads the better and effective utilization of scarce talents in the best interest of the organisation. Mondy and Noe (2006) concurred that workforce planning is the entry point of human resource management which has to do with the determination of human resource requirements, job analysis, recruitment, selection and socialisation. From this definition, one will argue that workforce planning forms the basis of key HRM activities such as job analysis, recruitment and selection. Similarly, Reilly (2003) considers workforce planning as a planned process where an organisation attempts to estimate the demand for labour and evaluate the size, nature and source of supply which will be required to meet the future demand.

Leung, Wu, Ho, Ip and Mou (2015) defined workforce planning as the systematic approach to assessing the number and quality of workers required through an institution and guaranteeing that people considerations are taken under consideration in business plans. The author believed that workforce planning leads to recruitment and selection, retention, succession and ability management plan. Aslam, Aslam,

Ali, Habib and Jabeen (2013) postulated that workforce planning is the process that identifies the number of employees a company requires in relations to high quality and quantity; therefore, it is seen as an ongoing process of regular and structured planning.

From the above definitions, it can be argued that workforce planning is a tool which assists organisations to determine the current and future human resource needs. The above definitions underscore the purpose of workforce planning which is to ensure that the right caliber of persons are recruited at the right place, at the right time, in the right cost and put at the right positions within the organisation (Al Wahshi, Omari & Barrett, 2013).

OBJECTIVES OF WORKFORCE PLANNING

There are several reasons why most organisations may consider initiating workforce planning. Butler, Ferris and Napier (1991) suggested that the importance reason for workforce planning because of competitive advantage. Ulrich (1987) suggested that HR planning is recognised as a source of development of organizational functions based on missions and objectives of the business. With the help of planning, areas that need better functioning are identified to make them grow and succeed.

Reilly (1999) points out that there are many reasons why most organisations choose to engage in human resource planning, namely: to estimate the number and quality of staff that will be required to achieve the desired goods; to ensure that there is no shortage and surplus of the number and skills of employees; to meet the future needs of the business; and to achieve sustainable competitive advantage.

Michael (2006) also advocates that the aims of workforce planning largely depend on its context. He contends that the overriding purpose of workforce planning is to forecast organisational needs for employees taking into consideration the internal and external supply of labour to meet staffing requirements. This implies that the aim of workforce planning is to identify the gap between the demand for and supply of human resource requirements of the organisation.

Santos, Zhang, Gonzalez and Byde (2009) contended that the objective of workforce planning is to forecast organisational needs for the workers taking into consideration the internal and external supply of labour to meet the staffing needs. Thus, to identify the gap between what is needed and available. Imison, Buchan and Xavier (2009) also argued that the main objective of workforce planning is to balance the right between the demand for labour and the supply of labour. Similarly, Anyim, Mba and Ekwoaba (2012) postulated the objective of workforce planning to ensure appropriate human capital is available to move the organisation forward.

Phutela (2016) has identified four objectives of workforce planning, namely: effective management of change; to reaslise the organisational goals; to promote employees; and to effectively utilise employees. With respect to effective management of changes, Phutela (2016) suggests that adequate workforce planning is required to cope with organisational changes in the various aspects which affect the organisation. According to Phutela (2016), the changes in the organisation requires continuation of allocation and effective utilization of HR in the organisation. In terms of realizing the organisational goals, the scholar believes that to achieve expansion of the business, HRP is very crucial. Concerning the promotion of employees, Phutela (2016) workforce planning provide feedback in the form of employee data which can be relied upon by the organisation when taking decision regarding promotional opportunities to be made within the organisation. Regarding the utilisation of HR, workforce planning is required to identify information such as surplus and deficiency in human resources.

FACTORS THAT INFLUENCE WORKFORCE PLANNING

The effectiveness of workforce planning in an organisation can be threatened by both internal and external. The internal factors are those factors within the organisation which affect the effectiveness of workforce while the external factors are those factors outside the organisation which present huge the challenge to the organisation in its effort to engage in workforce planning.

Internal Factors

Aslam et al. (2013) argued that the internal factors influencing workforce planning include the organisation's policy, the organisation's strategy, staffing needs of employees, responsibility of management, nature of work, financial position of the organisation, knowledge, skills and competency of the employees. Norhidayah, Dom, Kasim and Shamsudin (2012) carried out as study on framework of human resource planning (HRP) influencing factors for local workforce supply in Malaysian construction industry. The study confirmed that organisation strategy and nature of work were the internal factors which influence the effectiveness of workforce planning in organisations.

Shannon (2003) also identifies some internal factors affecting workforce planning in organisation including gathering information about the workforce in each institution, accurate information and analysis on personnel costs, the existing personnel policies of each institution, the capacity to understand the new job competencies needed and develop new staff roles and training for employees, mechanisms for improving organisational and employee performance and improvement in work processes, information about performance-based contracts and incentives and capacity to develop the necessary systems, change management process and Performance management and supervision systems.

External Factors

Norhidayah et al. (2012) in their study identified that the external factors which influence workforce planning are economic and demographic (social) changes. Sinclair (2004) also found that economic fluctuations are external factors which have important implications on workforce planning in organisations. Xie and Huang (2012) also identified that technological advancement is one of the most crucial factors which affects workforce planning in many undertakings. Xie and Huang (2012) suggests that communication technologies can enhance the engagement of workforce planning. Shyni (2005) argues that although technology can influence workforce planning, however, several benefits can be derived from it such as reduction in the processing cost.

Norma-Major and Gooden (2012) discovered that demography is one of the external factors which affects workforce planning. According to Edgar and Geare (2004), a study conducted in New Zealand reveals that HRM activities are influenced by factors such as demography, especially age, gender and ethnicity. Lars (2011) advocates that changes demographics will create fewer entry-level employees, which has the possibility to increase the level of competition among employers. According to Jacobson (2010), studies conducted in developed countries such as the United States, United Kingdom, Japan, Australia, New Zealand, and most European Union countries revealed that baby boomers are one of the major demographic challenges facing HRP in the public sector. The studies in these countries showed that only a small fraction of younger workers are available compared with the much larger number of baby boomers.

In a similar opinion, Shannon (2003) discovers that the external environmental factors affecting workforce planning in most organisations include macro environment of the firm, information about the labour laws and regulations as well as the dynamic nature of the environment of corporate planning. Shannon (2003) recommends that workforce planners must increasingly develop flexible planning scenarios leading to contingent plans. Thus planners, policymakers and heads of institutions require an up-to-date, accurate information on employees to be able to plan and implement changes in a rationale, efficient and humane way.

IMPORTANCE OF WORKFORCE PLANNING IN AN ORGANISATION

Several studies have confirmed that workforce planning impacts on all organisational or HRM activities within organisations worldwide. Armstrong (1992) discovered that a significant benefit of workforce planning is that it increases an organisation's productivity. Caine (1996) suggests that workforce planning helps organisations to avoid shortage and excess of manpower. Reilly (2003) believes that workforce planning practices assists organisations to determine the demand for labour and evaluate the size, nature, and sources of supply which will essentially be required to meet the demand. A study done by Gifford and Dina (2011) on "the development of human resource" shows that workforce planning helps to identify the skill requirements for various levels of jobs.

In a different study, Katua, Mukulu and Gachunga (2014) found that workforce planning strategies can enhance the performance of a firm. A study done by Amaratunga (2012) on how human resource planning can assure adequate staff levels, reveal that a primary function of workforce planning is to ensure that various company departments have sufficient staff to complete all the work required to meet the organisation's goals. Katua et al. (2014) found that workforce planning strategies can enhance the performance of an organistion. Arsad (2012) investigated into effect of workforce planning on organisational performance and found that there is a positive relationship between workforce planning and organisational performance. Johne (2009) also discovers that human resource planning plays an important role in organisational performance by providing team players.

Chand and Katou (2007) found that manpower planning has a strong relationship to productivity which impacts on organisational performance. Anya, Umoh and Worlu (2017) carried out a study on the link between workforce planning and organization performance in oil and gas firms in Port Harcourt Nigeria and found that human resource planning has a strong influence on organisational performance in forecasting future demand of business and environment which helps to manage human resource demand as required. Similarly, Ngui, Elegwa and Hazel (2014) explored the effect of employee resourcing strategies on the performance of commercial banks in Kenya. The results of the study showed that hat employee resourcing strategies have a significant positive effect on performance of the aforementioned banks. Mursi (2003) discovers that there is a significant positive relationship between HR planning and organisational performance.

In another study by Hiti (2000), HRP has a positive relationship with organisational performance. Ogunrinde (2001) examined the application of workforce planning and its relationship with organisational performance and discovered that most organisations initiated workforce planning performed better than those that did not.

Leng (2005) postulates that effective workforce planning plays a pivotal role in meeting internal and external organisational challenges in organisations, namely: skilled labour shortages, poor performance, lack of effective training and performance appraisals. Choudhury (2007) also argued that workforce planning adds value to an organisation by recognising that people are the key component of an institution's competitive advantage.

HARD VERSUS SOFT WORKFORCE PLANNING

According to Armstrong (2011) a distinction can be made between the 'hard and soft' manpower planning. Hard manpower planning according to Armstrong (2011) is based on quantitative analysis in order to ensure that the right numbers of the right sort of people are available when needed.

Soft manpower planning is also concerned with ensuring the availability of people with the right sort of attitudes and motivation who are committed to the organization and engaged in their work and behave accordingly (Armstrong, 2011). It is based on assessment of the requirement for these qualities and measurements of the extent to which they exist, by the use of staff surveys, the analysis of the outcomes of performance management reviews and opinions generated by focus groups.

STEPS IN WORKFORCE PLANNING

There are varied steps in workforce planning. These steps are discussed as follows.

Step One: Environmental Scanning

According to Ivancevich (2012) environmental scanning is the first step in workforce planning which helps human resource planners to identify and anticipate sources of problems, threats, and opportunities that should drive the organisation's strategic planning. Environmental scanning provides a better understanding of the context in which human decisions are made. Both internal and external environmental scanning are critical for effective planning. Environmental scanning is the systematic monitoring of the major external forces influencing the organisation. John (2008) postulates that internal scanning pays critical attention to the identification of factors have an effect on the organization's work force capabilities necessary to meet the departmental goals. Barrett and Richard (2006) asserted that internal environmental scanning gives attention to workforce trends including their age distribution, and portion of positions filled by internal candidates. From the organisational point of view, every department is tasked with the responsibility for identifying the internal opportunities and challenges. This internal scanning give the organisation the opportunity make and retain strengths to face and reduce the risks and challenges to attain success.

Unlike the internal environmental scanning, the external scanning is time consuming (Barnard et al., 2006). With this approach, the organisation or workforce planning team reviews all potential changes that may occur and their influences on the organisation (ibid). However, Barnard et al. (2006) recommended that a team should be formed whose term of office is to review how the changes impact the organization, its work and recruitment and selection patterns, process of training, retaining and developing the required workforce.

Changes in the external environment may have a direct impact on the way organisations are run and people are managed. Some of these changes represent opportunities, and some of them threats to the organisation. Whiles there can be (and often are) situation with ambiguous problems, threats and opportunities, the probability of reducing or eliminating the ambiguity is increased by a more thorough environmental scanning. The idea here is to at least attempt to turn a threat into an opportunity with information. In general, the greater the amount of relevant information that managers have about a problem, the more likely that problem can be turned into an opportunity (Akhigbe, 2013).

Step Two: Forecasting the Labour Demand

Labour demand forecasting projects how business needs will affect the human resources requirements using both qualitative and (e.g., Delphi, nominal) and quantitative methods (trend analysis, simple and multiple linear regression) (Snell & Bohlander, 2010). A forecast of labour demand derives from a projection of how business needs will affect human resource. Each of the environmental forces discussed above is likely to exert pressure on human resource demand both in terms of the number and the types of employees required, as well as the number and types of jobs utilized. In a nut shell the human resource planner must identify and predict or anticipate these needs, add focus to an otherwise confusing array of possibilities, and priorities for conflicting goals. Ulferts, Wirtz and Peterson (2009) claimed that when forecasting the possible demand for labour, it is important to first assess the challenges the college will have in meeting its staffing needs based on the external environment. The assessment should pay critical attention to how the external environment may impact human resource needs (Ulferts et al., 2019). Forecasting of labour demand will give an organisation information about the implications of different human resource strategies that can be used to support its goals. As stated earlier on, there are two methods of forecasting labour demand, namely: qualitative and quantitative techniques.

Quantitative Techniques

According to Snell and Bohlander (2010) quantitative approaches to forecasting involve the use of statistical or mathematical techniques, including trends and regression analysis.

Trend Analysis

With this, a firm's employment requirements are forecasted on the basis of some organizational index such as sales. To Bernardin (2003), trends analysis incorporates certain business factors (examples, units produced, revenue) and a productivity ratio (example employees per unit produced). Trend analysis is the most commonly used approaches for projecting HR demand and is typically done in several stages.

Regression Analysis

Regression analysis uses information from the past relationship between the organization's employment level and some criterion known to be related to employment. A company can establish a statistical relationship between sales or work output and level of employment (Randhawa, 2007).

Qualitative Analysis

The qualitative technique is the simplest method for projecting labour demand is a centralised approach in which the human resource department examines the current business situation and determines staffing requirements for the rest of the firm. While this approach is simple, it is generally not accurate. A top down approach assumes that the central human resource office has an accurate understanding of the business as well as the needs of each unit or function. In large complex assumptions typically do not hold (Snell & Bohlander, 2010). A more preferred method involves a decentralised process wherein each unit or functional manager subjectively drives his /her own staffing needs. These projections are aggregated to create an overall composite forecast for the company. With this method, the assumption is that forecasting is frequently more an art than a science, providing in exact approximations rather than absolute results. The ever-changing environment in which an organisation operates contributes to this situation (ibid).

Delphi Technique

Delphi technique is used to minimise interpersonal and jurisdictional conflicts. The Delphi technique avoids face- to-face group discussion by the use of an intermediary. Experts take turns at the presenting a forecast statement and assumptions. According to Das and Nayak (2015), Delphi technique consists of a panel of experts who responds in writing to a questionnaire dealing with a specific problem. With this technique, median response is calculated, and open-end opinions are further requested to respond which differ widely from it. The intermediary passes on the forecasts and assumptions to the others. Revisions are then made independently and anonymously by the experts. The intermediary then pools and summarises the judgments and gives them to the experts. Delphi technique has been shown to produce better one-year forecasts, but there can be difficulties in reaching consensus on complex problems. However, Delphi technique can take considerable time.

Nominal Technique

The nominal group technique is similar to the Delphi method. According to Bernardin (2002), with the nominal group technique, experts join at a conference table and independently list their ideas in writhing. The experts then share their ideas with the group in turn. As the ideas are presented, a master list of the ideas is compiled so that everyone can refer back them. The ideas are discussed and ranked by members by voting.

Step Three: Forecasting the Labour Supply

According to Snell and Bohlander (2010), just as an organization must forecast its future requirements for employees, it must also determine whether sufficient numbers and types of employees are available to staff the openings it anticipates having. As with the demand forecast, the process involves both tracking current employee level and making future projections about those levels. Supply forecasting measures the number of people likely to be available from within and outside the organization, having allowed for attrition (labour wastage and retirements), absenteeism, internal movements and promotions, and changes in hours and other conditions of work. There are two methods of forecasting the supply of labour, namely: internal and external. The methods of forecasting the labour supply are:

Staffing/Manning Tables

Staffing table is a pictorial representation of all organisational jobs along with number of employees currently occupying those jobs and future jobs. According to Mallela (2012), staffing table jointly indicates job analysis and time series. It shows the number of employees for each job title. It also indicates all jobs by title and number of employees engaged in it. Using the staffing table, the workforce many be classified as per the demographic variables like gender, age, marital status, physically challenged and other useful characteristics, as well as training time.

Rothwell and Kazanas (2003) also add that staffing tables or charts are special tables including all job categories within an organisation, the number of persons occupying those positions and the number of employees to be hired in a particular year. However, they do no indicate whether the planned new posts will be filled or not. They are merely used to show the total number of employees at the end of the budget period. Despite the limitations, staffing tables are found to be useful identifying manpower needs, training and development of employees (Das & Nayak, 2015).

Markov Analysis

This is a method for tracking the pattern of employee movement through the various jobs or positions within an organization. Heneman III and Sandver (1977) argued that examines the movement of personnel into, within, and out of the organization. In short, it uses past or historical rate of transfers, promotions, and turnover to estimate future availabilities in the workforce. Based on the past possibilities, one can estimate the number of employees who will be in various positions with the organisation in future. Reid and Taylor (1989) concurred that morkov analysis is used to determine the internal labour market, audit and control, career planning and development. However, it is the least used in supply forecasting.

Skill Inventories

This is an assessment of the knowledge, skills, abilities, experiences, and career aspirations of each of the current employees or employees in an organisation (Snell & Bohlander, 2010). It is a file of educational experience, interests, skills etc. that allow the human resource manager to quickly match job openings with employee's backgrounds (Ngui, Elegwa, & Hazel, 2014). However, these records must be updated at least every two years and must be confidence.

Replacement Chart

Replacement chart is the process/technique of listing of current jobholders and people who are potential replacement if an opening occurs (Rothwell & Kazanas 2003). In other words, replacement charts present a list of current employees, their positions, promotion possibilities and potential replacements. According to Rothwell and Kazanas (2003), replacement charts are prepared to secure the smooth transition of duties in case a sudden loss of certain key workers, especially the executives, occurs.

Succession Planning

Succession planning is the process of identifying, developing and tracking key individuals for existing positions. Succession management is a proactive approach to managing talent as it involves identification of high potentials for anticipated future needs and the tailored development of these people so that there is a talent pool or leadership pipeline available to meet organisational demands as they arise (Snell & Bohlander, 2010). Rothwell and Kazanas (2003) argued that succession planning contain more detailed information and cover not only managers but other workers. It is used for long-term planning of employees' development in the company. According to Rothwell and Kazanas (2003, p. 225), succession planning typically includes "data on candidates, job requirements and descriptions, formal procedure of systematic review of information on the candidates' qualifications in relation to the position requirements, development plans for employees, special assignments and testing methods for assessing their achievement, and candidates' succession summaries which point out their strengths and weaknesses". The HR domain of Succession Planning and Management (SPM) grew out of a recognised need to plan for CEO retirement in a tight labour market that had been caused by downsizing (particularly stripping layers of management), an increase in people reaching retirement age, as well as fewer entrants into the workforce. The importance of having the right people in these senior roles to act as role models was a key driver. Succession planning needs to focus on senior management positions, starting at the top of the organization (with particular attention paid to CEO and/or managing director) and going at least six or seven levels down, so as to include middle management positions. It's not necessary to continue down to team leader positions as these are more fluid." Succession Planning is a strategy of workforce planning. It is a process designed to ensure the organization recruits and develops new hires and in-house staff to fill each key role within the organization.

Step Four: Gap Analysis

Once a company has assessed both the supply and demand for employee skills, latent, and technical know-how, it can begin to understand its human capital readiness. The demand and supply forecasts can then be analysed to determine whether there are any deficits or surpluses. According to Ulferts et al. (2009), gap analysis involves identifying the number of staff and the skills and abilities required in the future. This provides the basis for recruitment, retention, and unavoidable downsizing plans. Computerised planning models can be used for this purpose. It is, however, not essential to rely on software planning package. The basic forecasting calculations can be carried out with a spreadsheet that sets out and calculates the number required for each occupation where plans need to be made (John, 2008). In analysising the gap, the results can be either labour shortages or surplus (Bechet & Maki, 1987). The gap will determine the kind of action plans to be employed by managers.

Step Five: Action Planning

Action plans are derived from broad resourcing strategies and more detailed analysis of demand and supply factors. However, the plans often must be short term and flexible because of the difficulty of making firm predictions about human resource requirements in times of rapid change. Plans need to be prepared in the areas of resourcing, flexibility and downsizing. Snell and Bohlander (2010) indicate that through manpower planning, organizations strive for a proper balance between demand considerations and supply considerations. Demand considerations are based on forecasted trends in business activity. Supply considerations also involve determining where and how candidates with required qualifications can be found to fill a firm's vacancies. Because of the difficulty in locating applicants for the increasing number of jobs that require advanced training, this aspect of planning has been receiving much more attention. Greater planning effort is also needed to recruit members of protected classes for managerial jobs and technical job that require advanced levels of education.

According to Snell and Bohlander (2010), if the organization is experiencing shortage of skilled labours, certain measures need to be taken to arrest/address the situation. The measures below will help organisations if they are faced with shortage of skilled labour.

Job Redesign

According to John and Slocum (1998), whenever a job is changed, a manager has a chance toincrease both the quality of the employees' work life and their on-the-job productivity. Job design is the deliberate purposeful planning of the job, including all its structural and social aspects and their effect on the employee. Job design is a broad concept that can refer to any part or combination of parts of the job. Restructuring the elements including tasks, duties and responsibilities of a specific job in order to make it more encouraging and inspiring for the employees or workers is known as job redesigning. The process includes revising, analyzing, altering, reforming and reshuffling the job-related content and dimensions to increase the variety of assignments and functions to motivate employees and make them feel as an important asset of the organization. The main objective of conducting job redesigning is to place the right person at the right job and get the maximum output while increasing their level of satisfaction. In deal with shortage of skilled labour, the organization must conduct a preview of job redesign in order to ensure that appropriate tasks/ responsibilities are reassigned to employees.

Zareen, Razzaq and Mujtaba (2013) discovered that a well job design brings involvement and satisfaction to the employees and they perform well by employing all their energies in the work. It also motivates workers towards task performance, and such employees become highly productive and loyal to the organisation. Generally, there are some methods of job redesign and they are explained below:

Job Rotation

This is the process of moving an employee or employees among different job within the same undertaken. Job rotation is a very important tool of job redesign because it enables management to test the viability of the employee to see if he/she can fit into any given position. The scholar, Meyer (1994), recognises job rotation as learning role in firms as employees get a chance to accomplish various task and changing roles. The purpose of job rotation in an organisation is to plan the job training phase because it proves helpful while transferring employees from one job to another in order to learn more and increase their knowledge by doing various jobs (ibid).

Job Enlargement

One of the ways of tackling the issue of employee performance and job satisfaction is to enhance the motivating factors of jobs. The term job enrichment was coined by Herzberg (1968) to denote the vertical enlargement of a job by adding responsibility and opportunity for personal growth, for example job enrichment needs to be distinguished from job enlargement which generally. Hackman and Oldham (1980) see job enlargement as the combination of different jobs and adding connected duties to job.

Job Enrichment

It goes beyond job enlargement to add greater autonomy and responsibility to a job and is based on the job characteristics approach. Job enrichment as proposed by Herzberg (1968) is not just increasing the number or variety of tasks; nor is it the provision of opportunities for job rotation. It is claimed by supporters of job enrichment that these approaches may relieve boredom, but they do not result in positive increases in motivation. The scholar argues that idea of job enrichment was to motivate employees by providing those opportunities of utilising their abilities so that productivity and performance of the employees increase and positively impacts the organisational environment and smoothing the way for achieving organisational goals.

Use Part-Time Workers

Houseman (2001) asserts that the rationale for the use of part-timers is the need to accommodate fluctuations in workload or absences in staff. Conversely, most organisations also utilise the part-time workers as a technique to screen candidates for regular positions. Additionally, one reason for the increasingly use of part-time workers is to save costs. The use of part-time workers is one of the measures of dealing with shortage of skilled labour in the short run. The use of part-time workers helps to ensure more scope for flexing hours worked, better utilization of plant and equipment by, for example, the introduction of a 'twilight shift'; and higher productivity on repetitive work because part-time workers can give more attention to their work during their shorter working day. Nelen, De Grip and Fouarge (2011) in their study discovered that the utilisation of part-time enables firms to allocate labour more efficiently. They argued that firms with part-time workers can bridge the gap between opening hours and a full-time work week.

Overtime Arrangements

According to Snell and Bohlander (2010), one of the measures an organization can employ when faced with issue of shortage of skilled labour is to encourage people to do over time. Over time is a situation where a person works beyond the normal hours of work. In this regard, the employee who works for extra hour will be entitled to an overtime pay or allowance. This system sometimes helped an organization to meet their production target. Therefore, it is very important for organisations that are faced with the issue of labour shortage to encourage their existing staff to do overtime.

Subcontractors

Guers, Martin and Wybo (2014) suggest that subcontracting has now becomes very widespread in contemporary socio-technical systems. Since the beginning of the twentieth century, there is a dramatic change in the way businesses are organised. There is no doubt that subcontracting is one of the key elements of the operation of new productive organisations and the subcontractor can be thought of as a fully-fledged actor in the system (Guers et al., 2014). Subcontractors are self -employed persons with the necessary technical know-how who perform certain vital tasks of organisations. They are specialised individual who manage projects on behalf of organizations. In crisis of shortage of skilled labour, management of such organizations can engage the services of subcontractors. Subcontracting enables resources to be concentrated on core business, activities; employment costs to be reduced; flexibility and productivity to be increased; job security for core employees to be enhanced.

Training and Development

In case of shortage of skills, the organisation can train and develop workers to enable them perform multiplicity of tasks. The purpose of training and development is to enable the employees to be versatile. It is observed that staff training, and development are activities that make significant contribution to the overall effectiveness and profitability to the organisation. Ganesh and Indradevi (2015) defined training as the acquisition of knowledge of skills, and the competencies. Training has specific goals of improving one's knowledge, skills and their capacity, capability, performance and their productivity. Armstrong (2011) sees training as the systematic development of the knowledge, skills and attitudes required by an individual to perform adequately a given task or job. Development on the other hand is enhancing up the already existing skills, knowledge and capabilities of the workforce. According to Janet Kottke (1999), employee development programmes comprises with core proficiencies, appropriate structure through which organizations develop their businesses at corporate level. It is said that only training and development is much important because it leads to the maximum utilisation of all the firm's resources (Armstrong, 2011).

Recruitment

Normally, recruitment is said to be the last measure if all other measures failed to work properly. This is because recruitment wastes time despite its advantages to the organisation. According to Harky, (2018), recruitment is the process that encourages many people to apply for a job. Opatha (2010) see recruitment as the process of finding and attracting suitably qualified people to apply for job vacancies in the organization. It is a set of activities an organisation uses to attract job candidates who have the needed abilities and attitudes. TO Ofori and Aryeetey (2011), recruitment is considered as the process of generating a pool of competent individuals to apply for employment within an organisation. Gamage (2014) argues that recruitment provides the organisation with a pool of potentially qualified job candidates. However, the quality of human resource in an organisation highly depends on the quality of applicants attracted because organisation is going to select employees from those who were attracted (Gamage, 2014). However, when there is labour surplus, the following measures should be employed:

Recruitment Freeze

Anytime an organisation is experiencing labour surplus the organization should stop recruiting immediately. Lashley (2001) postulates that constant repositioning of organisations is of utmost importance in an economy that is staggering towards stabilisation and firms have to choose either to change or remain constant and perish.

Recruitment freeze is one of the defensive strategies an organization can adopt to cut costs or to make the organization more productive and profitable. Baumolet et al. (2003) argue that recruitment freeze reduces organizational slack and operating costs, streamlines operations and enhances effectiveness towards making an organisation more competitive.

Nyasha (2017) suggests that hiring freeze becomes necessary to address the issue of labour costs and hedge organisation against collapse. Conversely, it was also found that freeze often results in increased stress, decreased morale and lack of work life balance for survivors because of increased responsibilities and obligation (Nyasha, 2017). A survey by Chartered Institute of Personnel Development (2009) to ascertain the impact of hiring freeze on cost reduction and organisational performance among 900 UK employers found that on average firms are saving approximately 27000 pounds per employee when using hiring freeze strategy and this enhances performance of firms.

A study done by A.T Kearney consultants (2009) among US Automakers reveals that United States firms were facing numerous problems ranging from organisational performance, growth, survivals and labour costs and to hedge their firms against collapse, they used the hiring freeze strategy. By contrast, a survey by DOT Public Transport Division (2006) on the effectiveness of hiring freeze as cost reduction strategy in the Public Transport Division in Europe found that hiring freeze created a backlog of hiring needs. Cascio (2009) postulates that hiring freeze often results in increased stress, decreased morale and lack of work life balance for survivors because of increased responsibilities and obligations. A research done by Gitonga (2010) on the effects of hiring freeze on employee and organisational performance in Kenya at Telkom Company (Embu) reveals that freezing recruitment at Telkom failed to improve employee and organisational performance. Madrick (1995) suggests that about 30% of the organisations which freeze recruitment are faced with deteriorate productivity and profitability. In support, Kim (2009) argues that recruitment freezes tear the organisation instead of improving organisational profitability and productivity.

Natural Attrition

Turner (1988) suggests that within official and academic discourse, natural attrition could be used as a tool to deal with redundancies, in part because it appears as equivalent to normal labour turnover and hence as a natural and normal process. The scholar argues that natural attrition was more complex than the running down of the workforce through normal labour turnover and that it was not necessarily the best redundancy practice in that situation. The author discovers that although the use of natural attrition was advantageous for the company in allowing it to produce a 'trim ship' without upsetting the hegemonic regime it had established with the workforce, it was not advantageous for either the members of the workforce or for the supervisory staff in immediate contact with them (ibid).

Job Sharing

A new and innovative method of work arrangement is job sharing. Although job sharing is nowadays practiced more in Europe, it was officially introduced in America in 1970s to do full time jobs which were usually done on one shift as part time. It was found that teaching and nursing were the first jobs which were done as job sharing because they were mostly done by women who wanted to balance their jobs with their family. Both "private sector and state sector presented their employees with this alternative" (Eick, 2001: 890). Job sharing is an "arrangement whereby two employees share the work of one fulltime position, dividing pay and benefits between them according to the time each works" (Robbins & Judge, 2007:232). Job sharing can involve splitting days or weeks, or less frequently working alternate weeks. (Armstrong 2010). Evidence suggests that job sharing increases employee's motivation and therefore their productivity due to equal job opportunities that it provides for everybody (Branine, 2004). It was further discovered that "increased flexibility, having the opportunity to use experienced employees as well as a vaster area of skills, increased commitment and motivations" (Harris, 1997, p. 30).

Reduce the Number of Contractors and Subcontractors

According to Armstrong (2010), this measure enables the organisation to reduce the number and size of its contractors and subcontractors. With this, the organization should terminate some of its contracts with the subcontractors and contractors. In doing this, it will enable the organization to reduce the size of the workforce thereby reducing the surplus problem.

Encourage Voluntary Retirement

With this measure, the organisation should encourage people to retire voluntarily by giving them attractive packages to enable those employees who wish to retire voluntarily retire. The term retirement refers to the state where a worker is out of active labor force, regardless of the reason for ceasing work and no matter whether an old-age pension is being drawn (Organisation for Economic Co-operation and Development (OECD, 1995). Dorn and Sousa-Poza (2010) suggested that voluntary or early retirement occurs as a result of employment challenges rather than from a preference for leisure relative to work. Using this method, organisations need to be very careful as to the number of ages a person should attain before going on voluntary retirement. Otherwise, people with the requisite kills and knowledge will take advantage of the attractive packages and retire voluntarily and later go and seek for employment opportunity in other organisations. Organisations could lose skilful employees when this is not done properly.

Downsizing

Downsizing should be considered as the last resort. The downsizing plan should be based on the timing of reductions and forecasts of the extent to which these can be achieved by natural wastage or voluntary. Decisions about layoffs are usually based on seniority and/ or performance. Organisational downsizing has recently become an increasingly important issue that needs to be addressed to ensure fair employment practices. Companies worldwide have used downsizing to improve employee competitiveness, profitability, organisational effectiveness, efficiency as well as to reduce the size of their workforce. Downsizing has ramifications for everyone in the organisation, regardless if employees are remaining in the organisation or those (Blomqvist, 2002; Tyler, 2003). Downsizing can be viewed as "a type re-organisation or restructuring, downsizing or workforce reduction is a strategy to streamline, tighten and shrink the organisational structure with respect to the number of personnel that the organisation employs" (Halley, 2001, p. 4)

Downsizing has been considered as HR practice which involves reduction in the number of workforce within the organisation, which can be achieved through several techniques including, retrenchments, early retirements or casualisation of staff (Hellgren, Näswell, & Sverke, 2005). On the contrary, Chew and Horwitz (2002) postulate that downsizing may not necessarily result in the loss of jobs where employees are retrained and re-deployed, or where other measures such as non-replacement of staff that leave occur. Vermeulen (2002, p.8) argues that "downsizing encompasses a broader range of activities than mere laying-off employees". One study suggests that competitive pressures require many companies to restructure themselves from rigid bureaucracies to leaner and more flexible designs (Cummings & Worley 2009). Organisational downsizing represents a set of activities, undertaken on the part of the management of an organisation, designed to improve productivity, organisational efficiency, and/or competitiveness (Cameron, Freeman & Mishra, 1993).

SOLUTION AND RECOMMENDATIONS

Workforce panning is the cornerstone of all HRM activities in an organisation. Effective and efficient workforce planning allows an organisation to achieve its goals, increase the effectiveness and competitiveness of enterprises in the labour market. Moreover, workforce planning enables firms to reduce future uncertainty and to better operate their business activities. However, workforce planning should ensure that there is the right number and structure of people in the right jobs at the right time. These people should be committed to the organisation's goals. Otherwise, there is a possibility that business goals and plans may not be realised and also the competitors can prevent the company from achieving their market position. For organisations to conduct workforce planning in the most effective and efficient way, they should consider outsourcing non-core activities including security and canteens and offering part-time employment to help reduce labour costs. Additionally, organisations should consider income generating projects to increase financial base to sustain human resource planning activities.

FUTURE AREAS OF RESEARCH

The chapter examined the future of workforce planning in organisation. Although the chapter explored both external and internal forces which could impact on the future of workforce planning in organisation, however, many studies have ignored the impact of technological advancement on workforce planning. Against this background, it is recommended that future book chapter should explore the influence of technology on the effectiveness of workforce planning. Additionally, it was observed that although many studies have confirmed that workforce planning has a significant impact on organisational performance, little has been down on the mediating variables of workforce planning and organisational performance, including employee creativity and innovation, organisational trust, employee commitment and engagement. Future book chapter should examine the interplay between the aforementioned variables, workforce planning and organisational performance.

CONCLUSION

The chapter examined the future of workforce planning in organisations. Evidence from the empirical research suggests that that workforce planning is a crucial HRM activity in the organisation that ensures the organisation is adequately staffed with the right number of employees who have the right skills now and in the future. It was discovered that the objectives of workforce planning in organisations include: to estimate the number and quality of staff that will be required to achieve the desired goods; to ensure that there is no shortage and surplus of the number and skills of employees; to meet the future needs of the business; and to achieve sustainable competitive advantage. It is evident that workforce planning influences HRM activities such as recruitment and selection, job analysis, training and development and compensation. Additionally, evidence shows that workforce planning in affected by both internal and external forces. The internal forces which affect workforce planning in organisations include gathering information about the workforce in each institution, accurate information and analysis on personnel costs, the existing personnel policies of each institution, the capacity to understand the new job competencies needed and develop new staff roles and training for employees, mechanisms for improving organisational and employee performance and improvement in work processes, information about performance-based contracts and incentives and capacity to develop the necessary systems, change management process and Performance management and supervision systems. On the other hand, the external forces which hinder effective workforce planning in organisations include economic conditions, political environment, government regulations or laws.

REFERENCES

Akhigbe, O. J. (2013). Human resource planning: A key factor in ensuring the effectiveness and efficiency of organization. *Journal of Emerging Trends in Economics and Management Science*, *4*(4), 388–397.

Al Wahshi, A. S., Omari, M., & Barrett, R. (2013). *Human resource planning: Sector specific considerations*. ECU Publications.

Anya, C. J. P., Umoh, G. I., & Worlu, G. (2017). Human resource planning and organizational performance in oil and gas firms in Port Harcourt. *International Journal of Academic Research*, *3*(9), 110–129.

Anyim, F., Mba, S., & Ekwoaba, J. (2012). The imperative of integrating corporate business plan with manpower planning. *International Journal of Business and Management*, *7*(8), 56–62. doi:10.5539/ijbm.v7n8p56

Armstrong, M. (2011). *Handbook of human resource management practice* (8th ed.). Kogan Page.

Arsad, M. (2012). *Human resource management practices and organizational performance: A study on administrators in Universiti Teknologi Mara* (Unpublished MSc Dissertation). Universiti Utara Malaysia.

Aslam, H. D., Aslam, M., Ali, N., Habib, B., & Jabeen, M. (2013). Human resource planning practice in managing human resource: A literature review. *Human Resource Planning*, *3*(1), 200–2012.

Aslam, H. D., Aslam, M., Ali, N., Habib, B., & Jabeen, M. (2014). Human resource planning practice in managing human resource: A literature review. *International Journal of Human Resource Studies*, *3*(1), 200–217. doi:10.5296/ijhrs.v3i1.6253

Barrett, K., & Richard, G. (2006). *Seven steps of effective workforce planning. When Boomers retire*. Governing Magazine.

Bechet, T. P., & Maki, W. R. (1987). Modeling and forecasting focusing on people as a strategic resource. *Human Resource Planning*, *10*(4), 12–25.

Bernardin, H. J. (2002). *Human resource management: An experiential approach*. Irwin Professional Pub.

Branine, M. (2004). Job sharing and equal opportunities under the new public management in local authorities. *International Journal of Public Sector Management*, *17*(2), 136–152. doi:10.1108/09513550410523269

Bulla, D. N., & Scott, P. M. (1994). Manpower requirement forecasting: A case example. In Human Resource forecasting and modeling. The Human Resource Planning Society.

Buradum, T. F. (2017). Influence of human resource planning on organizational performance of fast food companies in Port Harcourt, Nigeria. *Imperial Journal of Interdisciplinary Research*, *3*(11), 1–10.

Butler, J. E., Ferris, G. R., & Napier, N. K. (1991). *Strategy and human resource management*. Cincinnati, OH: South-Western Publishing Co.

Cameron, K. S., Freeman, S. J., & Mishra, A. K. (1993). Downsizing and redesigning organizations. In G. Huber & W. Glick (Eds.), *Organizational change and redesign* (pp. 19–63). New York: Oxford University Press.

Cascio, S. (2009). *Performance and staff freezes: how leading companies create sustained value*. New York: John Wiley & Sons.

Chand, M., & Katou, A. A. (2007). The impact of HRM practices on performance in the Indian hotel industry. *Employee Relations*, *29*(6), 576–594. doi:10.1108/01425450710826096

Choudhury, E. H. (2007). Workforce planning in small local governments. *Review of Public Personnel Administration*, *27*(3), 264–280. doi:10.1177/0734371X06297464

CIPD. (2009). *The cost to employer of redundancy*. Work Audit.

Colley, L., & Price, R. (2010). Where have all the workers gone? Exploring public sector workforce planning. *Australian Journal of Public Administration, 69*(2), 202–213. doi:10.1111/j.1467-8500.2010.00676.x

Cotten, A. (2007). *Seven steps of effective workforce planning*. IBM Center for the Business of Government.

Cummings, T. G., & Worley, C. G. (2009). *Organizational development and change* (9th ed.). South Western College Publishing.

Das, P. N., & Nayak, B. (2015). Measuring the effectiveness of human resource planning: A case of Nilachal Ispat Nigam Limited. *IJST, 8*(35), 1–9.

Dorn, D., & Sousa-Poza, A. (2010). Voluntary and involuntary early retirement: An international analysis. *Applied Economics, 42*(4), 427–438. doi:10.1080/00036840701663277

Dot Public Transport. (2006). Patterns of entry and exit in the U.S. manufacturing sector. *The Rand Journal of Economics, 19*(4), 495–515.

Edgar, F., & Geare, A. (2004). Employee demographics in human resource management research, Research and practice in human resource management. *Human Resource Management, 12*(1), 61–91.

Eick, C. J. (2001). Job sharing their first year: A narrative of two partnered teachers' induction into middle school science teaching. *Teaching and Teacher Education, 18*(7), 887–904. doi:10.1016/S0742-051X(02)00049-5

Ganesh, M., & Indradevi, R. (2015). Importance and effectiveness of training and development. *Mediterranean Journal of Social Sciences, 6*(1), 334.

Giffords, E. D., & Dina, R. P. (2011). Strategic planning in non-profit organizations: Continuous quality performance improvement - a case study. *International Journal of Organization Theory and Behavior, 7*(1), 66–80. doi:10.1108/IJOTB-07-01-2004-B004

Gittonga, T. R. (2012). *The impact of freezing recruitment on employee performance and productivity*. SENA.

Guers, C., Martin, C., & Wybo, J. L. (2014, September). *The impact of the use of subcontracting on organizational reliability and safety. In 24th European Safety and Reliability Conference-ESREL 2014* (pp. 1027–1035). London: Taylor & Francis Group.

Halley, A. A. (2001). *Downsizing*. Available: http://jobfunctions.bnet.com/thankyou.aspx?&docid=60722&view=60772&load=1

Harky, Y. F. M. (2018). *The Significance of Recruitment and Selection on Organizational Performance: The Case of Private owned Organizations in Erbil, North of Iraq* (Doctoral dissertation). Istanbul Aydin University Institute of Social Sciences.

Harris, P. (2007). Flexible work policies- mean business. *Training and Development Journal*, 32–36.

Hellgren, J., Naswell, K., & Sverke, M. (2005). There is more to the picture than meets the eye: A comparison of downsizing survivors with changed and unchanged job content. *SA Journal of Industrial Psychology*, *31*(4), 87–93. doi:10.4102ajip.v31i4.216

Heneman III, H. G., & Sandver, M. G. (1977). *Markov analysis in human resource administration, applications and limitations.* Management of Academy.

Houseman, S. N. (2001). Why employers use flexible staffing arrangements: Evidence from an establishment survey. *Industrial & Labor Relations Review*, *55*(1), 149–170. doi:10.1177/001979390105500109

Jacobson, W. (2010). Preparing for tomorrow: A case study of workforce planning in North Carolina municipal governments. *Public Personnel Management*, *39*(4), 1–21. doi:10.1177/009102601003900404

Johne, A. (2009). Insurance product development: Managing the Changes. *International Journal of Bank Marketing*, *11*(3), 5–14. doi:10.1108/02652329310027693

Kane, R. L., & Stanton, S. (1991). Human resource planning: Where are we now? *Asia Pacific Journal of Human Resources*, *29*(2), 5–20. doi:10.1177/103841119102900202

Karia, A., Omari, S., Mwanaongoro, S., & Ondieki, A. (2016). The role of human resource planning on performance of public water utilities in Tanzania. *African Journal of Business Management*, *2*(1), 72–77.

Katua, T., Mukulu, E., & Gachunga, H. (2014). Effect of employee resourcing strategies on the performance of commercial banks in Kenya. *International Journal of Education and Research*, *2*(1), 1–20.

Kim, R. (2009). *Reassessing the ins and outs of unemployment mimeo*. University of Chicago.

Lars, M. (2011). Work-life balance accounts, strategic human resource management and demographic change - the case of the German chemical industry. *International Journal of Employment Studies, 19*(1), 99–125.

Lashley, S. (2001). *Workplace strategies and facilities management: Building in value*. Burlington, MA: Buttersworth-Heinemann.

Leung, P. P. L., Wu, C. H., Ho, G. T. S., Ip, W. H., & Mou, W. L. (2015). Workforce modelling, analysis and planning: A feasibility study in a local nursing home. In *2015 IEEE International Conference on Industrial Engineering and Engineering Management (IEEM)* (pp. 1337–1341). IEEE.

Lunenburg, F. C. (2012). Human resource planning: Forecasting demand and supply. *International Journal of Management. Business Administration (London), 15*(1), 1–15.

Madrick, A. (1995). *Hiring freezes and employee performance*. London: Institute of Personnel Management.

Mallela, C. S. R. (2012). Human resource planning: Then and now. *Prabandhan: Indian Journal of Management, 5*(9), 27–31. doi:10.17010/pijom/2012/v5i9/60253

Milkovich, T. G., & Boudreau, J. W. (1993). *Human resource management*. Praha: Grada Publishing.

Mondy, W. R., & Noe, R. M. (2006). *Human Resource Management*. New Delhi, India: Pearson education.

Nelen, A., De Grip, A., & Fouarge, D. (2011). *Is part-time employment beneficial for firm productivity?* IZA Discussion Paper No. 5423.

Ngui, T. K., Elegwa, K., & Hazel, G. G. (2014). Effect of employee resourcing on the performance of commercial banks in Kenya. *International Journal of Education and Research, 2*(1), 1–20.

Niehaus, R. J. (1995). Evolution of the strategy and structure of a human resource planning DSS application. *Decision Support Systems, 14*(3), 187–204. doi:10.1016/0167-9236(94)00016-L

Norhidayah, D., Kasim, N., & Shamsudin, A. (2012). Framework of human resource planning (HRP) influencing factors for local workforce supply in Malaysian construction industry. *Journal of Technology Management in China, 7*(2), 177–197. doi:10.1108/17468771211242863

Norman-Major, K., & Gooden, S. (2012). *Cultural Competency for Public Administrators*. Armonk, NY: M.E. Sharpe Incorporated.

Ofori, D., & Aryeetey, M. (2011). Recruitment and selection practices in small and medium enterprises. *International Journal of Business Administration*, *2*(3), 45–60. doi:10.5430/ijba.v2n3p45

Opatha, H. H. D. N. P. (2010). *Human resource management*. Colombo: Author Published.

Pradeesh, N. M. (2011). *Human resource planning and development: Study material VI semester*. School of Distance Learning, University of Calicut.

Reid, W. M., & Taylor, R. G. (1989). An application of absorbing markov analysis to human resource issues in public administration. *Sage (Atlanta, Ga.)*, 76–74.

Reilly, P. (2003). Guide to workforce planning in local Authorities. Employer's Organization for Local Government.

Robbins, S., & Judge, T. (2007). *Essentials of organizational behavior*. Prentice Hal.

Robbins, S. P., & Judge, T. A. (2011). *Organizational behavior* (14th ed.). Upper Saddle River, NJ: Prentice Hall.

Snell, S., Bohlander, G. W., & Bohlander, G. (2010). *Principles of human resource management*. South-Western Cengage Learning.

Turner, K. (1988). Natural attrition: The preferred option? *The Journal of Industrial Relations*, *30*(3), 363–380. doi:10.1177/002218568803000302

Ulferts, G., Wirtz, P., & Peterson, E. (2009). Strategic human resource planning in academia. *American Journal of Business Education*, *2*(7), 1–10. doi:10.19030/ajbe.v2i7.4123

Vermeulen, L. P. (2002). A comparison of reasons and objectives for organisational downsizing in South Africa and Australia. *Management Dynamics*, *11*(2), 28–39.

Werner, S., Jackson, S. E., & Schuler, R. S. (2012). *Human resource management*. South Western Cengage Learning.

Xie, A., & Huang, X. (2012). *Advances in computer science and education*. London: Springer. doi:10.1007/978-3-642-27945-4

KEY TERMS AND DEFINITIONS

Delphi Technique: It consists of a panel of experts who responds in writing to a questionnaire dealing with a specific problem.

Downsizing: The reduction in the number of workforce within the organisation, which can be achieved through several techniques including, retrenchments, early retirements or casualization of staff.

Job Design: The deliberate purposeful planning of the job, including all its structural and social aspects and their effect on the employee.

Job Enlargement: The combination of different jobs and adding connected duties to job.

Job Rotation: The process of moving an employee or employees among different job within the same undertaken.

Job Sharing: It is an arrangement whereby two employees share the work of one fulltime position, dividing pay and benefits between them according to the time each works.

Labour Demand Forecasting: It projects how business needs will affect the human resources requirements using both qualitative and quantitative methods.

Labour Supply Forecasting: It measures the number of people likely to be available from within and outside the organisation, having allowed for attrition (labour wastage and retirements), absenteeism, internal movements and promotions, and changes in hours and other conditions of work.

Chapter 7
Reshaping Education for the New Labour Market in Sub-Saharan African Countries

Richard H. Afedzie
Pentecost University College, Ghana

James Aller
Georgia Southwestern State University, USA

Joseph Nketia
St. Edward University, USA

ABSTRACT

This chapter examines the vital role of education and training in the new labour market. It explores the relative importance of technical education and computer literacy for all able working citizens in sub-Saharan African countries. It states that heavy investment in education and training has a great return on productivity and has the potential to change societies for all citizens. The literature on new labour market documents that sub-Saharan African countries that have changed their educational system to reflect technical competency have been able to develop their workforce productivity and national economic development. It asserts that government policies on education and training should be of utmost priority to governance in order to enhance the labour market in the 21st century.

DOI: 10.4018/978-1-5225-9810-7.ch007

INTRODUCTION

The past four decades has witnessed a renewed focus on the link between education and training for the new labour market, especially in developing countries (Leuven & Oosterbeek, 2004). The new labour market is the collaborative economy which is facilitated by technologically skilled workforce and the prominent use of internet-based services. The new labour market thrives on factors such as the technological investment climate of a country, economic growth and productivity, financial markets, and the foreign direct investment (Lindahl, & Krueger, 2001). Similarly, investment by national governments in the areas of primary and secondary education often determines the availability of skilled labour force capable of meeting the needs of the new labour market. The impact of technology in the new labour market is also noted in many developing countries, since the development of a country's human resources and economic productivity are all connected to the introduction of technology in the economy. Since the new global order has intertwined organisations with markets through internet services, developing countries are gradually changing to the new labour market which seeks for a vibrant labour force equipped with technical skills and digital capabilities.

Not surprising, much of the research on the new labour market has focused on the state of educational reforms and its effects on the economic development of the economies in the developing countries (Mingat, 1998; Teal, 2011). The purpose of this chapter therefore seeks to examine the evolving role of both the educational and training development as well as its contributions to the new labour market.

BACKGROUND

The value of education and training is critical in the new labour market in achieving favourable economic outcomes (Autor, Levy, Murnane, 2003). Appropriate education along with training is essential for the new labour market which primarily requires technical expertise. The literature on labour market documents that technical education is important in developing human capital and the economy of a country (Hanushek & Woessmann, 2007). For developing countries in sub-Saharan African, the presence of natural resources such as crude oil, gold, diamond, bauxite, manganese and others imply that much concern should be devoted to the technical training and education of its citizens as a national development strategy. Likewise, the presence of large natural resources indicates that renew emphasis must be geared toward enhancing the skills of the labour force. Research studies on economic growth and development activities has focused on the important role of skilled labour force in attaining sustainable rate of output growth, lowering poverty and improving social development (Kurt, 2015). The study by Boccanfuso, Larouchet and Trandafir (2015) examine how improvement in higher education has impacted the labour market of highly-educated individuals in Senegal. It focuses on the short-term benefits of the country's educational reforms in the first decade of the twenty-first century. The authors also emphasized on likely contributions on the quality of the graduates on the labour market in Senegal.

The objectives of this book chapter seek to explore the background of the new labour market and the changes resulting from technological advancement over the past four decades. Similarly, this chapter will examine the historical contexts of the new labour market and its influence on growth and development of economies in developing countries. In so doing, this chapter will delve into the following educational and technological factors that influence the new labour market; (i) the role of education on the new labour market; (ii) the role of training on the new labour market; (iii) the role of technology on the new labour market; (iv) the impact of globalisation on the new labour market in developing countries and (v) the impact of migration on the new labour market. The chapter offers recommendations for enhancing the skilled workforce to meet the needs of the new labour market in developing countries and concludes with an analysis of the suitable policies necessary to foster the attainment of the required technical skills for the new labour market.

THE NEW LABOUR MARKET: A HISTORICAL PERSPECTIVE

Developing countries have been least impacted by the advancement of the technology which has been the driver of the new labour market (Codagnone, Abadie, & Biagi, 2016). The growth of the new labour market in the last four decades globally witnessed a big shift in the growth of major western countries and brought up emerging economies in eastern sections of Europe and many countries in Asia. The new labour market fostered increased productivity and ultimately enhancing per capital income and consumption (Hall, 2016). The infusion of new technologies has seen a breakthrough in several facets of life – from gene development to machine taking over most of the activities performed by man signifying the transformation of the global labour market landscape. Amid these development, most developing countries have not created the conducive environment to attract and utilize these technological revolutions which is fostering the new pattern of labour market across the globe. Since the turn of the twenty-first century, technological investment in developing economies have grown by 50% and some of major contributors to the growth include the technical, scientific, professional activities with their vastly digitalized engineering and research focus. However, over the last decade, the pace of technological development in the areas of artificial intelligence and workplace automation has given more currency to the importance of promoting economic growth and effective utilisation of the human resource in developing countries in Africa. Developing countries are often associated with common national developmental strategies and a key feature of the economies of developing countries include the following;

- A slow growth in the number of technical and educational labour force with large sector of the youth uneducated and unemployed.
- A higher number of men in the agricultural sector of the economy and majority of the women in petty trading (informal sector).
- The government sector seems to be the largest employer of the service industry with a growing manufacturing industry which employs a considerable number of men.
- A large emigration to the western countries in Europe and North America (highly educated and professional personnel) and remittances to the developing countries.
- A decline in the unionisation of institutions that have collective bargain are still vibrant in certain sectors of the economy such as ports, public utilities and public sector organisations (Jalilian, Tribe, Weiss, 2000).

EDUCATION IN SUB-SAHARAN AFRICAN COUNTRIES

Most developing countries in Sub-Saharan African countries have been agrarian oriented and exporters of raw materials to the developed nations. They also have large population size with little technical training in most of their tertiary institutions. In many cases, the education and training policies in developing countries have been planned to suit the needs of the new labour market, however, much of the education is focused on theory and little technical training (Acemoglu, & Jörn-Steffen, 1999). As such, there has been a trend of mismatch between education and the new labour market which requires technical trained labour force (Autor, Levy & Murnane, 2003).

Often the educational systems in developing countries are not fully reinforced with the relevant resources to improve the quality of human resources (Olaniyan & Okemakinde, 2008). This calls for the reshaping of education and training to meet the demands of the new labor market. Within this context, the identification of policies and planning tools are necessary in developing countries to restructure education and training in a manner that contribute and sustain economic development.

The reshaping of education could facilitate the brand of new labour force that corresponds largely to high employment in developing countries and consequently results in increase economic development. An educated labor force that is gainfully employed increase purchasing power and this also has the effect of increasing supply of goods and services in the economy. The net effect of increased demand and supply in a developing economy is economic growth and the expansion of the economy. This reveals that education in developing economies has multiplier effects that adds up to the acceleration of economic development.

Education reforms that meet the needs of the new labour market can also spearhead innovative ideas for the efficient running of the developing economy. Human capital development through the reshaping of education improves labor skills to solve problems and create products meant for pertinent challenges in the economy. The reshaping of education and training in the new field of digital technology has particularly enhanced the skill sets of technically competent labour force which has expedited the innovation processes in many developing countries. Improving the value of graduates specifically in the primary and secondary school system so that they can adequately prepared for the new labour market requires introduction of more resources into the educational system (teacher training, educational supplies and equipment). Graduates should be well equipped with the requisite practical skills and with a high level of literacy (reading, writing, numeracy and computer) tailored to fit into the dynamic new labour market. Restructuring education in a country is a huge task and one of the benefits is that more of their citizens will be either employable in industries or be self-employed. As such efforts for organizations to expand and grow are largely the result of technically driven developments.

Governments and organizations in developing countries in sub-Saharan African continue to invest more in education and training with several reforms such as universal primary and secondary level education, skills training program, tax incentives for private sector training, special vocational and technical training programs, entrepreneurial development programs and national technical training service. Most of the technical training initiatives began in the 1990s with the intention of making new graduates entrepreneurial and be financially self-sustaining in lieu of depending on their government for employment opportunities. Much of these developmental growths have been directed at the youth who are emerging as the new labour force in their various economies.

In Ghana, Cote d'Ivoire, Senegal and Rwanda, the primary schools' system has always been the platform for providing basic educational background which is the preparatory grounds for the development of technical and vocational training (Borghans, Grip& Heijke, 1996). In Ghana, the secondary school educational reform initiated the Senior secondary school system, by restructuring it to provide the youth with vocational and technical skills before tertiary education. The rationale behind it was to offer skilled based training to the youth who could not pass successful into the university to be self-sustaining with their own self-employed economic ventures. In Zambia, Malawi, Rwanda and Tanzania, the National Training Agency (NTA) was established to provide unemployed youth with skills for job opportunities in agriculture, industry and personally developed careers (Johanson & Adams, 2004). These vocational training agencies were created in the 1980s and were basically funded by the government through a world bank development support program. These programs are currently ongoing and providing support to technical training of the youth to be entrepreneurial in their self-interested career pursuits (Calvès, and Schoumaker (2004).

Further, a greater number of developing countries in sub-Saharan African countries are cognizant of the new labour market and its relevance in the economic transformation of their labour force and have made conscious efforts at adjusting their educational system to that pattern (Kozík, & Handlovská, 2011). To make educational reforms well connected to the new labour market, many countries are linking their educational program with a well-structured career guiding program for students; greater extra curricula activities to develop the "soft skills" of how individuals can relate better with each other, building conflict management skills, fostering better work ethics and time management, entrepreneurship and mentoring (Keevy, 2011). By establishing these practical and soft skills programs, it is anticipated that the youth would be better suited for the new labour market.

THE ROLE OF TRAINING ON THE NEW LABOUR MARKET

The role of training in the new labour market has been well emphasized in the literature on new labour market (Henderson, Dicken, Hess, Coe &Yeung, 2002) Significant transformation of developing economies has been achieved by means of investment in technical education and training of graduates. Major structural changes in economic productivity taking place in sub-Saharan African countries has largely been augmented by government policies and initiatives in the areas of training program for youth and on the job training (Salehi & Hajizad, 2010). The general notion is that training increases the prospects of gaining employment and socio-economic development in societies.

Researchers continue to emphasize the obvious link between technical training and economic development in developing economies (Sanders& Barth, 1968). Kuznets (1997) in his research on education and labour force participation, discovered that there is positive correlation between the labor force in agriculture and the training programs in an economy. Thus, the labor force in agriculture declines with increase in the number of people offered technical training in a society. By this trend, scholars in economic development conclude that training on the job and short-term training programs provide fundamental ingredient to economic development in other sectors of any economy.

Human resources development according to economic theories leads to employment and small business startups, that also impact economic development (Moog, 2002). The chain reaction from employment and business startups contributes to the acceleration of economic development. Lerman (2009) in a multiple-factor analysis of 32 developing countries, discovered that primary and post primary education coupled with technical training were better predictors of economic growth in those 32 countries. Thus, research has proven that education enhances economic development in many sectors of an economy.

Increasing, male participation rate in the labour force has been generally high for most sub-Saharan African countries primarily because of traditional cultural values about the role of women in the society. However, the female labour force has risen significantly over the past two decades because of the flourishing of western culture in developing nations, which provide equal rights to women. As such, women are now participating in higher numbers in the labour force for the following factors;

- Societal encouragement of women in education and training in the society.
- The growth of service industries such as banking, tourism and information services which has given more opportunities to women.
- Self-actualisation of women and the determination to be self-reliant financially.
- The decrease in fertility rates and the average household size lessens the desire to be a stay home mother for a long time.

Developing countries in their attempts to accelerate economic development need to create an enabling economy that is supportive of value adding educational systems (Everett, 1962).

TECHNOLOGY AND THE NEW LABOUR MARKET

The role of technology in the new labour market cannot be overlooked. The advancement of technology over the past four decades and the future trend of technological growth is expected to demand well-educated workers with special skills in technology. It has opened new frontiers in technological sectors of many developing economies and has seen the emergences of economic productivity and growth in several developing countries. With much of the economies of developing countries still under agrarian economic order, significant investment in education and training will help drive structural change into sustainable growth (Deming, 2015). More and highly qualified workers versed in current technology will demand more capital investment to enhance the welfare of the society (Autor, 2015). A technically educated and trained workforce facilitates more innovation and creates a competitive industrial base for global trade for developing countries. In general, both higher investment in technologically innovations and better qualified workers enhance average labour productivity.

Development in education and technology coexist in such a way that the need for technology is followed by the immediate need for education and development. These developments are often in isolation but they all require planning, analysis and data collection to be implemented effectively (Harris & Batty, 1993; Worrall, 1989).

Specifically, future employment growth is hinged on the economic productivity and the integration of technology in the production. Similarly, technology is facilitating the emergence of new work models such as total quality management and automation that may help solve some of the labour issues in developing economies (Autor, Levy, & Murnane, 2003). It is commonly believed that much of the shortfalls in the technical skill and highly professional labour force in the developing countries is attributed to structural factors such as the curriculum of the education system, the strategy of the economic development policies and its interface with the future labour market - new labour market (Acemoglu & Restrepo, 2015).

MIGRATION AND THE NEW LABOUR MARKET

Developing countries in Africa has historically been a place of migration – immigration and emigration (Bakewell & Jónsson, 2011). The new labour market in developing countries have encountered negative impact from emigration of the technically trained and professional workforce to developing countries (Galloway, Kelly & Keogh, 2006). Over the past four decades, organised migration has become a dominant feature among the young graduates from the tertiary institutions to countries such as USA, UK, Canada and Germany. The emigration of skilled labour and professional labour force to developed nations is known as the "brain drain".

The impact of the skilled and professional workforce migration has often resulted in lower productivity and reduced economic growth. (Fan & Oded, 2007). One key driver of the highly educated migration to the developed world has been the result of poor conditions of service and the remuneration difference for the same service in the developed nations (Bakewell, 2008). Migration of the best from the developing world to western nations has had a distortionary posture on the new labour market in developing countries of sub-Saharan Africa. It has reduced the economic incentives and rational for investors relocating in developing countries, simply because of the lack of skilled labour and trained workforce to undertake the technologically oriented jobs of the twenty-first century (Neiman & Karabarbounis, 2013). Similarly, potential entrepreneurs with the financial base to create employment opportunities in these developing countries end up transferring their capital and professional skills to the developed countries. Importantly, migration has had a severe economic impact in developing countries in the following areas:

- Economic downturn largely because of the loss of skilled labour force leading to low investment in the new labour market.
- Semi- skilled labour force who would have been an essential component of the new labour market in development have also migrated to developed nations to work as nurses, construction workers, transport workers, teachers, and pursue other career opportunities.
- Above all, the investment injected into the skilled professionals and educated workforce becomes a net loss of valuable human capital resources that could have ultimately benefited the developing country (Fan & Oded, 2007).

The sum effect of "brain drain" in developing countries of sub-Saharan Africa has been a perennial skilled workforce problem which would have been available for the new labour market. Government efforts to create more jobs to absorb the skilled workforce has often been piecemeal and the attraction of good conditions of service and better remuneration has often attracted more skilled workforce to developed countries (Hanushek, 2009).

It has been estimated that between 1990 and 2001, approximately six million skilled professionals and university graduates emigrated from developing countries in Africa to the Western Europe, United States of America and Canada (World Bank, 2012). The annual flow has declined over the period from 2012 to 2018 because of strict immigration enforcement in several Western nations. Given the small number of skilled labour and professionals in developing countries with heterogenous skills, an immigration of this magnitude does have a considerable impact on the emerging new labour market in developing countries. Curtailing the phenomenon of "brain drain" by creating good economic conditions to boost private investment and entrepreneurship will aid in stemming the tide of emigration of the skilled and technical labour force in the various developing countries.

GLOBALISATION AND THE NEW LABOUR MARKET

Globalisation is currently the dominant economic force dictating the role and pace of economic competition among countries and has considerably encouraged the use of technical labour force primarily to increase productivity with fewer input. Globalisation has prompted new labour market policy reforms in most developing countries (Matley, 2005). The new labour market has always been linked to the present economic revolution of globalisation which is characterized by change in which there is a continual necessity to adjust to new advances in technology and workforce technical literacy. Since economic productivity is integral to labour force development in developing economies, the development of human capital is essential to their productivity and international economic competitiveness (Werther, Ruch, & McClure, 1986).

The new labour market is constantly seeking for labour force with the capability to critically think through ideas in technology, science and numeracy. Likewise, the new labour market employers are looking for individuals with effective communication capabilities and entrepreneurial skills at the workplace. Developing the quality of human resources in developing countries entails greater investment in education and training with private institutional support to attain the goal of highly skilled labour force. For a considerable number of people in the developing nations, the labour force offers the primary means of income generating source (Alter, Ghilardi, & Hakura, 2017). The lack of economic opportunities to offer the labour force in most developing countries generates a host of problems such as poverty and economic deprivation among citizens of these countries (McKee-Ryan, Song, Wanberg, & Kinicki, 2005). Empirical evidence of economic conditions in developing countries reveals that availability of the labour market is directly related to greater economic competitiveness, better economic wellbeing, better education, training and economic productivity (Oosterbeek, & Webbink, 2007).

The engagement of technology is essential to any country, organization or team transitioning from one state of economic order to another (Samuel, Coombes, Miranda, Melvin, Young & Azarmina, 2004). Globalization has readily created the availability of technology transfer in both industrial and service industries. Similarly, globalization has enhanced the accessibility of technology in many developmental efforts in developing countries and this has enhanced the skill sets their workforce. In sum, increased globalization has also fuelled the development of the process of technology known as "skilled-Based Technological Change" or SBTC (Katz & Murphy, 1992). Research conducted by Biagi, Faggian, Rajbhandari and Venhorst, (2018) concluded that "the odds of being automatized decreases quickly as people attain higher formal qualifications" (p. 29).

COMMON INDICATORS FOR THE NEW LABOUR MARKET

Common indicators to examine the major economic stakeholders and resulting benchmarks conducive to a sustainable new labour market in developing countries. Among these indicators in include the following;

- available expertise
- political impact
- organization
- incremental development strategy
- suitable equipment
- ownership and origins
- types of indicators

Adaptation of these common economic and political indicators ensures the readiness of a country to transform its economy to the new labour market. For instance, the available of expertise guarantee the viable new labour market with existing skilled workforce contributing to it. Similarly, as organizations expand across country borders, continents and oceans, the preparation of these organizations to expand give insight as to the value of technology adoption in these developing countries. Likewise, adequate investment in education helps developing countries upgrade their human capital primarily to complement new technologies and improve the new labour market. A key benefit of the investment in education is the potential emergence of entrepreneurs to boost employment growth and economic development. A key indicator of the readiness for the new labour market is the shared benefits of the new technologies, constructive national development strategy, national policies that investigate the future economic development of the country.

The Labor Market's Contributions and Challenges in the 21st Century

Contributions to the New Labour Market

The key contributing factors and drawbacks to the new labour market is review in this section. Important socio-economic and political factors are highlighted in the figure 1 to indicate how the new labour market is impacted within a country. Major factors impacting the new labour market include the following;

1. Investment in education
2. Globalisation
3. Investment in human resource development
4. Political issues such as development strategy and endemic corruption
5. Migration

As the first and second industrial revolutions were crucial moments in turning around the evolution of modern economies, so has automation and computers equally

Table 1. Key socio-political and economic indicators to a viable new labour market

Key Indicators and Values	Major Expectations from Key Indicators
Available Expertise	• Does the expertise exist to deliver the education? • If the evolution is technology, are there personnel that can deliver the training needed?
Political Impact	• Does the country political environment support the change and support it? • Does it have the appropriate cultural norms and financial capability?
Organization	• What is the organization that is reshaping education in the location? • Is it a substantial organization that has the resources to bring needed talent, equipment or other forms of support?
Incremental Development Strategy	• When creating a development strategy, it is important to understand the national development context? • Is the strategy realistic to the national cultural expectations and financial capabilities?
Suitable Equipment	• Is suitable equipment part of the indication that a country is ready for reshaping education? • Is physical location for the equipment important to the success of manpower development?
Ownership and Origins	• One of the key indicators is where the need for change was initiated and who owns the change. • It is typically important for change initiatives to initiate from within. .
Types of Indicators	Indicators measure progress towards a goal: • Is funding available for equipment, building, and training? • What is the number of jobs created from reshaping education? • Is the emphasis on technical education creating emerging entrepreneurs?

Source: Own compilation

led developing countries the way forward in economic development (Kennedy, 2014). Technical training with heavy emphasis on technology has often enhanced worker's skills and capabilities and is currently pursued in many developing countries (Acemoglu, 2003). All these efforts have generated a surge of economic development in several developing countries in sub-Sahara Africa.

Challenges to the New Labour Market in Developing Countries

The structural adjustment of developing economies in the 1980s and early 1990s have reduced the level of government contribution in the provision of funding for greater skill development of the youth and offered the global financial institutions such as world Bank, International monetary fund, and African Development Bank more policy contributions on how developing countries' economies are planned. The wave of structural adjustment in countries such as Ghana, Benin, Togo, Nigeria, Kenya, Tanzania and Zambia in the 1990s created large unemployment because of the

Figure 1. Factors influencing the new labour markets in developing countries

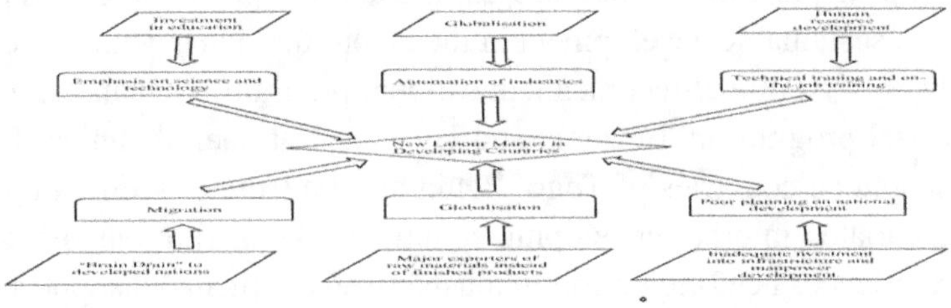

privatization of large number of public sector industries (Autor, Levy, & Murnane, 2003). This form of structural adjustment has handicapped investment of economic plans specific to the local economic needs of developing countries (Dao, 2004).

Above all, the high population growth and the low level of education among the labour force in developing countries continuous to be a hindering factor to achieving a balanced level of educated labour force ready to participate fully in the new labour market (Acemoglu, & Autor, (2011).

RECOMMENDATIONS

Since the last quarter of the twentieth century, the new labour market has seen greater growth in many developing countries because of the influx of technological know-how through vocational and technical education. However, change in education and technical development can be difficult even in the best of situations. Better planning, communication, and result based indicators will aide an organization and country in implementing an important change such as reshaping the education policies and practices. Without a desire to change or reshape the educational program of a third world country, the strategy of enhancing the technical development of the labour force will be doomed to fail if considerable focus is not given to it.

Creating good infrastructure base in these developing countries coupled with an investment climate of eradicating bribery and corruption will promote a conducive economic atmosphere for more private investment in developing countries, which will in the long term minimize the migration of skilled labour to western developed countries.

Besides the technical training and educational emphasis to develop the youth for the new labour market, there is the need to fully utilize the coaching and mentoring of the youth in developing countries to understand the constant changes and global economic flexibility associated with the new labour market (Calderón, & Servén, 2010).

A much better interface would be most required with employers who can offer apprenticeship support, work-study programs and other practical related programs to guarantee a sustainable development of the labour force in developing countries. Specifically, the vocational-technical educational program in Ghana, the National Entrepreneurial program in Tanzania and Uganda, National Technical Education in the Francophone countries of Togo, Benin and La Cote D'Ivoire are examples that can be initiated in other developing countries. The institutions offering these practical experiences needs to be continuously given the financial support essential to enhancing the technical and technological development of the labour force.

Special focus on small-scale industries for developing economies will go a long way of helping these local agro-based industries build for the 21st century technological process. Economics theories have indicated that skilled labor is a key component of factors of production and for developing economies to grow, the competencies and capabilities of its labor force need to be enhanced with primary on technical training.

FUTURE AREAS OF RESEARCH

The numerous factors positively influencing the growth of the new labour market in developing countries in sub-Sahara Africa needs to be empirically tested with data from world bank study. The empirical analysis will offer a greater understanding of the level of manpower challenges and educational factors likely to support the new labour market. Further, empirical analysis can also be used to compare some of the educational policies and reforms supporting new labour market in the other developing countries such as the Caribbean and South-East Asian countries. Future research should examine some of the monetary policies that has potential to encourage greater investment in technological development.

CONCLUSION

This chapter conclude that formulating educational policy meant to produce youth who are technically skilled and educated to fit the new labour market will benefit economies of developing countries. Many developing countries such as Ghana, Senegal, Cote d'Ivoire, Rwanda and Tanzania offer free primary and secondary level education and this policy continues to generate great returns to the economies of these economies. However, the degree of skilled labour returns on the economies of many developing nations depends on the country's stage of economic development. A country that takes more than 12 years to acquire basic educational skill and technical proficiency in basic professional skills has a system that is primarily incompetent to accommodate the demands of the new labour market (Parker, Van Alstyne & Choudar, 2016).

Specifically, small and medium size enterprises should be able to access government supported loan schemes to help grow their manpower training capabilities and sustainability in this new technological market environment. In so doing, more focus would be geared to the financial survival and technical resources of these industries to enable them to absorb the youth from national educational and training restructuring programs. To match the pace of population growth and emigration of educated youth to western nations, reshaping education and training to catch up with the level of technology in the new economic activities of the twenty-first century would be a massive boost to the new labour market in several developing countries.

REFERENCES

Acemoglu, D. (2003). Labour- and capital-augmenting technical change. *Journal of the European Economic Association*, *1*(1), 1–37. doi:10.1162/154247603322256756

Acemoglu, D., & Autor, D. (2011). Skills, tasks and technologies: Implications for employment and earnings. Handbook of Labour Economics, 4(4), 1043–1171

Acemoglu, D., & Jörn-Steffen, P. (1999). Beyond becker: Training in imperfect labour markets. *Economic Journal (London)*, *109*(453), 112–142. doi:10.1111/1468-0297.00405

Acemoglu, D., & Restrepo, P. (2015). The race between machine and man: Implications of technology for growth, factor shares and employment. *SSRN Electronic Journal*, *9*(5). doi:10.2139srn.2781320

Alter, A., Ghilardi, D., & Hakura, D. (2017). Public investment in a developing country facing resource depletion. *Journal of African Economies*, *26*(3), 295–321. doi:10.1093/jae/ejw031

Anderson, P. Y. (1987). Informal sector or modern labour market? Towards a synthesis. *Social and Economic Studies*, *36*(3), 149–176.

Autor, D. H., Levy, F., & Murnane, R. J. (2003). The skill content of recent technological change: An empirical exploration. *The Quarterly Journal of Economics*, *118*(4), 1279–1333. doi:10.1162/003355303322552801

Bakewell, O. (2008). Them in their place: The ambivalent relationship between development and migration in Africa. *Third World Quarterly, 29*(7), 1341–1358. doi:10.1080/01436590802386492

Bakewell, O., & Jónsson, G. (2011). Migration, mobility and the African city. Oxford, UK: IMI: International Migration Institute.

Biagi, B., Faggian, A., Rajbhandari, I., & Venhorst, V.A. (2018). New frontiers in interregional migration research. *Advances in Spatial Science*. . doi:10.1007/978-3-319-75886-2-4

Borghans, L. A. D., Grip, H., & Heijke, H. (1996). Labour market information and the choice of vocational specialization. *Economics of Education Review, 15*(1), 59–74. doi:10.1016/0272-7757(95)00041-0

Calderón, C., & Servén, L., S. (2010). Infrastructure and economic development in sub-Saharan Africa. *Journal of African Economies, 19*(3), 116–187.

Calvès, A., & Schoumaker, B. (2004). Deteriorating economic context and changing patterns of youth employment in urban Burkina Faso: 1980–2000. *World Development, 32*(8), 1341–1354. doi:10.1016/j.worlddev.2004.03.002

Codagnone, C., Abadie, F. & Biagi, F. (2016). *The future of work in the 'Sharing Economy'. Market efficiency and equitable opportunities or unfair precarisation?* Institute for Prospective Technological Studies, JRC Science for Policy Report EUR 27913 EN. doi:10.2791/431485

Crook, C.K. (2007). Learning science and learning technology: A place for cultural psychology. *British Journal of Educational Psychology Monograph Series, 11*(5), 1–17.

Dao, M. Q. (2004). Rural poverty in developing countries: An empirical analysis. *Journal of Economic Studies (Glasgow, Scotland), 31*(6), 500–508. doi:10.1108/01443580410569244

Deming, D. J. (2015). The growing importance of social skills in the labor market. *National Bureau of Economic Research, 9*(3), 300-330. doi:10.3386/w21473

Fan, C. S., & Stark, O. (2007). International migration and 'educated unemployment. *Journal of Development Economics, 83*(1), 76–87. doi:10.1016/j.jdeveco.2006.05.002

Fayolle, A. (2013). Personal views on the future of entrepreneurship education. Entrepreneurship and regional development. *International Journal (Toronto, Ont.), 25*(7-8), 692–701.

Hall, C. (2016). Does more general education reduce the risk of future unemployment? Evidence from an expansion of vocational upper secondary education. *Economics of Education Review*, *52*(9), 234–250.

Hanushek, E. A. (2009). School policy: Implications of recent research for human capital investments in South Asia and other developing countries. *Education Economics*, *17*(3), 291–313. doi:10.1080/09645290903142585

Hanushek, E. A., & Woessmann, L. (2007). *The role of education quality for economic growth. Policy Research Working Paper, No.4122*. Washington, DC: World Bank. Retrieved from https://openknowledge.worldbank.org/handle/10986/

Harris, B., & Batty, M. (1993). Locational models, geographic information and planning support systems. *Journal of Planning Education and Research*, *12*(3), 184–198. doi:10.1177/0739456X9301200302

Henderson, J. P., Dicken, M., Hess, M., Coe, N., & Yeung, H. W. C. (2002). Global production networks and the analysis of economic development. *Review of International Political Economy*, *9*(3), 436–464. doi:10.1080/09692290210150842

Henry, C., Hill, F., & Leitch, C. (2003). *Entrepreneurship education and training*. Aldershot, UK: Ashgate.

Jalilian, H. M., & Weiss, J. (2000). *Industrial development and policy in Africa: Issues of de-industrialisation and development strategy*. Cheltenham, UK: Edward Elgar.

Johanson, R. K., & Adams, A. V. (2004). *Skills development in sub-Saharan Africa*. Washington, DC: World Bank. doi:10.1596/0-8213-5680-1

Katz, L. F., & Murphy, K. M. (1992). Changes in relative wages, 1963-1987: Supply and demand factors. *The Quarterly Journal of Economics*, *107*(1), 35–78. doi:10.2307/2118323

Keevy, J. (2011). *The recognition of qualifications across borders: the contribution of regional qualifications frameworks. Background paper commissioned by UNESCO*. Pretoria: South African Qualifications Authority.

Kennedy, A. (2014). Understanding continuing professional development: The need for theory to impact on policy and practice. *Professional Development in Education, 40*(5), 688–697.

Kozík, T., & Handlovská, I. (2011b). The reduction of interest among elementary students in the field of technical education. *International Journal of Engineering Pedagogy*, *1*(3), 9–12. doi:10.3991/ijep.v1i3.1822

Kurt, S. (2015). Government health expenditures and economic growth: A federal approach for the case of Turkey. *International Journal of Economics and Financial Issues*, *5*(2), 441–447.

Kuznets, S. (1957). Quantitative aspects of the economic growth of nations. *Economic Development and Cultural Change*, *4*, 3–111.

Lerman, R. (2009). *Training tomorrow's workforce: Community college and apprenticeship as collaborative routes to rewarding careers*. Washington, DC: Centre for American Progress.

Leuven, E., & Oosterbeek, H. (2004). Evaluating the effect of tax deduction on training. *Journal of Labor Economics*, *22*(2), 461–488. doi:10.1086/381257

Lewin, K. (1947). Frontiers in group dynamics: Concepts, methods and reality in social; Social equilibria and social change. *Human Relations*, *1*(1), 1787–1812. doi:10.1177/001872674700100103

Lindahl, M., & Krueger, A. B. (2001). Education for growth: Why and for whom? *Journal of Economic Literature*, *39*(4), 1101–1136. doi:10.1257/jel.39.4.1101

Long, E. J. (1961). Economic basis of land reform in underdeveloped economies. *Land Economics*, *37*(2), 404–420. doi:10.2307/3159556

Matley, H. (2005). *Business school graduates as nascent entrepreneurs: Some policy considerations*. NCGE Policy Paper 6. Retrieved from www.ncge.com

McKee-Ryan, F., Song, Z., Wanberg, C. R., & Kinicki, A. J. (2005). Psychological and physical well-being during unemployment: A meta-analytic study. *The Journal of Applied Psychology*, *90*(5), 301–321. doi:10.1037/0021-9010.90.1.53 PMID:15641890

McMullan, W., Chrisman, J., & Vesper, K. (2001). Some problems in using subjective measures of effectiveness to evaluate entrepreneurial assistance programs. *Entrepreneurship Theory and Practice*, *26*(1), 37–54. doi:10.1177/104225870102600103

Mingat, A. (1998). The strategy used by high-performing Asian economies in education: Some lessons for developing countries. *World Development*, *26*(4), 695–715. doi:10.1016/S0305-750X(98)00001-1

Moog, P. (2002). Human capital and its influence on entrepreneurial success. *Historical Social Research (Köln)*, *27*(4), 157–180.

Mosely, C. (2005). The value of professional teaching portfolios to prospective employers: School administrators' views. *Professional Educator*, *27*(3), 58–72.

Neiman, B., & Karabarbounis, L. (2013). The global decline of the labour share. *The Quarterly Journal of Economics*, *129*(1), 61–103.

Olaniyan, D. A., & Okemakinde, T. (2008). Human capital theory: Implications for educational development. *European Journal of Scientific Research*, *24*(2), 157–162.

Oosterbeek, H., & Webbink, D. (2007). Wage Effects of an Extra Year of Basic Vocational Education. *Economics of Education Review*, *26*(4), 408–419. doi:10.1016/j.econedurev.2006.07.013

Parker, G. G., Van Alstyne, M. W., & Choudar, S. P. (2016). *Platform revolution: How networked markets are transforming the economy—And how to make them work for you*. New York: W.W. Norton & Company.

Sanders, D. P., & Barth, S. P. (1968). Education and economic development. *Review of Educational Research*, *38*(3), 213–230.

Svennilson, I. (1972). A note on his scientific achievement and a bibliography of his contributions to economics. *The Swedish Journal of Economics*, *74*(3), 313–332. doi:10.2307/3439072

Teal, F. (2011). Higher education and economic development in Africa: A review of channels and interactions. *Journal of African Economies*, *20*(3), 50–79.

Werther, W. B. Jr, Ruch, W. A., & McClure, L. (1986). *Productivity through people*. St. Paul, MN: West Publishing.

Worrall, J. (1989). Structural realism: The best of both worlds? *Dialectica*, *43*(1-2), 99–124. doi:10.1111/j.1746-8361.1989.tb00933.x

KEY TERMS AND DEFINITION

Educational Reforms: It is the name given to nation's goal of changing public education mainly to meet new priorities and objectives.

Emigration: The emigration of highly skilled personnel from one's own country to settled indefinitely in another country.

Globalisation: The process by which the world is assuming a new level of interconnection largely because of trade, technological advancement and cultural exchange.

Human Capital: The inherent personal attributes, expertise, skills expressed in the capability to perform a task in order to produce economic value.

Human Resource Development: Human resource development is the incorporated use of organisation, training, and professional development efforts to enhance personal, group, and organizational effectiveness.

Workforce: The available labour pool ready to offer their skills or expertise to an organization or job.

Chapter 8
Closing the Gender Gap in Human Capital Formation for the Fourth Industrial Revolution

Tinuke Fapohunda
Department of Industrial Relations and Human Resources Management, Lagos State University, Ojo, Nigeria

ABSTRACT

Disparities in gender calculations in several nations have originated turbulence in multinational platforms in the recent past. The United Nations Sustainable Development Goals list gender equality and women empowerment as the fifth of the eight goals. This study scrutinizes the gender gaps in human capital formation. It demonstrated the economic cost of gender inequality in human capital formation (losses in human capital attributable to gender inequality are estimated at $160.2 trillion) and considered some clear-cut involvements that can ease the realization of greater equality. To boost women's human capital formation, investments throughout the life cycle are obligatory. Successful involvements can be affected to tackle time use restrictions, support access to productive assets, and resolve market and institutional disappointments that reprimand women. Spending on girls and women is indispensable not only to boosting gender equality and the changing wealth of nations but also allowing nations to grow in maintainable manners.

DOI: 10.4018/978-1-5225-9810-7.ch008

INTRODUCTION

Human capital refers to the knowledge and skills people possess that allow them to generate value in the global economic system. It is not delineated exclusively through formal education and skilling; rather it could be improved ultimately throughout people's existences, increasing by being utilized - and reducing with non-utilization. The initiative and inventiveness at our combined disposal as human beings present us with the ways of tackling the huge contemporary tests and, significantly, to create a future characterized by additional inclusiveness and centred on human beings. Nevertheless, frequently, arising from inequity or idealistic and archaic convictions by policymakers, human potential remains unrealized and hindered.

Compared to almost any other feature, the way countries develop their human capital could constitute a more significant determinant of their long-term accomplishment. The global human capital report 2017 suggests a novel standard for leaders to build potential labour forces. The approach is founded on the belief that everyone merits identical prospects to develop their talents and it offers managers and leaders the devices for piloting the transformations already being observed from contemporary automation and effectively plots a course to transit to the fourth industrial revolution. The global human capital report observes that at national levels, there are human capital formation gaps which are largest in South Asia and Sub-Saharan Africa. Human capital is vital both to national productivity and the operation of political, social and civic foundations. Consequently, appreciating the present position and capability is important to a broad range of stakeholders. Essentially, this chapter centres on scrutinizing divergence in human capital formation outcomes by gender and examines the way forward in closing the existing gender gaps in human capital formation for the fourth industrial revolution. the chapter begins with an introduction and background to the study, and then discusses the purpose of this chapter. This is followed by a literature review which reviews three contemporary theories of human capital formation namely: the modernization theory, the dependence theory and the human capital theory, the concept of human capital formation, the significance of human capital formation in economic and national development and then the antecedents of gender gap in human capital formation. It also includes implications, solutions and recommendations and finally conclusion and future areas of research.

BACKGROUND

World Bank (2016) reports that globally, studies indicate that gender inequality has a tendency to dawdle economic development and further compound, the ascension from poverty. A nation's economy is jeopardized if the female half of its populace is without equal access to the economic contribution process. The economic price of gender gaps is high, because besides reducing the women's wellbeing, it also diminishes that of males and children and ultimately obstructs economic development. Blackden et al. (2016) developed a model where gender inequality has an adverse effect on asset accrual and factor productivity and affects economic development. Eliminating extremely qualified girls from the educational process, consequences in a decline in the broad typical quantity of human capital. Besides, limiting female education originates a decline in the human capital of the next generation because women's educational accomplishment has a tendency to considerably reduce child mortality and fertility. Studies on the causative influence of gender gaps on economic growth like King, Klasen, and Porter (2008) and World Bank (2016) indicate a significant negative effect of gender disparity on economic growth. The negative signs are attributable to an enormous gender gap in education, which could be regarded as a substitute for backwardness. The largest component of a country's wealth typically resides in her people. Singer (2018) affirms that worldwide, women comprise merely 38 percent of human capital wealth as against 62 percent for men. Two key dynamics cause women to have reduced incomes and poorer human capital wealth in contrast to men: inferior labour force participation rates and fewer hours worked in the labour market, and lesser pay. Owing partly to social norms consigning women to unpaid care and informal occupation, these dynamics keep many women in productivity ensnare. Lifelong investments are obliged to guarantee that both women and men gain equivalent access to openings and supplies and to increase women's earnings and human capital formation.

Successful involvements can be realized to awaken employment prospects and incomes for women. This comprises: decreasing the amount of time spent in unpaid labour and reallocating care duties; enhancing right of entry to and power over productive assets and tackling market and institutional frustrations. UNECA (2014) observes that ending gender inequity by investing in girls and women is crucial to enhancing the transforming wealth of nations and facilitating the development of countries in sustainable ways. High-quality human capital constitutes a vital element of economic viability worldwide because it is a central motivator of economic wealth and comfort in all countries. Consequently, economic literature repeatedly highlights numerous facets of human capital embracing in addition gender concerns and disparities in labour market results of both men and women.

The Purpose

No nation can attain sustainable development by overlooking and locking up the minds of over half of its population. There is an enormous wealth of human abilities globally. The resourcefulness and imagination at a people's disposal offers the way to deal with the huge challenges of our time and resolutely build a future that is more all-encompassing and human centric. Most often, human prospect is hampered either by inequality or impractical and obsolete beliefs by policymakers that investment in only little sub divisions of highly skilled human resources can compel sustainable, comprehensive growth. In the 1995 Beijing Declaration agreed to at the fourth World Conference on Women, participating Governments articulated their obligations "to move forward the goals of equality, development and peace for all women universally in the interest of humanity". This study focuses on examining the variance in human capital formation outcomes by gender and looks at how to close the subsisting gender gaps in human capital formation for the Fourth Industrial Revolution.

CONTEMPORARY THEORIES OF HUMAN CAPITAL FORMATION

This chapter reviews three contemporary theories of human capital formation namely: the modernization theory, the dependence theory and the human capital theory.

The Modernization Theory

Modernization Theory centres on the way education changes a person's values, principles and attitudes. Through experience obtained in modernizing establishments, like schools contemporary values and mind-sets are instilled in individuals. These attitudes comprise candidness to innovative ideas, autonomy from conventional authority, readiness to chart and analyze future requirements and a developing sagacity for individual and social effectiveness. The modernization thinkers such as Meier (1995) and Uwatt (2003) posit that these normative and attitudinal transformations persist all through the life cycle, everlastingly modifying a person's affiliation to the social arrangement. The more the amount of citizens open to the elements of modernizing organizations, the better the altitude of personal modernity achieved by the society. The speed of a nation's modernization and economic development becomes accelerated as soon as a significant part of the populace is transformed in this manner. In consequence, educational development by way of its consequences on personal principles and gains position the essential building blocks for a more dynamic labour force and for sustained economic development.

The Dependence Theory

Marxist conceptualizations constitute the foundation of the dependence theory. It originated from the dynamics of the world structure that configures that provision for economic revolutions in both the nucleus and border of the world economy is supported by human capital formation. The dependence theory contends that the pervasiveness of foreign investment capital, the incidence of transnational conglomerates, and attentiveness to exportation of prime products and reliance on imported technologies and man-made goods limit lasting economic development. Nevertheless, some elements of global polity could enhance economic enlargement in the developing world. Opponents of the theory refer to the proof of extensive unemployment and its unenthusiastic effects on economic growth. Also, they observe that educated persons with contemporary attitudes and values are sources of brain drain with its harmful effects on the reserve of trained human resources, prospective industrialists and, the rate of growth and development.

Several people have grown to be more guarded and sceptical regarding the assumed optimistic economic effect of education and human capital formation. For elevated human resources productivity, an essential part of technological advancement is outlays in human capital formation and this is called endogenous feature since accrual of physical capital is increased by the knowledge, skills, attitudes and health positions of the people who participate in those exercises. Consequently, there should be a significant and optimistic correlation between human capital formation and economic growth. An endogenous representation of economic growth proposes that endogenous features like government policies, political stability, market distortions, human capital etc., can considerably impinge on economic growth.

The Human Capital Theory

Human capital is the collective stock of a country's population that are available for the current and potential production and distribution of goods and services. UNECA (2014) asserts that it involves the knowledge, skill and attitudes obtainable in the country's human resources supply. Awopegba (2009) depicts human capital as the knowledge, skills, attitudes, physical and managerial effort needed to operate capital, technology, and land among other things, in order to produce goods and render services for human consumption. Human capital constitutes the entirety of human potentials in a nation's human resource stock and whose united effort, if appropriately developed and exploited, acquiesces elevated levels of labour productivity.

Studies like Schutlz (1992), Meier (1995) and Oladoyin (2010) initiated the conception that people invest in education to boost their reserve of human capital. Human capital is perceived as the accumulation of economically productive human capabilities, which can be shaped by merging inborn capabilities with investments in human beings. Human capital formation is distinguished as a creative investment in human capital, believed to be equally or even more valuable than that in physical capital. Human capital theorists like Schutlz, Becker and Mince institute that fundamental literacy boosts the efficiency of workers in low-skill jobs and additionally declare that a teaching that requires rational or critical reckoning, or offers technical and specialized knowledge, augments the marginal productivity of workers in high-skill posts. Human capital denotes the stock of competences, knowledge and personality attributes represented in the capacity to perform work in order to generate economic value.

Babalola (2015) emphasizes that the contribution of the human capital theory to economic thoughts and development arises from its capability to augment the productivity of existing human resources in diverse ways. Therefore, the Human Capital Theory seems to be the most prominent economic theory of Western education, positioning the outline of government policies since the early 1960's. It is perceived more and more as a significant function in economic performance. A vital approach in establishing economic performance has involved utilizing an idea of individuals as human capital. Fitzsimons (2006) observes that Smith, (1776) originated the foundation of what was later to develop into the science of human capital. A modern reformulation of the Human Capital Theory emphasizes the implication of education and training as the answer to involvement in the new global economy.

The OECD (2014) asserts that the drastic transformations to the public and private sectors of the economy initiated in modern times in reaction to globalization will be relentless and alarming to numerous instituted principles and methods. Foray and Lundvall (2016) note that, consistent with the Human Capital Theory, it has been argued that, the general economic performance of the OECD countries is progressively more openly founded on their knowledge stock and their learning capabilities. Undoubtedly, the OECD is endeavouring to create a novel function for education as regards the human capital subject needed in 'globalised' institutions. Furthermore, the Human capital theory initiates the investment risk of human capital which includes illiquidity and suppositions about reimbursement periods and opportunity cost. Moreover, the theory sees human beings as economic elements acting as their own economy. The role of human capital is commonly accepted in economic development, productivity analysis, innovation, public policy and evaluation.

Harbison (2014) affirms that Human capital constitutes the ultimate basis for the wealth of the nations. Capital and natural resources are passive factors of production; human beings are the active agents who accumulate capital, exploit natural resources, build social, economic and political organizations and carry forward national development. Schutlz (2004) affirms that irrespective of this awareness, most early economists nevertheless considered physical capital as the foremost constituent of a nation's productive wealth; and continued to consign natural and human resources to the background. Adamu (2003) indicates that reviving the importance of human capital took the effort of Schutlz and others which resulted in more current attempts to integrate investment in education into the typical economic analysis.

The Human Capital Theory has however been censured on several counts. In the Marxist renaissance of the 1960s, it was hit for legitimizing so-called bourgeois individualism, especially in the United States where the theory began and thrived. Again, it was accused of holding individuals culpable for the imperfections of the system, making counterfeit capitalists out of employees, and misrepresenting the real conflict of interest between the two. Nevertheless, even marking down these fundamentally political censures, the human-capital theory can be considered a species of rational-exchange theory and susceptible to a standard analysis, by sociologists, of individualist rationalizations of economic ideas.

The most obvious declaration of the deficits of the human capital theory goes to the heart of neo-classical economics. The revival of economic sociology, especially by Block (1990), aims to dispute the fundamental postulations motivating the methodology of neo-classical economics. Block (1990) maintains that this is hinged on crucial building blocks. One is the suggestion that the economy is an analytically separate realm of society that can be understood in terms of its own internal dynamics. Economists are absolutely conscious that politics and culture control economy, but they distinguish these as exogenous dynamics that can be securely grouped as one develops a framework that centres on solely economic factors.

The human capital theory constitutes a contemporary expansion of Adam Smith's clarification of wage disparities by the so-called net (dis)advantages between diverse employments. Okojie (2014) observes that the costs of learning the job constitutes a very vital element of net advantage and has made economists like Gary Becker and Jacob Mince to maintain that, all things being equal, personal incomes differ in line with the amount of investment in human capital. Another expectation is that extensive investment in human capital generates in the labour-force the skill-base that is obligatory for economic growth. Any investment capable of assisting employees to increase productivity due to factors connected to their health, knowledge and experience is an investment in human capital. Even in economics, censors of the human-capital theory allude to the complexity of measuring significant concepts, like future income and the central thought of human capital itself. Not every investment in education assures a progress in productivity as evaluated by employers or the market. Particularly, there is the quandary of measuring both worker productivity and the future income connected to career openings, apart from near-tautological manner by reference to actual earnings disparities which the theory claims to elucidate. Olaniyi (2010) affirms that empirical studies have proposed that, while several of the detected disparities in incomes are probably attributable to skills learned, the percentage of unexplained difference remains elevated, and has to be a characteristic of the imperfect structure and functioning of the labour-market, sooner than of individual productivities comprising the labour supply.

HUMAN CAPITAL FORMATION

Studies like Odia (2007), Kerr (2001) and Akintayo (2007) submit that human capital formation is the process of building the human skills, the work habits and capacity for productive employment. Human capital formation is the procedure of developing the skills, knowledge and the competencies of all the people of the society and which are required in the labour market for the production of goods and services. UNDP (2012) delineates human capital formation as the process of developing people's options, by increasing human functioning and competencies. The fundamental constituents of human capital formation include: leading a long and healthy life, being well-informed, and having right of entry to resources necessitated for a respectable standard of living. Okojie (2014) affirms that human capital formation involves the process of attaining and enhancing the number of persons with the skills, education and understanding that are vital for the economic growth and development of a nation. It is therefore linked with investment in man and his development as an ingenious and dynamic individual.

Human capital formation should include practically the entire populace as its object. It is a lifelong process, which is compulsory for any society desirous of surviving under the intricate dares of a dynamic world. Previously, economic development programmes principally in developing economies, greatly highlighted, and struggled for, speedy economic growth with the belief that economic growth is tantamount to economic development. Significantly, human beings and their potentials were regarded simply as factors of production of economic growth. Disparities and poverty among a few sectors of the population were frequently deemed as obligatory prices of economic growth and development.

Nevertheless, in contemporary times, there is the recognition that such restricted visions of development were more injurious in the procedure of sustainable economic development. Consequently, a methodical and human approach to development, which regards human capital formation as the core of any significant economic development programme has developed. In accepting this novel approach to development, different Human Development Reports (HDR) have since offered insightful and wide-ranging examination on the prospects and challenges of human capital formation, encouraging policy discuss and proffering policy suggestions for both worldwide and nationwide actions. At the national level, countries are persuaded to develop a procedure of enlarging alternatives and development potentials of the people in all economic, social and cultural activities for a more prosperous, more vigorous, more educated and significant life.

The human capital formation strategy constitutes a means of realizing the potentials of people by expanding their competencies and this unavoidably entails the empowerment of people, and facilitating their active participation in their own development. The disparities in the level of socio-economic development across nations are credited not really to endowments of natural and physical capital but to the quality and quantity of human capital. Human capital formation perks up the quality and productivity of human resources which, sequentially, results in economic growth.

Moreover, Harbison (2004) contends that performing as an imperative medium of attaining fair income distribution; human capital formation is in addition a powerful means of tackling the dilemma of poverty. Schutlz (2004) observes that the significance of human capital formation has been appreciated in the economic development process since the times of Adam Smith who particularly incorporated the acquired and useful abilities of all the citizens in his notion of fixed capital in addition to accentuating the significance of education at different points in the wealth of Nations. Alfred Marshall also underlined the significance of education as a national investment and, opined that the most valuable of all capital is that invested in the human beings.

Significance of Human Capital Formation in Economic and National Development

Kingsley (2011) proposes that the world is not inert and the technological advances in relation to the general unstable changing work environments are becoming a persistent phenomenon. As such, employees are obliged to renew their knowledge, skills and attitudes to function efficiently and to adhere to the tempo of innovative techniques of production, human relations, enhancement in their world view and communication system. Olaniyi (2010) states that human capital formation significantly persuades attainment of organizational goals. Furthermore, Hassan (2007), Shimry and Leohard (2012), Akintimile (2012) and Kingsley (2014) detail a significant correlation between human capital formation and skill utilization, improved morale, increased productivity and development of technology competence. Phillips and Thomas (2017) also state a positive influence of human capital formation on job stability and wage increment, especially when they obtained jobs relevant to the skills acquired. Investment in human capital enhances versatility, mobility and consciousness of unemployment opportunities, and the higher the level of education, the greater the contribution of the worker, to the national product. While in the procedure of economic growth, it is routine to place additional significance to the accrual of physical capital, currently it is progressively distinguished that the expansion of tangible capital stock relies to a substantial degree on human capital formation.

Studies by Schultz (1975, 2004), Harbison (1973), Denison (1996) and Becker (1994) disclose that a vital feature accountable for the speedy growth of the American economy has been the comparatively escalating expenditures on education. They contend that similar sums of money devoted to education, results in a larger enhancement in national income, than that depleted on tangible capital goods as evident in developing economies. The superior fraction of industrial growth is obtained not from additional capital investment, but from investment in men and development initiated by superior men. Technological knowledge and skills outline the society's intangible assets without which capital cannot be exploited productively. Education and human capital formation are thus perceived as national investments and the most important of all investment in capital is observed as that devoted to human beings. Ojo (2011) scrutinizes that studies carried out in the advanced countries like the USA, the defunct Soviet Union, Denmark and Japan during the period they accomplished speedy economic growth demonstrated a positive correlation between economic growths and the quantity and kind of human capital formation in the labour force of these countries. Human capital formation also played a prominent role in guaranteeing the resurgence of various countries that experienced extensive devastation of infrastructures in the World Wars. Previously, economists had been unsuccessful in recognizing the control of human capital in the production process and thus undervalued its import in post-war recovery. The enormous achievement of the Marshall plan (through which the United States pushed massive amounts of financial and material resources to the countries of Western Europe, to revitalize their economies after the World War II) exhibits the foremost role of human capital formation.

Comparatively, developing countries were unable to take in even a humble portion of such capital inflow; the strategic missing connection was linked to poor human capital formation. The same factor was accountable for the status of underdevelopment of the Organization of Petroleum Exporting Countries (OPEC) despite the financial bonuses which they got numerous times. The remarkable victory of the defunct Soviet Union in the post war race in arms and space Conquest illustrated palpably, the significance of human capital formation. Also underscoring the human capital formation factor in development is the exceptional success of countries like Japan and Israel, that boast modest natural resources, but copious highly trained human capital. More generally, developed countries have remained in the vanguard of global technological break-through owing largely to the availability of diverse classes of intelligence and scientific capabilities similarly, the technological gap between the developed and developing countries are expanding. All these corroborate that the larger fraction of industrial development is got, from investment in man and enhancements brought about by improved men.

Recently, there has been an obvious boost in the consideration for human capital formation. Specifically, a good deal of the spotlight has been on education and human capital formation with a necessitated apprehension about the enhancement of the quality of life for the individual. In Nigeria, the 2010-2015 National Development Plan, asserts that an imperative part of the labour force is its quality. Thus, it is not just the overall requisites but as well the right balance that is of importance in economic and national development.

Ojo (2011) affirms that the availability, organization and use of the resources determine the development of a country. The more advanced the level of education, the greater will be the contribution of employees to the national product. In contrast to physical capital, human capital formation is considered both as an investment and consumption good. This is attributable to the reality that outlays on human capital gratify wants directly, besides, the function of formation and maintenance of human skills. Raw human beings can be converted into productive 'human capital' by instilling skills obliged by the economy and increasing individual productivity, both to the market place and in the household. Fapohunda (2013) contends that human capital adds to national growth through its capacity to enhance the productivity of the population of the labour force resulting in boost in economic growth. Therefore, to eliminate economic diffidence and inculcate the capacities and motivations to progress, it is obligatory to augment the knowledge and skills of people. The necessity for investment in human capital consequently becomes of supreme significance. A dearth of apposite skills and knowledge represents a restricting feature to economic growth.

UNDP (2018) indicates that several countries, particularly in today's developing economies, continue to follow lanes to establishment of economic value by exclusively centring on maximizing exploitation of their people's existing human capital with modest consideration for skill diversification and acquiring more advanced expertise. The technological transformations engendered by the Fourth Industrial Revolution demands a very factual likelihood of disturbing such economic development corridors past all possibility. On the other hand, economic value creation in a rising number of developed economies is anchored in extremely specialized expertise although the jobs and sectors compelling these movements hazard leaving behind an increasing portion of the workforce.

Gender Gap in Human Capital Formation

A nation's population is typically approximately divided equally between males and females with the exception of atypical situations for example war or extremely selective immigration which usually influence males more than females. Nevertheless, throughout the ages, the distribution of power, wealth, influence, employment etc. between men and women has by no means been near equality. Formerly, a woman's economic position was delineated by that of her father or her husband. Women spent little, if any, years outside the parental or marital home. However, considerable transformations in marriage and divorce models have made it increasingly possible that a woman either offers substantive involvements to the household income or supplies the principal source of income. Women have joined the labour force in growing numbers. The World Bank (2016) reports that globally, studies designate that gender inequality has a propensity for delaying economic development and making the rise from poverty more complex. Evidently, a nation's economic development is jeopardized if the female half of its population is deprived of equal access to the economic contribution process. The economic price of gender gaps is thus great, since besides decreasing women's welfare it is also predisposed to weakening that of males and children and eventually frustrating economic development.

The World Bank (2016) reports that worldwide, women represent only 38 percent of human capital wealth as opposed to 62 percent for men. In low and lower-middle income countries, women represent a third or less of human capital wealth. The World Bank (2016) adds that on a per capita basis, gender inequality in earnings could initiate losses in wealth of $23,620 per person globally. The losses vary between regions and countries since degrees of human capital wealth, and thus losses in wealth attributable to gender inequality, is inclined to rise in absolute values with economic development. Universally, for the 141 countries incorporated in the World Bank Analysis, the forfeiture in human capital wealth as a result of gender inequality is estimated at $160.2 trillion by just assuming that women would earn as much as men. This is about double the value of GDP globally. This implies that globally, with gender equality in earnings, human capital wealth could increase by 21.7 percent and total wealth by 14.0 percent. These approximations of the costs of gender inequality are associated only with dissimilarities in lifetime labour earnings and consequently human capital affluence concerning women and men. Several other losses are connected to gender equality besides those estimated.

Women stand for roughly 50% of Nigeria's population and thus half of the labour force but a 2012 study by the Federal Office of Statistics designates that 32.8percent of Nigerian women age 16 and older were in the labour force compared with 23.4 percent in 2001. Fapohunda (2017) reports that, for the ten year period between 2007 and 2017, the average labour force participation rate (LFPR) was 60.3 percent for women and 74.2 percent for men. In 2016, the national labour force participation rate for women and men in the ages 15-64 years was 64.7 percent. The proportion of men was 82.6 percent while women accounted for 72.4 percent.

Collectively, women do as much work as men if not more but the natures of work in addition to the circumstances under which they work and their access to prospects for development varies from men. Women frequently, have drawbacks in access to employment openings and work stipulations; additionally, several women give up or limit employment owing to family duties. Fapohunda (2013) observes that bearing in mind the mounting chances that a woman is obliged to accept some if not all financial responsibility for herself and her children, her hopes for employment and earnings have become vital to the welfare of women and children. There has been substantial progress in expanding women's potentials, despite the fact that their involvement in economic and political decision making remains very restricted. As earlier observed, women involvement in the labour market has progressively enlarged and the gender gap in labour force involvement has remarkably reduced, nevertheless gender gaps in human capital formation continue to be significantly high. Even in the most developed nations, gender inequality has lingered as a live subject.

The world is bequeathed with an immense wealth of human capacity. Most frequently though, human potential is hindered either by inequality or an impractical and obsolete faith on the part of policymakers that investment in small sub sections of highly skilled labour alone can drive sustainable, inclusive growth. The Global Human Capital Report 2017 recommends an innovative benchmark for leaders to assemble the workforces of the future. The approach which derives from the belief that all people irrespective of gender, merit an equal opportunity to develop their talents, offer leaders the methods and the instruments to pilot the changes we are by now seeing from the contemporary wave of automation and successfully navigate the transition to the Fourth Industrial Revolution. The belief in the idea of human development strategy possibly encouraged the Federal Government of Nigeria, to pronounce in its guiding principles in the 2010-2013 economic policy that the economy exists for and belongs to the people, and at all times the general well-being of all the people shall be the proper measure of performance. It adds that the strategy to be utilized shall be to empower Nigerians in both rural and urban areas to become more economically productive, with a view to improving their quality of life. To avoid the errors of the past, projects and measures to be implemented must be people- oriented.

Managing the evolution to deeper investment in human prospects within the milieu of the Fourth Industrial Revolution is one of the most significant societal, economic and moral challenges being currently experienced. The development of education that fits future requirements, a labour force that boasts enhanced preparation for shifts in labour markets, chances for employment creation and structures that permit gains and opportunities to be distributed equally, despite gender, age or origin must be promoted. The Global Human Capital Report 2017 affirms that averagely, the world has developed only 62% of its human capital or, on the contrary, nations are ignoring or wasting, on average, 38% of their talent. Only 25 nations have tapped 70% or more of their people's human capital. In addition, 50 countries score between 60% and 70% while 41 countries score between 50% and 60%, and 14 countries remain below 50%, meaning these nations are currently leveraging less than half of their human capital. The leaders of the Human Capital Index are commonly economies with a venerable dedication to their people's educational achievement and that have positioned an extensive share of their workforce in skill-intensive occupations across a wide range of sectors. Predictably, they are principally today's high-income economies.

The human capital formation gap is smallest in North America and Western and Eastern Europe but largest in South Asia and Sub-Saharan Africa. According to the report economies such as Nigeria, countenance an array of human capital challenges, together with low levels of literacy and basic education. With an overall average score of 52.97, the Sub-Saharan African region is the lowest-ranked region in the Index. Nigeria, Sub-Saharan Africa's largest economy and most heavily populated country ranked in the lower midfield of the region, and has a comparatively large pool of tertiary-educated workers, particularly amongst its older generations, and reasonably strong staff training. Nevertheless, it concurrently evidences low primary and secondary education achievement across all age groups and one of the lowest current primary school enrolment rates globally, indicating exceptionally uneven human capital formation results and the untapped opportunities of pursuing a more inclusive human capital development approach.

In United Nations Intergovernmental milieus, the international community has made tough, comprehensive commitments to gender fairness and women's rights in access to and power over financial and monetary resources. Also, human rights pacts, schemes and machineries have dealt with the issues of women's admission to and control over resources. Governments nevertheless have the major responsibility for implementing these responsibilities. Robert (2014) designates that women in the paid labour force are differentiated by limited and uneasy employment panoramas and apparent poorer wages, pitiable employment situations, tremulous hours and unfavourable employment contracts. Women are predominantly employed in low income jobs or extremely small level systems that push them into secluded employments and boring labour-intensive production. Accomplishing gender equality portends remarkable advantages for the wellbeing and organization of women and girls'. Table 1 presents a tabulation of the analysis of losses from Gender Inequality by Region for the years 1995-2017.

Again it assists their families, societies, and nation in attaining complete development prospect. The Global Human Capital Report (2017) affirms that worldwide, women comprise only 38 percent of human capital wealth as opposed to 62 percent for men. In low- and lower-middle income countries, women comprise

Table 1. Losses from gender inequality by region, 1995-2017

	1995 ($ 2014)	2000 ($ 2014)	2006 ($ 2014)	2012 ($ 2014)	2017 ($ 2014)
East Asia & Pacific					
Loss in human capital ($ trillions)	34.2	35.8	37.7	42.1	49.9
Loss in human capital per capita ($)	18,627	18,450	18,663	20,130	23,253
% loss in total wealth	24.5%	22.1%	20.8%	17.1%	16.6%
Europe & Central Asia					
Loss in human capital ($ trillions)	32.4	36.3	37.2	38.8	41.6
Loss in human capital per capita ($)	39,892	44,511	45,045	46,261	48,884
% loss in total wealth	14.3%	14.8%	13.7%	13.0%	13.3%
Latin America & Caribbean					
Loss in human capital ($ trillions)	7.3	5.9	6.5	6.7	6.7
Loss in human capital per capita ($)	15,500	11,558	11,945	11,468	10,940
% loss in total wealth	14.3%	10.5%	10.2%	8.8%	7.9%
Middle East & North Africa					
Loss in human capital ($ trillions)	1.6	2.1	2.4	2.7	3.1
Loss in human capital per capita ($)	9,275	11,261	11,220	11,150	11,757
% loss in total wealth	10.2%	11.8%	9.9%	7.7%	7.4%
North America					
Loss in human capital ($ trillions)	43.4	55.1	51.3	43.3	47.2
Loss in human capital per capita ($)	146,791	175,923	156,600	126,052	133,299
% loss in total wealth	18.8%	19.5%	16.3%	13.3%	13.5%
South Asia					
Loss in human capital ($ trillions)	3.3	4.6	6.5	7.4	9.1
Loss in human capital per capita ($)	2,664	3,383	4,374	4,613	5,405
% loss in total wealth	28.8%	32.2%	35.0%	29.4%	29.4%
Sub-Saharan Africa					
Loss in human capital ($ trillions)	1.1	1.1	1.0	1.9	2.5
Loss in human capital per capita ($)	2,016	1,927	1,435	2,480	2,914
% loss in total wealth	7.6%	8.8%	6.3%	9.8%	11.4%

Source: Wodon (2018, p. 34)

a third or less of human capital wealth. The report states that, on a per capita basis, gender inequality in human capital formation, could initiate losses in wealth of $23,620 per person worldwide. These losses vary between regions and countries owing to levels of human capital formation and wealth, and thus losses in prosperity attributable to gender inequality, has a tendency to increase in total values with economic development.

The report adds that because of these explanations, in absolute terms the losses are biggest in OECD countries. As shown in Table 1, globally, for all the countries incorporated in the 2017 analysis, the loss in human capital wealth due to gender inequality in human capital formation is approximated at $160.2 trillion by merely presupposing that women would earn as much as men. The Global Human Capital Report 2017 observes that this $160.2 trillion is about double the value of GDP globally. Put in another way, human capital wealth could increase by 21.7 percent globally, and total wealth by 14.0 percent with gender equality in Human Capital Formation. These estimates of the losses from gender inequality are related only to differences in human capital formation and wealth between women and men.

Antecedents of Gender Gap in Human Capital Formation

Gender inequality makes women and girls powerless in behaviours that dispossess them of their fundamental human rights. Such deficiency in prospects for girls and women bring about great economic costs for them, their households and countries. The position of women continues to be subordinate to that of men. The typical educational accomplishment for girls' continues to be lesser than for boys and adult women are less educated than men. Moreover, prejudices and social norms outline the conditions of female labour force participation. Women have less probability than men to participate in the labour force and to work for pay and when they do, there is a greater tendency for them to work part-time, in the informal sector, or in jobs that have lower compensation. These drawbacks turn into considerable gender gaps in human capital formation and earnings, which eventually reduce women's negotiating power and voice. Besides, several girls are married or have children prior to the age of 18, ahead of their being physically and emotionally ready to become wives and mothers. Das Gupta (2007) emphasizes that there has long been significant anxiety over the obvious gender inequalities in human capital formation and outcomes in numerous developing countries. Sen (2018) avows that in India for example, the female adult literacy rate is only 48%, in contrast to 73% for men.

Extremely archaic divergences in the gender allotment of economic and monetary resources have positioned women at a disadvantage in contrast to men in their ability to undertake, subscribe to and gain from more extensive human capital formation and development processes. Deeply instituted differences continue owing to unjust customs and practices, despite significant development on several components of women's economic empowerment despite improvements in educational accomplishment and share of paid work. Additionally, the pace of revolution has been lethargic and uneven particularly across regions in the same country. Moreover, gender inequality persists because women are constantly omitted from vital decision-making roundtables deciding the allocation of financial and pecuniary resources and outlooks.

Again, a nation's response to economic recession principally by way of slashes in public expenditures on health and education along with increased risk of reductions in allocations to gender parity and women's empowerment often boasts unequal consequences for women and girls, probably reversing gains achieved. In addition, Olomu (2014) proposes that national cultures differ regarding views of women's actual or probable inputs to the paid labour force. Cultural stereotypes regarding women may possibly take a momentous position in shaping the educational, legal, and organizational panoramas offered to women. Thomas (2013) and Oloko (2015) assign a discrimination against women in the majority of organisations in Nigerian organisations mainly concerning the ranks and the autonomy billed to them. Ikpe (2013) insists that most employers prefer to employ men more readily than women principally in positions that oblige either characteristic intellect or those characterized by technology, and where women are employed, the level of sustenance they obtain from colleagues is normally low. Routinely, women have been quick to be home keepers and mothers and where they worked, it was not expected that such employment would be external to the home. The cultural system in Nigeria believes that while men must be overriding and powerful, women are expected to exhibit obedient and dependent traits. Even so the world is rapidly changing and an excellent modification is in the province of women emancipation, which demands the coming out of women from the seclusion of their homes to business activities outside the home.

By accomplishing gender equality in human capital formation, countries can enhance their human capital assets, and in so doing their total affluence considerably. This would facilitate them reinforcing the sustainability of their growth conduit. Also among the major factors that cause women not to have as much of human capital wealth as men involves inferior labour force participation speeds and less hours worked in the labour market, and poorer pay. These factors keep countless women in efficiency ensnare owing partly to social customs consigning them to unpaid care and informal work. Investments right through the life cycle is required to enhance women's human capital formation and wealth.

IMPLICATIONS

The foregoing implies that some issues are possibly prominent from the several explanations for the huge disparities between men and women in human capital formation and wealth. One is that, men boast superior labour force participation levels compared to women and they are inclined to work more hours in paid work.

Women are predisposed to work on average more hours than men generally, however a much better portion of this endeavour is committed to unpaid work, therefore they are inclined to boast poorer human capital and earnings. Also, men are apt to earn more than women hourly at work. While there is improvement, in the last twenty years towards decreasing disparity in educational achievement between boys and girls, the gender gaps in human capital formation that still subsist for adults is moreover owing to disparities in educational attainment between men and women, which are frequently themselves owing partly to profoundly ingrained social norms that are still very much pertinent nowadays.

Globally, there is an immense wealth of human talent and the cleverness and creativeness at the joint disposal of all humanity offers the means of tackling contemporary grand and, decisively to building a more comprehensive and human centric prospect. However, owing to inequity or an unworkable and obsolete faith by policymakers that investment in minute sub sections of highly skilled labour only can compel sustainable, comprehensive growth human potential is unrealized or hampered. To develop future workforces this study suggests a novel standard for leaders. Founded on the belief that all people merit equivalent chances to develop their talents, the approach this study sponsors, presents leaders with the means and the implements to steer the transformations already being observed in the contemporary wave of automation and effectively pilot the shift to the Fourth Industrial Revolution. A mainly imperative political, societal, economic and moral tests being faced today is managing this evolution towards deeper investment in human potential within the context of the Fourth Industrial Revolution. This chapter encourages the development of education that matches future requirements, a workforce with improved preparation for shifts in labour markets, opportunities for job creation and structures that permit equal distribution of gains and opportunities, not considering gender, age or origin. It presents the most recent knowledge for more enlightened decision-making. The ways in which nations develop their human capital can constitute a more vital determinant of their long-term accomplishment than almost any other factor.

SOLUTIONS AND RECOMMENDATIONS

Technological transformations and its influence on employment markets require a restored spotlight on the methods of global human capital formation and leverage for social well-being and economic wealth for everyone including women. Ageing economies will countenance a historical cycle earliest, as increasingly more of their populations cross into the 65 and over age group and the labour forces contract more, obliging an improved incorporation of minority groups like female workers.

Regardless of the prospective theoretical vagueness, a lot of studies like Kishor (2005), Agnihotri, Palmer-Jones and Parikh 2012 and Qian (2013) report that increased female labour force participation and human capital formation are undeniably related to improved human capital and continued existence results for girls. The World Gender Development Report (2012) puts forward that the divergences emanate from: disparate allocation of time use and career duties between men and women and between domestic and public/private service provision; imbalanced access to and management of productive assets; and market and institutional malfunctions (right of entry to information and networks, legal and economic hindrances, restraining social norms). These distinctions could influence all women, be they wage workers, farmers, or self-employed workers/entrepreneurs. The disparities also frequently reciprocally strengthen each other and initiate efficiency ensnares for women. This is expensive for the women, their family units, communities, and societies as exhibited by the approximations of the losses in human capital formation and wealth from gender inequality. Besides, the disparities symbolize a severe discouragement to investments in tomorrow's women. To help lessen the disparities in human capital formation between men and women potential policies to be adapted could comprise several initiatives.

The first is investments throughout the life cycle. Successful involvements can be executed in numerous parts to advance employment prospects, human capital formation and eventually earnings for women. This consists of: decreasing time depleted in unpaid work (especially subsistence and domestic work) and reallocating care responsibilities; enhancing right of entry to and rule over productive asset (principally land, credit, insurance, savings and major skills); and tackling market and institutional malfunctions (like admittance to information and networks, legal and monetary obstacles, and limiting social standards). As UNDP (2018) suggests, more extensive investments in women (and men) along the life cycle might assist in improving accumulation of human capital more commonly. Winkler (2016) notes that within an economic examination structure, a woman's choice to join the labour force is primarily established by factors that concern her reservation wage (the remuneration at which she is prepared to join the labour market), and factors that concern the wage she can receive in the market. The reservation wage fluctuates openly with the availability of market alternatives for household production and technology; inversely with the husband's (or other earners) earnings. Connecting the proceeds from increased female labour force participation with activities creating more earnings implies levelling the playing field and dealing with the prospectively complex re allotment of time between paid employment and other activities plus unrelenting and invasive gender disparities in output and earnings across diverse segments and jobs.

Next is to deal with time use constraints. Practically all societies have a division of labour founded on gender norms which involves women concentrating on reproductive work and men in productive work. Rubiano and Viollaz (2018) reports that a current evaluation of time use surveys from 19 countries demonstrates important distinctions in the manner women and men distribute their daily time between leisure, unpaid work (domestic tasks and child/elderly care) and labour market employment. Typically, women expend about 5 hours in unpaid domestic work, 2.3 hours in labour market work while men expend 5hours in labour market work and 1.9 hours in unpaid domestic work. Earlier work employing time use data for sub-Saharan Africa like Blackden and Wodon, (2006) had similar results. Consequently, to release a considerable quantity of time for women to partake in labour market work and human capital formation, unpaid work would have to be recognized, reduced and redistributed. Again, as Estache and Wodon (2014) affirm, the function of infrastructure in releasing useful time for women has long been distinguished so at home, access to fundamental infrastructure services and child and elderly care services can liberate woman's time.

Access to fundamental infrastructural services adds to women's economic empowerment by adding to the duration of the work day, decreasing time for domestic work and providing home-based business prospects. World Bank (2003) affirms that in Morocco, in an area where a project was intended to decrease the weight of girls customarily concerned with fetching water to enhance their school attendance, the girls' school turnout rose by 20 percent in four years. Reimo et al. (2017) found that the provision of child care in Latin America enhanced female employment and human capital formation by between 10 and 30 percent. International Finance Corporation (2017) suggests that affiliations and teamwork between the public and private sectors and civil society organizations can facilitate the provision of inexpensive and excellent child care provided that the expenditures on provision do not negatively influence women's employment prospects.

Studies in both developing and developed countries demonstrate a negative relationship between travel time and women's participation in the labour force and by extension human capital formation. Black et al. (2014) reports that in the United States, an addition of a minute to travel time in urban areas is linked to a 0.3 percentage point reduction in women's labour force participation. Also flexible schedules and mode of work, and legislation on retirement ages can all make a difference in the workplace. Policies that facilitate workers balancing paid work and family tasks include parental leave. The prospect for workers to resume their pre-leave jobs or employers not only amplifies labour force participation but assists employees preserve firm-specific human capital. Workplace flexibility also helps workers balance the requirements of paid employment and family duties. However, for both leave and flexible work arrangements, it is imperative to guarantee the involvement of both women and men and to standardize the liberality of leave/ flexibility and reduce possible disadvantages for women as regards more dawdling career development or occupational segregation. It must be noted though that as Fapohunda (2017) reports, in several developing nations like Nigeria, flexibility is only obtainable in the informal sector where women are inclined to be concentrated in those jobs that are frequently the only jobs allowing them (though at an elevated outlay in foregone income) to stabilize income-creation and family duties. Market and institutional failures also have to be resolved. In broad terms, market failures are circumstances where markets do not produce most favourable resource allotments while institutional failures denote organizations not performing appropriately and consequently not accomplishing their assignments. Both kinds of malfunctions can be enveloping with prospectively severe inferences for gender inequality. Access to information to tackle occupational segregation and human capital formation gaps can also aid improvement in gender equality. Campos et al (2015) designates that access to information concerning probable profits for women in male-dominated areas can facilitate female entrepreneurs cross over and sector shifts, in as much as they in addition get support from male mentors in the field and can withstand sexual harassment and barriers to access credit. Another imperative area for restructuring is legal and economic structures. This embraces labour market policies meant to guarantee equal opportunities in the labour market like anti-discrimination laws and the abolition of laws limiting women's labour force participation and human capital formation in several sectors. This chapter centres on the correlation between gender variation in human capital formation and economic growth. It maintains the UNPF point that economic growth and social equality should ensue concurrently, since gender inequality sets boundaries on individual growth, national development, and societal advancement. Enhancements to gender equality increases employment rates and GDP per capita.

In developing economies like Nigeria, establishing substantiated underlying relationships between gender inequality in human capital formation and a country's growth and development has been tough on account of dearth in available sex-disaggregated data. But the growth with equity approach to economic growth articulates that the method of 'growth first and then agonizing about equity later' generates a spurious option and contains human development. It presents the pledge of more rapid decline in poverty and inequity, permitting more of the poor (who are mostly women) to have access to productive and stable occupations, improved health and literacy, greater earnings and augmented hopes of contributing dynamically in the life of their societies. Hence, growth with equity especially in human capital formation supports national advancement from merely enlarging earnings to achieving higher levels of human development.

To achieve sustainable and rapid economic growth which would inspire structural transformation of the economy especially for the Fourth Industrial Revolution; gender equality must be dealt with headfirst. Government are obliged to dedicate to plans to advance standards of education, generate employment prospects, and decrease the impediments that instigate gender inequality in admittance to education and employment, in an endeavor to provoke appropriate productivity that is obligatory for the realization of the much wanted economic growth.

FUTURE AREAS OF RESEARCH

This study has focused on discussing improvement in gender equality in education, income, and female labor-force participation result from a development process in which the driving force for technological progress is the increase in the average level human capital. A consideration of the contemporary situation human capital and capacity is important to a wide variety of stakeholders because human capital is significant both to societal productivity and the functioning of its political, social and civic institutions, the beliefs that this paper can offer support to stakeholders like governments, businesses, education providers and civil society groups in identifying major areas for focus and investment. Future research could address areas of the roles that sexism and stereotyping play in human capital formation, and the way in which these interact with other processes to contribute to impeding women from education and human capital formation. Such research could also examine whether other minority groups, which are also under-represented in the national growth and development (and that may share stereotypes with women), are correspondingly at risk of being excluded from education and human capital formation.

CONCLUSION

This chapter examines how to close the gender gaps in the area of human capital formation and underlines the disparities in human capital formation as a constituent of current life. It exhibited the economic cost from gender inequality in human capital formation and wealth; and appraised some of the wide plans and precise involvements that can facilitate the attainment of greater equality. The financial case for investing in girls and women is now extremely strong. Losses in human capital attributable to gender inequality are estimated at $160.2 trillion. To boost women's incomes and human capital formation, investments throughout the life cycle are required. Successful involvements can be executed to tackle time use limitations, assist access to productive assets, and resolve market and institutional disappointments that punish women. Removing the obstacles and inequalities that women face regarding employment and human capital formation is a step towards realizing their potential in the economy and enhancing their contribution to economic and social development. Putting an end to gender inequality in human capital formation by spending on girls and women is indispensable to boosting the changing wealth of nations and allowing nations to grow in maintainable manners. This not only makes economic sense, it also constitutes the correct thing to do.

REFERENCES

Adamu, P. A. (2003). Tariff policy and the development of Nigeria's Manufacturing sector. In *The Structure Growth and development of the Nigerian economy*. Essays in Honour of T.M. Yesufu. Iyoha.

Agnihotri, S., Palmer-Jones, R., & Parikh, A. (2012). Missing women in Indian Districts: A quantitative analysis. *Structural Change and Economic Dynamics*, *13*(3), 285–314. doi:10.1016/S0954-349X(02)00023-1

Akintayo, D. I. (2007). Access to education, manpower development and job performance effectiveness of workers: The relevance of distance education programmes in Oyo and Lagos State of Nigeria. *Trends in Educational Studies Journal*, *2*(1), 29–41.

Akintimile, M. (2012). Women empowerment and economic development. *Journal of Economic Literature*, *50*(4), 1051–1079. doi:10.1257/jel.50.4.1051

Awopegba, P. O. (2009). *Human resources, high level manpower and the development of the Nigerian economy*. Lagos: Processed.

Babalola, J. (2015). Investment in human capital and personal income distribution. *Journal of Political Economy*, *66*(4), 281–302.

Becker, G. S. (1994). Human capital (3rd ed.). Chicago: The University of Chicago Press.

Black, D., Kolesnikova, N., & Taylor, L. (2014). Why do so few women work in New York (and so many in Minneapolis)? Labor supply of married women across U.S. cities. *Journal of Urban Economics*, *79*, 59–71. doi:10.1016/j.jue.2013.03.003

Blackden, M., Canagarajah, S., Klasen, S., & Lawson, D. (2016). *Gender and growth in Sub-Saharan Africa*. UNU-WIDER Research Paper No. 2006/37. Accessed on 17th January, 2019 at http://www.rrojasdatabank.info/rp2006-37.pdf

Blackden, M., & Wodon, Q. (2006). *Gender, time use, and poverty in sub-Saharan Africa*. World Bank Working Paper No. 73. Washington, DC: The World Bank.

Block, J. (1990). Family size, outcomes for children, and gender disparities. *Economic and Political Weekly*, *28*(1), 1811–1821.

Campos, F. M., Goldstein, L., McGorman, A. M., Boudet, M., & Pimhidzai, O. (2015). *Breaking the Metal Ceiling: Female Entrepreneurs Who Succeed in Male-dominated Sectors in Uganda. Africa Gender Innovations Lab*. Washington, DC: The World Bank. doi:10.1596/1813-9450-7503

Das Gupta, M. (2007). Selective Discrimination against Female Children in Rural Punjab, India. *Population and Development Review*, *13*(1), 77–100. doi:10.2307/1972121

Denison, D. (1996). What is the difference between organizational culture and organizational climate? A native's point of view on a decade of paradigm wars. *Academy of Management Review*, *27*(3), 619–654. doi:10.5465/amr.1996.9702100310

Estache, A., & Wodon, Q. (2014). *Infrastructure and Poverty in sub-Saharan Africa*. New York: Palgrave Macmillan. doi:10.1057/9781137348487

Fapohunda, T.M. (2017). An exploration of the effects of work life balance on productivity. *Journal of Human Resources Management and Labor Studies, 2*(2), 71-89.

Federal Office of Statistics. (2012). *Annual Abstract of Statistics* (2012 edition). Abuja: Author.

Fitzsimons, H. O. (2006). *Gender inequality, income and growth: are good times for women?* Washington, DC: The World Bank.

Foray, M., & Lundvall, Y. (2016). The gender gap, fertility, and growth. *The American Economic Review*, *126*(3), 374–387.

Harbison, F. H. (1973). *Human Resources as the Wealth of Nations*. London: OxfordUniversity Press.

Harbison, F. H. (2004). *Education Manpower and Economic Growth.* Delhi: Oxford & IBH Publication Co.

Harbison, F. H. (2014). Human resources development planning in modernization economics. *International Labour Review*.

Hassan, T. (2007). *Women and National Development: The Way Forward.* Ibadan: The Bama Mathal Lecture Radcliffe College.

Ikpe, D. (2013). *The world bank: development, poverty, and hegemony*. University of Kwazulu: National Press.

International Finance Corporation. (2017). *Tackling Childcare: The Business Case for Employer-supported Childcare*. Washington, DC: International Finance Corporation.

Kerr, A. (2001). The effect of bias on the advancement of working mothers: Disentangling legitimate concerns from inaccurate stereotypes as predictors of advancement in academe. *Human Relations*, *61*, 1677–1711.

King, E. M., Klasen, S., & Porter, M. (2008). *Gender and development challenge paper*. Paper Prepared for the 2008 Round of Copenhagen Consensus Project.

Kingsley, W. O. (2011). Work-life 'balance' in Nigeria. *Acta Sociologica*, *49*(4), 379–393.

Kingsley, W. O. (2014). *Globalization and employment generation. Evaluating the impact of trade on aggregate employment in Nigeria in Industrial Sector*. NES 2014 Annual Conference Nigeria.

Kishor, S. (2005). *Gender Differentials in Child Mortality in India: A Review of Evidence" in Women's Health in India*. Bombay: Oxford University Press.

Meier, G. M. (1995). *Leading Issues in Economic Development* (2nd ed.). Oxford, UK: Oxford University Press.

Mince, J. (2013). Occupational stress, work-home interference and burnout among Belgian veterinary practitioners. *Irish Veterinary Journal*, *61*(4), 233–241. PMID:21851711

Odia, G. (2007). *Gender equality as development framework of women integration in economic development. African Journal of Social and Policy Studies, 12(1).*

OECD, PISA. (2015). Results Universal Basic Skills: What Countries Stand to Gain. Author.

OECD. (2017). *Concepts, measurement and trends. Is Informal Normal? Towards More and Better Jobs in Developing Countries*. Paris: Jutting and Laiglesia.

Ojo, F. (2011). *Youth employment and youth employment programmes in Africa: The case of Nigeria, Addis Ababa, Jobs & Skills*. Presented at *UN Economic and Social Commission for Asia and the Pacific Conference*.

Okojie, P. (2014). *Gender poverty and educational human capital investment in Nigeria*. Nigerian Economic and Financial Review.

Oladoyin, R. D. (2010). *The role human capital development: an empirical study of Nigerian case, Oxford Business and Economics Conference Program*. Oxford, UK: St. Hugh's College, Oxford University.

Olaniyi, J. O. (2010). Implications of women's work for children's nutritional status in Sub Saharan Africa. *Social Science & Medicine, 56*(10), 2109–2121.

Oloko, R. (2015). Concept and measurement of Women's work in Nigeria and their implication for social change. In L. Olurode (Ed.), *Women and Social Change in Nigeria*. Lagos: Unity Publishing and Research Co.

Olomu, Y. (2014). The role of psychological well-being in job performance: A fresh look at an age-old quest. *Organizational Dynamics, 33*(4), 338–351.

Phillips, D., & Thomas, G. (2017). *Within and between gender disparities in income and education: Benefits from Democracy*. IZA Discussion Paper Series, No. 3221. Institute for the Study of Labor (IZA). Retrieved from ftp:// repec.iz.org/RePEc/ Discussionpaper/dp3221.pdf

Qian, N. (2013). Missing women and the price of tea in China: The effect of sex specific earnings on sex imbalance. *The Quarterly Journal of Economics, 123*(3), 1251–1285. doi:10.1162/qjec.2008.123.3.1251

Reimo, A. M., & Revenga, A. A. (2017). What works for women's work. Washington, DC: The World Bank.

Robert, T. (2014). The (perceived) returns to education and the demand for schooling. *The Quarterly Journal of Economics*, *25*(2), 515–548.

Rubiano, M. E., & Viollaz, M. (2018). *Gender Differences in Time Use: Allocating Time between the Market and the Household*. Washington, DC: The World Bank.

Schultz, T. (2004). Investments in the schooling and health of women and men quantities and returns. *The Journal of Human Resources*, *28*(1).

Schultz, T. P. (1992). *Human Capital and Economic Development*. New Haven, CT: Economic Growth Center, Yale University.

Schultz, T. W. (1975). Investment in human capital. *The American Economic Review*, *51*(1), 1–17.

Sen, A. (2018). More than 100 Million Women are Missing. *The New York Review of Books*, (December): 2018.

Shimry, T. J., & Leohard, Y. (2012). *Schooling, Experience, and Earnings*. New York: NBER Press.

Singer, H. L. (2018). Impact of education and health on employment. *European Journal of Administrative Sciences, 13*(18).

Smith, A. (1776). *The Wealth of Nations*. Harmondsworth, UK: Penguin.

Thomas, D. (2013). Intra-household resource allocation: An inferential approach. *The Journal of Human Resources, 25*(4), 635–646. doi:10.2307/145670

UNDP. (2012). *Human Development Report 2012*. New York: Oxford University Press.

UNDP. (2012). *Human Development Report 2012: Work for Human Development*. UNDP.

UNDP Nigeria. (2018). Global Human Capital Report 2018. UNDP.

UNECA. (2014). *Africa Women's Report 2014*. UNECA.

United Nations Population Division. (2018). *World Population Prospects*. Revision. Author.

Uwatt, M. (2003). Human Resource Development and Economic Growth in Nigeria, 1960-2000 Human Resource Development in Africa. In *Selected Papers for 2002 NES Annual Conference*. Nigerian Economic Society.

Winkler, A. (2016). *Women's labor force participation. Family-friendly policies increase women's labor force participation, benefiting them, their families, and society at large*. IZA World of Labor, Paper 289.

Wodon, Q. (2018). *What Is the Cost of Gender Inequality in Lost Earnings? Global Estimates Based on the Changing Wealth of Nations. Mimeo*. Washington, DC: The World Bank.

World Bank. (2003). *Operationalizing the 2003 World Development Report: Conflict, Security and Development*. Washington, DC: The World Bank.

World Bank. (2016). *World Development Report 2016: Learning to Realize Education's Promise*. Washington, DC: The World Bank.

World Gender Development Report. (2012). *World Economic Forum*. The Global Gender Gap Report.

ADDITIONAL READING

Lange, G. M., Wodon, Q., & Carey, K. (2018). *The Changing Wealth of Nations 2018: Sustainability into the 21st Century*. Washington: The World Bank.

McKinsey Global Institute. (2015). *The Power of Parity: How Advancing Women's Equality Can Add $12 Trillion to Global Growth*. London: McKinsey Global Institute.

World Bank. (2012). *World Development Indicators*. New York: Oxford University Press.

KEY TERMS AND DEFINITIONS

Economic Development: The process a nation employs in improving then economic, political, and social wellbeing of its people.

Gender Equality: Involves treating everyone identically in terms of access to and control over resources and opportunities.

Gender Gap: The gap between men and women in education, health, politics, and economics, etc.

Human Capital: The stock of knowledge, skills abilities and attributes to perform to produce economic value.

Human Capital Formation: Transforming a country's citizens to workers with the capacity to efficiently produce goods and render services.

Occupational Segregation: Distribution of workers across and in occupations founded on demographic features like gender.

Sustainable Development: Development that is pro-poor, pro nature, pro jobs, pro-women, pro-men, and pro-children.

Women Empowerment: Women taking control over their lives; setting their own agenda, gaining skills, increasing self-confidence, solving problems, and developing self-reliance.

Chapter 9
Human Capital Formation for the Fourth Industrial Revolution:
The Role of Women

Paul Adjei Onyina
Pentecost University College, Ghana

ABSTRACT

This chapter focuses on the drivers of human capital development in the fourth industrial revolution by examining the role of women. It discusses the role of women in economic development since 570BC. Women are ignored in most important areas in society whereas men are found at the frontline. However, available empirical analyses suggest that when women are empowered, they are able to turn the tables in their favour. The chapter outlines development role played by selected women across time and uses data from studies to show poor representation of women on international bodies and parliamentary seats. Selected women that have led and continue to lead various countries all over the world are presented. This chapter argues that women are important stakeholders in economic freedom. The chapter suggests encouraging society and men in particular to help women become front line participants in the human capital development for the fourth industrial revolution.

DOI: 10.4018/978-1-5225-9810-7.ch009

INTRODUCTION

The world had witnessed production process going through changes over time. The changes are put into stages called industrial revolution. As Sentryo (2019) states, water and steam were used to automate production in the first industrial revolution, the second industrial revolution saw the use of electric energy to generate and manufacture in bulk, the third witnessed electronics and information technology to automate production. There is a fourth industrial revolution on going based on building upon the ideas of the third industrial revolution starting from the middle of the last century. However, the role of women in the earlier industrial revolutions is not well known.

Throughout history, women have made great contribution to development in various ways, but the role tend to be unnoticed in the earlier revolutions. As noted by Foundations for Western Culture (FWC, 2018), the First Industrial Revolution had different impact on women, however; were mostly employed to work under difficult conditions. Women from less wealthy families worked to earn income to feed their families from 6.00 am and end at 7.00 pm with only a lunch break of 45 minutes; some started to work even as children. As the FWC (2018) narrations show, women worked under dangerous conditions even in some situations women worked with men who were half-naked (in the coalmines) at a lower wage rate. Unfortunately, during the First Industrial Revolution, salaries paid depended on gender at the expense of women. Thus, women earned about a third or half of male counterparts. Low salaries to women and children benefited the employers who made "good" use by exploiting them.

Again, available evidence indicates that some women worked in the mines under harsh conditions; they wore belts around their waste with chains in between their legs joined to the carts that transported the coal into the pits. Despite these poor conditions, women worked hard to contribute to development in their era. Some societies relegate women to the background and ignored, thus, women are restricted in doing certain things and must obtain permission from their husbands before they can do certain things; once they are able to go beyond that, they are considered to be empowered (see Rahman, 2007, and Garikipati, 2008 for some findings on women empowerment). It is important to note that though women have not been at the forefront and have been abandoned in terms of leadership position; their contributions have been tremendous to economic development. In the light of this, the chapter is of the view that women's contributions to the human capital development of the Fourth Industrial Revolution, is very crucial such that all and sundry have to ensure that the hindrances are removed to allow their participation for better society. In the next section, the role played by selected women in economic development is outlined. The rationale is to portray the importance of women in development despite low recognition, and this low recognition must not continue.

ROLE OF SELECTED WOMEN IN HELPING SOCIETY IN ECONOMIC DEVELOPMENT OVERTIME

The role of selected women in their quest for helping society is outline in this section of the chapter. This intends to show that women play an important integral part of any society and must be included and recognized in the quest for development. Thus, the role of gender is portrayed here to be important from the beginning of creation. Here specific role played by selected women since 570BC are listed for readers to see the important role that women spearheaded years back and continue to play to date, and thus in the Fourth Industrial Revolution, women cannot be left out. Thus, highlights of various contributions by selected celebrated women whose efforts changed the world are portrayed, they have been grouped into: i) Women Right Activists and Humanitarians ii) Poets and Writers iii) Musicians and Actress iv) Politicians and Leaders – war leaders and queens v) Scientists and vi) Entrepreneurs. Unless otherwise stated, the study adopted the presentation below from Pettinger (2014). Though brief, what most of them did and to some extend how it affected humanity is provided. It ranges from 570 BC to date.

Women Right Activists and Humanitarians

The following are women who were able to change the world on women right activities and or affected people's life on humanitarian grounds. One of such womenwas Sojourner Truth_(1797 – 1883).She was an African-American abolitionist who championed the rights of women; delivered a celebrated extemporaneous speech in 1851 with the title "Ain't I a woman?". This speech provided in basic language equality between men and women.

Another one is Margaret Fuller_(1810 –1850).She was a women's right advocate. She authored a book *Women in the Nineteenth Century* (1845) which was very significant in ensuing that people's view about men and women changed. The book was credited among the pioneer feminist works. Her argument was that men and women were equal and there was no need for women to depend on men. This, in a way put gender issues on its rightful position. Harriet Beecher Stowe_(1811–1896) is another woman worthy to present. She led a campaign against slavery throughout her life. Along the same life and time wrote a novel "*Uncle Tom's Cabin*" which was a bestseller that became instrumental to the success of the anti-slavery campaign. Her achievements were so strong that Abraham Lincoln later commented that her writings played a significant role in the wake of the American civil war. Here is another hero, a woman leading the fight against slavery, which was anti-human.

Elizabeth Cady Stanton (1815–1902) is the next woman on the roll whose effort affected the world. She was an American social activist, and one of the leaders in the early women's rights movement. She was an influential person who assisted in the establishment of the early women's suffrage movements in the US. In 1848, she became famous as the writer of "*Declaration of Sentiment*".

We cannot leave out Florence Nightingale (1820–1910). Florence Nightingale was a British and a world-celebrated nurse believed to be the mother of nursing. During the Crimean War, she was influential in changing the responsibility and awareness of the nursing career. Her committed service won extensive approbation and was responsible for the considerable enhancement in the treatment of injured military men. In addition, Susan B. Anthony (1820–1906) follows. She was another anti-slavery campaigner in the American and fought for the endorsement of women's and employees rights. Her campaign started within the self-control movement and this persuaded the need for women to take part in an election. She travelled all over the US and presented numerous speeches with human rights as the focus.

Another one is Millicent Fawcett.(1846–1929). She was another leading suffragist and equal women rights activist. Fawcett was the leader of the Britain's biggest suffrage movement, the anti-violent (NUWSS) and was at the forefront to ensure that women have the chance to vote. She was a founding member of the Newnham College, Cambridge. Another woman's activist is Emmeline Pankhurst (1858–1928). She was another British suffragist who devoted her life to the support of women's rights. She made use of all means of protest such as violence, public demonstrations and hunger strikes. However, she died three weeks prior to the passing of an act in 1928, which gave women above 21 years the right to vote.

Emily Murphy (1868–1933) is the next on the list. She became the pioneer woman magistrate in the British Empire. In 1927, together with four other Canadian women, they sought after and tested an old Canadian law that rejected "women as human beings". Eleanor Roosevelt (1884–1962) is another one. As a wife and an aide de camp of the U.S. President, F.D. Roosevelt, Eleanor Roosevelt made an important input to human rights activities, an area she crusaded during her entire lifetime. At a point in time, she headed the UN Human Rights Commission and led to draw up the UN Human Rights Declaration in 1948. The last but not the least in this group is the cerebrated Mother Teresa (1910–1997). Mother Teresa was an Albanian nun and charity worker. She dedicated her life serving the poor and homeless, this made her to be recognised worldwide as an emblem of voluntary service to humanity. During her Missionary of Charities activities, she is remembered for her devotional services caring for several sick and dying people in Calcutta, India. In 1979, she received the Nobel Peace prize.

Poets and Writers

In this category, a presentation of women whose poets and books have influenced humanity in so many ways is provided. The first is Sappho (620 - 570 BCE) as stated by Cartwright (2013). She was among the first ever known female writers. Even though a lot of her poetry cannot be traced, her enormous repute has remained. Plato confirmed that Sappho was among the great 10 poets of his time. She is a woman poet who carried of her work over centuries ago, have influenced mankind to date. Hildegard of Bingen (1098–1179) continues the list. She was a mystic, writer and composer. Hildegard of Bingen lived a reserved life; as a living, she was all the time at the back of convent walls. However, her works including the writings, poetry and music were revelatory during her days. She was a consultant to popes, kings and influential people in her time. To date, most people are still influenced by her writings and music. Most male leaders found Bingen a source of reliable consultant for their various activities.

The next on the list is St Teresa of Avila (1515–1582). She was a mystic woman, a Spanish poet, and a Carmelite reformer. St Teresa of Avila lived throughout the Spanish inquisition; nevertheless, she was not put to trial despite her magical revelations. She was instrumental in reforming the traditions of the Catholic Church and guided the religion away from passion. Saint Teresa was an influential woman in religion and in the Catholic Church in particular. Another writer is Mary Wollstonecraft (1759–1797). She was an author in England who wrote an important book in the early days of the feminist pressure group. Her leaflet titled "*A Vindication of the Rights of Women*" prepared the ground for an ethical and useful foundation in expanding human and political rights to women. Mary Wollstonecraft led the way in the fight for female suffrage. A known argument is that the role played by Mary Wollstonecraft was possible because she was at the forefront of women's activist.

Jane Austen (1775–1817) is another woman to have influenced the world. She is one of the celebrated female authors to date; she authored numerous novels well recognized in contemporary days among the well-known works. They include *Pride and Prejudice, Emma* and *Northanger Abbey*. At the time of her writings, female authors were not encouraged, but Jane helped to provide a medium for potential writers to follow; this is something that have changed the world. In addition, mention is made ofEmily Dickinson (1830–1886). She was recognised as one of America's greatest poets; Emily Dickinson lived most of her life in isolation. The poems that she wrote were available posthumously, and received extensive literary admiration for their brave and exceptional approach. The way she presented her poems became a significant legacy in the 20th Century poetry.

Musicians and Actress

Few of the women in this group isKatharine Hepburn (1907–2003). She was an actress in American and an iconic personality in the Twentieth Century film industry. In addition to the four Oscars that she won, Katharine Hepburn was noted for twelve Oscar nominations. Her way of life was irregular for the period and all the way through her performing life, she helped redefine customary ideas the role of women in society. Then Billie Holiday (1915–1959) follows. She was referred to as "First Lady of the Blues", and was American jazz singer. Billie Holiday was generally acknowledged as the famous and most expressive jazz vocalist second to none. Her voice was met with touching, in its emotional passion and poignancy. She died at a tender age of 44, she was associated with the definition of jazz era and her albums are extensively at the shops for sales today.

Politicians and Leaders (War Leaders and Queens)

This category has legend women who either led people to war or ruled as a Queen, or was in both positions at the same time. Such women ruled over men and or commanded men at the battlegrounds. The first in the series is the influential Cleopatra (69 BCE–30). She was the very last Ptolemaic ruler of Egypt. Cleopatra was able to defend Egypt from the expanding Roman Empire; her efforts ensured that Egypt was not annexed by the then fearful Roman Empire. To ensure this, she made sure to become an ally of the two most powerful and influential Roman leaders, Marc Anthony and Julius Caesar. As a fact to date, allies do not engage in fighting among themselves. An important point here is that, in those days, the Romans over powered the jurisdictions of male rulers, but Cleopatra was a female ruler whose kingdom was intact. Another one is Boudicca (30 – 61 AD); one of the motivating leaders of the Britons during the First Century. She was the pivot in leading a number of tribes' insurgency in opposition to the Roman occupation. In the beginning, she was victorious, and her army of 100,000 sacked Colchester and then went to London, but was later defeated. An important question here probably is when a woman led an army numbering over 100,000 "Where were the men"?

Also, Eleanor of Aquitaine (1122–1204) is one of such women. She was the first Queen of France. Her two sons Richard and John reigned as King of England. As a well-informed, gorgeous and highly eloquent woman, Eleanor became an influential politician in Western Europe with the assistance of her sons. If the sons of a France Queen could rule England, then it is important to say that the woman was instrumental in the development of the two nations. A teenager girl that is worth of mentioning is Joan of Arc (1412–1431). At age 17, Joan of Arc, a patron saint of France, stirred a French rebellion in opposition to the occupation of the English. A not likely hero, the little Joan, under her leadership was able to become victorious at Orleans. She was later tired, found guilty and burnt alive; this only portrayed her heightened and charisma. The question that needs an answer here is "Was Joan of Arc tried and burned alive because the men feared for her leadership"?

Catherine de Medici (1519–1589) is another woman that comes into mind. She was an Italian from Florence, the King of France at a time married Catherine when she was 14 years. She participated in endless political manoeuvrings and sought to augment the authority of her favourite offspring who were all male. This resulted in the catastrophic St Bartholomew's Day Massacre. Another cerebrated ruler is Elizabeth I (1533–1603). She was the Queen of England at some stage in a time of enormous economic and social transformation; she led England to become a cemented Protestant nation. It was her regime that Britain overpowered the Spanish Armada, which was a major step allowing Britain to develop into one of the world's leading superpower. Here a woman became the leader in the development efforts of the nation.

The list continues with Catherine the Great (1729–1796). Catherine the Great was among the greatest political heads during the Eighteenth Century. It is believed that she was instrumental in ensuring that the wellbeing of Russian serfs improved. She positioned the arts and aided to strengthen Russia as a dominant European country. A woman leading the development of Russia to become an instrumental force to reckon with in Europe. Again, Queen Victoria (1819–1901) cannot be left out. She was a British Queen. Her reign as Head of State from 1837 to 1901 saw her rule as one of the biggest empires ever seen. Though Queen Victoria was an influential figure in British politics, she was detached from political beliefs; her entire regime became known as the era of Victorian values. She influenced people's life without political power.

A cerebrated woman in the person of Yaa Asantewaa (1840 – 1921) needs to be mentioned. She was the Queen Mother of Ejisu in Ghana. Though a farmer, she was an intellectual politician and a human right activist who led the Asantes to fight the British in a war that became known as the "Yaa Asantewaa War" during the Colonial Days (1900), when the British have arrested and deported all the powerful Asante Chiefs to Seychelles Island. The cause of the war was that the British demanded the Asantes to surrender their Golden Stool to them, which the Asantes refused, to them (Asantes), the Golden Stool is sacred and must not be surrendered to any stranger causing the arrest of all the powerful men. Yaa Asantewaa then, took the mantle as the leader of the Asantes to fight the British. For her brevity, people have named their children after her (See Mensah, 2010 for details). Another ruler is Indira Gandhi (1917–1984). Indira Gandhi was the first woman Prime Minister of India. Her regimes were between 1966–77 and 1980–84. She was regarded as very influential and strict leader; she by a whisker escaped a military take over when she accepted a call for election, when the "emergency period" of 1977 ended. Her Sikh bodyguards assassinated her in 1984 because of her role in the attack, and probably her entry of the Golden Temple[1].

Scientists

There is another category made up of women scientists. The first on the list here is Elizabeth Blackwell (1821–1910). In Elizabeth Blackwell, she is not only the first Britain born woman to obtain a medical degree in America, but also the first female member to be on the medical register in the UK. She was instrumental in breaking down social barriers, facilitated women to be acknowledged as doctors, and became accepted in the well sought for medical profession in all nations. Then, the Nobel Prize Winer Marie Curie (1867–1934) follows. She was a Polish/French scientist, became the first female to break the men dominated award, not only did she receive the Nobel Prize, but also the first winner of the Nobel Prize for two different categories - the first for research into radioactivity Physics, 1903, and the second for Chemistry in 1911. Some years later, she teamed up with other scientist to develop the first ever X-ray machines. A for-runner as an inventor of medical equipment.

It continues with Dorothy Hodgkin (1910–1994). She was a British chemist who received the Nobel Prize based on the significant discoveries of the composition of both penicillin and afterwards insulin. Her discoveries brought a considerable improvement in the delivery of health care services. An exceptional chemist, Dorothy additionally dedicated most part of her life to the peace pressure group and supported nuclear disarmament campaign. Rosalind Franklin (1920 – 1958) is another woman hero. Rosalind was another British Chemist who made great contributions to the composition of DNA and RNA for people to understand, and this paved the way to the discovery of the DNA double helix. Franklin was influential in the chemistry of coal and viruses.

Entrepreneurs

The entrepreneurs are the last but not the least. These businesspersons have made great contributions to the development of humanity. One of them is Helena Rubinstein (1870–1965). As a businessperson, Rubinstein established the world's first cosmetic firms. This American businessperson's ventures proved enormously flourishing and, in later years, she became a philanthropist and use the profit earned to support benevolent enterprises in the area of learning, art and health. Thus, she was a successful entrepreneur. Another one is Coco Chanel (1883–1971). Coco Chanel was French fashion designer and celebrated as a renowned innovative fashion designer. She helped define the role of women as fore –runners in development and was influential in women fashion and wear, throughout the 20th Century. She revealed revolutionary opinions, as an innovation and specific contribution to the society; she redesigned men's traditional clothes such that they benefited women.

In addition to these women of substance, the same applies to Rachel Carson (1907 – 1964) who was an American conservationist and a pioneering environmentalist. Also, Simone de Beauvoir (1908–1986), a French existentialist philosopher, who wrote a book with the title "The Second Sex" which portrayed the customs of sexism that dominated society and history. The first women Prime Minister of Great Britain Margaret Thatcher (1925–2013) is on the list, she ruled for over 10 years and promoted free markets. Anne Frank (1929–1945) of Dutch Jewish ancestry was an author of the most extensively read books in the world. More can be said about Wangari Maathai (1940–2011), who was a Kenyan-born environmentalist, pro-democracy advocator and women's rights campaigner and a winner of Nobel Peace Prize for hard work to prevent conflict among others. The first woman Prime Minister of a Muslim country Benazir Bhutto (1953–2007) of Pakistan is worth mentioning. She led Pakistan to move from a dictatorship to democracy, became the Prime Minister in 1988, put in place social reforms and assassinated in 2007.

There are other women who are living legends as of January 2019 such as Queen Elizabeth II (1926–) of Great British ruling since 1952. Her rule has seen quick social and economic transformation for Britain and her Commonwealth countries. Betty Williams (1943–) joined forces with Mairead Corrigan in a crusade to end the sectarian violence in Northern Ireland. The duo founded the Community for Peace and received the Nobel Peace Prize in 1977 (post-dated for 1976). Then, an Iranian lawyer, Shirin Ebadi (1947–) is another woman in the category. She is a human rights activist in Iran, stands for political dissidents and other activities to support democracy and human rights, won the Nobel Peace Prize in 2003.

Oprah Winfrey (1954–) of the US, talk show host and businesswoman is another influential woman activist. She was the pioneer woman to have possession of her own talk show. More can be said about the current German Chancellor Angela Merkel (1954 -). She has ruled since 2005 and have become one of the most influential women in the world. Madonna (1958 –), an American pop star is also another woman living legend. She is believed to be the most successful female musician. She is credited with over 250 million records sold. Additionally, she features in films. The British J.K. Rowling (1965–) author of the extraordinary best-selling Harry Potter series also comes into the picture. Hilary Clinton (1947 –), a US politician who was the first women to context for the high office of US on the ticket of a main political party (Democrats) and lost to Donald Trump. She was the Secretary of State from 2009 to 2013.

The list is endless, amongst them female activists who have contributed enormously, influenced their communities, and the world at large not listed above, they affected diverse facets of life despite the challenging moments. As noted earlier, a young woman tried, and burnt alive, but her influential role found in the book of annals. Others being consultants, their clients include powerful men in society such as pope, kings and many more. Some were able to lead their nation to war, activists took a frontline in various campaigns, and scientists invented medicines and machines. Despite these roles undertaken by the female gender, their recognition at local and international levels fall below expectations. The next section presents representation of women at various levels in society and at the international scene. An major outcome is when it will emerge that there is a need for vigorous campaign across the globe to ensure that the important role women play in development are seen in the Fourth Industrial Revolution.

EVIDENCE OF NEGLIGENCE OF WOMEN IN DECISION MAKING

Despite the role played by women in society and how they have influence people, they have very poor representation at various levels in the decision making process. For example, according to Inter Parliamentary Union (IPU, 2016), in 2015, there were two different forms of parliamentary elections held in 58 countries across the globe. First, countries that have quota system, and then those with no quota system. In 28 countries, a type of quota system used was on gender basis; out of the 34 chambers that conducted elections, women won only 28.3 percent. For the remaining 30 countries that did not use any quota system for 36 chambers, women won only 13.5 percent of the representations. This is a clear indication that should there be a quota system based on gender; there is an increase in women representation.

Based on the IPU (2016) report, there were some situations where quota for gender representation were ignored; however, the electoral process allowed "more" women to be elected as was the case in Denmark and Finland of the Nordic Region in Europe, and then Argentina and Guyana in Latin America. These arrangements helped women representations to increase to 25.8 percent compared to 22.3 percent in countries that elected women through the majoritarian elections. Table 1on the next page depicts the countries involved and the actual number of women involved in the various elections.

As seen from the Table 1, the highest women representation was 50 percent in Mexico's lower house, the only statutory requirement that shows equal representation. The least was Federal States of Micronesia with no woman representation. Another observation is that only four countries with no quota required, had women representations that crossed the 30 percent mark. However, empirical evidence suggests that countries with discrimination based on gender appear to experienced lower economic growth and poverty reduction compared to countries that have equality between genders; again where there is unequal gender treatment leads to inefficient outcomes (Bradshaw, Castellino and Diop, 2013). The focus now is on the representation of women on both international and governmental bodies discussed below after the table.

Women Representation at International and Governments Bodies

This section gives evidence from United Nations and Governments bodies to show low participation of women in the decision making process. The intention is to depict how women have been ignored by the "powers" that have the "ability to bite" but do not take actions. Women representations at various bodies (both international and governments to conferences) have not been encouraging. For example, the United Nations has been campaigning for the increase of women on all bodies and had been guided by the following "Normative Framework" table below to ensure women compete and have equivalent membership as men when it comes to participating in United Nations Governing Bodies activities (see U. N. Women, 2017 for details).

Based on the above framework, there are various actions to ensure that the number of women participating in United Nations governing bodies increase. Along these lines, there are several calls for exceptional actions, precise targets and capacity-building programmes (UN Women. 2017). However, there may be the needed legal, executive actions, and other regulatory frameworks. Through the above framework portrayed in the table, and the United Nations System-wide Action Plan, there has been an increase in gender representations. The following remarks from UN Women (2017) shows the general progress in this respect:

"Progress towards achieving equal representation of women across the United Nation system remains slow. The lessons learned from reporting through UN-SWAP show that without intensified efforts and appropriate human and financial investments in this area, as well as in others such as organizational culture and resources allocation, the overall rate of progress in women's participation will stagnate or decline" (p. 8).

The situation at other international bodies is not different; Krsticevic (2015) details the under-representation of women in international bodies as of September 2015, noting that gender parity requires a 50 percent representation. The study analyzed women representation of 84 international bodies over the years, and show the involvement of women on these bodies to be very poor and worrying. The poor representation of women indicated by Krsticevic (2015) showsa glooming picture. For example, since the establishment of the International Court of Justice (ICJ) in 1945, only four women have served as members, though there have been 106 members for the ICJ. As noted, three of the four members are still members of the ICJ. This

Table 1. Candidates that contested for election in 2015

Majority Electoral System	Total Seats	No. of Men	No. of Women	% Women	Success Rate	Quota
Comoros	203	198	5	2.5	20.0	No
Ethiopia (lower house)	1828	1527	301	16.5	70.4	Yes**
Haiti (lower house)	1621	1492	129	8.0	0.0	Yes*
Haiti (upper house	232	209	23	9.9	0.0	Yes*
Marshall Islands	98	93	5	5.1	60.0	No
Nigeria (lower house)	1730	1504	226	13.1	8.8	No
Nigeria (upper house)	747	619	128	17.1	5.5	No
Poland (upper house)	423	305	58	13.	22.4	No
Tuvalu	32	29	3	9.4	33.3	No
United Arab Emirates	330	262	78	23.6	1105	No
United Kingdom (lower house)	3971	2938	1033	26.0	18.5	Yes**
United Republic of Tanzania	1260	1012	238	19.0	57.1	Yes*
Majority and Appointed						
Afghanistan (upper house)	73	58	15	20.5	20.0	Yes*
Saint Kitts & the Nevis	23	22	1	4.3	100.0	No
Saint Vincent & the Grenadines	43	37	6	14.0	0.0	No
Singapore	181	148	35	19.3	62.9	No
Mixed Electoral System						
Andorra	106	72	34	32.1	29.4	No
Egypt	2573	2638	210	8.2	42.4	Yes*
Lesotho (lower house)	1136	799	337	29.7	8.9	Yes*
Mexico (lower house)	4436	2248	2248	50.0	9.4	Yes*
Micronesia (Fed. States of)	34	34	0	0.0	0.0	No
Switzerland (lower house)	3788	2480	1308	34.5	4.9	Yes**
Tajikistan (lower house)	285	255	30	10.5	40.0	No
Venezuela	1799	1128	671	37.3	3.6	No
Proportional Representation						
Burkina Faso	6944	4870	2074	29.9	0.6	No
Croatia	2311	1354	957	41.1	2.4	Yes*
Denmark	799	549	250	31.3	26.8	No
Estonia	872	636	236	27.1	10.2	No
Finland	2146	1301	845	39.4	9.8	Yes**
Netherlands (upper house)	261	178	83	31.8	31.3	Yes**

continued on following page

Table 1. Continued

Majority Electoral System	Total Seats	No. of Men	No. of Women	% Women	Success Rate	Quota
Oman (lower house)	596	576	20	3.4	5.0	Yes**
Pakistan (upper house)	121	103	18	14.9	61.1	Yes*
Poland (lower house)	7858	4530	3328	42.4	3.8	Yes*
Portugal	4453	2553	1900	42.7	3.8	Yes*
Sri Lanka	6151	5595	556	9.0	2.0	No
Surinam	387	259	128	33.1	10.2	No
Turkey	8426	6400	2026	24.0	4.0	Yes**

Source: IPU (2016)

Legend: Yes* Statutory quota, Yes** voluntary party quota, Success rate~ Total number of women candidates divided by the total number of women elected (not shown in table).

is not different from the International Tribunal of the Law of the Sea (ITLOS), it started to operate from 1994 and has seen 40 judges who have served on its bench. Sadly, only one woman has served and continue to serve on the ITLOS. International Criminal Tribunals have not been different. In Rwanda, the International Criminal

Table 2. Normative framework

Year	Expected Framework
1979	Convention on the Elimination of all forms of Discrimination against women
1980	Resolution 1990/15 of the Economic and Social Council
1985	Beijing Declaration and Platform for Action
2003	Resolution 58/142 of the General Assembly
2006	50th Session Commission on the Status of Women
2015	2030 Agenda for Sustainable Development

Source: Culled from UN Women (2017).

Table 3. Percentage of women as members since establishment of some international courts

Court	Percentage of Women Representation
International Court of Justice	3.8
European Court of Justice	8,4
International Tribunal of the Law of the Sea	2.5

Source: Krsticevic (2015).

Court compose of 10 permanent members with just two women as members. The Yugoslavian version has 17 permanent members with two women. Perhaps, the only exception is the International Criminal Courts with 17 permanent members; the three current serving women hold the top positions of that court namely the President, Vice President and the prosecutor. The table below shows the poor representation of women on some international courts.

Women representation of major international tribunals is just 17 percent on the average (Krsticevic, 2015). Not only did she looked at the under representation of women, but also presented areas where women have both high and low representations at the United Nations treaty bodies as indicated below in Table 4.

The next area of another interest is at the national level, both government bodies and parliamentary seats. The U. N. Women (2017) states that representation of women at the highest level of governments, public and private organizations are insignificant. The table below shows the view of the UN Women. Further analysis shows a very disappointing situation, for example, the five countries where 50 percent of the ministers were women are Finland, France, Liechtenstein, and Sweden all in Europe, and only Cabo Verde in Africa. The American countries, Pacific countries and the Asians "could not pass the test". As shown above, the percentage of women representation is insignificant. Per the analysis of UN Women (2017), it is only 30 countries in the world that have more than 30 percent of their ministers to be women, 46 countries have women ministers below 10 percent.

Table 4. UN treaty bodies with high and low representation of women

Treaty Body	Percentage of Women	Remarks
Committee of the Elimination of Description against Women	96	High
Committee on the Rights of the Child	61	High
Committee on the Prevention of Torture	52	High
Committee on the Rights of Persons with Disabilities	33	Low
Committee against Torture	30	Low
Human Rights Committee	27	Low
Committee on the Elimination of Racial Discrimination	22	Low
Committee on the Protection of the Rights of Migrants Workers and their Families	21	Low
Committee on Economic, Social and Cultural Rights	17	Low
Committee on Enforced Disappearances	10	Low

Source: Krsticevic (2015).

Table 5. Women in national governments globally as at January 2017

Area	Women Representation
Number, Head of State	10
Number, Heads of Governments	19
National Parliamentarians	23%
Countries with 50% + Women ministers	5
Countries with 50% + Women Parliamentarians	2

Source: UN Women (2017).

The other dynamics is that most of the women ministers have social related portfolios namely family, education and culture. Such powerful portfolios as defense, finance, and economic sectors mostly do not have women as ministers. In terms of parliamentary seats across countries and regional level, admittedly there have been increases over the years. The table below portrays averages in the world and regional parliamentary seats occupied by women for 1995 and 2016.

The percentages do not take into account parliaments for which data is not available

As shown, there has been an improvement of the parliamentary seats of women for the past two decades. The good news is that for each region, there have been improvement in the parliamentary seats between 1995 and 2016. Apart from the Arab States and the Asian regions, the rest all saw an improvement by at least 100 percent increase in the number of parliament seats occupied by women. However, the percentages still fall below the 50 percent equality or parity. Country specific data from 1998 to 2017 is available from World Bank (2018).

Table 6. World and regional averages of women parliamentarians in july 1995 and january 2016 [regional ranking in the order of the percentage point change]

Region	Average	1995	2016
World Average	11.3	11.3	22.6
Americans	+14.5	12.7	27.2
Sub-Saharan Africa	+13.4	9.8	23.2
Arab States	+13.2	13.2	17.5
Europe (Nordic Countries included)	+ 12.2	13.2	25.4
Pacific	+ 9.5	6.3	15.8
Asia	+5.6	13.2	18.8

Source: IPU (2015).

The above presentation shows that participation of women at the decision-making level at international bodies and government bodies are very poor, and this does not encourage economic development. This is not the best because Bradshaw et al. (2013) indicated that available evidence show that when there is gender equality on various bodies, there is rapid economic development. UN Women affirmed this in the following quote:

"Established evidence reveals that women's participation improves political decision-making and can contribute to the formulation and implementation of policies and strategies that better respond to the rights and interests of women and girls. Women demonstrate leadership by working across party lines through women's caucuses and by taken on issues of gender equality, including the elimination of gender based violence, parental leave and childcare, as well as gender-equality laws and electoral reforms. Women's participation in United Nations-led peace processes correlates with a greater likelihood of agreements reached and implemented. Similarly, peace agreements brokered with the involvement of women are more likely to be gender-responsive, sustainable, enhance civil society participation and ensure broader community acceptance" (UN Women 2017:8).

The religious bodies' recognition of women is not different from the international and government bodies as discussed above. The fact is that to date, no woman has been ordained as a Pope, the highest office in the Roman Catholic Church; moreover, all the Cardinals that meet to appoint a new Pope when the seat becomes vacant are men. Whereas some churches ordain women as priests, others do not. For example, the Church of Pentecost in Ghana (one of the fastest growing Pentecostal Church in Africa if not the world) has no ordained woman as a minister. By December 2018, the church has 1,476, ordained men ministers, 36,412 ordained elders (men), 25,936 ordained deacons (men), but only 49, 103 ordained deaconesses (women) (see The Church of Pentecost 2019). However, women form over 70% of the overall adult membership. Apea (2019) provides a case for the ordination of women from the Pentecostal perspective in Ghana. Another example of unrecognition of women is that in the Moslem world, a woman Islamic cleric is unknown.

EMPIRICAL EVIDENCE OF WOMEN'S CONTRIBUTION IN SOCIETY

Below is an important point from Bradshaw et al. (2013) on the effectiveness of women on development approach:

"World Bank research has highlighted how the poor are less likely to engage in higher risk return activities and the result is that the return on their assets is 25-50% lower than for wealthier households, ... While not a gendered analysis, women's relative poverty, lack of assets, and lack of experience might mean they are particularly risk averse keeping them from higher return economic initiatives. *However, women have been shown to use micro-finance effectively to develop small enterprises and are recognised as good at paying back loans*" (p. 9) emphasis added.

This statement confirms the following empirical microfinance finding from different studies as shown below. Many studies such as Pitt and Khandker (1998), Pitt, Khandker, McKernan, and Latif (1999), Pitt, Khandker, Choudhury, and Millimet (2003), Pitt (2001) have established that the impacts of programme membership vary significantly by the gender of those involved in the programme. For instance, in Bangladesh, Pitt and Khandker (1998) establish that the stream of expenses on consumption rises 18 *taka*[2] when 100 *taka* is provided as credit to women; in contrast, 100 *taka* credit to men was found to increase consumption expenditure by only 11 *taka*.

Pitt et al. (2003) investigated how credit programs affect the poor and health status of children in rural Bangladesh. Among others the study found that an increase in loan to women by 10% bring about 6.3% increase in the arm circumference of their female children, this was two times the increase on comparable credit granted to men. Again, loans granted to women were found to positively affect, though little outcome on, the arm circumference of their male children (noting that the actual factor was not determined). On the average, an increase of credit to women by 10% brought an increase in the arm circumference of girls by 0.45 cm and boys by 0.39 cm. At the same time, the same increase in credit to men increase the arm circumference in girls and boys by 0.21 cm and 0.14 cm respectively. The study found that loans granted to women when estimated bring a large, positive, and statistically significant outcomes on the heights based on age for boys and girls. The result listed specific elasticities as 1.53 for male children and 1.14 for the female. The increase in the height of girls was 0.36 and for boys was 0.56 centimeters every year on the average, when credit to women increases by 10%. However, same credit to male had negative point estimates though not significant. Thus, when credit to men increases by 10%, analysis found that it reduced the height of girls by 0.16 cm and boys by 0.11 cm yearly.

Pitt, Khandker and Cartwright (2006) investigated the outcome when male and female participate in group-based loan programmes. The outcome indicated that when women take part in credit programmes, they become empowered, are more involved in decision-making process in the household, have access to both pecuniary and economic resources. The study also found that women become more enhanced in terms of social network activities, are more active with better bargaining power compared with their spouses. Credit to women allow them to discuss important issues such as how to ensure good parental care and family planning very well. On the other hand, credit provided to men tend to have negative impact on numerous areas of women empowerment. The areas are physic all mobility access to services and financial possessions, influence to achieve domestic transactions.

In India, Garikipati (2008) found that the households of women that joined self-help groups (SHG) that provided credit were less vulnerable and better placed than their counterparts who were not members of the SHG. More importantly, the results suggested that the longer a woman participate in the credit programme, the possibility of her household coping with drought and income diversification rises.

D'Espallier, Guerin, and Mersland (2013) gave an empirical evidence when female gender becomes the focus of microfinance lending programme using dataset across the world. Among others, the study found targeting women for microfinance ensure repayment, but steep cost does not allow complete financial performance. In addition, in Ghana, Onyina (2014) found female household heads 2.2 times higher placed to make purchases of food items for the entire household when they are involved in microfinance credit programme than men household heads. Sivagandhi and Dash (2017) investigate how women are empowered through Self Help Groups and women employment prospects in India. They found that the two complement one another. Additionally, they stated that a change in the per capita income and poverty rate offer the opportunity for female employment and outreach of women SHGs throughout the Indian states. The study provided a list of reasons such as women having access to bank loans, credit facilities and women being educated as added advantage to increase the rate at which women empowerment initiative.

Again, in Ghana, Addai (2017) found that there was a statistically significant positive correlation between microfinance and women empowerment, in two areas namely economic and social, though the relationship depends on two things, a married person or otherwise and level of education, marital status and educational level of the women with age having no controlling effect.

SOLUTIONS AND RECOMMENDATIONS

From the above discussions, it is clear that women play important role in economic development. However, marginalized at all levels in life including representations at both domestic and international levels, as well leaders in religious organizations. To actually benefit from the fantastic role women play that can help bring the development of human capital for the Fourth Industrial Revolution into reality, the following have been outlined for all and sundry to help ensure that women come out of the doldrums to the forefront of various activities.

First, there must be a strong political will to ensure that women are not marginalized, all political appointments and or representations are gender based. To be able to arrive at a balance in gender to participate in the decision-making processes at all levels, the UN Women (2017) put up the following recommendations to for consideration.

An expectation is that all agree to introduce ad hoc measures in the forms of quota for all delegations to the various governing bodies so that women will compose of at least 30 percent with the aim of increasing it up to 50 percent. UN Women (2017) echoed IPU (2015) recommendation on how to treat women on electoral activities. Among others, the IPU (2015) stated that a lot of the existing electoral system in most countries have closed their doors to women, for women find it very difficult to break through when it comes to electoral system. More resources committed to women issues will go a long way to minimize the difficulties. Even coverage of women candidates relegated to the background. Hence, the IPU recommends political leaders to come out with polices that will allow women to participate in the electoral processes without hindrances. Placing them at better areas or at constituencies where they can easily win their contested seats. To the IPU (2015), in 2015, there was an improvement in this; however, there is a need for more action. It will go a long way to increase the number of women at the decision-making process, and ensure that women representation at international levels improves. Thus, more commitment is needed are all levels.

At the national levels, delegates should be composed of equal gender, starting from 30 percent to be at par with men at the 50 percent with time. To achieve this requires explicit policies and mandated targets put in place and followed. The use of enforcement measures so that expected targets become reality in going forward. Ensuring that leadership positions in conferences and committees will also have Chairs and Co-Chairs for both male and female members, the headship may rotate from time to on gender bases. More education, campaign, training, and capacity building for women will help bring women to the forefront in the development of human capital for the Fourth Industrial revolution. Along the same line, Bradshaw et al. (2013) have called for the need to support women's access to official or unofficial justice systems, and to task them to be responsible for the promotion of all women's equal privileges, prospect, and involvement. With the implementation of these, women will become leaders at the forefront of the Fourth Industrial Revolution.

In addition, there must be a focus on capacity building programmes for women representatives to help increase women's involvement in leadership and other technical positions. Increase awareness so that both men and women will be trained on gender related issues so that there will be understanding by all for capacity building in favour of women involvement. In this case, there is a need for more financial support for such a gender related training for men and women.

Designate a fund for women in terms of travelling to international bodies to ensure they fully participate in all activities. Here there is a need to re tool provision of basic services as a whole. For example, according to Bradshaw et al. (2013), if we consider financial, environmental, and health predicaments, women are the most affected. Consequently, there is a need to intensify the provision of such services to women and girls. Again, it is important to come out with policies to deliver inexpensive, excellence childcare and satisfactory healthcare delivery; this in the end would help women's accessibility to paid work, to ensure that they are not vulnerable. Meantime, it is required that full time employment avenues are equally accessible to men and women. For women and access to finance, as well as continue to provide social protection, and many more areas in favour of women.

Establish strategies so that it will build on the awareness for equal gender representation and ensuring that nominations and appointment to attend conferences and meetings and announcements of notices of polls are gender balanced. Promote opportunities to brainstorm with robust advocacy to ensure that there is strong network and collaboration among female representatives and between the delegates that represent women organizations. It cannot be otherwise but agree with Bradshaw et al. (2013) that "Key for economic growth is the promotion of women's economic rights which entails promoting a range of women's rights: their sexual and reproductive rights and rights to education, to mobility, to voice, to ownership, and to live free from violence" (p. 13). At the same time, it requires robust communication strategies put in place to educate people on the need for gender equality, for the human capital development as expected in the Fourth Industrial Revolution.

FUTURE AREAS OF RESEARCH

From the above analysis, a need arises for future research direction. Such research direction on the acceptability of women in the society in general, as to what monitor women contribute in the economic development. Future research to depict the increasing number of women representation on various international and governmental bodies to portray the involvement of women in decision-making will be a step in the right direction. This will go a way not only to know the progress of under representation of women discussed in this chapter, but also the direction of much needed further campaign and education.

CONCLUSION

This chapter has presented the need for women, the mostly marginalized in society projected very high in all areas in achieving their role in the development of human capital for Fourth Industrial Revolution. It argued that women have poor recognition in society and relegated to the background, such that what society expect from them become a reality. It listed some women and the role they played over the years. The chapter portrayed that, the role of women cut across all spheres of life. Nonetheless, the important roles that these women played at various times in history show an avoidable vulnerability of women, in expectation of recognized role in economic development. That's, women resisted all decisions and barriers to ensure that they contribute their part in economic development. In conclusion, the argument is that women must be involved in other decision-making in economic development to be part of the development of the human capital for the Fourth Industrial Revolution process. In addition, encouraging women in all areas in the society will be an important activity in this respect.

REFERENCES

Addai, B. (2017). Women Empowerment through Microfinance: Empirical Evidence from Ghana. *Journal of Finance and Accounting, 5*, 1-11.. doi:10.11648/j.jfa.20170501.11

Apea, E. (2019). *Are the Churches flying with One Wing? A New Look at Ordination of Women*. Emmanuel Apea.

Bradshaw, S; Castellino, J., & Diop, B (2013). *Women's Role in Economic Development: Overcoming the Constraints. Sustainable Development Solution Network.* A Global Imitative for the United Nations.

Cartwright, M. (2013). *Sappho of Lesbos, Palazzo Massimo. Ancient History Encyclopedia*. Retrieved June 10, 2019, from https://www.ancient.eu/image/2123/

D'Espallier, B., Guérin, I., & Mersland, R. (2013). Focus on Women in Microfinance Institutions. *Journal of Development Studies, 49*. doi:10.1080/00220388.2012.720364

Foundations of Western Culture (FWC). (2018). *Industrial Revolution: Women's Roles in the Industrial Revolution.* Retrieved November, 19, 2018 from http://foundations.uwgb.org/womensroles/

Franck, R., & Galor, O. (2015). *The Complementarity between Technology and Human Capital in the Early Phase of Industrialization*. Retrieved August 27, 2018 from http://d.repec.org/n?u=RePEc:bro:econwp:2015-3&r=his

Garikipati, S. (2008). The Impact of Lending to Women on Households Vulnerability and Women's Empowerment: Evidence from India. *World Development, 36*(12), 2620–2642. doi:10.1016/j.worlddev.2007.11.008

IPU. (2016). Women in Parliament in 2015 The year in review. Geneva: IPU.

Krsticevic, V. (2015). *Gender Equality in International Tribunals and Bodies: A global campaign for gender parity in international representation an achievable step with global impact*. Academic Press.

Mensah, N. P. W. (2010). *Nana Yaa Asantewaa, The Queen Mother of Ejisu: The Unsung Heroine of Feminism in Ghana* (An unpublished Master of Arts thesis). University of Toronto.

Onyina, P. A. (2014). The Impact of a Microfinance Programme on Clients: Evidence from Ghana. Scholar's Press.

Pettinger, T. (2014). *Women who changed the world*. Retrieved on April 21, 2018 from www.biographyonline.net

Pitt, M., & Khandker, S. R. (1998). The Impact of Group-Based Credit Programs on Poor Households in Bangladesh: Does the Gender of the Participant Matter? *Journal of Political Economy*, *106*(5), 958–996. doi:10.1086/250037

Pitt, M. M. (2001). The Effect of Nonagricultural Self-Employment Credit on Contractual Relations and Employment in Agriculture: The Case of Microcredit Programs in Bangladesh. *Bangladesh Development Studies*.

Pitt, M. M., Khandker, S. R., & Cartwright, J. (2006). Empowering Women with Micro Finance: Evidence from Bangladesh. *Economic Development and Cultural Change*, *54*(4), 791–831.

Pitt, M. M., Khandker, S. R., Chowdhury, O. H., & Millimet, D. L. (2003). Credit Programs for the Poor and the Health Status of Children in Rural Bangladesh. *International Economic Review*, *44*(1), 87–118. doi:10.1111/1468-2354.t01-1-00063

Pitt, M. M., Khandker, S. R., McKeman, S.-M., & Latif, M. A. (1999). Credit Programs for the Poor and Reproductive Behavior in Low Income Countries: Are the Reported Causal Relationships the Result of Heterogeneity Bias? *Demography*, *36*(February), 1–21. doi:10.2307/2648131 PMID:10036590

Rahman, S. (2007). *The Impact of Microcredit on Poverty and Women's Empowerment: A Case of Bangladesh* (Unpublished PhD Thesis). University of Western Sydney.

Sentryo. (2019). *The 4 Industrial Revolutions*. Retrieved on February 23, 2019 from https://www.sentro_net/the 4

Sivagandhi, S., & Dash, D. P. (2017). Microfinance and women Empowerment-Empirical evidence from the Indian states. *Regional and Sectoral Economic Studies*, *17*(2), 61–74.

The Church of Pentecost. (2019). *General Headquarters 16th Extraordinary Council Meeting*. Accra: The Church of Pentecost.

Women, U. N. (2017). *Shaping the International Agenda: Raising Women's Voices in International in Intergovernmental Forums*. Geneva: International Gender Champions.

World Bank. (2018). *World Development Indicators.* Available at https://data.worldbank.org/indicator/SG.GEN.PARL.ZS

World Economic Forum. (2016). *The Future of Jobs: Employment, Skills and Workforce Strategy for the Fourth Industrial Revolution.* Retrieved August 27, 2018 from https://www.weforum.org/reports/the-future-of-jobs

World Economic Forum. (2017). *System Innovative on Shaping the Future of Education Gender and Work.* Retrieved August 27, 2018 from https://www.weforum.org/systeminitiatives/shaping-the-future-of-education-gender-and-work

KEY TERMS AND DEFINITIONS

Activist: A person who believes strongly in political or social change and works hard to try and make this happen.

Approbation: Approval or agreement, often given by an official group or praise.

Carmelite Reformer: Someone who made an attempt to reform a friar or nun of a contemplative Catholic order at Mount Carmel during the Crusades and dedicated to Our Lady.

Feminist: A person who believes in feminism, often being involved in activities that are intended to achieve change.

Development: When someone or something grows or changes and becomes more advanced.

Gender: The physical and/or social condition of being male or female.

Human Rights: The basic rights which it is generally considered all people should have, such as justice and the freedom to say what you think.

Mystic: Someone who attempts to be united with God through prayer.

Nobel Prize: A set of annual international awards bestowed in several categories by Swedish and Norwegian institutions in recognition of academic, cultural, or scientific advances.

Oscar: One of a set of American prizes given each year to the best film, the best male and female actor in any film and to other people involved in the production of films.

Ptolemaic Ruler: The Roya family which ruled the Ptolemaic Kingdom in Egypt in the Hellenistic period between 305 to 30 BC.

Spanish Inquisition: An organization within the Roman Catholic Church that existed from 1542 to 1834 and which was established to punish people whose religious beliefs were considered wrong.

St. Bartholomew's Day Massacre: Was in 1572, a targeted group of assassinations and a wave of Catholic mob, directed against the Huguenots (French Calvinist Protestants) during the French Wars of Religion. Modern estimates for the number of dead across France vary widely, from 5,000 to 30,000.

Suffrage: Refers to the right to vote in an election, especially for representatives in a parliament or similar organization.

Suffragette: A woman in Britain, Australia and the United States in the early 20th century who was a member of a group that demanded the right of women to vote and that increased knowledge of the subject with a series of public protests.

ENDNOTES

1 Women are not allowed to enter the Golden Temple in India.

2 Taka is the currency used in Bangladesh the country of the study.

Chapter 10
Leadership for Enhancing Organisational Performance Through Workforce Reskilling

Neeta Baporikar
https://orcid.org/0000-0003-0676-9913
Namibia University of Science and Technology, Namibia & University of Pune, India

ABSTRACT

Leadership styles adopted influence employee performance, but merely appropriate style without workforce reskilling cannot ensure sustainable and holistic organizational performance. The objective of this chapter is to explore and analyze leadership for enhancing organizational performance through workforce reskilling in the context of a local authority, namely municipality. Adopting mixed method approach, the primary data was collected by administering questionnaires. A sample size of 100 respondents participated in the study with the aid of convenience sampling technique for proportionate representation from each department. However, out of 100 questionnaires distributed, only 96 were completed and returned. Analysis is done by STATISTICA Software. The findings reflect that both democratic and autocratic leadership are adopted and there was insufficient workforce reskilling required to meet the current needs of the organization.

DOI: 10.4018/978-1-5225-9810-7.ch010

INTRODUCTION

As other organizational and managerial factors have changed, shared values and norms of society and its organizations have also shifted (Kim & Bae, 2017). Over the past 15 years or so, human resource management (HRM) systems and practices have gone through tremendous changes globally. Traditionally HRM policies and practices aimed at tenure and seniority approach. With advent of ICT and knowledge shits from early 21 century, performance-based systems with greater emphasis on rationality, fairness and competence came into use (Kim & Bae, 2017). Today, organizations have started to intensively train and develop managers to enhance their professional competences. Hence, the challenge for leadership is to transform its role and ensure that human capital formation takes the priority. Municipality of Swakopmund is no exception to this dynamics of leadership and human resource management issues.

The Municipality of Swakopmund is a local Authority established under the Namibia Local Authority Act, 1992 (Act 23 of 1992). This town is situated in the Namib Desert along the western coast of Namibia. Swakopmund is the fourth largest populated city in Namibia (Erongo Regional Profile, 2010). The Municipality of Swakopmund is grouped under a category called part one Municipality. Being a part, one Municipality means that the institution is autonomous and does not depend on the central government for funding. It literally approves its own budget and runs its own affairs. In general, municipalities are responsible for the management of the provision of services to local communities in a sustainable and equitable manner. Swakopmund Municipality has a staff compliment of 388, comprised of five departments namely; Corporate, Community Development, Engineering, Finance and Health Services. Ten political councillors represent the Municipality from different political parties. The Mayor of Swakopmund is the chairperson of the Council who plays the leading role among her fellow Councillors. There is a management committee responsible for ensuring that the decisions of the Council are carried out and Council approves those budgets. The Chief Executive Officer is the highest administrative authority responsible for ensuring that the set Council policies are executed.

In line with the Municipality of Swakopmund's mission statement, the organisation creates an environment that promotes earning income, respect, trust, support, personal growth and productivity in order to develop effective and committed employees. The Municipality of Swakopmund commits to accepting a high degree of open communication, a participative management style and lead by example. For the Municipality to fulfil its mission and achieve its objectives it undertook a "*Free to Grow exercise*" in 2015, which was aimed at identifying factors influencing or affecting employees' performance. The *Free to Grow* exercise was conducted within the organisation where employees were engaged through a workshop. This exercise revealed that most of the employees said that there was lack of recognition and lack of appreciation, lack of trust, inconsistent treatment, favouritism, and lack of communication and coordination of resources as factors negatively influencing employees' performance (Botha, 2015).

Free to Grow exercise did not dig deeper at what level the identified factors influence and affect the performance of employees. According to Ojokuku, Odetayo, and Sajuyigbe (2012), the ultimate goal of every organisation is not only to survive, but also to sustain its existence by improving performance. The prime motive of many organisations is to achieve their stated objectives, hence the need to effectively coordinate and motivate the workers by an effective leader (Ojokuku et al., 2012). Leaders play crucial roles in realising the organisational goals while boosting employees' performance by satisfying them with their jobs that becomes the crux of issues in the corporate world of today. Leaders are responsible of integrating and coordinating both human and material resources to produce the output or services. The study of leadership attracted the attention of different researchers over the years and both focused on different definitions. Mintzberg (2010) posits that leadership is fundamental and trust emanates from respect of others. Ngambi, Cant,, and Van Heerden, (2010) and Ngambi (2011) define leadership as a process of influencing followers to commit towards realising their full potential in achieving the organisational value and shared vision with passion and honesty. Leadership maintains a relationship between a leader and individual followers. Adair (2005) refers to leaders as a reflection of what they expect from their followers as the success of any organisation largely depends on the quality of employees' performance. This articulation is apt as one of the factors of production classified in economics literature among the four categories namely; labour (employees), capital and entrepreneurship as well as other natural resources including land. Employees are the most valuable assets in any organisation and associations will not succeed without them. Armstrong (2004) refers to employee performance as measured in terms of outcomes.

Further, motivated employees produce quality performance and they complain less (Makkonen, Pohjola, Olkkonen & Koponen, 2014). Employee performance like any other system does not function when not all components are coordinated to work well and efficiently. According to Chandrasekhar (2011), employees that are dissatisfied because of poor workplace environment also lead to a decrease in productivity. On the same note Judge, Bono, Ilies & Gerhardt (2002) show organisational performance will also decline, as more production time will be lost since dissatisfied employees are likely to take more leave days. The work environment has a significant impact upon employee performance and productivity (Ollukkaran & Gunaseelan, 2012). Workforce is an important component in an organisation since employees are the promoters of excellent organisational performance (Mafini & Pooe, 2013). With this perspective, the chapter appraises what is the leadership and how it enhances organisational performance in general and in particular what is the role of workforce reskilling to achieve the goals and objectives to ensure superior performance of the municipality. It also proposes strategies for improving employees' performance through the workforce reskilling approach.

LITERATURE REVIEW

Leadership is collective, understood to involve persuasion and explanation as well as ability to identify, affirm and enhance the values of the group, which the leader represents. Taiwo (2013) argues that leadership is very complex and diverse so much that different contexts ranging from business to politics and various organisations influence leading to various differences and definitions of leadership. Leadership is both a research area and a practical skill encompassing the ability of an individual or organisation to lead or guide other individuals, teams or entire organizations. Some scholars including Zhu, Chew and Spangler, (2005) illustrate that it is important to understand the effects of leadership on performance, as it is one of the key driving forces for improving a firm's performance.

Fu-Jin, Shieh and Tang (2010) indicated that often leaders demonstrate support for employees, which breed confidence and lead to better performance, thereby affecting employee's job satisfaction positively. Peterson (2003) suggests that the role of leadership is crucial for an organisation to achieve a high level of performance, whereas Meindl, Ehrlich and Dukerich, (1985) advocate that the role of leadership is not that important in achieving the organisational performance. Previous studies claim that leadership has identified a number of different leadership styles, which leaders adopt in managing organisations (Chen and Chen 2008; Belete, 2015). London (2001) emphasised that the importance of organisational objectives assists executives in performing and executing leadership roles by coordinating efforts of the employees. Organisations attain identity, recognition and maintain status when achieving the set objectives. According to Dubrin (2007) needs are classified into physical, social and egoistic, while job satisfaction is often associated with human needs and condition. Many researches also note that there is a link between leadership and management because it involves directing and controlling, to an extent that the nature and degree of activities change within the organisation.

Moreover, if the organisation is to achieve its objectives, leadership of an organisation should be accorded sufficient attention. The practice of leadership evolves taking charge and aligning the activities of an organisation to ensure that the desired results are achieved. Dubrin (2007) lists the management functions as planning, organising, directing, controlling and co-ordination of activities to achieve the organisational set objectives. Planning is a process of looking forward to determine the course of actions; an organisation may follow to achieve the set objectives be it in short or long term for organisation's success (Paley, 2004). Further, directing in most organisations involve face-to-face supervision of duties and responsibilities. Thus, in a daily routine of business, the success of the organisation is determined by the effectiveness of a leader or manager in directing the affairs of the organisation. Controlling is another factor and a function that provides the manager or leader with the means to ensure that the organisational plans are adequately addressed and executed. Huisman, Wissen and Leo (2004) explain that control involves possessing the capacity to guide and correct activities, which does not promote achieving the organisational goals.

Leadership Theories and Models

Due to ever-growing interest in the field of leadership, researchers began to analyse the possible consequences of leadership behaviours. Following are some of the theories related to leadership:

Trait Theories of Leadership: Trait theory was developed based on the content theory that leaders are born with certain distinguished personalities traits, which include social, personal and social characteristics. Physical traits are associated with physical appearances such as leader being tall, energetic, young, handsome and beautiful. Social traits are linked to educational background, prominent schools and being socially prominent. Personal traits cover emotional stable, adaptable and self-confidence. Judge et al., (2002) argue that traits matter in prediction of leadership effectiveness.

Behavioural Leadership Theory: Behavioural theory suggested that good leaders are not born but trained. This theory proposes that trained leaders are better as compared to born leaders, hence a contradiction to the previous theory, which suggests that born leaders, are better than trained leaders. This theory further highlights that normally people do not work in isolation, thus always observe others conduct and observe the occasions on which is rewarded or punished.

Theory X and Theory Y: In theory X employees are mainly motivated through reward of monetary gifts and other fringe benefits (Douglas, Robert & Stephen, 2013). This theory further highlights that people avoid responsibility and prefer to be directed and have job security. As a result, most of the employees' characteristics should be controlled and directed through punishment in order to increase the habit of achieving organisational objectives. In Theory Y managers believes that employees are hardworking, cooperative, self–motivated with a good attitude toward achieving the organisation goals (Douglas, et al 2013). Generally, employees under this theory are positive to contribute to the set goals and targets of the organisation. The key aspects of this theory are to encourage integration, creating conducive working environment for all to prosper.

Participatory Theory: proposes that an ideal leadership style is the one that recognise other input and put them into account. Under this theory, the leader encourage participation and contribution from employees and help employees feel more relevant and committed to the decision making process.

Fiedler's Contingency Model: Hughes, Guttorp and Charles (1999) argued that some researchers consider Fiedler's Contingency Leadership Theory as the most validated of all leadership theories. It is against this background that the researcher focused on the Contingency Leadership Theory with special focus on Fiedler Contingency. According to House and Aditya (1997), Fiedler developed the first contingency leadership theory in 1951. It was the first theory that focused on how leader's personality and behaviour interact with situational variables. Fiedler proposed that effective employee performance depended upon the proper match between a leader's ability to lead, contingent upon situational factors that include the leaders' capabilities, preferred style and behaviour competency of employees (Iqbal, Anwar & Haider, 2015).

Leadership Styles

Daniel (2002) categorises different leadership styles and proposed a scaling, ranging from autocratic through democratic to participative to show the degree of authority and decision making power of leaders and employees in the organisations. Some of the main leadership styles are:

Autocratic Leadership: is a classic "do as I say" type of approach which is corporate equivalent to dictatorship. (Ojokuku et al., 2012) argue that autocratic leaders are inexperienced with leadership thrust upon them in the form of a new position or assignment that involves people management. Autocratic leaders instruct employees and closely supervise them (Likert, 1967). Autocratic leaders maintain decision making within them. As a result, these leaders may damage the organisational reputation because followers are forced to execute strategies and duties in a very narrow way, based on subjective ideas of what success looks like. In autocratic leadership, there is no shared vision, decisions are quick and work is done faster. Opinions from employees are rarely appreciated. According to Michael (2010), most followers under these leaders are described as biding their time, waiting for the inevitable failure this leadership produces and the removal of the leaders that follows. Proponents of this leadership style advocate it as ideal approach to achieve high employee performance without necessarily putting them under stress. It is argued that there is a close supervision under this leadership and leaders assume full responsibility for their actions (Naile & Selesho, 2014).

Democratic Leadership: style is considered to benefit most organisations. These leaders provide guidance and assistance to teams while accepting and receiving inputs from individual team members (Ittner &. Larcker, 2002). Under this leadership style, managers give employees full control and responsibilities in executing duties. Managers also encourage the employees to become good leaders and involve them in employee personal development and growth. Thus, communication barriers and gaps are identified and reduced. (Belete, 2015). According to Kirega (2006), this style of leadership appreciates other people's skills, experience and ideas but the final decisions remain in the leaders' hands. These leaders provide proper recognition and delegate duties and responsibilities. Democratic leadership is known to improve employee performance in both short and long-term situations and can be used for any type of work. According to Debashis (2000), this leadership style provides employees with creativity in problem solving; participate in trainings, meetings, and motivation, which enhance employees' confidence. Belete (2015) concludes that democratic leadership is quite effective for manufacturing industries, professional entities, non-profit organisations and creative fields such as advertising where everyone's input matters and makes a difference.

Laissez – Faire Leadership: is known as a passive kind of leadership style. Leaders displaying this type of leadership are perceived as not caring at all about other individual issues. Laissez –Faire leaders are resistant in decision making, which delays taking action and mostly absent when wanted, may avoid responsibilities, not respond to problems, and fail to follow up, resist expressing views and delay responses. Leaders do not have just one style of leadership, but varying styles depending on the situation at hand (Hersey, Blanchard, & Johnson, 2000). Balete (2015) maintains that laissez-faire leadership style can be effective in situations where team members are highly skilled, motivated, empowered and able to work independently.

Moral/Servant Leadership: is a new and recently established model of leadership. This model is dedicated to a collective transformation, totally committed to moral values and principles, and guided by the exercise of capabilities in service to the common goal. Servant leadership has moved away from the old traditional way where leaders give instructions to followers to a situation, where leaders commit to service and listen to the followers. What prevails today is moral leadership consisting of service-oriented leadership and does not focus on satisfying the immediate needs of the employees or community only, but assist each member to develop capabilities needed in order to contribute to personal intellectual and well-being of individuals as employees, as an organisation and the entire community. Personal and social transformation if not motivated by the desire to contribute to social transformation, a person runs a risk of falling into self-centredness. Investigating and applying the truth refers to ideal truth which point to the way things should not be. Belief in the essential nobility of human nature is based on a profound and unshakable conviction in the essential and potential goodness of humanity (Azedah, 2012).

LEADERSHIP STYLE AND ORGANISATIONAL PERFORMANCE

Autocratic Leadership and Organisational Performance

Leaders of this calibre have absolute power over the employees and leave no room for followers to make suggestions even if it is in the best interest of the organisation (Armstrong, 2002). Cole (2002) suggests that this style works in organisations where change needs to be encouraged, particularly in situations where conflicts such as strikes have occurred. Cole (2002) further argued that if this leadership is applied in suitable situations, it is likely to reap organisational effectiveness. In his research, Belete (2015) indicates that for this leadership to be effective, it should be based on both political and administrative issues in their relevant situations to be effective. It is noted that most of the issues rose from the nature of the administrative structure. This study noted that the respondents at the Municipality of Swakopmund revealed that autocratic leadership affected the organisational culture because employees are not provided with adequate feedback and mostly their views are not considered. Further, rules and regulations are imposed on them without their input.

Democratic Leadership and Organisational Performance

Maurik (2001) argues that the task of a leader applying this leadership nurtures the roots of organisational values, which consist of nothing but a basic human aspiration. Researchers argue that democratic style is needed to have efficiency and proper employee management that leads to improved organisational performance (Belete, 2015). In local government settings for example, transparency and openness are as much part of leadership because that leads to performance and effective evaluations. Nkata (2004) gives some solutions to the challenges raised in the "*Free to Grow*" exercise that the role of recognition, employee involvement, and training are some factors that have demonstrated to be able to promote both employee effectiveness and organisational performance.

Laissez – Faire and Organisational Performance

Northouse (2001; 2013) indicates that the contingency theories to leadership support realistic freedom to leadership, which is laissez-faire style. Laissez-faire carries the belief that the most effective way of leading depends on the ability to allow some degree of freedom to employees. Belete (2015) argues that the challenge with the latter in the African context is that this leadership has been hardly practiced in completeness due to political interferences. Thus, organisational performance is a process to enhance the effectiveness of the organisation and the well-being of employees through planned interventions (Mustaffa, 2012). Jon and Randy (2009) indicate that the actual output or results of an organisation performance are measured against its intended outputs, goals and objectives. Literature reveal that there are four measures for organisational performance namely; human resources, organisational outcomes, financial outcomes and capital market outcome. In this study, the focus is on human resources. According to Mustaffa (2012), human resource outcome relates to change in employee behaviour, employee satisfaction, employee turnover and absenteeism. Eventually, organisational performance outcome consist of labour productivity, customer service which results in customer satisfaction and quality of products and services. In terms of financial accounting, outcomes are measured in terms of returns on assets, returns on equity and organisational profitability.

Work performance is defined as the way employees diligently perform their duties. High performance work systems and practices have been identified as key factors in improving organisational effectiveness and thereby realise organisational goals (Rowold, 2011). It is argued that high performance work systems influence and align employees' attitude and behaviours with the organisational performance and eventually increase employee commitment and subsequently the overall organisational performance. Performance measurement is essential to ensure that organisation works to achieve the set objectives and hence, it is crucial to have clear goals and objectives so that performance can be rationally measured.

Many researchers have discussed the relationship between leadership style and organisational performance. The contingency theory illustrates that there is no universal leadership theory fitting all employees or all organisations. Different situations call for different measures. Leadership is required to consider different approaches in handling situations, which produce high levels of productivity. Many studies show leadership style has significant relation with organisational performance (Ojokuku et al., 2012). McGrath and MacMillan (2000) confirm that there is a relationship between leadership styles and organisational performance. Businesses attribute their successes to leadership efficiency; the leadership style of administrative supervisors has a considerable effect on the organisational performance (Sun, 2002).

Effective leadership and management are regarded as key priority for national and regional development, however the process by which they are enhanced is by training and development yet how they affects upon performance remain poorly understood (Babatunde and Ikenga, 2015). Behery (2008) agrees that the global environment is very competitive as such companies need to revaluate the roles of leadership in order to avoid wasting resources which enables the organisation to remain competitive. Further, the performance and effectiveness of an organisation are evaluated by parameters such as financial reports, bottom lines, and revenue and market shares.

Factors Affecting Employees Performance

The "*Free to Grow*" exercise conducted in 2015 at the Municipality of Swakopmund revealed some of the factors affecting employee performance. Some of the identified factors were lack of recognition, lack of trust, inconsistent treatment, favouritism, lack of communication and coordination. Further leadership style in an organisation encourages or deters employees' performance (Thao and Hwang, 2015). Coaching on the other hand addresses the belief and behaviours that hinder job performance (Toit, 2007). In essence, coaching assists the workforce to perform better (Starr, 2004). Empowerment positively correlates with both satisfaction and performance (Bartman & Casimir, 2007). A study conducted by Chen and Tjosvold (2006) reveal that participation leadership involves employees in decision making and assists them to feel that they are considered in problem solving and can influence organisational decisions. Participation leadership increases employee job performance and reduces labour turnover. Norms and values of organisational culture also effect those who are directly or indirectly involved and though these norms cannot be seen easily, yet have a significant impact on the performance of employees and organisational productivity.

INFLUENCE OF LEADERS ON EMPLOYEES' PERFORMANCE

Leadership is a process of encouraging and helping others to work towards achieving organizational goals. The human factor binds a group of people together and motivates it towards goals transforming the group's potential into reality. According to Voon, Lo, Ngui & Ayob (2011), a capable leader provides organizational directions and lead employees or followers towards achieving desired goals. Mat (2008) stressed that followers generally emulate the leaders' actions and behaviours thus leading to the achievement of the desired goals. Thus, leaders have a mammoth task to inspire their subordinates through calculated actions. Managers also adopt different leadership styles depending on their orientation. The orientations may be influenced by the manager's historical background ranging from culture, education system or the organizational environment. Different leadership style adopted by a particular manager in a way has an impact on staff motivation, performance and organizational commitment, which eventually influence the employees' decision either to stay or leave the organization. It is vital to retain employees to the continuation of the organization because of the skills acquired and accumulated in the period of organizational service (Wakabi, 2013). An organization with a high labour turnover experience high costs and effort of recruiting, inducting and training new recruits while risking business operation disruptions.

The conceptual framework is given in figure 1, which depicts that the leadership styles namely autocratic, democratic, and laissez-faire which are regarded as independent variables, whereas employee performance and organisational performance are regarded as dependent variables. The researcher adopted this conceptual model on their relationship to examine which leadership style is most appropriate to enhance employees' performance in an organisation. In this context, performance is professed as team inputs, meeting deadlines and achieving departmental goals. Iqbal, et al (2015) maintain that these factors should lead to work efficiency, effective feedback and good organisational communication and improved relations. Thus, leadership and employee performance cohesion should be proven through styles and approaches in an effort to cause efficiency.

DATA PRESENTATION AND ANALYSIS

100 questionnaires were distributed to the targeted sample and 96 received were filled-in. The total response rate is 96%. The target sample represents 29% of the

Figure 1. Leadership styles and organisational performance

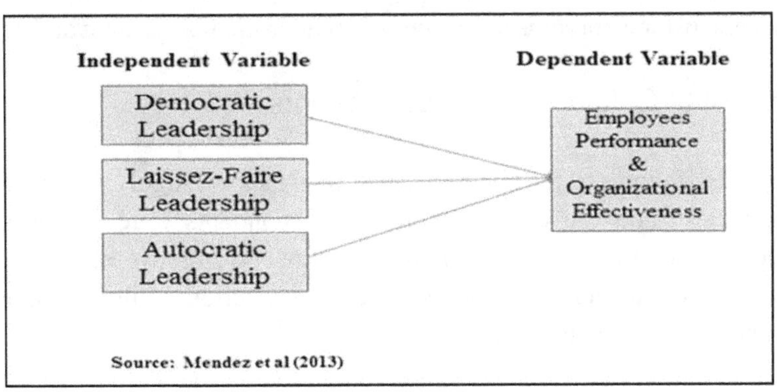

total employees of the Municipality of Swakopmund; hence constitute a realistic sample size. Demographics of the respondents includes gender, age of respondents, years of service, highest education qualification attained and department. Majority of the respondents (54%) are female and 46% are male. This represents a strong gender balance, accounting for almost equal sample number of male and female. The data on the age groups of the respondents obtained from the questionnaires shows that 66% of the respondents were below the age of 41 years. This implies that the majority of the workforce at Municipality of Swakopmund comprises mainly of young and energetic segment of the population. Hence, the workforce at the Municipality of Swakopmund is within the most productive age. It is evident that the respondents hold a range of educational qualifications and the majority of the respondents (77%) have attained a Diploma as the highest academic qualification, indicating a limitation in skill capacity amongst the employees at the Municipality of Swakopmund. Hence, workforce reskilling by training may be a very important requirement to improve employees' skills to improve their performance at work and to create a knowledge-based workforce. Further, data based on years of service shows that 45% of the respondents have worked for the Municipality of Swakopmund for less than 6 years. This shows that most of the respondents have been with the Municipality of Swakopmund consistently for over 6 years and are more likely to know the organisation performance. The results indicate that the Municipality of Swakopmund has a good employee retention system.

Organisational Culture by Department

The variation in the departmental response to issues related to organisational culture (Figure 3). Highly variable responses were observed in all departments, with community development mainly disagreeing while the health department respondents agreeing to all questions related to the organisational culture (Figure 2). The remaining departments provided variable responses but mainly agreeing to issues related to organisational culture (Figure 2). Most of the departments disagreed that managers foster an organisational culture that promotes learning and creativity.

Organisational Culture By All Respondents

The aggregated findings on the organisational culture show a highly variable response rate with a mean above average (Figure 3). Respondents were neutral on three components; communication between management and employees, management is competent and ethical and that managers foster organisational culture that promotes learning and creativity (Figure 3).

Figure 2. Organisational culture segregated by department

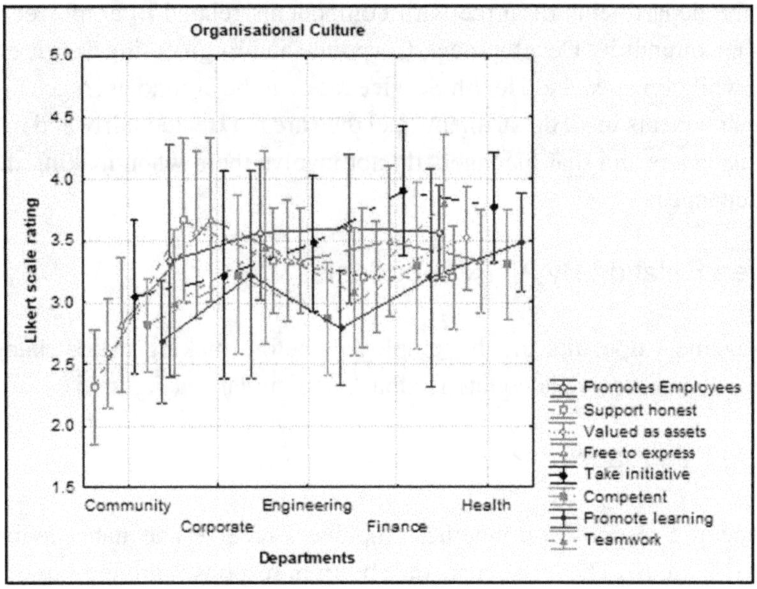

Employee Relations by Department

Figure 3. Likert scale ratings as per components

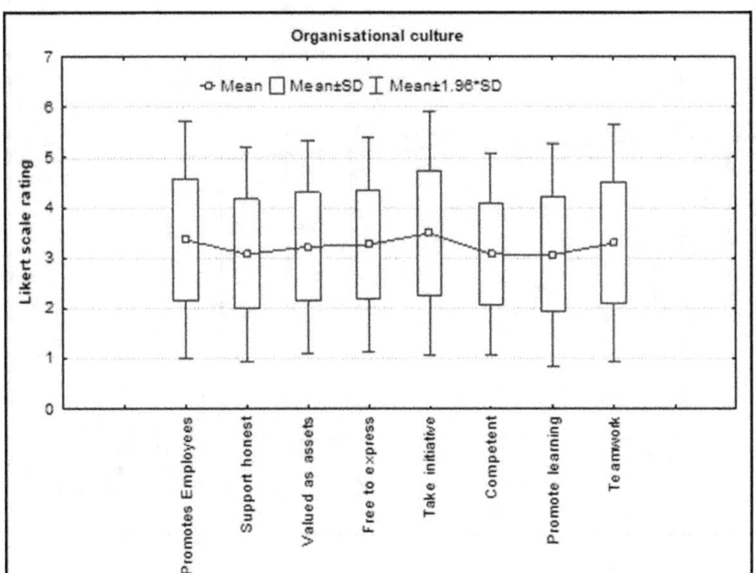

The figure shows the departmental response to the issues related to employee relation. Most of the departments disagree with components related to employee relation (Figure 4). Community Development, Corporate and Engineering Services mainly disagree, while Finance and Health Service rate it to be around average (Figure 4). Overall respondents in all departments feel they are not treated fairly and respectful by their managers and that managers do not involve them when making decisions of major changes.

Employee Relation By All Respondents

The management does not involve employees before making major changes and employees do not receive adequate feedback and guidance (Figure 5).

Adequate Feedback

Gender specific response on whether employees receive adequate feedback and guidance (Figure 6). The trends and variability in responses are the same between the genders and the respective years of service, except for females that worked

Figure 4. Employee relations per department

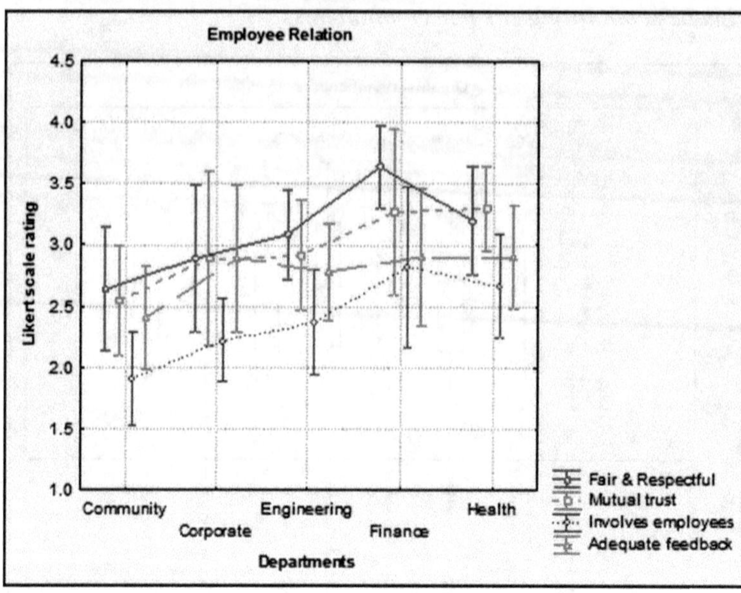

Figure 5. Employee relations by all respondents

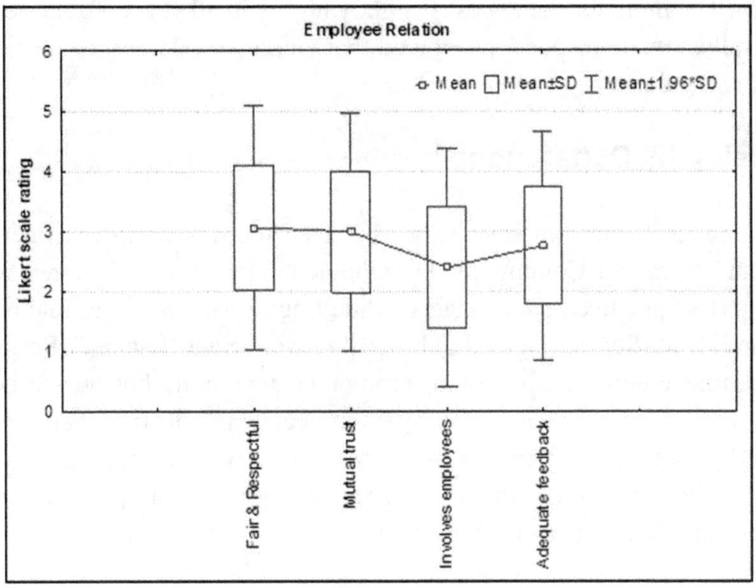

for the organisation for more than 20 years, where a higher variability is observed

Figure 6. Response Re Managers Adequate Feedback, Guidance Based On Gender and Service Years With 95% Confidence Interval

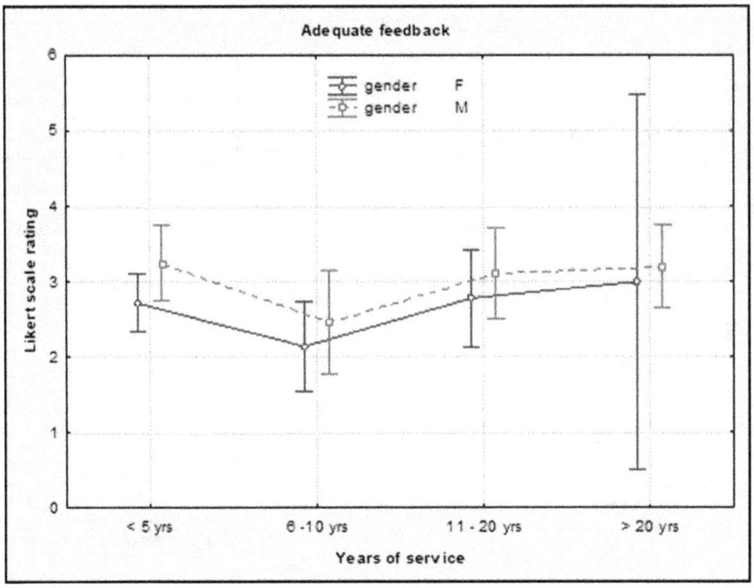

(Figure 6). The trend for the males is slightly higher in all years of service (Figure 6). Generally, female respondents agreed that employees do not receive adequate feedback and guidance.

Leadership by Department

The response to leadership style varies between the different departments. The respondents from the Community Development Department disagree with the leadership style practiced by managers, while Engineering Services rate is around average and Health Services agreed and rated it above average (Figure 7). Respondents in all departments agree that leadership promotes team morale, but most respondents disagree that managers involve employees in decisions affecting their work. The responses by the three departments were less variable when compared to Corporate and Finance department (Figure 7). The variability was more pronounced in the Corporate Service Department (Figure 7).

Leadership By All Respondents

There is a general agreement that leadership promotes team morale and build organisational commitment and that leaders view mistakes as opportunities to learn

Figure 7. Response on leadership style segregated by department

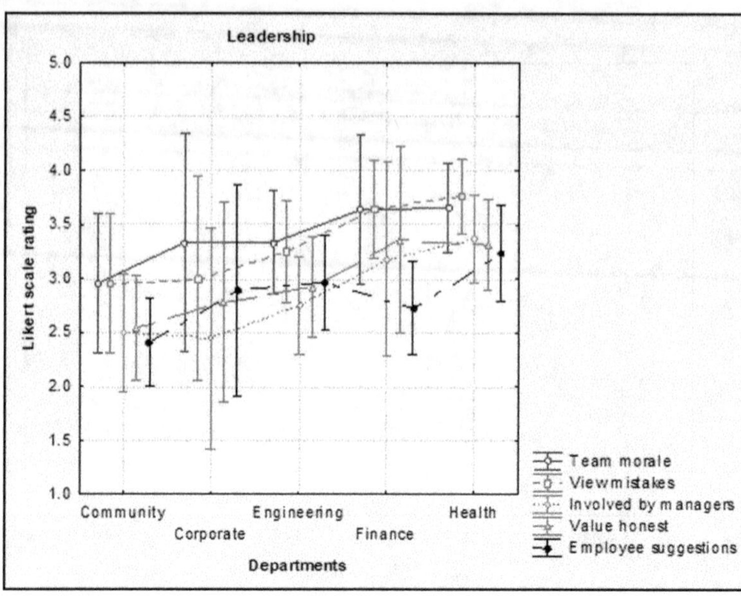

(Figure 8). However, the team feels that managers do not involve them in decisions affecting their work and they do not take note of employee's suggestions.

Team Morale

Gender specific response on whether the leadership promotes team morale and builds organisational commitment (Figure 9). The trends are slightly different, with females in different service groups agreeing that leadership does promote team moral and commitments (Figure 9). The difference in the gender-segregated response is more pronounced in respondents that have worked for the organisation between 6-10 years. Respondents with the least and highest number of years of service agree that the organisation does promote team morale and builds commitments (Figure 9).

Employees Suggestions

Gender segregated response on whether management takes note of employee suggestions (Figure 10). Respondents with less than five years of service and those with more than 20 years of service agreed that management does take note of employees' suggestions, while the respondents between 6 and 20 years of service disagree (Figure 10). Generally, males have slight higher rating than females in all the different groups of years of service.

Figure 8. Likert scale rating on segments related to leadership with their respective 95% confidence interval

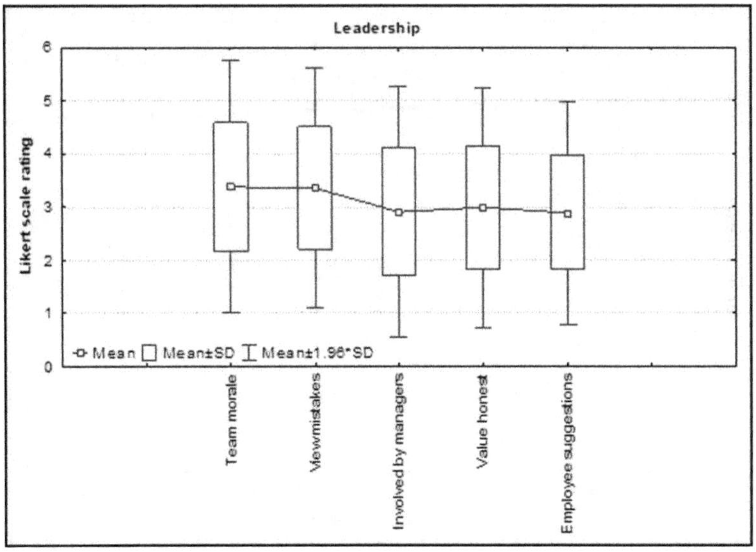

Figure 9. Respondents, response on if managers promote team morale, segregated by gender and years of service, with their respective 95% confidence interval

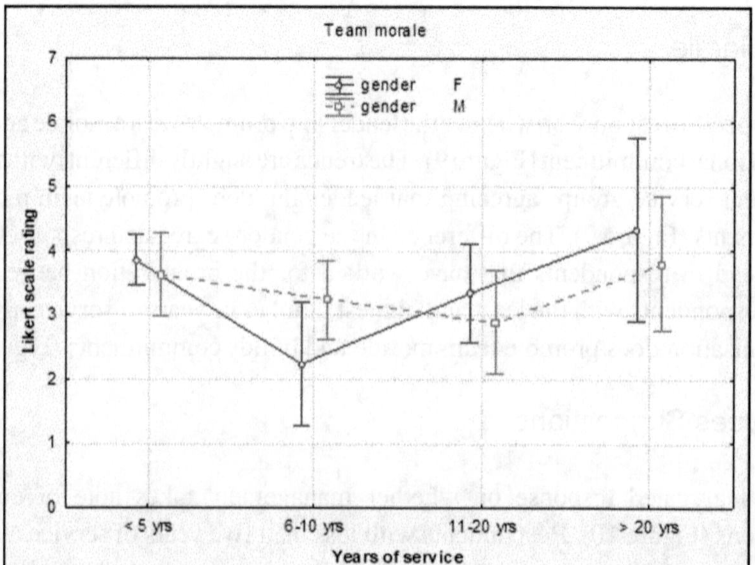

Figure 10. Respondents, response on if their suggestions are considered by managers, segregated by gender and years of service, with their respective 95% confidence interval

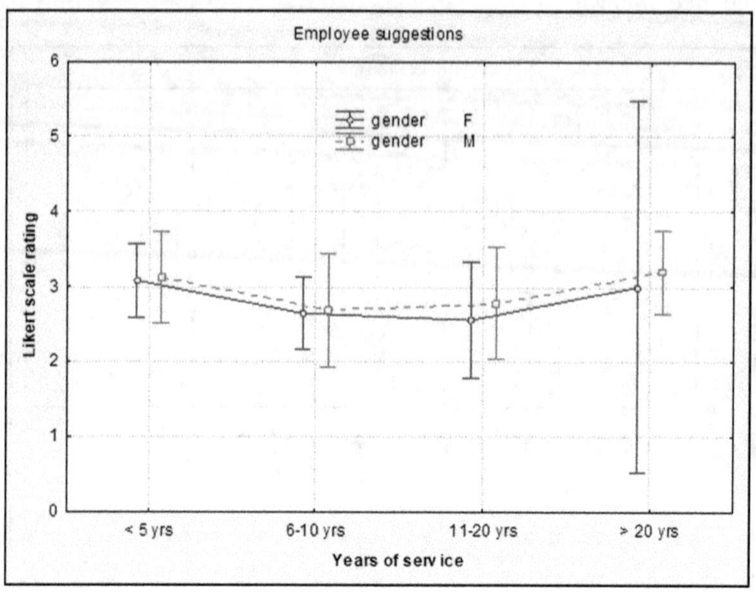

Performance By Department

Employees under Community Development and Engineering Services were neutral about the execution of an action, while Finance and Health Services agreed to a higher Likert scale rating (Figure 11). Corporate Service provided highly variable responses (Figure 11). All departments but Engineering Services felt that the organisation maintains competitive pay and benefit packages. On the other hand, only the Finance Services felt that they are recognized for higher performance, the other department rated it the lowest (Figure 11).

Performance By All Respondents

Figure 12 shows higher variability in the respondent's views about performance. In general, there is a neutral feeling among staff on lack of recognition for high performance. Respondents felt that they are competitively remunerated, and the organisation has the ability to maximize employees' potential (Figure 12).

High Performance

Gender segregated response on employees' performance (Figure 13). The gender segregated response follow the same trend except for the employees that have worked

Figure 11. Response on performance segregated by department

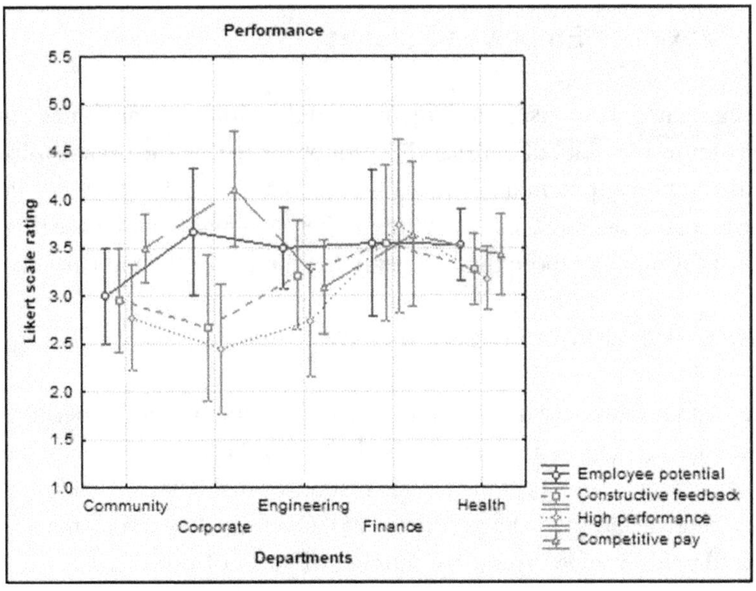

Figure 12. Likert scale rating of components related to performance with their respective 95% confidence interval

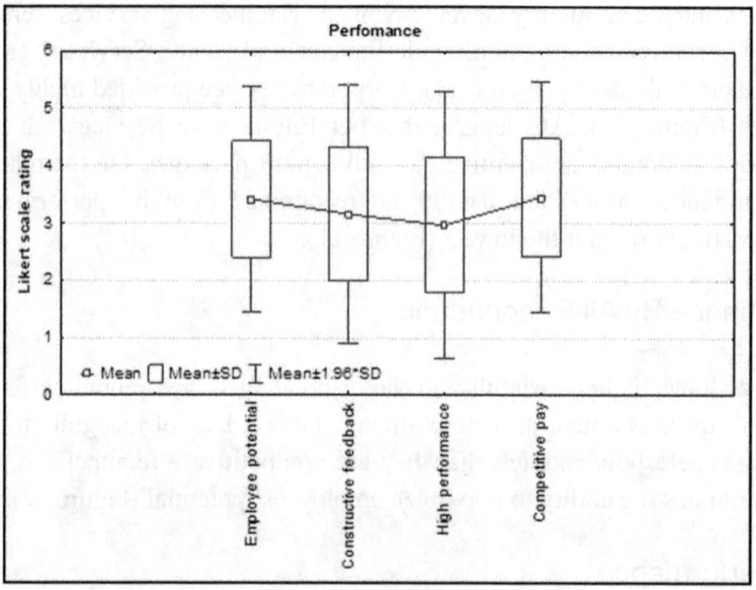

for the organisation for more than 20 years, where the responses are highly variable within and between the genders (Figure 13). Generally, among the respondents few females have worked for the Municipality of Swakopmund for more than 20 years, hence a higher variability in this group.

Ability to Maximize Employee Potential

Gender segregated responses on organisational ability to maximize employee potential (Figure 14). All but one, service groups agree that the organisation is able to maximize employee potential. Female respondents that worked for the organisation between 6 and 20 years rate these activities higher than males, and those that worked for less than 5 years and more than 20 years rated it lower than males (Figure 14).

Employees' Are Competitively Remunerated

Gender segregated response if the organization has maintained a competitive pay and benefit packages (Figure 15). The results shows less variation between the gender and the years of service, expect the female responses that have served for more than 20 years, where variability is huge (Figure 15). Overall, all respondents agreed that they are well paid, irrespective of the number of years of service.

Figure 13. Respondents, response on whether employees feel that they are recognized for high performance, segregated by gender and years of service, with their respective 95% confidence interval

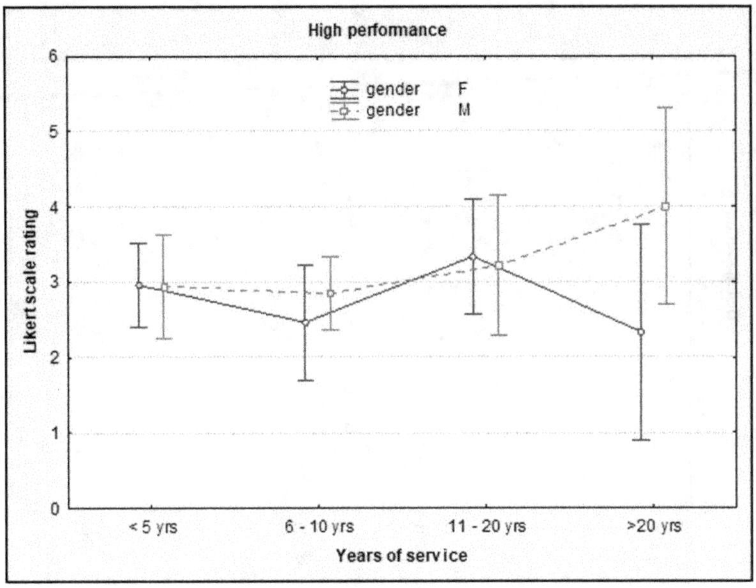

Figure 14. Respondents, response on if the Municipality of Swakopmund has the ability to maximize the employees' potential, segregated by gender and years of service, with their respective 95% confidence interval

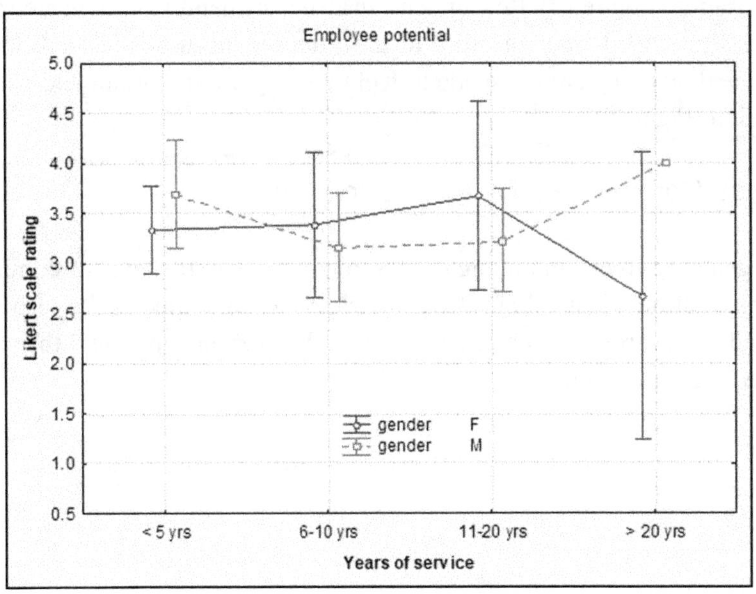

Figure 15. Respondents, response on the Municipality of Swakopmund remuneration and service benefit, segregated by gender and years of service, with their respective 95% confidence interval

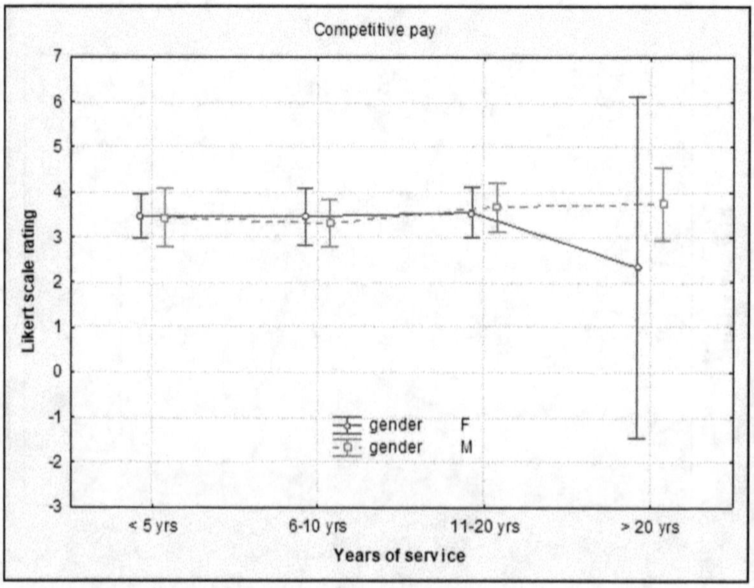

Employee Commitment By Department

Generally, employees in all departments agreed to be committed to the objective of the organisation (Figure 16). Respondents in all departments have indicated a higher willingness to work harder in order to have the organisation succeed. However, they also feel that they are not made to feel that they are important and part of the organisation (Figure 16).

Employee Commitment By All Respondents

There is general agreement among the respondents about the level of commitment to the organisation (Figure 17). There is a clear variation among the respondents, but overall mean provide a positive response. The respondents' feel that they are not made to feel important.

Figure 16. Response on employee commitment segregated by department

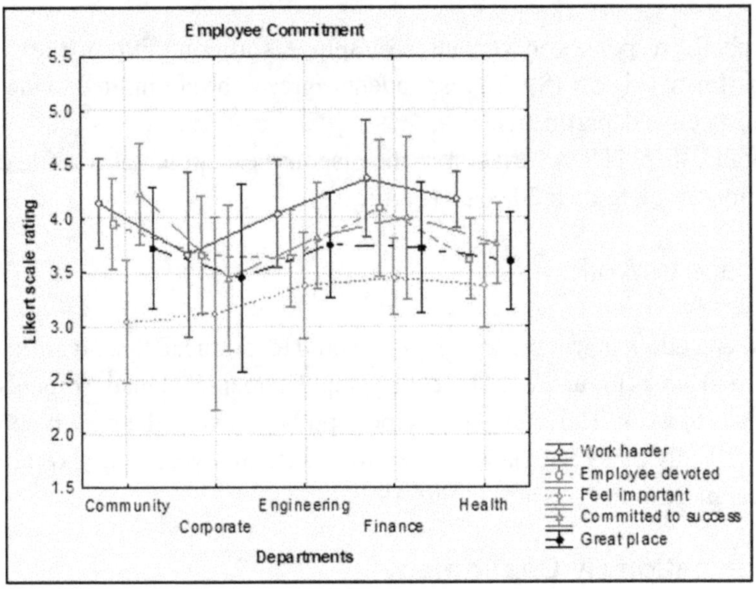

Figure 17. Likert scale rating on employee commitment with the respective 95% confidence interval

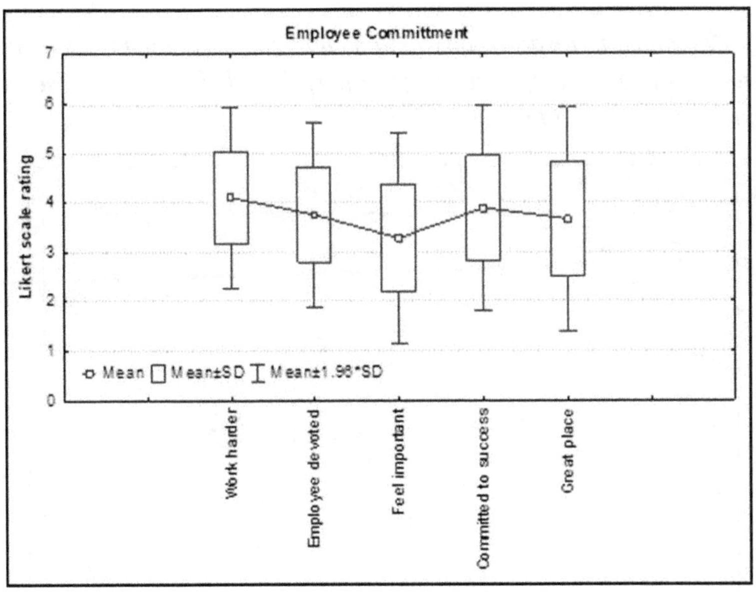

Employees Are Committed to Success

Gender specific responses on whether the employees are committed to the success of their department (Figure 18). All respondents agree to be committed to the success of their respective departments.

Generally, there is less variation in the response except females worked for the organisation for more than 20 years (Figure 18).

Great Place to Work

Gender segregation on whether employees would recommend this organisation as a great place to work (Figure 19). There is a general agreement that the organisation is a great place to work. The agreement is more pronounced by the male respondents, more specifically those that have worked for less than 5 years and those that have worked for more than 11 years (Figure 19)

Communication By Department

All departments' respondents agree that they can speak freely to their supervisors, but supervisors do not involve employees in the goal setting of the organisation.

Figure 18. Respondents, response on whether employees are committed to the success of the Municipality of Swakopmund, segregated by gender and years of service, with their respective 95% confidence interval

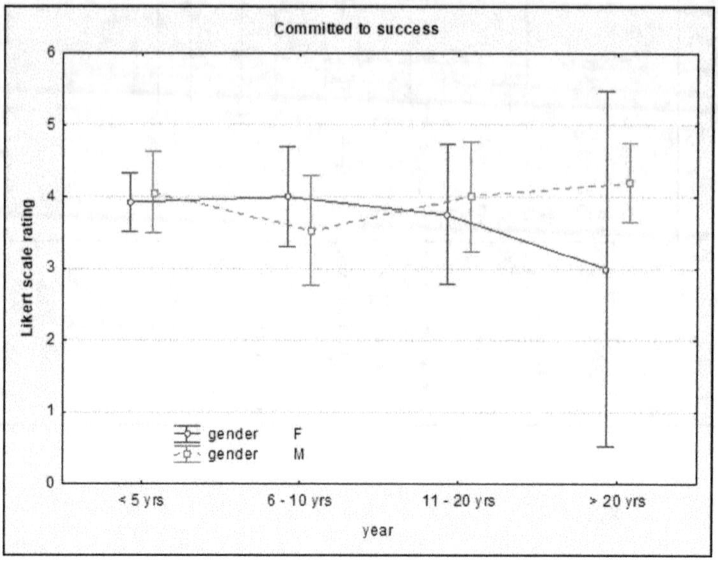

Figure 19. Gender and years of service-segregated responses on whether respondents, feel that Municipality of Swakopmund is a great place to work, with their respective 95% confidence interval

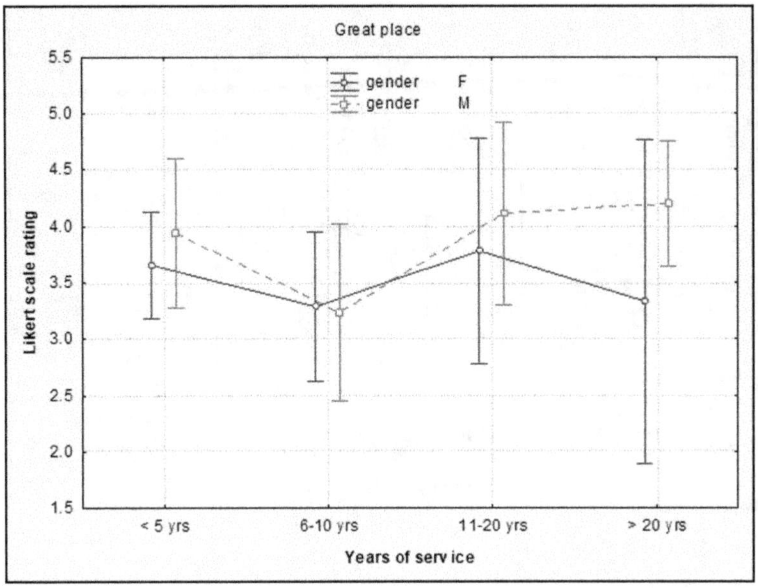

Respondents have also indicated that there are some barriers to open and efficient communication between departments, more pronounced in the Engineering Services (Figure 20).

Communication By All Respondents

Figure 21 shows the response on communication within the organisation. The responses on communication are highly variable. The mean shows that there is good communication within the organisation, although the mean response on open communication and involvement in goal setting are around the average.

Opinions Valued

Figure 22 shows a gender-segregated response on communication tied with the years of service. Generally, there is a higher variation between male and female respondents. Male respondents that have worked for the Municipality of Swakopmund for less than 5 years and for more than 20 years felt that their opinions are valued. Female respondents felt that their opinions are valued, the same opinions is expressed by the

Figure 20. Response on communication segregated by department

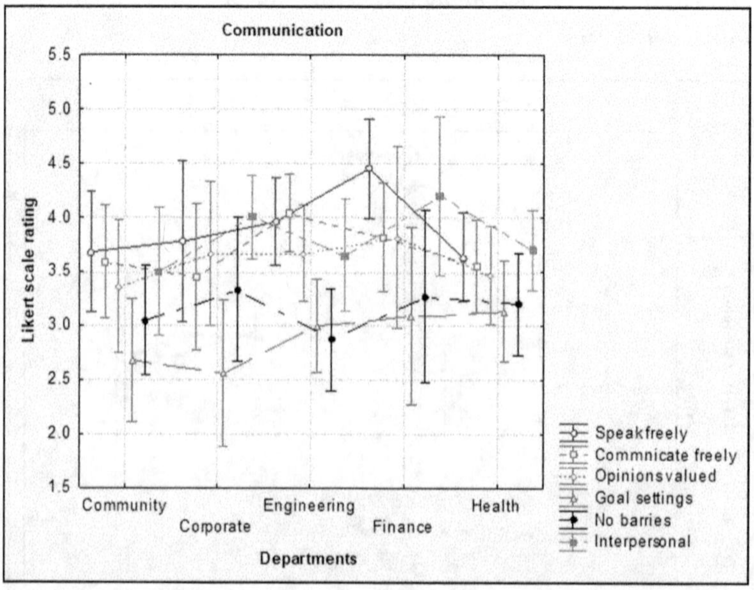

male respondents except those males that have been with the organisation between 11-20 years, who felt that their opinions are not valued (Figure 22).

No Communication Barriers

Gender specific response on whether there are barriers to open and efficient communication between departments (Figure 23). There is a general agreement between the genders except, the males that have worked for between 11-20 years who ffelt that there are barriers in communiccation between the departments (Figure 23).

Section C contained structured interview questions targeting employees in leadership positions, such as managers, general managers and head of departments, who are involved in overseeing the day-to-day operations of their respective departments. The section seeks their understanding of the role of leadership, type of leadership styles and the effect of leadership on employees' performance. Respondents believe that employees' performance is an output or contribution that each employee delivers as per their daily work sheet. These employees' daily work sheets are aligned to the overall organisational goals. Variable responses were provided concerning organisation modes of communication and their effectiveness. Respondents listed various modes of communication ranging from face-to-face meetings, email, internal memorandum, social media etc. Some respondents felt that these modes of communication are not always very effective. Generally, respondents

Figure 21. Likert scale rating on communication with their respective 95% confidence interval

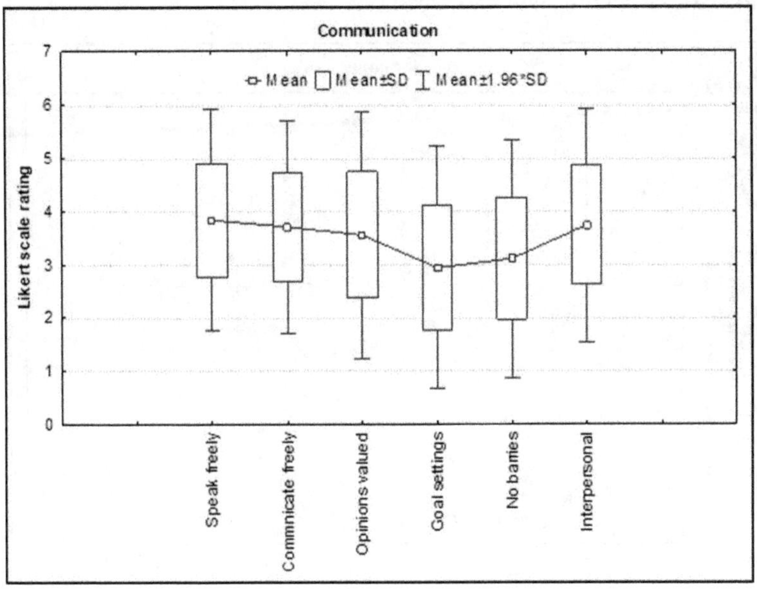

Figure 22. Respondents, response on if their opinions are valued by managers, segregated by gender and years of service, with their respective 95% confidence interval

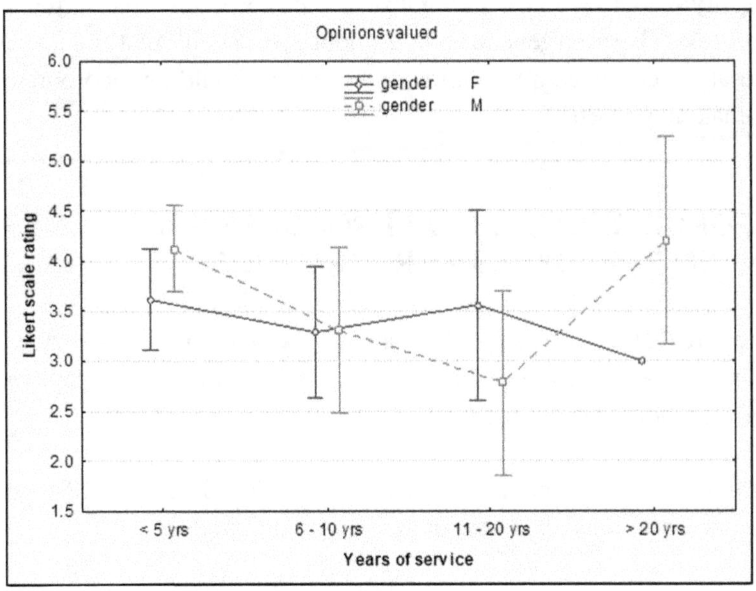

Figure 23. Respondents, response on whether there are communication barriers between the different departments, segregated by gender and years of service, with their respective 95% confidence interval

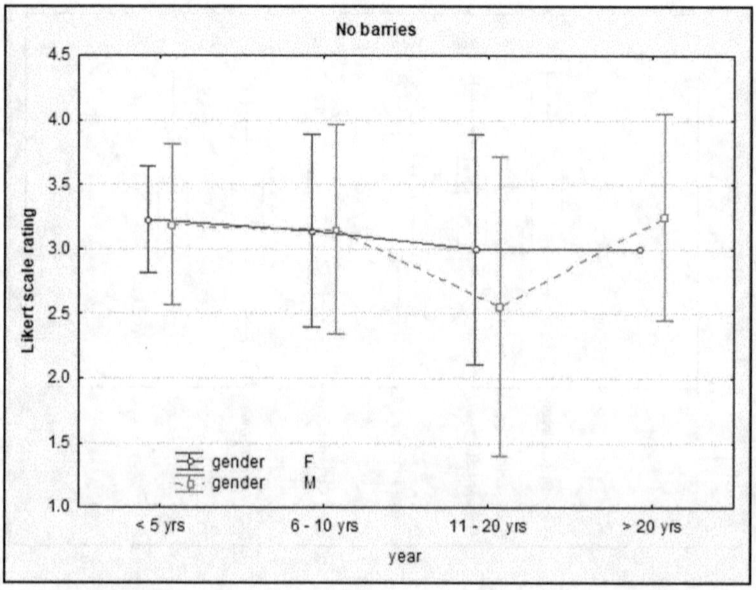

believe that there is a relationship between employees' performance and leadership style. Respondents felt that managers' leadership style plays vital roles in ensuring employees are motivated and inspired. Respondents recommended the democratic leadership style, as they felt that employees need to be involved in the decision-making process. There is a general feeling among respondents that employees should be valued and recognized all the time, their inputs should be incorporated in the decision-making process.

WORKFORCE RESKILLING APPROACHES FOR ENHANCED EMPLOYEES' PERFORMANCE

Turbulence are difficult times for all organisations, but more so for service entities it is to survive these difficult times. That is possible when they adopt workforce reskilling approaches. These include:

- Right skilling of labour force as the interdependency of the employer/ employee relationship is now more important than ever.

- Re-skilling to work on service cost reductions, and to apply all of the principles of service efficiency, quality. It is an essential time to make sure all of that training is put to use. With reduced margins, there is absolutely no room for quality problems, for waste, or misunderstanding.
- Thriving on positive attitude and training work force to think positive to achieve the required savings means leveraging the workforce. The expectation has to be that all employees have a responsibility to secure the future of the organisation. The role of leaders is not to draw up lists for redundancy, but facilitate cost savings, through communicating clear expectations and implementing programs that enhance teamwork and help all employees to make a positive contribution.
- Learning newer skills, the uncertainty created by the current economic climate can affect the confidence of employees and indeed their own performance. Leaders have many levers to put into play that, if used correctly, can be of great value to both the performance of organisations and the employee. The most critical area of impact is the organisational culture.
- Right skilling on the culture like training "how things are done" in an organisation. More importantly in times of crisis, culture takes the driver's seat. A constructive culture where people treat each other with respect and work together effectively provides a solid foundation to handle external pressures more positively. So, in uncertain times, it is imperative that the culture is one in which employees can strive to do their personal best; one in which they wish to stay to pursue a career and one in which they actively promote the organisation as a great place to work. A culture that encourages people in these ways is one in which its people are actively engaged. Thus, creating an engaging environment in which people are inspired to do their best does not happen by accident. These environments typically have leaders that are open and honest and act with humility – these leaders love to coach and develop their people. Leaders that take full accountability for their actions and do not get into the blame game. They also are generally very curious about what is happening around them, genuinely interested in their people and keen to be constantly learning.
- Focus on revenue generation and cost opportunities: there is a need to continue to know the organisation inside out, the business levers, revenue and cost savings opportunities, and continue to drive the organisations to innovate really to survive and create advantage in these times.
- Engagement becomes even more important: leaders also need to develop strategies to continue to keep the current employees focused, engaged and productive in this challenging environment. Further, service organisations like municipalities will need more change-oriented leaders and they will be

more valuable than ever in these times. Finally, having the right systems and processes to motivate people and reinforce a positive culture is imperative.

RECOMMENDATIONS

The life cycle of knowledge required to accomplish many jobs has become ever shorter as new concepts and technology are introduced more frequently. This has increased pressure to renew workforce competency through training/retraining or recruitment of new personnel. Competency requirements must be anticipated and acted on proactively to avoid serious lags in achieving strategic goals. The private sector increasingly states that workforce knowledge is a key competitive issue and promotes workforce reskilling (Karthikeyan, 2015). Public service providers also require this as the public is not likely to accept less from the workforce in terms of up-to-date competencies, nor should it. The private sector has begun actively to encourage older workers to stay by providing increased flexibility to work part-time, or to perform projects where their wisdom and organizational knowledge, gained through years of experience.

The results clearly indicate that there is a need for vocational education, training and higher education to be flexible in their course offerings, work with industry to ensure that it is delivering consistent and quality learning outcomes, thus creating a culture of communication and collaboration by mutual understanding of education and training, possibilities and constraints. The skills base needed in the twenty-first century is one that encompasses a mastery of core knowledge in a key field along with a number of well-developed workplace skills such as critical thinking, effective communication and willingness to engage in continued lifelong learning (Business-Higher Education Forum, 2013). Multiple changes in career are now likely expected in the workforce; having strong base knowledge to understand emerging digital technologies and new approaches to problem solving will be required (Deloitte Australia, 2014). The workforce needs attributes such as team spirit, willingness to learn, commitment to the organisation, capacity to foster innovation and improve business performance (Mendes and Machado 2015).

Based on the above discussion and analysis the following are the recommendations to the management of the Municipality of Swakopmund:

- The democratic leadership style practiced in the Swakopmund Municipality should be encouraged as this style has a potential to further empower employees by developing teams and delegate some measures of power and authority to employees.

- It is also important for the Municipality of Swakopmund provide professional guidelines that create a sense of responsibility to employees coupled with an intense on job training and skills development.
- More twinning agreements with other regional or international local authorities, especially those that are faced with similar challenges in terms of service delivery and exchange best practices.
- Finally, yet importantly, it is highly recommended that the Municipality of Swakopmund provide its leaders with comprehensive leadership programmes to enhance mutual understanding between the employees. In addition, the Municipality of Swakopmund may also explore and study the servant leadership style, which may improve relationship with employees.

FUTURE AREAS FOR RESEARCH

For future studies, it would be desirable to repeat this exercise, by expanding the questionnaires to include the community of Swakopmund, thus increasing the number of participants. Such exercise will gain valuable inputs from the community, which the Municipality of Swakopmund management can utilize to improve the organisational performance. Additional further research is needed to understand how best education and training providers can work effectively with these local authorities to address the skills needs.

CONCLUSION

The finding of this study echoed with the main objective was to explore and analyse leadership styles adopted by the Municipality of Swakopmund and thereby examine the influence it has on employees' performance and overall employees' performance. Leadership style is one of the factors identified. Leadership style refers to a leader's conduct, behaviour and attitude of governing, leading and supervising. Leadership style can be influenced by personality traits, understanding, approach and attitude towards the subject matter. The findings of this study indicated that managers do not involve employees in decision-making process and provide adequate feedback and guidance. Furthermore, employees said that they are not involved in decision affecting their work and their suggestions are not considered. Respondents reported that there is a communication barrier between the departments. At the Municipality of Swakopmund, leadership style seems to affect all implementers including the new entrants. Leadership can create a corporate culture that has an influence on employees' performance. It is acknowledged through this research that employee's performance, which leads to the organisation's performance, is a difficult concept and not easily measured especially in the absence of performance agreements. Even the morale factor is important as high morale contributes to high levels productivity, high returns to shareholders and employee loyalty. David and Nigel (2009) concluded that team morale play a significant role in motivating employees more than the money. The findings also indicate that the Municipality of Swakopmund practices both democratic and autocratic leadership styles. It should be noted that democratic and autocratic leadership are two contradictory styles Given the effectiveness of each leadership style, if the Municipality of Swakopmund has to adopt and operate both styles well, it could gain some benefits. Of course, it should also be noted sole reliance on leadership style can be damaging and cause unintended consequences. According to Dawson (2002), autocratic style may show great results in a short period. However, excessive use of authority will distort productivity in the long term. People would either get bored or get dissatisfied and leave. In contrast, democratic leadership using institutional mechanisms such as remuneration, compensation, communication policies and procedures may create a dynamic empowerment culture with an active, strong, dynamic and innovative workforce.

According to Meyer and Herscovitch (2001), continuous learning improves career-development and career growth and organisations that provide such opportunities tend to attract and retain high-performing employees. Through performance management systems, relevant training and career path could be identified. It is recommended that the Municipality of Swakopmund should introduce the performance management system and consider workforce reskilling. Training motivates new employees to be more productive and efficient, while making old employees more motivated to familiarize themselves with new techniques and new machines. This is largely in line with Wright and Geory (2001) findings that employee competencies change through effective training programs. The findings of this study revealed that training is not a high priority. Guest (1997) discussed abundantly that training is proven to generate performance improvement related benefit for the employee as well as for the organization, by positively influencing employee performance through the development of employee knowledge, skills, ability, competencies and behavior. On a positive note, most of the respondents believed that, the Municipality of Swakopmund is a great place to work. Respondents feel that they are competitively remunerated and benefit packages are irresistible. Respondents also feel that the organisation has the ability to maximize employees' potential. The majority of the respondents feel that they are working hard to help the organisation achieve its set goals. Respondents feel that a democratic leadership style is practiced as managers promote team morale and commitment. This support the earlier findings by McNeese (1997) who concluded that giving grants and bonuses to employees will motivate them because such practices indicate recognition, creation of tailored incentives to recognize and motivate a range of employees working in different departments.

To conclude, the study provided an understanding on the issues identified during the "*Free to Grow Exercise*" in 2015. There is strong evidence that communication in the Municipality of Swakopmund is a major problem, between departments and within departments. There is also evidence that autocratic leadership style is practiced in some departments, which affects the performance of employees in those specific departments. It is therefore recommended that the Municipality of Swakopmund management use the findings and recommendations of this study to address the gaps within the organisation. Thus, fair compensation with benefit packages, morale and motivation, career growth and development as well as training and reskilling will influence performance and commitment in the workplace. Apart from that it provides employees with the opportunities to make a difference to the job, be innovative to try out new skills, exercise own discretions yet receive timely feedback on their performance.

REFERENCES

Adair, J. (2005). Not Bosses But Leaders: How to lead the way to success. *MPG Book Limited*. Bodmin, Cornwall. *Administrative Science Quarterly*, *30*, 78–102.

Armstrong, M. (2004). *Managing Performance: Performance Management in Action* (1st ed.). London: Chartered Institute of Personnel & Development.

Azadeh, S. (2012). *Moral Leadership: Transformational Leadership*. Paper presented at the Southern African Management Conference, Windhoek, Namibia.

Babatunde, O., & Ikenga, E. (2015). The Impact of Leadership Style in Employee's Performance in an Organisation. Nigeria. *Public Policy and Administration Research.*, *5*(1), 194–204.

Bartram, T., & Casimir, G. (2007). The relationship between leadership and follower in-role performance and satisfaction with the leaders: The mediating effects of empowerment and trust in the leader. *Leadership and Organization Development Journal*, *208*(1), 4–9. doi:10.1108/01437730710718218

Behery, M. (2008). Leadership, knowledge sharing and organizational benefits within UAE. *The Journal of American Academy of Business, Cambridge*, *12*, 227–236.

Belete, J. (2015). *Effects of leadership style on employees' performance in case of Kaffa Zone Higher Public Educational Institutions*. Jimma University.

Botha, D. (2015). *Free to Grow Report. Municipality of Swakopmund.*

Business-Higher Education Forum. (2013). *The National Higher Education and Workforce Initiative: Forging Strategic Partnerships for Undergraduate Innovation and Workforce Development.* Retrieved from http://www. bhef.com/publications/ national-higher-education-andworkforce-initiative-forging-strategic-partnerships

Chandrasekar, K. (2011). Workplace environment and its impact on organisational behaviors in the Public Sector. *International Journal of Enterprise Computing and Business Systems.* Retrieved from http://www.ijecbs.com/January2011/N4Jan2011.pdf

Chen, K. J., & Chen, S. I. (2008). Personal traits and leadership styles of Taiwan' higher educational institution in innovative operations. *The Journal of American Academy of Business, Cambridge, 12*(2), 145–150.

Chen, Y. F., & Tjosvold, D. (2006). Participative leadership by American and Chinese managers in China: The role of relationships. *Journal of Management Studies, 43*(8), 1727–1752. doi:10.1111/j.1467-6486.2006.00657.x

Cole, G. A. (2002). *Personnel and Human Resource Management* (5th ed.). London: Continuum Publisher.

Daniel, G. (2002). *The New leaders: Transforming the Art of Leadership into the Science of Results. Little brown.* London: Zancaster Press.

David, W. C., & Nigel, F. P. (2009). *Strategic Marketing* (9th ed.). McGraw-Hill.

Debashis, C. (2000). *Leading consciously: A pilgrimage toward self-mastery.* Butterworth.

Deloitte Australia. (2014). *Positioning for Prosperity: Catching the Next Wave. Building the Lucky Country Series.* Author.

Douglas, A. S., Robert, A. R., & Stephen, C. R. (2013). *On-Demand Supply Management, World-Class Strategies, Practices and Technology.* Ross Publishing.

Dubrin, A. J. (2007). *Leadership Research Findings, Practice and Skills* (5th ed.). Houghton Mifflin Company.

Erongo Regional Profile. (2013). *Swakopmund Local Economic Development Strategy.* Retrieved from www.swkmun.com.na

Fu-Jin, W., Shieh, C., & Tang, M. (2011). Effect of Leadership Style on Organisational Performance as viewed from human resources management strategy. *African Journal of Business Management, 4*(18), 3924–3936.

Guest, D. E. (1997). Human resources management and industrial relations. *Journal of Management Studies*, *24*(5), 503–521. doi:10.1111/j.1467-6486.1987.tb00460.x

Hersey, P., Blanchard, K. H., & Johnson, D. E. (2000). *Management of organizational behaviour: Leading human resources* (8th ed.). Englewood Cliffs, NJ: Prentice Hall.

House, R. J., & Aditya, R. N. (1971). The social scientific study of leadership: Quo Vadis. *Journal of Management*, *23*(3), 409–473. doi:10.1177/014920639702300306

Hughes, J. P., Guttorp, P., & Charles, S. P. (1999). A non-homogeneous hidden Markov model for precipitation occurrence. *Applied Statistics*, *48*(1), 15–30. doi:10.1111/1467-9876.00136

Huisman, C., Wissen, V., & Leo, J. (2004). Localization effects of firm start-ups and closures in the Netherland. *The Annals of Regional Science*, *38*(2), 291–310. doi:10.100700168-004-0196-7

Iqbal, N., Anwar, S., & Haider, N. (2015). Effect of leadership style on employee performance. *Arabic Journal of Business and Management Review.*, *5*(5), 1–6.

Ittner, C. D., & Larcker, D. F. (2002). Empirical managerial accounting research: Are we just describing management-consulting practice? *European Accounting Review*, *11*(4), 787–794. doi:10.1080/0963818022000047082

Jon, M., & Randy, L. D. (2009). *Human Resources Development* (6th ed.). South Western.

Judge, T. A., Bono, J. E., Ilies, R., & Gerhardt, M. W. (2002). Personality and leadership: A qualitative and quantitative review. *The Journal of Applied Psychology*, *87*(4), 765–780. doi:10.1037/0021-9010.87.4.765 PMID:12184579

Karthikeyan, C. (2015). Re-Skilling and Right-Skilling HR Component to Sustain in Turbulent Business Scenario: A Conceptual Study on Prevailing Strategies. *European Journal of Commerce and Management Research, SI*(1), 51-53.

Kim, D. O., & Bae, J. (2017). *Employment relations and HRM in South Korea*. Routledge. doi:10.4324/9781315256566

Kirega, V. P. G. (2006). *Kampala City Handbook*. Kampala, Uganda: Gava Associated Services.

Likert, R. (1967). *The human organization: Its management and value* (1st ed.). New York: McGraw-Hill.

London, M. (2001). *Leadership Development: Paths to Self-Insight and Professional Growth* (1st ed.). Lawrence Erlbaum Associates, Incorporated Publisher. doi:10.4324/9781410604514

Mafini, C., & Pooe, D. (2013). The relationship between employee satisfaction and organisational performance: Evidence from a South African government department. *SA Journal of Industrial Psychology*, *39*(1), 1–9. doi:10.4102ajip.v39i1.1090

Makkonen, H., Pohjola, M., Olkkonen, R., & Koponen, A. (2014). Dynamic capabilities and firm performance. *DBA Africa Management Review.*, *2*(3), 614–626.

Mat, J. (2008). *The Influence of Leadership Style on Internal Marketing in Retailing* (PhD Thesis). University of Stirling.

Maurik, J. V. (2001). Writers on Leadership. London: Penguin Books.

McGrath, G. R., & MacMillan, I. C. (2000). *Entrepreneurial Mindset: Strategies for continuously creating opportunity in an age of uncertainty*. Harvard Business School Press Books.

McNeese, G. (1997). Factors Contributing to Nurses Demotivation with Recognition Initiatives: A Review of the Research Literature. *International Journal of Nursing Studies*, *44*, 297–314.

Meindl, J. R., Ehrlich, S. B., & Dukerich, J. M. (1985). The romance of leadership. *Administrative Science Quarterly*, *30*(1), 78–102. doi:10.2307/2392813

Mendes, L., & Machado, J. (2015). Employees' Skills, Manufacturing Flexibility and Performance: A Structural Equation Modelling Applied to the Automotive Industry. *International Journal of Production Research*, *53*(13), 4087–4101. doi:10.1080/00207543.2014.993772

Meyer, J. P., & Herscovitch, L. (2001). Commitment in the workplace: Towards a general Model. *Human Resource Management Review*, *11*(3), 299–326. doi:10.1016/S1053-4822(00)00053-X

Michael, A. (2010). *Leadership style and organizational impact*. Retrieved from http://www.ala-apa.org

Mintzberg, H. (2010). Shifting the trajectory of civilisation. *Oxford Leadership Journal*, *1*(2), 1–10.

Mustaffa, Y. M. B. (2012). *Factors influencing organisational performance in Metro Specialist Hospital, Sungai Petani*. Universiti Utara.

Naile, I., & Selesho, J. (2014). The Role of Leadership in Employee Motivation. *Mediterranean Journal of Social Sciences*, *5*(3), 175–181.

Ngambi, H. C., Cant, M. C., & Van Heerden, C. H. (2010). *Marketing Management: A South African perspective*. Cape Town, South Africa: Juta.

Nkata, J.L. (2004). *Private higher education in Uganda: the case of its distribution, Contribution to access and costs*. Academic Press. doi:10.1177/1356389011411610

Northouse, P. G. (2010). *Leadership theory and practice* (5th ed.). Thousand Oaks, CA: SAGE Publication.

Northouse, P. G. (2013). *Leadership Theory and Practice* (6th ed.). London: SAGE Publication.

Ojokuku, R. M., Odetayo, T. A., & Sajuyigbe, A. S. (2012). Impact of Leadership Style on Organizational Performance: A case Study of Nigerian Banks. *American Journal of Business and Management*, *1*(4), 202–207.

Ollukkaran, B. A., & Gunaseelan, D. R. (2012). A study on the impact of work environment on employee performance. *International Journal of Management Research*, *2*(2), 71–85.

Paley, N. (2004). *Successful Business Planning: Energizing Your Company's Potential*. London Thorogood.

Peterson, R. S., Smith, D. B., Martorana, P. V., & Owens, P. D. (2003). The Impact of Chief Executive Officer Personality on Top Management Team Dynamics: One Mechanism by Which Leadership Affects Organizational Performance. *The Journal of Applied Psychology*, *88*(5), 795–808. doi:10.1037/0021-9010.88.5.795 PMID:14516245

Rowold, J. (2011). Relationship between leadership behaviors and performance: The moderating role of a work team's level of age, gender and culture heterogeneity. *Leadership and Organization Development Journal*, *32*(6), 628–647. doi:10.1108/01437731111161094

Starr, J. (2004). The manager's role in coaching overcoming barriers to success. Development and Learning in Organisations. *International Journal (Toronto, Ont.)*, *18*(2), 9–12.

Sun, R. Y. (2002). The relationship among the leadership style, organisational culture and organisational effectiveness based on competing value framework: An empirical study. Institute of Technology in Taiwan.

Taiwo, O. (2013). *Leadership Style: Impact on Employees*. Lahti University of Applied Sciences.

Thao, L. T., & Hwang, C. (2015). *Factors affecting employee performance*. PetroVietnam Engineering Consultancy J.S.C.

Toit, A. D. (2007). Making sense through coaching. *Journal of Management Development*, *26*(3), 282–291. doi:10.1108/02621710710732164

Voon, M. L., Lo, M. C., Ngui, K. J., & Ayob, N. B. (2011). The influence of leadership styles on employees' job satisfaction in public sector organizations in Malaysia. International *Journal of Business. Management and Social Sciences*, *2*(1), 24–32.

Wakabi, B. M. (2013). Leadership Style and Staff Retention in Organisations. *International Journal of Science and Research*, *5*(1), 412–416.

Wright, P., & Geroy, D. G. (2001). Changing the mindset: The training myth and the need for word-class performance. *International Journal of Human Resource Management*, *12*(4), 586–600. doi:10.1080/09585190122342

Zhu, W., Chew, I., & Spangler, W. (2005). CEO transformational leadership and organizational outcomes: The mediating role of human-capital-enhancing human resource management. *The Leadership Quarterly*, *16*(1), 39–52. doi:10.1016/j.leaqua.2004.06.001

KEY TERMS AND DEFINITIONS

Challenges: Something that by its nature or character serves as a call to make special effort, a demand to explain, justify, or difficulty in a undertaking that is stimulating to one engaged in it.

Competence: Refers to the capacity of individuals/employees to act in a wide variety of situations. It consists of education, skills, experience, energy and their attitudes that will make or mar relationships with the customers and the products or services they provide.

Decision-Making: A rational and logical process of choosing the best alternative or course of action among the available options.

Development: Means 'steady progress' and stresses effective assisting in hastening a process or bringing about a desired end, a significant consequence or event, the act or process of growing, progressing, or developing.

Government: The organization, machinery, or agency through which a political unit exercises authority and performs functions and which is usually classified according to the distribution of power within it.

Knowledge Management: The systematic process of finding, selecting, organizing, distilling and presenting information that improves the comprehension in a specific area of interest. It is also as a synonym for content management or information management, but incorporates communities of practice, learning from experience, and knowledge retention and transfer.

Leader: Head, superior, a person who rules, guides, motivates, encourages, stimulates and inspires others.

Manager: A person who has the authority and responsibility for getting the work done, making decisions, and is accountable.

Organization: A group of persons organized for some end or work; an organized structure or whole for a business or administrative concern united and constructed for a particular end.

Training: Organized activity aimed at imparting information and/or instructions to improvc the recipient's performance or to help him or her attain a required level of knowledge or skill.

Transformation: The act or process of transforming, change in form, appearance, nature, or character or alteration, especially a radical one. A change in position or direction of the reference axes in a coordinate system without an alteration in their relative angle.

Chapter 11
Effective Integration of Technology and Human Capital Development in Healthcare

Terrence Duncan
https://orcid.org/0000-0002-5456-6013
Liberty University, USA

Gary James Hanney
South University, USA

Darrell Norman Burrell
The Florida Institute of Technology, USA

Emad Rahim
Bellevue University, USA

ABSTRACT

Human capital development is important for organizations and most industries in the United States of America (USA). In the healthcare industry, human capital development is a priority due to the variety of skilled and unique positions within one of the most regulated industries within the USA. Integration of work processes, operational efficiencies, and assimilating regulatory changes are a pre-requisite for human resource professionals to remain competitive as well as remain operationally relevant. Information technology adoption in healthcare must continue to improve to address some of the industry's largest challenges: turnover, retention, and education. The intent of this chapter is to outline the existing challenges of human capital development in healthcare and how information technology provides significant value to closing the gaps of the alarming trends that exist in the industry.

DOI: 10.4018/978-1-5225-9810-7.ch011

INTRODUCTION

The integration of technology into everyday life and operations continues to expand at a prolific rate. Benefits of technology include increased efficiencies, improved communication, effective integration of logistics between buyer and supplier, as well as improved decision-making using business analytics. The healthcare industry benefits from technology and improved technological advances; however, it remains to be under-utilized.

The healthcare industry is one of the largest industries in the United States according to the U.S. Gross Domestic Product (G.D.P.). According to the Centers for Medicare and Medicaid Services, healthcare is approximately 18% of U.S. G.D.P., with a growth rate as of 2016 at 4.3% (Duncan, Rahim, & Burrell, 2018). Numerous intervening factors exist that will continue to grow the cost of healthcare and the industry itself. Such factors include a projected increase of an aging population with chronic health disorders; expansions of different specialties to address healthcare treatment needs; and cost of care.

Coupled with the anticipated growth of the industry is the increased need for skilled laborers. Despite the demand required to fill these specialty positions and to care for the aging population and address other healthcare needs, significant shortages in physicians and nurses are anticipated over the next decade (Kirch & Petelle, 2017). As the likelihood of hiring to meet the expected demand will fall short, providers and facilities operating within the healthcare industry must consider different ways to attract and retain employees.

Employee turnover compounds shortages in crucial staffing areas. Management often focuses on reactive measures on addressing turnover. One of the root causes related to turnover derives from the lack of training, whether it is during the orientation period or other situations requiring critical decision-making that may affect someone's life. Although most positions involving a professional license requires continuing education in core competency and skills, the combination of a lack of adequate staffing, personnel, and time compete against these requirements. This creates additional strain on existing resources to meet the needs and demand of the patients.

Technology provides employers with strategic advantages for human resources development. Qualitative and quantitative data can be extrapolated from surveys, exit interviews, and other means of data collection to assist in identifying critical opportunities for improvement. Investments in human capital stimulate innovation. The nurturing effect of change from within provide organizations an opportunity to add new knowledge to previous existing knowledge (Kong, 2015). As healthcare organizations must demonstrate the ability to adapt and improve flexibility due to a confluence of regulatory, economic, and political changes, innovation is vital for organizational success.

Human capital development is a critical stage of development globally. Traditional methods of human capital development are not as applicable in this current era. Economic, social, and technological factors are factors that affect most industries as the boundaries are either being eliminated or redefined. Coupled with the fact that current and future generations of workers are becoming more reliant on technology for dissemination of information and productivity, global industries are at a crux for developing human capital.

From the 2000s to the present, the Fourth Revolution is defined by advances in technology vis a vis global industrial networks, the Internet of Things, cloud computing, and innovations in the delivery of information (Mamedov, Mienva, & Glinchevsky, 2019). Ongoing dialogue and research continue to exist examining the development of human capital; efficiently integrating technology; and understanding the combination of the two to address significant and dramatic shifts in business models and globalization. Advancements in technology continue to create new opportunities for industries to spurn innovation, streamline work processes, and improve the overall quality of life.

BACKGROUND

Technological advances in human capital development continue to play a significant role in numerous industries as organizations continue to seek ways to improve efficiencies of scale, minimize disruption in employment, improve education, and connect the employees to the organization's vision and strategic business plans. Human resources play a vital role in the desired success of healthcare organizations. In an effort to continue the sustainability of organizational objectives, human resources must continue to be recognized and accepted as a significant stakeholder towards operational success in healthcare. Quality of care and patient satisfaction are significant determinants that dictate the success or failure of a healthcare operation's ability to maintain relevancy. Failure to properly integrate human resources appropriately may affect the triple bottom line of community, planet, and profit (Rahim & Duncan, 2017).

With an aging population also comes an aging workforce. Scott et al. (2017) noted the combination of the rapid growth of an aging population requiring care along with an aging workforce that contributes to the destabilization of quality of care outcomes as well as an increase of occupational injuries. The underlying impact of occupational injuries is not often discussed as a contributing factor towards a decline in productivity. Developing innovative educational programs assisting the healthcare workforce to mitigate against such losses is as important as the ongoing required education of performing the essential functions of employment.

Integration of technology into human capital development is essential in healthcare due to the delivery model of education changing as well. As distance learning has grown since the early 2000s, the delivery of healthcare education evolved as well. Although face to face learning is still a prerequisite for most programs using accumulating clinical hours, delivery of education continues to shift through mobile or advanced technology learning. Such modalities of learning include virtual simulation, webinars, and teleconferencing. Education is the most effective if it is adaptive of the society it leads. Therefore, additional research on understanding the value of technology and position-based learning programs is necessary.

Social intelligence is another vital element of human capital development. The healthcare industry is an industry that relies on the ability of its employees to demonstrate that the concepts of cooperating with others, strengthen human relations, and interact positively with its external stakeholders (Kong, 2015). Developing tacit and interpersonal skills is an ongoing requirement to nurture employee growth and promoting positive quality of care outcomes, as well as patient satisfaction.

The nursing and physician shortage continues to plague quality of care outcomes. As the shortage is anticipated to continue for at least another decade, continued research is necessary to address two different fronts. One front is to understand some of the underlying causes of the shortages. The second front, which is the intent of this proposal, is to outline the benefits of technology to help retain, educate, and address some of the known needs that exist within the healthcare industry. Continuing education is a vital element for an employee's success upon completion of licensure. Successfully integrating technology into human resources management will assist in relieving some of the strains that exist within the healthcare industry.

Nursing and Physician Shortages

The healthcare industry has several contributing factors for nursing and physician shortages. A combination of an aging population, expansion of healthcare providers, expansion of healthcare specialties, and more attractive fields contribute in their respective ways towards shortages. Demographics play a significant factor as well. As of 2017, projections revealed between 2015 and 2030, a 12% increase of the U.S. population will occur, with the individuals aged 65 and over to increase by 55% (Kirch & Pettele, 2017). From a physician standpoint, projection reveals that shortages will range between 40,800 and 104,900 (Kirch & Pettele, 2017).

The need for advanced technology integration in the industry may help reduce the over-reliance of the sheer number of physicians required. Advanced technology such as in areas of telemedicine may improve care to underserved communities;

improve efficiency in communication between the patient-physician dynamic; and improve overall lifespan in the U.S. Advanced technology also benefits the field by developing better care practice models for study. Integration of advanced technology benefits the greater good for those in the U.S.

Nursing shortages continue as a cause for concern for those within the healthcare industry. Projections reveal a shortage of nurses between 154,018 and 510,394. The nursing shortage is unique based on the projected distributions of (Zhang, Thai, Pforsich, & Lin, 2018). According to Zhang et al. (2018), the shortage will be more defined in the U.S. regions South and the West compared to the Northeast and the Midwest. Furthermore, Zhang et al. (2018) concluded in their research that 37 out of 50 states would experience significant nursing shortages by 2030. The states projected with extreme shortages may be due to shifting migration patterns of the elderly based on economic and climate-related reasons.

Health informatics continues to grow as an essential field of study in the healthcare industry. Health informatics provides the means to streamline healthcare delivery processes, improve overall clinical and operational efficiency, and improve financial outcomes. Continuing education in informatics may assist nurses in becoming more integrated into the healthcare delivery system processes, and provide an opportunity to decrease medical errors, burnout, and improve clinical expertise amongst the field (Lloyd & Ferguson, 2017). Nurses could further benefit from technology tools such as dashboards to provide real-time clinical solutions and improve communication within the organization.

Nursing shortages continue to be a core focus of study for numerous researchers in clinical and operational research. Understanding how technology can bring efficiency to current core processes along with automating certain activities that could help reduce shortage projections or used as a tool to increase recruitment and enrollment activities in the field of study. Developing and promoting continuing education that is not stagnant is critical to address the need of the patients, which demand will grow significantly in the future.

The U.S. spends more per capita on healthcare than any other country in the world. Nonetheless, Americans are less healthy than other industrialized nations. Physician shortages do factor into some of the declining numbers; however, it is not likely that an increase of physicians will occur at a feasible rate. Some research contends that changing the community care model will mitigate the shortage and improve quality of care. Others contend that advances in technology could decrease the gap of the perceived need of additional physicians versus developing more complex needs of delivery healthcare (Corso, Dorrance, & LaRochelle, 2018).

Although not as extensive or chronic as the nursing shortage, the projected physician shortage relates to projections for future demand of care. The shortage of physician is a global phenomenon that captured the attention of the World Health Organization

(WHO). According to WHO, combined physician and nursing shortages, along with other key healthcare professionals, are projected to be at approximately 4 million (Xue et al., 2018). This global phenomenon is anticipated to shift the availability of care based on geographic and financial reasons capitalized by clustered population centers. The results will continue to exacerbate the need for care in rural communities and underdeveloped nations.

INFORMATION TECHNOLOGY AND EDUCATION IN HEALTHCARE

The United States healthcare industry has been behind information technology compared to other industries. The high cost of technology with regards to capital equipment is a theoretical concern why healthcare administrators did not invest in technology. A demand for information technology in the healthcare industry continues to grow, as well as the need for technology to foster educational opportunities. In 1990, investments in technology were constrained due to fiscal challenges (Wilson & Tulu, 2010). As technology continues to grow in other fields, it is reasonable to anticipate healthcare information technology can be used to improve, quality, safety, and productivity.

It has widely been recognized that physicians, nurse, and other healthcare professionals rely on information technology to complete everyday responsibilities and work processes. Despite the ongoing need for advancements in technology in healthcare, opportunities provided through legislation have not yielded the desired results. For example, healthcare organizations struggled to implement the Health Information Technology for Economic and Clinical Health (HITECH) Act. Utilization of HITECH intended to encourage the adoption and meaningful use of health information technology and certified electronic health record technology (CEHRT). The use of computers increased in use in medical practices, from diagnosis to prognosis, patient education, surgery, and hospital care. Although adoption did increase, overall adoption did not achieve several of its core purposes, such as improving interoperability.

The use of the Electronic Health Record (EHR) was the first phase of the HITECH and the importance of training healthcare professionals (Lee, Moy, Kruck, & Rabang, 2014). The number of challenges with the rollout of technology being integrated with healthcare displayed the adoption of these tools. Healthcare organizations are looking for healthcare professionals that can integrate business skillsets and information technology with healthcare and academic programs to provide enhanced quality healthcare (Wilson & Tulu, 2010). The use of innovative technologies to facilitate teamwork in health care is also a growing trend. However, the inability for the different EHRs to "talk" to each other has been a primary concern. This inability has resulted in additional administrative functions which increased a healthcare professional's time away from providing direct patient care and increased potential medical errors.

Academia is the nexus of research and knowledge sharing when it comes to evidence-based medicine (EBM) methods. EBM methods are developed and practiced throughout the healthcare industry. The use of information technology combined with the EBMs could enhance innovation and best practices during the continued pursuit of increased information technology usage. Educating healthcare professionals on the use of information technology like telemedicine has shown how healthcare is mobile.

Telemedicine is the use of communication and information technology to treat patients at a distance and able to treat patients globally (Katzenstein, Yrle, Chrispin, Hartman, & Lundberg, 2012). This technology could be used synchronously or asynchronously allowing the physicians to treat patients afar. Another potential opportunity when it comes to information technology is enabling personal mobile device use via a bring-your-own-device (BYOD). Utilizing BYOD in healthcare facilities and medical schools provided convenience to the end-user, as well as cost-effectiveness. There has been international interest in the use of telemedicine to help improve the quality, safety, and cost-effectiveness. Telemedicine has been found useful in treating and managing long-term conditions globally (McLean et al., 2013).

Mobility devices have shown some promise when it comes to healthcare information technology and for healthcare professionals to be more mobile. In observing improved wired and high-speed wireless capabilities, healthcare professionals can now work more remotely which has shown to be more affordable and efficient (Lee et al., 2014). Smartphones and tablets can be used to provide healthcare in unlimited capacity anytime and anywhere. Mobility devices have increased in use in higher learning, the workplace, and clinically (Lumsden, Byrne-Davis, Mooney, & Sandars, 2015). These mobile devices now can allow up-to-date clinical data at the clinician's fingertips.

Traditional learning theories of accessing documents at the library changed with the increased use of technology. Now with the internet, obtaining information can be done quickly and accurately. Accessing databases on laptops has become the status quo to improve the efficiency of data collection and research. The increased use of technology in healthcare has helped to foster quality healthcare continuously.

Healthcare and Online Learning

Professional development refers to many types of educational experiences related to an individual's work. Nurses, social workers, doctors, and people use various forms of professional development to learn and apply new knowledge and skills that will improve their performance in the workplace. In most clinical occupations in healthcare require practitioners to participate in ongoing learning approved by the career associations or licensing boards, sometimes as a requirement for keeping their jobs. The development and use of online education create new, effective, and useful approaches for the improvement of human capital skills through collaborative learning approaches.

Lave and Wenger (1991) demarcated situated learning theory, specifying that group cognition occurs through the adoption of group distinctiveness, knowledge sharing, and group knowledge construction as a benefit of the collaborative interaction. Hargreaves's (2001) research on learning development and collaboration proposed a robust connection between open, expressive sharing and collective learning as valuable tools that can be leveraged for professional development. Thus, supporting the importance of communities of practice as avenues to help professionals increase their knowledge and improve their skills in their selected fields (Webber, 2018).

Lave and Wenger (1991) delineated communities of practice as groups of individuals who share their knowledge, expertise, and experiences through a form of intentional and purposeful group interaction. Online graduate programs and video conference-based tools for training like ZOOM and Adobe Connect now provide new platforms for online communities of practice, and offering health care professionals learning opportunities online. Cloud computing and collaboration offers the ability to collaborate asynchronously and modify artifacts of collaborative learning (Liu, 2014). Exchanging materials references posting or accessing materials digitally through online courses (Liu, 2014). Technology allows for health care professionals to quickly post links or documents on the selected site for the community to download (Baker, 2011). The use of online course sites allows for conversations, assignments, videos, and lectures to be archived and kept indefinitely to be accessed at any time. Online learning approaches will enable videos, handbooks, and case studies to be posted as downloadable files, links to download sites, or embedded within posts. These materials become the artifacts of the learning community interaction that can be accessed both others regardless of geography. Learning community collaboration consists of co-creation of new knowledge through collaboration between members (Valez, 2015). Examples might include a discussion of best practices around how to address a problem or process (Baker, 2011).

Vygotsky's (1978) seminal research explored the concept of social development theory. Social development theory projects that social interface forms the underpinning for cerebral and intellectual growth as the by-product of active participants learning through a communal investigation of challenges (Vygotsky, 1978). In the context of collaborative learning, the members each contribute their unique skills and prior experience to understand difficult concepts, to improve processes, and solve complex problems (Webber, 2018). Through the development of community and social interaction, members construct knowledge and create mental conceptual models (Lave & Wenger, 1991). Through communal inquiry, professionals improve their skills by leveraging the benefit of each other's experiences, levels of expertise, and previous education (Valez, 2015). Bandura (1977) described social learning theory as significant learning that takes place by learning participants' observations of how other group members critically think, share their ideas, and solve problems. Learning participants learn from one another through observation, imitation, and modeling of behavior that they perceive and witness as most practical and useful (Bandura, 1977).

Lave and Wenger (1991) outlined the crux of effective communities of practice relies on situated learning theory (SLT). SLT suggests the active, participatory, and hands-on engagement of learning is critical for an active collaborative learning community (Lave & Wenger, 1991). Social interaction and collaboration are vital components of engaged learning communities of practice (Lave & Wenger, 1991). Through collaboration and sharing learning participants improve their skills through the co-construction of knowledge (Webber, 2018).

De Castro, Shapleigh, Bruck, and Salazar (2015) outlined the tremendous value of online and hybrid approaches for professional development. Their research noted the collaborative benefits of being able to pool the collective intelligence of health professionals with that were geographically isolated from one another but brought the benefit of different levels of experience and perspectives (De Castro, Shapleigh, Bruck, & Salazar, 2015). Now many universities even offer online degree programs that allow health professionals to complete undergraduate, graduate, and even doctoral degrees entirely online. Examples of universities that are offering these options include the University of Lynchburg in Lynchburg, VA; the Jefferson College of Health Sciences in Roanoke, VA; Rocky Mountain University of Health Professions in Provo, UT; and A.T. Still University in Kirksville, MO. The power of these programs and their ability to leverage technology is that it allows professionals to engage learning in ways that will enable health problems and critical thinking around solving them to be viewed by national and global viewpoints as classes and programs have participants from all over the world that can share the power of their unique perspectives (Ruggeri, Farrington, & Brayne, 2013).

Cloud Computing, Internet of Things, and Robotics in Healthcare

Diversification in healthcare delivery systems and solving complex problems in healthcare requires innovation and increased integration of information technology. Such information technology that would benefit the healthcare industry similar to other larger industrial counterparts includes cloud computing, Internet of Things (IoT), and robotics in healthcare. Benchmarking results from other industries such as logistics, aerospace, automotive, and electronic manufacturing could provide improved economies of scale, efficiency in supply chain methods, and improved quality of care outcomes. Healthcare continues to lag in adopting new and emergent technologies compared to other industries that have embraced improved IT in areas such as fast food, big-box retail centers, and even grocery stores.

In addition to obtaining a competitive edge by implementing different variations of IT, the speed of the information and data flow from the user to the customer will provide financial benefits which can be redistributed to the primary user. Such relationships that could benefit from improved use of IoT, cloud computing, and robots include pharma, patient and physician relationships, and geriatric care to name a few. Thus, it is essential that as government entities continue to consider how to improve quality of care outcomes, an improvement of public-private investments into such ventures would theoretically improve potential returns on investment.

A case study conducted by Karaca, Moonis, Zhang, and Gezgez (2019) examined the benefits of a mobile cloud computing based stroke healthcare system. The use and application of data in healthcare continue to grow, thus creating challenges in managing and conducting appropriate data analysis. Furthermore, the space to hold data via older traditional methods such as files and paperwork continued to prove costly for providers and increased the probability of medical errors due to missing critical data information required on the patient, as well as identifying trends in quality of care outcomes.

By utilizing larger CPUs and storage, data becomes more liquid and easier to transfer between locations and entities. Although challenges still exist in managing, storing, and disseminating data, physicians and patients continue to benefit from creating a shared decision-making process. This is vital as patients value the ability to feel as if they have some form of control over decision-making making critical choices with their physician. Both parties, patient and physician, benefit from making an informed decision together, although in most situations, the physician is cognizant of what the ideal treatment or method of care is required.

Although complex to those not familiar with its concepts, the Internet of Things (IoT) provides intelligent healthcare systems that rely on prediction capabilities. The ability to create a prediction of particular events provide a value-added benefit for daily life, as well as hospital systems. Similar to cloud computing, IoT relies on data transmitted across the Internet utilizing a gateway between a particular type of infrastructure network and the smart home or hospital. Although relatively new in terms of adaptability in the healthcare industry, the integration of the concepts related to IoT provides long-term benefits for the end-user and identified stakeholders of the designed systems.

Growing in acceptance worldwide, IoT provides a more structured and systemic approach towards smart healthcare solutions. Rahmani et al. (2018) noted that IoT-based systems could fundamentally alter and transform social benefits as well as promoting cost-efficiencies in the healthcare sector. IoT provides users the ability to automate specific processes that could not be accomplished before its adoption. The enhancement of tasks via automation provides an improvement from tasks completed by humans.

A common prevailing theme with the adoption of effective IT continues the acknowledgment that improvements in automation and IT will likely lead to a decrease in medical errors, improve quality of care outcomes, and improve surgical as well as life expectancy outcomes. By effectively integrating a variety of means of collecting data through various architectural means, the desired data to conduct predictive analysis, regression analysis, as well as descriptive statistics will give end-users as well as patients and other stakeholders increased access to data to make informed decisions.

Industrialized nations have capitalized on the use of information technology effectively. Whereas in the past, the United States was once considered the best healthcare system in the world, the current rankings now show the U.S. lagging behind other industrialized nations such as the U.K., Sweden, Australia, and Germany. Such rankings included variables such as quality, access, efficiency, equity, and healthy lives (Bigoli, 2018). Although several factors affect the ratings overall, a constant variable tied to higher rankings include the use of robotics and increased use of developing an e-health environment featuring integrated use of information technology.

Rapidly growing in use and application globally, robotics presents a myriad of opportunities and challenges for e-health in the 21st century. Such use of robotics provides healthcare providers to improve quality, safety, efficiency, and productivity. Application of robotic use includes surgery, logical and mechanical tasks, and complex cognitive tasks (Cresswell, Cunningham-Burley, & Sheikh, 2018). The attractiveness of increased use of robots continues to grow due to external pressure to control costs, access to improved technological capabilities, and reducing costs associated with labor (Cresswell et al., 2018). Despite opportunities existing for increased use of robotics, sociotechnical challenges exist that requires additional studies and research in order to provide effective integration of these devices as part of the Fourth Revolution.

RECOMMENDATIONS

Collectively, the healthcare industry should continue to strive for improvements in adoption of information technology. The benefits of the combination of IT and end-users provide unlimited opportunities for addressing significant disparities in care. Advancements of technology provide an opportunity to significantly expand access to those in rural areas or under-developed countries.

An emphasis towards expanding education to those seeking to enter the healthcare field would benefit the industry as a whole. Human capital development involves not only involves the internal stakeholders within the industry, it should plan and advance interests toward ensuring that future generations of leaders, practitioners, and labor receive exposure to the benefits of technology to limit any potential resistance to technology adoption. Such education could come in form of including thematic topics related to information technology; exposure of robotics and cloud computing; and integrating health IT topics into secondary education and vocational programs. Providing low cost alternatives to learning and development would eliminate deterrents in shortages related to physicians and nursing programs.

Post-secondary education would benefit eliminating barriers included in the healthcare education dynamic. Although the skills and acumen needed for clinically based occupation is desperately needed, cross-functional education in non-clinical occupational fields would provide additional labor, potential for innovation, and expand opportunities for additional integration of IT to occur. Similar to other degree programs at the university level, the healthcare industry would benefit from benchmarking in certain degree fields such as engineering, information systems, logistics, and business administration programs. Expanding knowledge-based learning opportunities will help further develop talent for the future.

FUTURE AREAS OF RESEARCH

The Fourth Revolution is still in its relevant infancy in terms of content, data, research, and discussion. Thus, additional opportunities for research exist to continue a more robust discussion on topics related to human capital development. Such research would benefit identified external and stakeholders who are affected within the confines of the healthcare industry.

It is widely known that certain identified end-users are slow adopters of information technology. Various research using several theories to conduct quantitative studies reflected on end-user resistance, predicting information technology acceptance, and understanding perceptions related to end-user resistance. Most research focused on physicians and nurses as end-users due to the work processes required in a clinical setting. It is recommended that additional research is conducted to further understand if the level of resistance remains the same or increased due to the perception of potential impact of robotics and workload efficiency. Understanding these themes may provide an opportunity for developing training or additional tools to assist or improve the adoption process throughout the industry.

Healthcare disparities should continue to remain as a paramount concern not only in the U.S. but globally. Controlling or curbing healthcare costs provides significant economic benefits and improves overall quality of life. Additional research should be emphasized in determining the cost determinants of those in disadvantaged communities, rural locations, or underdeveloped nations to examine how information technology could benefit the affected population, lower costs, and improve healthcare outcomes. The overall impact of such research and improvement to access could provide significant benefits to millions of the affected population.

Intertwining tools from distance learning education, which is also a slow adopter, and healthcare could benefit the industry as whole. Additional research is required in examining the retention of information disseminated digitally affects clinical related positions in comparison to traditional learning settings (i.e. brick and mortar). Human capital development could improve if determining what works and what does not for those who are obtaining their education via distance learning. Understanding the pros and cons of this type of learning could enhance the amount of time required to develop and cultivate additional talent, or it could improve the talent skill set for those currently within the industry. Improving the delivery time of knowledge-based transfer could create efficiencies in time-management, productivity, and improved economies of scale.

CONCLUSION

Nursing and physician shortages are a key priority that information technology may help close such gaps. The appropriate integration of information technology provides an effective mean of disseminating educational tools to assist in ongoing professional development, improve employee retention, and minimize the economic effects of employee turnover. Providing a more useful measure of information technology adoption could provide more access to more real-time learning that could also decrease medical errors and improve quality of care outcomes.

Information technology and education in healthcare should remain in sync. Despite the lack of urgency demonstrated by the industry to embrace information technology, the industry has taken measures to improve its usage and implementation. The U.S. government attempted to help stimulate adoption rates by passing legislation with incentives to improve adoption. Although compliance was not 100 percent, the efforts of government legislation stimulated the ongoing discussion and additional research that is needed to understand the importance of information technology and healthcare. Understanding the link between the two variables will provide valuable ongoing research by those interested in human capital development and improving the educational component that is required within the industry.

The healthcare industry could benefit from the use of information technology and learning similar to the effective and growing adoption rates of technology and distance learning. In a manner that is somewhat identical to the healthcare industry, education was a slow adopter of information technology. As academia noted its benefits for disseminating information and archiving artifacts, online education continues to benefit the field of academia, as well as the changing demographics and demands of students.

As one of the most significant and rapidly growing industries globally, healthcare continues to deal with significant challenges that could provide economic disruption and affect the overall quality of care. Some of the more pressing challenges include high turnover rates, staffing shortages, and lack of interoperability between providers and administrators. Despite the size and continued growth of the industry, healthcare under-utilizes information technology in a manner that could address such problems. It is incumbent for those interested in academia and industry interested in human capital development to appropriately acquire and utilize information technology efficient in a manner that could narrow the gaps of these challenges.

The evolution of technology extends more than basic integration. Globally, industrialized nations continue to promulgate the direct and indirect benefits of information technology. Known in some circles as the Fourth Revolution, the slow adopting nature of the healthcare industry has changed its course towards new methods and ideology in improving human capital development within the industry. Such innovation includes the reliance on cloud computing, Internet of Things, and Robotics. These financial and labor-intensive investments reap benefits for those who capitalized in integrative information technology. The increased use of these three areas provided improved quality of care outcomes, decrease in medical errors, and improvements in surgery, as well as improved efficiencies in healthcare delivery systems.

External and internal costs within the healthcare industry provide pressure on providers to discover innovative ways to improve the delivery of healthcare. Patients continue to be more informed and desire to position themselves as an active stakeholder in determining healthcare planning decisions. As such, it is incumbent of those within the industry to use the combination of knowledge, integrated technology, and aptitude to provide new dynamics worth exploring within the healthcare industry. These advances will prompt additional research qualitatively and quantitatively; however, the results will provide improved benefits for all parties involved.

Recognizing and proactively developing measures, e-learning tools, and deploying advancements in technology towards the healthcare industry solves one of the more significant, and more silent, global crisis that exists in the 21st century. Despite the advances of technology in other industries globally, healthcare historically adopts slowly towards change and innovation. A combination of new and emerging technology along with benchmarking existing technology in other industries may prove valuable for external and internal stakeholders.

Human capital development remains a priority within the industry to address the myriad of challenges that currently exist. A smarter, more educated workforce that can effectively utilize technology may improve quality of care outcomes. Use of different technology provides an opportunity for faster dissemination of information, automation of work processes, and provide enhanced opportunities to take part in the Fourth Revolution by significantly removing economic, social, and global borders that exist.

REFERENCES

Baker, C. B. (2011). *Beginning to understand why New Hampshire's rural educators chose not to join New Hampshire's newly developed on-line professional learning communities: A quantitative and qualitative study (Order No. 3588428)*. Retrieved from ProQuest Dissertations & Theses Global.

Bandura, A. (1977). *Social learning theory*. New York, NY: General Learning Press.

Bidgoli, H. (2018). Successful integration of information technology in healthcare: Guides for managers. *Journal of Strategic Innovation and Sustainability*, *13*(3), 22–37.

Corso, K. A., Dorrance, K. A., & LaRochelle, U. (2018). The physician shortage: A red herring in American health care reform. *Military Medicine, 183*(3), 220-224. doi:10.1093/milmed/usy211

Cresswell, K., Cunningham-Burley, S., & Sheikh, A. (2018). Health care robotics: Qualitative exploration of key challenges and future directions. *Journal of Medical Internet Research*, *20*(7), e10410. doi:10.2196/10410 PMID:29973336

De Castro, A. B., Shapleigh, E., Bruck, A., & Salazar, M. K. (2015). Developing blended online and classroom strategies to deliver an occupational health nursing overview course in a multi-state region in the United States. *Workplace Health & Safety*, *63*(3), 121–126. doi:10.1177/2165079915576919 PMID:25994977

Duncan, T. D., Rahim, E., & Burrell, D. N. (2018). A panel on challenge in healthcare post-EMR adoption. Presented at Midwest Association for Information Systems, St. Louis, MO.

Ferguson, S. L., & Lloyd, J. (2017). Innovative information technology solutions: Addressing current and emerging nurse shortages and staffing challenges worldwide. *Nursing Economics*, *35*(4), 211.

Hargreaves, A. (2001). Emotional geographies of teaching. *Teachers College Record*, *103*(6), 1056–1080. doi:10.1111/0161-4681.00142

Karaca, Y., Moonis, M., Zhang, Y., & Gezgez, C. (2019). Mobile cloud computing based stroke healthcare system. *International Journal of Information Management*, *45*, 250–261. doi:10.1016/j.ijinfomgt.2018.09.012

Kirch, D. G., & Petelle, K. (2017). Addressing the physician shortage: The peril of ignoring demography. *JAMA Network*, *317*(19), 1947–1948. doi:10.1001/jama.2017.2714 PMID:28319233

Kong, E. (2014). A qualitative analysis of social intelligence in nonprofit organizations: External knowledge acquisition for human capital development. *Knowledge Management Research and Practice*, *13*(4), 463–474. doi:10.1057/kmrp.2013.63

Lave, J., & Wenger, E. (1991). *Situated learning: Legitimate peripheral participation*. New York, NY: Cambridge University Press. doi:10.1017/CBO9780511815355

Lee, A., Moy, L., Kruck, S. E., & Rabang, J. (2014). The Doctor is in, but is academia? Re-Tooling IT education for a new era in healthcare. *Journal of Information Systems Education*, *25*(4), 275–281.

Liu, H. (2014). Cloud computing in music theory: Using in universities. *Applied Mechanics & Materials,* (556-562), 6758.

Lumsden, C. J., Byrne-Davis, L., Mooney, J. S., & Sandars, J. (2015). Using mobile devices for teaching and learning in clinical medicine. *Archives of Disease in Childhood - Education and Practice*, *100*(5), 244–251. doi:10.1136/archdischild-2014-306620 PMID:26033788

Mamedov, Z. F., Mineva, O. K., & Glinchevskiy, E. I. (2019). Innovative Approach To Human Capital Management Under Conditions Of Strong Turbulence of Fourth Industrial Revolution. Varazdin: Varazdin Development and Entrepreneurship Agency (VADEA).

McLean, S., Sheikh, A., Cresswell, K., Nurmatov, U., Mukherjee, M., Hemmi, A., & Pagliari, C. (2013). The impact of telehealthcare on the quality and safety of care: A systematic overview. *PLoS One*, *8*(8), 1–11. doi:10.1371/journal.pone.0071238 PMID:23977001

Rahim, E., & Duncan, T. D. (2018). *Examining the evolution of sustainable leadership. In Contemporary Multicultural Orientations and Practices for Global Leadership*. IGI Global.

Rahmani, A. M., Gia, T. N., Negash, B., Anzanpour, A., Azimi, I., Jiang, M., & Liljeberg, P. (2018). Exploiting smart e-health gateways at the edge of healthcare internet-of-things: A fog computing approach. *Future Generation Computer Systems*, *78*, 641–658. doi:10.1016/j.future.2017.02.014

Ruggeri, K., Farrington, C., & Brayne, C. (2013). A global model for effective use and evaluation of e-learning in health. *Telemedicine Journal and e-Health*, *19*(4), 312–321. doi:10.1089/tmj.2012.0175 PMID:23472702

Scott, K. A., Fisher, G. G., Baron, A. E., Tompa, E., Stallones, L., & DiGuiseppi, C. (2017). Same-level fall injuries in U.S. workplaces by age, group, gender, and industry. *American Journal of Industrial Medicine*, *61*(2), 111–119. doi:10.1002/ajim.22796 PMID:29193187

Velez, V. (2015). *Implementing child maltreatment prevention into the clinical setting: An on-line learning tutorial for advanced practice nurses (Order No. 3701612). Retrieved from ProQuest Central*. ProQuest Dissertations & Theses Global.

Vygotsky, L. S. (1978). *Mind in society: The development of higher psychological processes*. Cambridge, MA: Harvard University Press.

Webber, E. (2018). *Building Successful Communities of Practice*. San Francisco: Blurb Publishing.

Wilson, E. V., & Tulu, B. (2010). The rise of a Health-IT academic focus. *Communications of the ACM*, *53*(5), 147–150. doi:10.1145/1735223.1735259

Xue, Y., Greener, E., Kannan, V., Smith, J. A., Brewer, C., & Spetz, J. (2018). Federally qualified health centers reduce the primary care provider gap in health professional shortage counties. *Nursing Outlook*, *66*(3), 263–272. doi:10.1016/j.outlook.2018.02.003 PMID:29685322

Zhang, X., Tai, D., Pforsich, H., & Lin, V. W. (2018). United States registered nurse's workforce report card and shortage forecast: A revisit. *American Journal of Medical Quality*, *33*(3), 229–236. doi:10.1177/1062860617738328 PMID:29183169

KEY TERMS AND DEFINITIONS

Bring Your Own Device (BYOD): Refers to the practice or the allowance of staff and personnel to bring their own personal device which could include smartphones, tablets, and laptops.

Cloud Computing: Provides users the ability to save or retrieve data information for the use of storage and continue ongoing work process without an active hardline management or data retrieval system.

Evidenced-Based Medicine (EBM): Practice of medicine by medical professionals in the field using well-documented and research to provide optimal treatment results and outcomes.

Health Informatics: The study, design, and implementation of information technology innovations in the healthcare industry.

Human Capital: Defines human resources in terms of assets which includes knowledge, skills, and abilities of individuals.

Internet of Things: Defines connectivity between the Internet and everyday objects, activities, and devices.

Social Intelligence: The ability and the capacity of an individual to know oneself and others around the social spectrum. Derives from self-awareness and relationships among others.

Chapter 12
Technology Incubator and Entrepreneurship Development

Saidi Adedeji Adelekan
Mountain Top University, Nigeria

Benneth Uchenna Eze
Hallmark University, Nigeria

ABSTRACT

The importance of technology in advancing experiential learning and building entrepreneurs that can withstand the challenges and explore the opportunities in the fourth industrial revolution are enormous. The chapter adopted a literature review approach to establish the link between technology incubator and entrepreneurship development. The concepts of technology incubator and entrepreneurship development as well as other related concepts were extensively discussed. It identifies the need for adequate investments toward tech entrepreneurship development and tech-savvy for the future through technology incubation programmes. Such programmes set to aid innovativeness, creating jobs, fast-tracking research to industry linkages, building wealth by fostering the formation of new ventures, among others. The chapter concludes that institutions for entrepreneurship development need to shift their tents to cover major areas of technological revolution, particularly technological incubation to promote entrepreneurship development in Industry 4.0.

DOI: 10.4018/978-1-5225-9810-7.ch012

INTRODUCTION

Technology incubation has played a significant role as an instrument for entrepreneurship development. Technology incubators are economic development toolsutilised for advancing and promoting the idea of development. These are achieved through support for economic development strategies for small business development, innovation and application of technology, and promotion of growth from within local economies, while additionally giving a tool for technology transmission. Technology incubation is the transitory, facilitative assistance given to start-up ventures through the transfer of complex administration and unique environment with the objective of enhancing their opportunities of survival in the early period of life expectancy, and building up their later development (Bubou & Okrigwe, 2012; Dutta, 2018; Ndagi, 2017).

Technology incubation programmes generally have the objectives of aiding innovativeness, creating jobs, fast-tracking research to industry linkages, building wealth by fostering the formation of new ventures, among others (Yusubova, Andries & Clarysse, 2019; Bose & Goyal, 2019; Ikebuaku & Dinbabo, 2018; Kapinga, Montero, Mwandosya, & Mbise, 2018).In achieving these objectives, incubators utilise approaches such as technical and business management training, creation of access to credit facilities, increased access to capital, contract procurement assistance, the one-stop-shop approach, creation of networking opportunities through clustering, export assistance and technology transfer assistance (Mainoma & Aruwa, 2012; Adelekan, Majekodunmi, & Omotayo, 2018).

The rules of technology incubation are designed at ensuring a fast track of entrepreneurship development as institutions and government give incubates the essential support that kindles their interests and develops their ideas into practical and self-sustaining ventures (Mansur & A buga, 2017; Oladele-Emmanuel, Redlich & Wulfsberg, 2018). There is a close link between technology incubation and entrepreneurship, as the procedure of incubation tends to enhance entrepreneurship development.

This chapter specifically explores the concept of technology incubation and entrepreneurship development. The benefits of technology incubation as well as the basic requirements of technology incubation towards the enhancement of entrepreneurship development are extensively discussed.

BACKGROUND

The formal concept of technology incubation began in the United States in 1959, when Joseph L. Mancuso opened the Batavia Industrial Centre inBatavia, New York warehouse (CSES, 2002). Incubation expanded in the United States in the 1980s and spread to the United Kingdom and other parts of Europe through a variety of incubation vehicles such as innovation centres, enterprise centres, technology and science parks.

According to the International Business Innovation Association, there are about 7,000 incubation centres worldwide. A study funded by the European Commission in 2002 acknowledged about 900 incubation environments in Western Europe (CSES, 2002). In 1980, there were only 12 incubators in North America. This increased to more than 1,400 incubators as of October 2006 in the same continent. The treasury unit of Her Majesty identified about 25 incubation centres in the United Kingdom in 1997. By 2005, UKBI identified about 270 incubation centres across the country. Knopp (2007) explains that North American incubation programmes aided more than 27,000 companies that provided employment for more than 100,000 workers and generated annual revenues of $17 billion in the year 2005.

Technology Incubation in Africa

Incubation activity has not been limited to developed countries; incubation environments are also implemented in developing countries, particularly in Africa. The introduction of incubation programmes in Africa can be traced to the year 1988, when the United Nations Development Programme (UNDP) testran the concept on a pilot scheme in four countries: Coted'Ivoire, Nigeria, Zimbabwe and Equatorial Guinea. Ndagi (2017) observes that the incubation programmes have spread across Africa with one hundred incubation centres. Nigeria has about forty-four incubation centres; South Africa with about thirty-six, while the other African countries have the remaining twenty.

Technology Incubation in Nigeria

The introduction of a technology incubation programme in Nigeria in the year 1988 led to the conduct of a feasibility study for the establishment of pilot centres at Aba, Kano and Lagos. The feasibility study was to ascertain the viability of technology incubation centres in these commercial cities. The feasibility study led to the establishment of a centrein Lagos in 1993, anotherin Kano in 1994 the thirdin Aba in 1995. The success of these centres led to the establishment ofcentres in Minna, Nnewi and Calabar in 1998. By 2012, there were about forty-four incubation centres in Nigeria (Agri, Kennedy, Bonmwa & Acha, 2018; Guerrero & Urbano, 2019; Ndagi, 2017; Kiani-Mavi, Gheibdoust, Khanfar & Kiani-Mavi, 2019; Olaolu, 2018; Sanyal & Hisam, 2018).

In the year 1993, the Federal Government of Nigeria established the National Board for technology incubation, with the aim of pursuing the commercialisation of technical and technological innovations, using technology incubation as a tool. This is in order to enhance the attainment of industrial, social, technological, and economic competitiveness of the nation and increase in the quality of life of its residents.

The general aim of the programme is to encourage the foundation and co-ordinate the exercise of Technology Incubation Centres and Science and Technology Parks, which are intended to sustain technology-based start-up ventures across the country. The more explicit objectives of the board comprise the following:

- To provide institutional infrastructure and mechanisms for the development and commercialisation of R&D outputs and inventions;
- To source entrepreneurs and investors for the commercialisation of chosen technologies; to sensitise all stakeholders for the establishment;
- To ensure continuous innovations in material processing and equipment, supervision and regulation of Technology Incubation Centres,
- To confirm competitiveness of the products of the programme through value-added service support and effective linkages to knowledge providers,
- To efficiently include all important stakeholders in the establishment of Technology Incubation Centres nationwide;
- To source funds for the implementation of the programme; and to source and develop commercially practical indigenous and foreign technologies.
- Other explicit objectives include ensuring conformity with policy and regulations of the programme;affirming effective and efficient performance leading to accelerated growth of entrepreneurs in the programme and providing post-incubation survival schemes for the enterprises.
- Toencourage the growth of the private sector through the creation of competitive SMEs as the engine of growth of wealth creation, poverty reduction and employment generation;subsidising all services provided by the technology incubation programme in order to decrease the overhead burdens of start-up enterprises;
- To encourage value re-orientation so as to promote hard work, transparency and accountability in business operations; and interfacing with research establishments and tertiary institutions for the commercialisation of their research and development outputs (Volkmann, Tokarski & Grunhagen, 2010).

ENTREPRENEUR

The term, entrepreneur, refers to a person who organises, manages, owns, controls and assumes the risk of a business venture (Eckhardt& Shane, 2003; Adegbite, 2001; Adelowo, Olaopa & Siyanbola, 2012). The word entrepreneur originated from the French word, 'entreprende' which means 'to undertake' (Akanni, 2010). In a business context, it means to start a business, identify a business opportunity, organise resources, manage and assume the risk of a business or an enterprise. It is also used to describe those who (take charge) lead a project, which will deliver valuable benefits, and bring it to completion. It refers to individuals who, at the end of the day, can manage vulnerability and get achievement, with the presence of overwhelming difficulties that could obliterate a less managed business. According to Hornby (2006), an entrepreneur is an individual who makes money by beginning or running businesses, particularly when this includes taking financial risks.

Drucker (1995) characterises an entrepreneur as somebody who shifts economic resources out of a zone of lower productivity and into a territory of a higher one and greater yield. This definition has two viewpoints that need to be emphasised. In the first place, there are resources that are manipulated. Second, the action is aimed at accomplishing higher profitability and more prominent yields. In the science of economics, how to enhance the factors of production and seek to accomplish equilibrium in the circulation of wealth are studied. Also, there is the attempt to capitalise on the current resources and to establish equilibrium. The entrepreneur is a person who considers change to be ordinary and healthy. For the most part, the entrepreneur does not realise change. Maybe, he 'scans' for change, reacts to it, and exploits it as an opportunity. Entrepreneurs are driven by the need to be independent, adding esteem and values to families and societies, being rich or, regularly, not being jobless. Potential entrepreneurs are active and unequivocal; they have aspirations, negotiating prudence and foreknowledge. They are agents of change who quicken the age, application and spread of innovative ideas (UNDP, 2009).

According to UNIDO (1999), entrepreneurship is the process of utilising initiative to transform a business concept to a new enterprise and diversify existing enterprises to high growing business potentials. The entrepreneur acts in an unexpected way. They bring to light something distinctive which represents value in the eyes of the consumer. The idea is that the individual at the helm should see the organisation as operating under a procedure planned to give 'value' to the customers. At the point when all parts of the business are equipped towards accomplishing this objective – that is, value to the consumer or an insight of it – then such an organisation is entrepreneurial.

Abraham Maslow, the American human psychologist, characterises entrepreneurs as persons who 'discern change, enjoy it and invent or improvise without being prepared'. He also discusses that the entrepreneur is a 'here-now' creator, an improviser, who is not afraid of being viewed as operating in disagreement with the general practice and conviction. An entrepreneur is a person who senses or perceives an opportunity where others fear rejection; he will not talk of problems or obstacles but challenges. His mentality and mindset are tuned to progress, and though he knows about the likelihood of disappointment, itdoes not engross him.

Entrepreneurs are usually inclined to manage-risk schemes, than get-rich quick schemes (Baradaran, Yadollahi-Farsi, Hejazi & Akbari, 2019; Chen, Cai, Bruton& Sheng, 2019; Carpenter &Dunung, 2012). Eckhardt and Shane (2003) differentiate entrepreneurs from small-venture owners because entrepreneurs innovate by introducingnew processes, products, or markets to rapidly enhance their businesses, while small-venture owners characteristically attempt the provision of long-established products.

However, Hsueh and Tu (2004) argue that at whatever time new firms are formed, irrespective of their sizes, the entrepreneurs behind their establishment usually believe that they have identified a niche either in terms of a new process, a new market or a new product. Therefore, it can be presumed that the early development phase of an organisation's life cycle (start-up phase) is perceived as being entrepreneurial to some degree.

According to Carpenter and Dunung (2012), entrepreneurs venture into profit and non-profit endeavours. The commonest entrepreneurial undertaking is the profit-oriented enterprises whose owners venture into business with the intent of making profit. Some entrepreneurs also initiate a non-profit venture with the intent of attaining some pre-determined social goals rather than making profit. Non-profit ventures usually work towards the betterment of society. This kind of entrepreneurs is referred to as 'social entrepreneurs'. Social entrepreneurs focus on coming up with creative solutions to social challenges. They identify and utilise opportunities, manage and organise projects and people with the major aim of benefitting humanity, thereby utilising the same skills and tools as other entrepreneurs (Carpenter & Dunung, 2012; Eze, 2018; Adelekan & Tijani, 2017).

Characteristics of Entrepreneurs

There are numerous thought processes present in beginning a new business. A few entrepreneurs gain good examples from that of an effective family. A couple launch into an entrepreneurial vocation by way of inventing a new product and building a business around it. Others end up noticeably disappointed with corporate professions and find that entrepreneurship gives an appealing arrangement of difficulties and rewards. For the achievement and accomplishment of entrepreneurship, Timons

(1978) affirms that entrepreneurs must have the accompanying attributes which he additionally calls the entrepreneurial spirit. This includes:

- **The Readiness to Take Risks:** An entrepreneur takes on some level of risk when trying to start a new venture. Now and again, entrepreneurs may risk their own capital as well as reserves contributed by family, companions, and other speculators. The business-person may leave the security of a corporate profession and still be indeterminate that the new pursuit introduces a superior open door. Be that as it may, entrepreneurs, as a group, may not experience as much danger of disappointment as they may have thought beforehand.
- **Insistent Critical Thinking:** Innovation is what really matters to entrepreneurship and this incorporates critical thinking. Entrepreneurs must be individuals that can readily identify problems and come up with workable solutions for them. Likewise, such an individual predicts a particular need and/or the needs of the general public and makes a special effort to address this issue. Along these lines, entrepreneurship is tied in with doing something new or exploiting old things in a new way.
- **Goal-Setter:** All entrepreneurs must exude objectivity. The goal ought to be unmistakably characterised, achievable and moving. This in turn provides inspiration for the accomplishment of the business objective or aims.
- **A High Requirement for Accomplishment:** People with a high requirement for accomplishment want to take care of issues without the help of others. They appreciate defining objectives and accomplishing them through their own particular endeavours. They also like accepting the inputs of others on how they are getting along. These attributes assist business people to be more proactive as well as identify future issues, needs, or changes. Furthermore, business visionaries are high in McClelland's hypothesis of need achievement.
- **Tolerance of Vulnerability and Equivocality:** Occasionally, instability and vagueness are unavoidable in business. An entrepreneur's ability to withstand ambiguity and vulnerability decides the outcome s/he gets. The individual's vulnerability depends on her/his response towards people's complaints in business, including, murmuring and criticism, all of which can rob the individual of both the quality and activity to effectively manage resistance.
- **Distinctive Ability:** Another characteristic that separates business visionaries is simply the capacity to fight against a forced standard. This is the capacity for the entrepreneur to set a standard for her or himself and putting exercises in place towards developing a strong determination towards finishing this standard. This keeps up and manages the business in an energetic fashion.
- **Locus of Control:** Generally, this is the ability that people possess—not fortunes or destiny—that controls their own lives. Entrepreneurs and

supervisors both jump at the chance to think they are pulling their own particular strings. An entrepreneur is probably going to have an inward locus of control, with a solid confidence in her or his capacity to succeed. At the point when an individual with an inner locus of control fails or commits an error, that individual is probably going to acknowledge duty regarding the result and invest more energy, as opposed to hunting down exterior reasons to clarify their disappointment. Here, the entrepreneur is tireless in this pursuit and spurred on to conquer obstructions that would otherwise discourage others. Then again, individuals with an outside locus of control trust that what transpires is because of good fortune, destiny or factors outside their ability to control. At the point when individuals with an outer locus of control fail, they will probably feel defenseless and are more averse to manage or increase their objective in looking for future business ventures.

- **Self-Certainty:** Entrepreneurs feel sure that they can ace the abilities expected to maintain a business and that they can conquer unanticipated hindrances. This self-assurance can be utilised to energies and inspire others. Fearlessness empowers business visionaries to *ad lib* and discovers novel answers to business problems that may dishearten other weaker individuals.
- **Working for a More Drawn Out Period:** One of the attributes of enterprise is drive supplemented by vitality, which begins from within due to the energy the individual has for the business. A business visionary ought to be able to work for a more drawn out timeframe without becoming grumpy with exhaustion.
- **Dealing With Disappointment:** An entrepreneur ought to be prepared to manage disappointment. S/he ought not to consider inability to be an end; rather, disappointment should spur the individual towards determining how not to do a thing. As Timons (1978) has stated, 'people who fear disappointment will kill whatever accomplishment inspiration disappointment has and will have a tendency to participate in a simple errand, where there is minimal shot of disappointment, or in a troublesome circumstance where they can't be considered dependable on the off chance that they don't succeed.'

According to Meredith *et al.*, (1991), the following table represents a summary of characteristics and traits of entrepreneurs.

Entrepreneurship

Entrepreneurship can be defined as a process, which involves looking out for opportunities and creating what will meet these opportunities. Freiling and Schelhowe (2014) explain that entrepreneurship is both exploitative and explorative in nature,

Table 1. Characteristics and traits of entrepreneurs (Meredith et al., 1991)

CHARACTERISTICS	TRAITS
Self-confidence	Exudes confidence, is independent, displays individuality, is cheerful, optimistic and sanguine
Task-result oriented	Need for achievement, is profit-oriented, perseverant, possesses determination, is hardworking, maintains high levels of energy.
Risk-taker	Risk-taking ability, likes challenges.
Leadership	Leadership behaviour, gets along well with others.
Originality	Is innovative, creative, flexible (openness of mind), resourceful
Future-oriented	Expresses forethought, insight and is discerning.

Source: Meredith *et al.*, (1991)

based on the combination of the creative, innovative, risk management, internal management and arbitrage role it plays. The first roles aremainly exploratory, while the last two are exploitative in nature. Obasan (2005) views entrepreneurship as a dynamic process formed and managed by an individual or group of people who strive to take advantage of economic innovation to generate new value in the market.

Entrepreneurship focuses mainly on recognition and exploitation of opportunities as well as innovation, and adding value (Oladimeji, *et al* 2018; Volkmann, *et al.*, 2010). According to Abosede and Onakoya (2013), entrepreneurship is a process that offers job opportunities, brings about new ideas and inventions, and stimulates economic growth and development through the enhancement of national income.

Two schools of thought are prominent in the field of entrepreneurship: the trait and the behavioural schools of thought. The trait school of thought focuses on individual traits or characteristics in distinguishing entrepreneurs from non-entrepreneurs. The traits of the entrepreneur are seen as the major factor determining entrepreneurship. Some of the identified entrepreneurial traits in literature includezeal for achievement, locus of control, risk taking, age and personal value system (Adelekan, 2017; Begley & Boyd, 1987; Gartner, 1989). In spite of the attention that the trait approach has received in literature, the approach seems to be unable to capture the entrepreneurship phenomenon fully. The deficiency of the trait approach in capturing creativity led to the development of the behavioural approach.

The behavioural approach views entrepreneurship as the procedure for creating new organisations. Unlike the trait approach that takes the individual as the primary level of analysis, the behavioural approach sees the entrepreneurial entity being created as the fundamental or primary level of analysis. The aim is not to find out who the entrepreneur is but to understand what brought about the entrepreneurial achievement. In essence, the behavioural school is more interested in how the entrepreneur's traits are converted into actions, leading to creation of entities.

Important Skills for Entrepreneurial Success

Together with the traits and characteristics that are found in entrepreneurs, there are additional skills which have been identified with progress and success in business. An entrepreneur utilises an assortment of business skills to make and operate an enterprise successfully (Enikanselu & Oyende, 2010). Among these are:

- **Negotiation Skills:** Whenever an exchange of goods or services between two parties takes place, quality appeasement aptitudes are helpful. A meeting which utilises negotiation skills proficiently ensures good terms for the two parties in the exchange by virtue of their shared opinion. This critical style of thinking often results in a Win-Win negotiation for both parties. Likewise, it requires the person to act in compliance with common decency to produce a relationship in light of trust and collaboration. This makes it simpler to discover a premise of trade that is alluring to the two parties. Entrepreneur's often use negotiation skills to accomplish assets expected to keep an organisation going forward.
- **Networking Skills:** Collecting data and building alliances entails quality networking. The networking skills are applied to both:
    a. **The Personal Network:** This is based on the connections between the entrepreneur and other entrepreneurs, providers, leasers, financial specialists, companions, and others. These individual contacts can enable an entrepreneur to settle on viable choices by giving information that lessens instability in the business. For example: A previous lecturer may give free specialised counselling guidance and understudy volunteers to help develop a promoting system for the new venture. Talking with kindred entrepreneurs who have experienced the way toward building a business from the ground-up can give important criticism and enthusiastic help. Entrepreneurs construct individual networks by effectively searching out people with comparable interests, keeping in contact with them, and searching for chances to make the relationship commonly fulfilling. By being receptive to the requirements and enthusiastic reception of the general population to their own systems, business visionaries assemble trust and goodwill. A personal network can be shaped through interest in proficient social orders, business clubs, beneficent associations, trade fair and networks of entrepreneurs.
    b. **The Business Network:** This is an arrangement of coalitions and alliances between different businesses to accomplish commonly advantageous objectives. A larger organisation may enter into an association with a smaller enterprise keeping in mind the end goal to increase a portion

of the advantages of the new and modernisation product or service the entrepreneurship is developing.

- **Leadership Skills:** Excellence in leadership offers a mutual vision for others to progress in the direction of similar goals. Entrepreneurs are pioneers who stimulate and inspire workers to do what is useful for the undertaking, notwithstanding when it is not to their immediate advantage. The entrepreneurs rely upon leadership skills to fortify representative assurance and guide the endeavour toward the goal of defeating problems that hinder business.
- **Opportunity Recognition Skills:** Entrepreneurs can recognise opportunities and ideas they emerge. To be effective, an entrepreneur must scan the environment, searching for opportunities and ideas. At times, an entrepreneur may find an issue to be illuminated or discover a market requires that is not being filled. Under differing circumstances, an individual may turn into a business-person and afterward search for potential business opportunities. In either case, the entrepreneur must know that an open door exists and have the capacity to exploit the circumstances as they arrive.
- **Opportunity Fit Assessment Skills:** Not every person can succeed at everything. To be fruitful and successful, an entrepreneur must have the capacity to work things out, regardless of whether his identity, ability and leadership style harmonises with the opportunities. This incorporates the specialised and business aptitudes that are required notwithstanding individual inclination and talent.
- **Implementation Skills:** Successful business visionaries have a tendency to have a high requirement for accomplishment, have an inner locus of control, be daring people or risk takers, and be sure about their capacity to ace unexpected difficulties.

ENTREPRENEURSHIP DEVELOPMENT

Abianga (2010) characterises development as the demonstration or procedure of progress, growth, advancement and enhancement inside a physical setting. Hornby (2006) comparably characterises development as the steady growth of something such that it turns out to be further developed and more grounded.

A universal consensus on the decisive role of competitive markets and entrepreneurs in economic development has emerged in the most recent decades. In developing nations, essential obstruction or barrier to economic growth is characterised by a shortage of capital, land and labour, but it is the presence of dynamic entrepreneurs that can combine these assets with market mechanisms and expedite the task to ensure economic growth.

Entrepreneurship development therefore refers to the process of improving entrepreneurial knowledge and skills through institution-building programmes and structured training. It is aimed atincreasing the base of entrepreneurs in order to accelerate the pace at which new businesses are created (UNDP, 2010). This speeds up economic development and ensures employment generation. It focuses on the person or individual who desires to begin or enlarge a venture. Additionally, it focuses more on growth potential and innovation.

The Federal Government of Nigeria, in recognition of the role entrepreneurship could play in speeding up the growth and development of the economy, introduced two educational policies in 2009. The first policy states that entrepreneurship education should be made a general studies course for all undergraduates of tertiary institutions. The second emphasises that a centre for entrepreneurial development be established in each of the tertiary institutions where different skills would be taught. This is to enhance the entrepreneurial skills of students.

Technology Incubator and Entrepreneurship Development

Technology incubation has played an important role as a tool for entrepreneurship development. It is equally a tool for economic development, through the promotion of creativity and the application of technology, which propels economic growth. Technology incubators support economic development strategies for small business development, and encourage growth within local economies, while providing a mechanism for technology transfer. Technology incubation provides support to start-ups through the delivery of complex services and special environment with the aim of enhancing their survival, especially in the early phase of the life span of the enterprise (Ikebuaku & Dinbabo, 2018; Kapinga *et al.,* 2018; Ndagi, 2017).

Technology incubation programmes, as an entrepreneurship development tool, generally have the economic development goals of creating jobs, building wealth by fostering the formation of a new venture, ensuring the fast track of research to industry linkages and facilitating creativity. In accomplishing these goals, technology incubators employ series of strategies. These strategies includetechnical and business management training, increased access to capital, the one-stop shop approach, creating networking opportunities through clustering, contract procurement assistance, export assistance and technology transfer assistance, as well as creating access to credit facility (Mainoma & Aruwa, 2012). These services are provided through synergy, collaboration and liaison with other economic development and entrepreneurship development associations in the same region.

Technology incubation and entrepreneurship development are intimately linked, in that the process of incubation aids entrepreneurship development (Oladimeji *et al.*, 2018). Most policies of technology incubation are aimed at ensuringthe fast track of entrepreneurship development, as the government and institutions provide incubated entrepreneurs with the necessary support that stimulate their interests and nurture their ideas into realistic and self-sustaining enterprises.

Theoretical Framework on Innovation and Entrepreneurship

Schumpeter's (1934) theory of innovation underscores the function of entrepreneurship. It evaluates entrepreneurial profits, and the search for opportunities for new value creation and idea generating activities which would expand and transform the circular flow of income through proactivity, innovation and risk taking by the entrepreneur. This aims at advancing the identification of opportunities, through the intellectual capital of the entrepreneur to maximise potential growth and profit.

Schumpeter's theory of innovation (1934) belongs to the sphere of economic theory. He describes entrepreneurs as creators, innovators and catalysts for change. According to Schumpeter, an entrepreneur is someone who brings about change through introduction of new technological products or processes. His 'creative destruction' postulation projects the internal displacement of old processes with new ones (Eze, 2018)

Schumpeter creates a clear distinction between intellectual and physical capital, and between saving, which enhances physical capital, and innovation, which enhances intellectual capital. He assumes that technological improvement results from innovative activities implemented by organizations driven by the motive of making profit, and that it entails what he refers to as creative destruction. It implies that innovation brings about the creation of a new product, process or market, which gives its creator a competitive advantage over its competitors. The creation of a new product renders some earlier innovations obsolete. Subsequently,these new products, processes or markets are also most likely to be rendered obsolete by prospective innovations (Schumpeter, 1934).

The entrepreneur is propelled by the craving for power and independence, the will to succeed and the fulfillment of getting things done (Swedberg, 2000). Technology incubation entails high level of innovation, which is also a very important determinant of entrepreneurial development. Therefore, technology incubation as well as entrepreneurship development is highly linked to Schumpeterian theory of innovation.

IMPLICATIONS

It was deduced from the literature that incubation centres require the development of several models to meet the technological needs of the 21st Century. Furthermore, the major objectives of technology incubation programmesare: aiding innovativeness, creating jobs, fast-tracking research to industry linkages and building wealth by fostering the formation of new ventures. Therefore, both local and global industry players need some creativity that emerges from various incubation centres (Ikebuaku & Dinbabo, 2018; Kapinga, *et al*, 2018; Dutta, 2018; Ndagi, 2017). However,in this book chapter, the Schumpeterian theory on innovation was adopted in postulating the link between technological incubation and innovation and how it can enhance entrepreneurship development. This is because Schumpeter focused on creative destruction, which refers to innovativeness that renders existing technology obsolete.

RECOMMENDATIONS

As a result of the findings from literature, it can be deduced that technology incubators aid economic growth and development through the development of micro and small enterprises, and encourage growth within local economies, while providing a mechanism for technology transfer. Technology incubation provides support to start-ups through the delivery of complex services and special environment with the aim of enhancing their survival, especially in the early phase of the enterprise life cycle. The government at all levels should create more incubation centres as well as provide adequate funding for the operations of existing incubation centres. Furthermore, entrepreneurs should take advantage of incubation centres, as it provides an easy and inexpensive way of acquiring skills as well as birthing innovativeness.

FUTURE AREAS OF RESEARCH

Thus, future research should be conducted to see how technology incubation could propel entrepreneurship development. Such studies could focus on the micro, small and medium enterprises' (MSMEs) segment of the entrepreneurship sphere, since some studies have shown that the outcome of most incubation activities is usually the development of new MSMEs. Therefore, it becomes necessary to examine to what extent technology incubation has aided the development of MSMEs. In conducting such studies, it is recommended that the mixed method should be employed, that is, the combination of qualitative and quantitative methods (qual-quant) and preferably the use of structured questionnaire and in depth interview.

CONCLUSION

This chapter conceptually evaluated the link between technology incubators and entrepreneurship development. Findings from literature revealed that technology incubators have aided entrepreneurship development, particularly, the development of micro, small and medium enterprises. Additionally, technology incubation centres represent an effective tool for entrepreneurship development. They can facilitate and build confidence within the entrepreneurship space, support start-ups and foster a culture of entrepreneurship. It can also aid enterprises outside the incubators by acting as a catalyst for the development of wider business support structure.

REFERENCES

Abianga, E. U. (2010). Effective leadership and fellowship drives community development. *International Journal of Management and Enterprises*, *7*(2).

Abosede, A. J., &Onakoya, A. B. (2013). Entrepreneurship, economic development and inclusive growth. *International Journal of Social Sciences and Entrepreneurship*, *1*(3), 375-387.

Adegbite, O. (2001). Business incubators and small enterprise development: The Nigerian experience. *Small Business Economics*, *17*(3), 157–166. doi:10.1023/A:1011801018398

Adelekan, S.A. (2017). Impact of financial crisis on entrepreneurial effort in developing SMES in Nigeria. *LASU Journal of Business Review*, *4*(1).

Adelekan, S. A., Majekodunmi, S. A., & Omotayo, A. O. (2018). Impact of Entrepreneurship Development Programme on Economic Development of Lagos State, Nigeria. *IOSR Journal of Business and Management*, *20*(9), 74–81.

Adelekan, S. A., & Tijani, A. A. (2017). Effect of support for entrepreneurship development on economic growth and development in Nigeria. *European Scientific Journal*, *13*(13), 426–448. doi:10.19044/esj.2017.v13n13p426

Adelowo Caleb, M., Olaopa, R. O., & Siyanbola, W. O. (2012). Technology business incubation as strategy for SME development: How far and how well in Nigeria. *Science and Technology*, *2*(6), 172–181. doi:10.5923/j.scit.20120206.06

Agri, E. M., Kennedy, N. D., Bonmwa, G. O., &Acha, O. F. (2018). *Technology innovation and sustainable entrepreneurship development in Nigeria: Stakeholders' impact assessment in central Nigeria*. Academic Press.

Akanni, O.W. (2008). Entrepreneurship in Nigeria: Problem, challenges and prospects. *Nigeria Management Review, 14*(1&2).

Baradaran, M. S., Yadollahi Farsi, J., Hejazi, S. R., & Akbari, M. (2019). A Competency-based Typology of Technology Entrepreneurs: A Systematic Review of the Empirical Studies. *Iranian Journal of Management Studies*, *12*(2), 17–37.

Begley, T. M., & Boyd, D. P. (1987). Psychological characteristics associated with performance in entrepreneurial firms and smaller businesses. *Journal of Business Venturing*, *2*(1), 79–93. doi:10.1016/0883-9026(87)90020-6

Bose, M. S., & Goyal, D. (2019). Critical success factors of agri-business incubators and their impact on business. *CUSTOS E AGRONEGOCIO ON LINE*, *15*(1), 352–378.

Brown, B. J., & Clow, J. E. (1997). *Introduction to business: Our business and economics world*. Westerville, OH: Glencoe Mc- Graw-Hill.

Bubou, G. M., & Okrigwe, F. (2012). Fostering technological entrepreneurship for socioeconomic development: A case for technology incubation in Bayelsa State, Nigeria. *Journal of Sustainable Development*, *4*(6), 138–149.

Carpenter, M., & Dunung, S. (2012). *Challenges and opportunities in international business*. Retrieved from http://2012books.lardbucket.org/pdfs/challenges-and-opportunities-in international-business.pdf

Centre for Strategy and Evaluation Services (CSES). (2002). *Benchmarking of business incubator.* Brussels: European Commission Enterprise Directorate.

Chen, J., Cai, L., Bruton, G. D., & Sheng, N. (2019). Entrepreneurial ecosystems: What we know and where we move as we build an understanding of China. *Entrepreneurship and Regional Development*, 1–19.

Drucker, P. (1995). *Managing in a time of great change. E.P.* New York, NY: Dutton.

Dutta, C. (2018). The role of business incubators in entrepreneurship development: A brief review of literatures. *Research Bulletin*, *44*(1), 105–120.

Eckhardt, J. T., & Shane, S. A. (2003). Opportunities and entrepreneurship. *Journal of Management*, *29*(3), 333–349. doi:10.1177/014920630302900304

Enikanselu, S. A., & Oyende, A. I. (2010). *Introduction to Entrepreneurship*. Lagos, Nigeria: Enykon Consult.

Eze, B. U. (2018). Corporate entrepreneurship and manufacturing firms' performance. *Emerging Market Journal*, *8*(1), 12–17. doi:10.5195/EMAJ.2018.146

Freiling, J., & Schelhowe, C. (2014). The impact of entrepreneurial orientation on the performance of internationalisation. *Journal of Entrepreneurship. Management and Innovation*, *10*(4), 169–199.

Gartner, W. B. (1989). Who is an entrepreneur? Is the wrong question. *Entrepreneurship Theory and Practice*, *13*(4), 47–68. doi:10.1177/104225878901300406

Guerrero, M., &Urbano, D. (2019). A research agenda for entrepreneurship and innovation: the role of entrepreneurial universities. *A Research Agenda for Entrepreneurship and Innovation*, 107.

Hsueh, L., & Tu, Y. (2004). Innovation and the operational performance of newly established small and medium enterprises in Taiwan. *Small Business Economics*, *23*(2), 99–113. doi:10.1023/B:SBEJ.0000027663.84972.ac

Ikebuaku, K., & Dinbabo, M. (2018). Beyond entrepreneurship education: Business incubation and entrepreneurial capabilities. *Journal of Entrepreneurship in Emerging Economies*, *10*(1), 154–174. doi:10.1108/JEEE-03-2017-0022

Kapinga, A. F., Montero, C. S., Mwandosya, G. I., & Mbise, E. R. (2018). Exploring the contribution of business and technology incubators to women entrepreneurs' business development in Dar es Salaam, Tanzania. *Journal of Global Entrepreneurship Research*, *8*(1), 23. doi:10.118640497-018-0111-9

KianiMavi, R., Gheibdoust, H., Khanfar, A. A., & KianiMavi, N. (2019). Ranking factors influencing strategic management of university business incubators with ANP. *Management Decision*.

Knopp, L. (2007). *2006 state of the business incubation industry*. Athens, OH: National Business Incubation Association.

Mainoma, M. A., & Aruwa, S. A. S. (2012). *Entrepreneurship: Principles, processes and development*. Kaduna, Nigeria: Felicity Publishing.

Mansur, M. S., & Abuga, I. (2017). Incubator Based Activities and Technology Entrepreneurship Growth in North Western Nigeria. *KIU Journal of Humanities*, *2*(1), 157–168.

Meredith, G. G., Nelson, R. E., & Neck, P. A. (1991). *The practice of entrepreneurship*. University of Lagos Press.

Ndagi, A. (2017). Role of technology incubation on entrepreneurship development in Nigeria: A case of Minna technology incubation centre. *International Journal of Advanced Studies in Economics and Public Sector Management*, *5*(3), 131–138.

Obasan, K.A. (2005). *Entrepreneurship Theory and Practice*. Ogun: Gratia Associates International.

Oladele-Emmanuel, B. D., Redlich, T., & Wulfsberg, J. (2018, June). Measuring Innovation: Insight from Nigeria's Innovation Incubators. In *2018 IEEE International Conference on Engineering, Technology and Innovation (ICE/ITMC)* (pp 1-9). IEEE. 10.1109/ICE.2018.8436304

Oladimeji, M. S., Abosede, A. J., & Eze, B. U. (2018). Innovation and internationalization of Nigeria deposit money banks. *Emerging Market Journal*, *8*(1), 1–11. doi:10.5195/EMAJ.2018.144

Olaolu, D. (2018). An integrated framework for the critical success factors and incubator performance in Nigeria. Academy of Entrepreneurship Journal, 24(1).

Sanyal, S., & Hisam, M. W. (2018). The role of business incubators in creating an entrepreneurial ecosystem: A study of the sultanate of Oman. *Indian Journal of Commerce and Management Studies*, *9*(3), 9–16. doi:10.18843/ijcms/v9i3/02

Schumpeter, J. (1934). *The theory of economic development*. Cambridge, MA: Harvard.

Swedberg, R. (2000). *Entrepreneurship. The Social Science View*. Oxford, UK: Oxford University Press.

Timmons, J. A. (1978). Characteristics and role demands of entrepreneurship. *American Journal of Small Business*, *3*(1), 5–17. doi:10.1177/104225877800300102

UNIDO. (1999). *SMEs in Africa survive against all odds*. Retrieved from http://www.unido.org/doc/view?document_id=3927&language_code=en

United Nations Development Programme (UNDP). (2010). *Human development report 2010- 20th Anniversary Edition. The real wealth of Nations: Pathways to human development*. New York: University Press.

Volkmann, C. K., Tokarski, K. O., & Grunhagen, M. (2010). *Entrepreneurship in a European perspective*. Berlin: Gabler Verlag. doi:10.1007/978-3-8349-8752-5

Yusubova, A., Andries, P., & Clarysse, B. (2019). The role of incubators in overcoming technology ventures' resource gaps at different development stages. *R & D Management*, radm.12378. doi:10.1111/radm.12378

KEY TERMS AND DEFINITIONS

Entrepreneurs: An entrepreneur is a person who organises, manages, owns, controls, and assumes the risk of a business venture.

Entrepreneurship: This is a process, which involves looking out for opportunities and creating what will meet these opportunities, through innovativeness, proactiveness and risk-taking.

Entrepreneurship Development: This refers to the steady growth of entrepreneurial activities, such that it turns out to be further developed and more grounded.

Incubation Centre: These are centres where transitory and facilitative assistance is given to small enterprises or start-ups. It is geared towards small business development, innovation and application of technology, and promotion of growth from within local economies, while additionally giving a tool for technology transmission.

Startups: A startup is an enterprise initiated by individual founders or entrepreneurs to take advantage of identified business opportunities and scale the enterprise over-time. Startups usually search for a repeatable and scalable business model.

Technology: These are methods, systems, and devices which are the result of scientific knowledge being used to aid business operations and to propel the growth and development of business entities.

Technology Incubation: These are assistance given to start-ups ventures through the transfer of complex administration and unique environment with the objective of enhancing their opportunities of survival in the early period of enterprise life cycle, and building up their later development.

Chapter 13
Intellectual Capital Reporting and Disclosure Practices in Sri Lanka

Kennedy D. Gunawardana
https://orcid.org/0000-0003-3381-9058
University of Sri Jayewardenepura, Sri Lanka

ABSTRACT

This chapter examines disclosure practices of intellectual capital in the Sri Lankan context. The chapter provides an empirical analysis to showcase the relationship between intellectual capital reporting and the management perception. The three capital components identified in the intellectual capital are human capital, organizational capital, and social capital. Those capitals give a considerable contribution on the wealth of the organization and the main problem is the subjectivity and complexity of the disclosure practices of the listed companies in Colombo Stock Exchange from 2013 – 2016. This study is based on the intellectual capital disclosure practices published in annual reports for the period of 3 years. The managerial perception and company characteristics were linked with the intellectual capital disclosure practices. The study found no common procedure for disclosure among the annual reports while the details of intellectual capital disclosures vary considerably from one annual report to another.

DOI: 10.4018/978-1-5225-9810-7.ch013

INTRODUCTION

In modern day, due to the lack of resources, global economic behavior is dynamic. Therefore, the economist try to find out the optimum methods to get best use of resources. Generally, all the physical resources are always deprecating while the human abilities and capacities are always appreciating. The value of the physical resources are not changed from one company to another. But the human capacity and the outcomes of the human works are different from man to man even if they have same qualifications.

The main point of this chapter is that the companies are really facing the barriers of enjoying the benefits of intellectual capital due the high complexity of that. The main reasons for the complexity are the changing behavior and too sensitiveness of intellectual capital. Therefore there is no any common method to disclose the intellectual capital. The researcher is aimed to examine the disclosure practices of intellectual capital in Sri Lankan context. Also there is no any proper method to disclose the intellectual capital even in the intentional businesses. Basically there are three capital components that can be identified in the Intellectual Capital as Human Capital, Organizational Capital and Social Capital. Those capitals give a considerable contribution on the wealth of the organization and the main problem is the subjectivity and complexity of the disclosure. According to the argument of Dzinkowski (2000) clear identification of the Intellectual Capital is a real issue in the business organizations. Due to the subjectivity of the disclosure of intellectual capital, it is hard to compare and get a clear idea about the intellectual capital of the organizations.

In Sri Lankan companies there are no any proper practices of intellectual capital. There are nearly 250 listed companies in Sri Lanka and some of the best companies have mentioned about some of their disclosure practices of intellectual capital under the intangible assets and in various sections of annual reports. But in Sri Lankan context there is no any proper attraction on the intellectual capital as an asset. The main problem is the complexity and the subjectivity of disclosing part of the intellectual capital. If there is a proper standard for the intellectual capital, it is easy to disclosure it in a proper manner. In relation to the intellectual capital in Sri Lankan context;

- To find out the relationships between managerial perception and intellectual capital discourses and value practices.
- To study the existing intellectual capital disclosure practices from 2013 – 2016, practiced by listed companies in Colombo Stock Exchange.

This study carried out on the disclosure practices of intellectual capital that are being carried out by listed public quoted companies in Sri Lanka. The public quoted companies mean the companies which are registered in the Colombo Stock Exchange. It focused on the managerial perceptions and the company characteristics of the companies and how they affected on disclosure practices of intellectual capital. Therefore generally the width of the research was the listed public companies in Colombo Stock Exchange.

INTELLECTUAL CAPITAL (IC)

Intellectual capital is knowledge that can be exploited for some money-making or other useful purpose. The term combines the idea of the intellect or brain-power with the economic concept of capital, the saving of entitled benefits so that they can be invested in producing more goods and services. Intellectual capital can include the skills and knowledge that a company has developed about how to make its goods or services; individual employees or groups of employees whose knowledge is deemed critical to a company's continued success; and its aggregation of documents about processes, customers, research results, and other information that might have value for a competitor that is not common knowledge. Intellectual Capital has three components as follows.

Intellectual Capital = Human Capital + Organizational Capital + Social Capital

Also Emerald Early has said the intellectual capital is the knowledge, applied experience, enterprise processes and technology customer relationships and professional skills which are valuable assets to an organization.

Human Capital (HC)

The value that the employees of a business provide through the application of skills, know how and expertise. Human capital is an organization's combined human capability for solving business problems. Human capital is inherent in people and cannot be owned by an organization. Therefore, human capital can leave an organization when people leave.

Human capital also encompasses how effectively an organization uses its people resources as measured by creativity and innovation. Therefore in this study, leadership styles, employee motivation and satisfaction, work related knowledge and competency, entrepreneurial sprit and innovativeness of the employee of the listed companies have been investigated under the human capital as a major part of intellectual capital. The main point here is that the knowledge is different from one company to another company even they have same headcounts and qualifications.

Figure 1. Components of intellectual capital (knowledge flow)
Source: Petrash (1996)

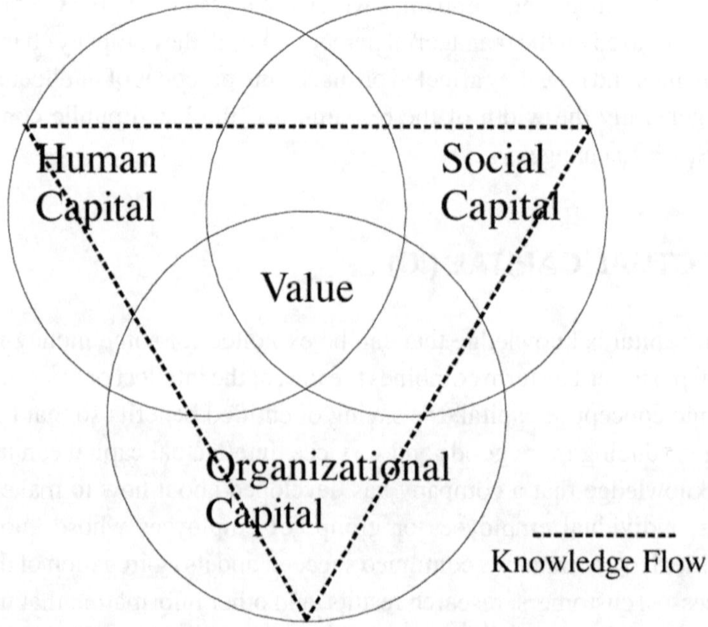

Organizational Capital (OC)

Organizational capital means the knowledge flow of the structure of the organizations. It includes corporate strategies, processes, corporate culture, systems, financial relations and management credibility of the organizations. It calls Structural Capital also. This is internal. All the internal knowledge flow raised from the organizational structure has been discussed under the organizational capital as a main part of intellectual capital.

Social Capital (SC)

Social capital is directly related with the external environment of the organization. Basically it includes the customer based whole society. Here the customer loyalty, customer satisfaction, growth of the business in the market, customer complaints, market share and favorable contracts and contacts with the peer groups have been discussed under the social capital as a major part of the intellectual capital. This social capital is called as Customer Capital.

CURRENT KNOWLEDGE

The article named "A rational management perspective within the managerial mind frame" written by Chaharbaghi and Cripps (2008) have said that the rational management model is thus a normalizing, disciplinary technology aimed at transforming the polyphony of voices within an organization into a solo so that regulation and order can be imposed over diversity. Through this normalizing process, individuals' choices for action become aligned with the organizational goals and the meaning of those choices becomes reduced to their capabilities to carry out what is expected. Thus, individuals can only use expressions such as, "I can", and that is to say "I am competent to do so", or "I cannot", that is to say "I am not competent to do so" and the language of obligation such as "I must" (Schabracq and Cooper, 1998). This technology allows the control of the individual and the control of choice, making individuals thoughtless in the name of economic interests. From the rational management perspective, "intellectual capital" only becomes meaningful when it is defined in a way that gives an illusion of inclusion and excludes choice by allowing the dominant discourse of rational management to impose what kind of intellectual labour is legitimate. This illusion serves to hide a preference for a disembodied worldview and an intolerance of the embodied world. The illusion of inclusion is necessary to obscure the crucial difference objectives of management and the non-rational criteria and objectives that are born out of individual's intellectual labour.

As the non managerial perspective in this article said that intellectuel capital: A non-rational management perspective, rational behaviour cannot be reduced to managerial rationality. Behaviour can be non-rational in managerial and yet rational in extra-managerial terms (i.e. managerially irrational and non-managerially rational). It is possible to develop an alternative way of thinking about intellectual capital through a non-managerially rational or non-rational management perspective. The logic of the non-rational management perspective instigates trust and diversity as opposed to the disciplinary, normalizing technology for individual regulation and collective control used in the rational management perspective.

The non-rational management model is characterized and described in terms of an embodied whole, where each inner part contributes to the determination of the whole. From this perspective, organizations are seen as a nexus of social treaties created by a diversity of interests. Trust is the key value and guiding principle driving the non-rational management model. It places faith in the capability of individuals to maximize their potential and determine what needs to be done. From this perspective, social cohesion is perceived not through sameness or uniformity but through unity in diversity. The non-rational management model is based on the assumption that organizational life is about making choices in a world where truth is a nebulous notion.

According to their non-rational management model therefore represents an ecological model of thinking in that it celebrates mutual dependency and interdependency. It supports the notion that reality is uncontrolled, and that individuals and organizations are located and embedded in a dynamic, uncertain context. That it is not possible to know in advance when journeying along an unknown road that it might lead to a dead-end.

Nelson and Winter (1982) said that learning is derived from the history associated with trial and error processes causing change to be incremental and choice to be limited. What emerges is a track record through which change can be traced. Choices are sometimes planned, sometimes unrealized and sometimes emergent (Mintzberg, 1994). Individual learning is both conditioned by the technology used to assess it and an individual's response to that technology and its meaning (Weick, 1995). However, whilst a shared understanding may be developed and social order may exist this does not imply that meaning is universal. Individuals are quite capable of doing one thing and thinking another. Thus, knowledge and knowing are independent of one another and determined by individual meaning. As a result, differences rather than consensus are the state of play.

According to their ecological model each individual has an interdependent and antagonistic relationship with the context within which they are placed. These tensions are balanced by the trust that exists between individuals, where trust is considered to be the self-assertive state of being responsible for the conscientious performance of some task and the integrative state which allows others to use or do something in the belief that they will behave responsibly and honestly.

In this conclusion, intellectual capital has the potential of unveiling what really matters for the survival and sustainable performance of organizations in the perceived, emerging, post-industrial and knowledge intensive society. This, however, requires a critical approach that provides an insight into the way different discourses are promoted and what their promoters gain from its use. Without the knowledge of such discourses it is not possible to make sense of intellectual capital. By adopting a critical approach, this study has argued that the measurement of intellectual capital does not have any explanatory power.

The adoption of measurement of intellectual capital can only serve as a device for control through biasing organizational conversations and legitimizing intervention when it assists management need for control. A radical alternative perspective of intellectual capital requires a fundamental change in the assumptions of what management is about and that forcing the discourse about intellectual capital into existing working frameworks will not bring about a change in the attitude of mind of managers or workers. The rational management perspective of intellectual capital has ignored, and made insignificant, the non-rational dimension, and vice versa.

Also in the article of Kannan (2008) has done a broad literature survey. The literature surveyed included financial and accounting measurement techniques, perceptual measures, process and systems measures, social networks analysis techniques, and econometric techniques for intangibles measurement. It is discussed in detail about the seminal studies and popular frameworks for intellectual capital measurement.

Brennan and Connell (2007) have done a prior research analysis on intellectual capital. According to that much research, both theoretical and empirical, has been undertaken on intellectual capital in recent years, Early research focused on defining intellectual capital and on methods of classification (e.g. Brooking, 1996; Edvinsson and Malone, 1997; Sveiby, 1997; Roos et al., 1997). Kaplan and Norton (1992), Sveiby (1997) and Edvinsson and Malone (1997) proposed different frameworks for classifying intellectual capital. These frameworks are broadly similar, but show different interrelationships among the elements of intellectual capital.

Edvinsson and Malone (1997) are in a supplement to Skandia's annual report, used for the first time the word ``intellectual capital'' instead of the accounting term ``intangible assets'' Skandia AFS, a Swedish financial services company, was one of the first companies to report the "hidden'' intellectual capital assets of the business. Skandia went on to develop one of the most important models, the Skandia Navigator, for managing intellectual capital. Another important researcher in intellectual capital is Karl- Erik Sveiby (1997) who has carried out a considerable amount of the pioneering research on intellectual capital management. He further points out that the increasing importance of intellectual capital may require a fundamental shift in the way we think about organizations. Two companies, Skandia AFS (Edvinsson, 1997) and Dow Chemical (Petrash, 1996) were involved in much of the pioneering efforts of intellectual capital management. Each company also developed its own framework for managing intellectual capital. Against this background, empirical research was carried out in many countries to examine how companies account for intellectual capital assets. Indicators of intellectual capital, intellectual capital statements and measurement of intangibles were analyzed by them for the purpose of identifying best. In the article of Lim and Dallimore (2008), there were best findings on intellectual capital. The managerial implication on intellectual capital has been identified in a perfect way. It can be mentioned as follows.

Intellectual capital is of substantial and growing importance in innovation, productivity, growth, enterprise competitiveness, and economic performance. The unpredictability and volatility of the business environment should require companies to look into their intangible assets, including their management know-how and marketing know-how. The purpose of setting standards for indicators of these assets is to ensure that non-financial information is presented in a way that enables decision-makers to make informed judgment based on a comparative standard. The results showed that the management know-how capitals are relatively similar in its significance based on the top five indicators. As for the marketing know-how capitals, customer capital stands up to be more significant than other capitals. These indicators would provide significant benefits to existing and prospective investors as well as the quality of the services provided by the companies. Research has also been conducted with fund managers in the investment community on their perception towards the importance of disclosing the indicators of the different forms of capital assets (Lim and Dallimore, 2002).

The fund managers were also asked about their level of understanding of how these indicators are being measured and how they can be evaluated. Similarly, the results have shown that the investment community stressed more emphases on human capital and customer capital. They also questioned whether organizations would disclose information on indicators to the public.

Some say that this is unlikely unless there is a mandatory requirement set by regulators. Nevertheless, when the public see the new reporting of this intellectual capital information, they may develop a new attitude toward the company. An on-going study is being conducted with the listed companies to determine their perceptions of the importance of disclosing these indicators as well as determining their willingness to disclose them if they were given a choice not to disclose such information.

Richard Petty and James Guthrie (2008) have written an article on intellectual capital and they have mentioned there the evolution of intellectual capital. It is really important to understand continues evolution of intellectual capital. The evolution has been mentioned as follows based on the particular article.

- Early 1980s - General notion of intangible value (often generically, labeled “goodwill”).
- Mid 1980s - The “information age'' takes hold and the gap between book value and market value widens noticeably for many companies.
- Late 1980s - Early attempts by practitioner consultants to construct statements/ accounts that measure intellectual capital (Sveiby, 1988).
- Early 1990s - Initiatives systematically to measure and report on company stocks of intellectual capital to external parties (e.g. Celemi and Skandia; SCSI, 1995).
- In 1990 - Skandia AFS appoints Leif Edvinsson ``Director of intellectual capital''. This is the first time that the role of managing intellectual capital is elevated to a position of formal status and given an air of corporate legitimacy.
- In 1992 - Kaplan and Norton introduce the concept of a balanced scorecard. The scorecard evolved around the premise that ``what you measure is what you get''.

- Mid 1990s - Nonaka and Takeuchi (1995) present their highly influential work on "the knowledge creating company". Although the book concentrates on "knowledge", the distinction between knowledge and intellectual capital is sufficiently fine as to make the book relevant to those with a pure focus on intellectual capital Celemi's Tango simulation tool is launched in 1994.
- In 1994 - A supplement to Skandia's annual report is produced which focuses on presenting an evaluation of the company's stock of intellectual capital. "Visualizing Intellectual Capital'' generates a great deal of interest from other companies seeking to follow Skandia's lead (Edvinsson, 1997).
- In 1995 - Another sensation is caused when Celemi uses a ``knowledge audit'' to offer a detailed assessment of the state of its intellectual capital. Pioneers of the intellectual capital movement publish bestselling books on the topic (Kaplan and Norton, 1996; Edvinsson and Malone, 1997; Sveiby 1997).
- Late 1990s - Intellectual capital becomes a popular topic with researchers and academic conferences, working papers, and other publications find an audience. An increasing number of large-scale projects commence which aim, in part, to introduce some academic rigor into research on intellectual capital
- In 1999 - An international symposium in Amsterdam on intellectual capital.

Stephen Chen (2008) has written an article on intellectual capital. His aim was to find the application of intellectual capital using the game theory. The examples of how game theory may be used to better assess the strategic value of intellectual capital are shown below.

Brands can be considered as a method of signaling quality and other product characteristics to consumers. This allows various models developed in game theory to be applied, such as Akerlof's (1970) classic "market for lemons" model in which price signals quality. In this model, Akerlof shows that relying on high prices as a signal of quality can lead to market failure, if producers of low quality can just as easily charge high prices as producers of high quality goods. Brands may thus be a better signal of quality by virtue of the fact that they are costly investments for firms to make. Thus, the commitment of the firm as evidenced by its advertising for the brand can signal to the buyer that the seller has enough confidence in the product to invest in the brand. For example, Brandenburg et al. (1997) cite the example of Gillette, which spent more than $100 million on the launch of its Sensor shaving system in 1990 and argue that it was not only the information content in the advertisements, about the technological superiority of the system, that was responsible for the success of the campaign, but also the obviously expensive nature of the advertisements, which demonstrated Gillette's confidence in the new product. Such an analysis would suggest that, in determining the value of the brand, one should seek to include a measure of how much the brand increased consumer confidence in the product, above and beyond the indication provided by the price.

From an options perspective, additional value may also be derived from the strategic options made possible by that increased confidence. For example, investment in the Sensor brand might open up other markets such as branded after-shave. This could be valued as a call option (an option to buy or make additional investments). Alternatively, a failure of the test marketing might be of value in preventing additional losses in similar projects. This could be valued as a put option (the option to sell or cancel proposed investments). Therefore all the above things are directly related with the intellectual capital of the organizations. Therefore intellectual capital acts a vital role.

Leon (2008) said that the managerial perceptions of organizational knowledge resources. According to his findings and recommendations, he has given some guidelines for future direction on intellectual capital researches. The author posiions that the phenomenon of intellectual capital belongs to the broad area of "knowledge management" (Stwart, 1999). The conclusions reached above suggest the presence of several issues that underlay the emerging practice of knowledge management. These issue lie in the areas of

- The communication of knowledge management
- The impact of gender on knowledge management
- The impact of youth on knowledge management; and
- The impediments to knowledge management

According to the above literature review researcher realized that the intellectual capital valuation and also disclosure practices of intellectual capital is really important to do a research study.

The researcher found that the best way to adopt the intellectual capital to Sri Lankan context is to propose some guidelines to disclosure practices of intellectual capital. Also according to the literature survey it has been found that the valuation parts of intellectual capital is also a major part of the disclosure of intellectual capital. That means how the values are taken into accounts, especially to the balance sheet. Therefore how they disclosure their valuation practices also were taken under the disclosure practices for better findings. According to that the valuation and disclosure practices are taken as the dependent variables.

According to the literature review it has no doubt that the dependent variable should be the managerial perceptions. Under managerial perception there are three elements has been taken as human capital, social capital and organizational capital. Company characteristics such as profitability, size, etc. make an effect on the relationship between managerial perceptions of intellectual capital and disclosure

& value of intellectual capital. Therefore the company characteristics have been taken as the controllable variable and the real relationships have been tested after adjusting the effects of controllable variable to the independent and dependent variables. All those things have been identified from the methods which were used by the past researchers.

Brennan and Conell (2000) said thatsome of the research projects still in progress, proposals for developing guidelines and accounting standards for intellectual capital at an early stage. The primary goal of much of the research is to establish a set of guidelines for managing, measuring and reporting on intellectual capital. Intellectual capital must be measured in a way that is useful for decision making.

Nerdrum and Erikson (2001) said that it is needed to make a theoretical framework for human capital. Also he argued that intellectual capital necessarily comprises a set of complementary capacities. It means that all the capitals which are related to intellectual capital are intergrated. Moreover, they have shown that economic theory possesses the theoretical arguments to justify the notion of intellectual capital. Because human capital theory traditionally does not account for the great potential embedded in the more unique characteristics dealt with here, they have extended the theory to include the notion of intellectual capital, and as such, placed the theory within a broader framework of value creation.

According to Caddy (2000) intellectual liabilities have to be taken in to considerations when disclosing and valuing of intellectual capital. As a further area of research, if categories of intellectual liabilities can be elucidated, then attention should be devoted in the first instance towards assessing if these categories can be ranked in terms of size of impact, possible duration, level of organization response required, even if direct measurement and valuation cannot be performed.

Jeewantha et al. (2015) studied about the voluntary disclosure practices in the annual reports including intellectual capital disclosure practices. Most of the researchers have mentioned that the IC is a voluntary non-financial disclosure practices which can be mentioned in the annual report. It was mentioned that the voluntary disclosure will be depended on the firm size, profitability level, leverage of the firm, nature of the audit firm, industry, etc..

The understanding of intellectual capital and the current knowledge of intellectual capital have been mentioned. According to all the literature it is stated that the neediness and importance of a common procedure to disclose of intellectual capital. Therefore researcher realized that it is needed to do a research study on disclosing the IC of the companies specially based on Sri Lankan context.

EVOLUTION AND CONTEMPORARY DEVELOPMENT OF INTELLECTUAL CAPITAL

The researcher divided the time duration of the evolution in to four periods based on some considerable turning points to study the evolution of intellectual capital in Sri Lanka. The first period has been taken as "before 1948" period. The aim was to highlight the practices which were done before the independency of Sri Lanka. The second time period has been taken as the duration between 1948 to 1977. That means the period after the independency and before the open economy. There was a close economy which was handled by the government without intervention of the United Kingdom. The third period has been taken as the duration between 1977 to 2009. The base is the open economy. Most of the international things were experienced during this time and public sector acquired the market comparing to the government.

Before 1948 Period

Year 1948 was a turning point of Sri Lanka. Actually the British period was the period that the companies were established in a systematic way. Before that there were some businesses in Sri Lanka. But the record keeping and all other things had not been properly maintained. Next the researcher will discuss about the evolution of the disclosure practices of intellectual capital in the above era specially focus on the British period.

1948 – 1977 Period

In this era there was a turning point to be established in an independent way to Sri Lanka after the independency. Therefore the Sri Lankan government initially started to enter the private sector market in a considerable level. Especially the Institute of Chartered Accountants of Sri Lanka was established in 1959. That gave a clear picture and proper guidance to how to keep the records in an organization. Also Central Bank of Sri Lanka was established in this period and government transaction also properly recorded in this era. It seems that there may be properly recorded some details on intellectual capital rather than the British period. Generally, the formal annual report procedures were come to the market in this period.

- 1955, Central Bank Report, Annual Report – Couldn't find any information regarding intellectual capital.
- 1960 / 1975, Central Bank Report, Annual Report – Couldn't find any information regarding intellectual capital and there were no any information regarding knowledge and workforce.

- 1968, Ceylon Tyre Corporation, p. 6 -7 – There were some information regarding changes of the staff, categorization of staff, separate executive posits, etc..
- 1969/1970, Ceylon Tyre Corporation p. 8-9 - There were some information regarding increases of staff, separate executive posits, etc.
- 1971, Sri Lanka Sugar Corporation – Couldn't find any information regarding intellectual capital even there were no any information regarding knowledge and workforce.
- 1971/1972, Mahaweli Development Board, p 27, There were some information regarding recruitment of staff, staff grade appointments, etc.
- 1972, Port Tally and Protective Services Cooperation - There were some information regarding about employment carder, etc.
- 1972, Bank of Ceylon, p 15 - There were some information regarding labour force increases.
- 1972, Marga Institute, p 6, 1st annual report - There were some information regarding full qualified persons were in the board of directors.
- 1972, Peoples Bank, p 9 - There were some information regarding director information, etc.
- 1972, State printing corporation, p 23 - There were some information regarding remuneration for directors.
- 1977, BOC, p 21, There were some information regarding officers details.
- 1977, Sri Lanka Broadcasting Corporation, p 13 - There were some information regarding library books, disk assets and royalties as an expense.
- 1977, Peoples Bank, p 2 - There were some information regarding open economy, staff, etc.
- 1977, Ceylon Steel Cooperation, p 12, There were some information regarding administration, human relations, personnel carder, Training and Development, etc.
- 1977, Sri Lanka State Trading Corporation, p 20- 21, - There were some information regarding there are details of employees, contribution to state revenue, customer satisfaction, profitability.
- 1977, National Textile Cooperation, p 2 - There were some information regarding employees.

In this period there is a proper evolution on annual report and it has a continuous growth. Also proper accounting procedures are there and some kind of information of intellectual capital were also there even it didn't have a proper logical manner. But there were some features of human capital, organizational capital and customer capital.

1978 – 2009 Period

This is a turning point of Sri Lankan economy due to the openness it to the global. So lots of imports and exports were there and public section came to the Sri Lankan market at a considerable level. Therefore the market has been expended.

There was the proper established accounting standard introduced by Institute of Chartered Accountants of Sri Lanka. Special in 1994 there was a huge changed of accounting standards and also in 1995 the auditing standards were introduced in a proper way. There were some provisions on preparation of financial statements. But researcher couldn't find anything related to intellectual capital in the Sri Lankan Accounting Standards. As examples;

- Framework for the preparation and presentation of financial statements 1995 (revised 1994).
- SLAS 15 – Presentation of current assets and liabilities - current and noncurrent assets were divided based on liquidity.
- No any stranded on intangible assets and intellectual capital
- Stranded for intangible asset was there as SLAS 37. But there is no any disclosure and value practices of intellectual capital.

Data Collection

Data collection was mainly done here in three parts. Those are annual reports, documents of visited places, international documents.

Annual Reports

According to the sample the researcher has collected annual reports in listed companies in Colombo Stock Exchange (CSE). Mainly 90 companies were selected covering all the sectors. There are nearly 20 sectors in CSE. Nearly 250 companies can be seen under those 20 sectors. Therefore the researched has selected 90 companies out of 250 companies covering all the sectors using a relevant sampling method as mentioned in All the annual reports were collected covering three financial years as 2013/2014, 2014/2015, 2015/2016. Therefore altogether 270 annual reports were collected. Basic aim of collecting the annual reports was to check the existing practices of intellectual capital disclosure practices.

Figure 2. Secondary data analysis flow

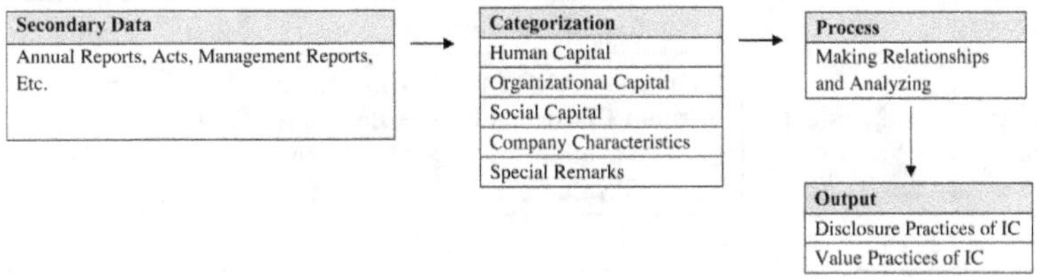

Content Analysis

There were lots of data gathered to analyze the IC practices. To get them to a common way a Content Analysis was basically done. The main headings of content analysis were human capital, organizational capital, social capital, company characteristics and special remarks.

Hypothesis Testing

The relationship between the managerial perception of human capital and the intellectual capital disclosure practices. The independent variable was the managerial perception of human capital and the dependent variable was intellectual capital disclosure practices. The thinking pattern of human capital in intellectual capital disclosure practices were tested through this hypothesis.

The significance of each hypothesis without controllable variable was calculated to check the difference of the significance with controllable variable and without it. Significances are different. But all are below 0.050 at 95% confident level. Therefore the entire alternative hypotheses were accepted and null hypotheses were rejected.

Correlation

Correlations of the variables were investigated to check the relationship among the independent and dependent variables. The SPSS output can be mentioned as follows. The independent and dependent variables have been taken after adjusting the effect of control variable. The Pearson Correlation was used.

According to the correlations, only two are in significance level. Dependent variables are correlated with the independent variable called organizational capital. Only the organizational capital is significantly correlated with the dependent variables. The other independent variables are not significantly correlated with the dependent variables.

Table 1. Hypotheses testing

Hypotheses Testing					
Independent Variables	**Dependent Variables**	**One Way ANOVA without Controllable Variable P value**	**One Way ANOVA with Controllable Variable P value**	**H_0**	**H_1**
MPHC	ICDP	0.001	0.045	Reject	Accept
MPOC	ICDP	0.002	0.021	Reject	Accept
MPSC	ICDP	0.000	0.027	Reject	Accept
MPHC	ICVP	0.001	0.008	Reject	Accept
MPOC	ICVP	0.001	0.006	Reject	Accept
MPSC	ICVP	0.000	0.008	Reject	Accept
MPHC	Managerial Perception of Human Capital				
MPOC	Managerial Perception of Organizational Capital				
MPSC	Managerial Perception of Social Capital				
ICDP	Intellectual Capital Disclosure Practices				
ICVP	Intellectual Capital Value Practices				
Control Variable	Company Characteristics				

According to the availability of intellectual capital 29% from the sample stated that they have practice disclosing of IC previously. That means the companies have been trying to establish the IC disclosure practices in their companies even they did not have a common procedure. Most important thing here is that 55% of companies are currently practicing IC disclosure practices. Others are in a positive way to practice it in near future. Only 8% of the companies do not have even an intention to practice it. But that it not a considerable figure.

Academically and professionally educated staff is a common figure in the annual reports. Also some kind of disclosing part of experienced staff related to IC is also there. General trend is to disclose the details of talented staff.

According to the availability of intellectual capital 13% from the sample stated that they have practice valuing of IC previously. That means the companies have been trying to establish the IC value practices in their companies even they did not have a common procedure. Most important thing here is that 53% of companies are currently intention to practice IC value practices. Because there is no any proper procedure to value of IC. Therefore currently usage of valuing of IC is in 28%. Also

Table 2. Correlations

		Human Capital Residual	**Organizational Capital Residual**	**Social Capital Residual**	**Disclosure Practices Residual**	**Value Practices Residual**
Human Capital Residual	Pearson Correlation	1				
	Sig. (2-tailed)					
	N	51				
Organizational Capital Residual	Pearson Correlation	.219	1			
	Sig. (2-tailed)	.123				
	N	51	51			
Social Capital Residual	Pearson Correlation	.663**	.386**	1		
	Sig. (2-tailed)	.000	.005			
	N	51	51	51		
Disclosure Practices Residual	Pearson Correlation	-.036	**.410****	.018	1	
	Sig. (2-tailed)	.045	**.021**	.027		
	N	51	**51**	51	51	
Value Practices Residual	Pearson Correlation	.056	**.322***	.145	.894**	1
	Sig. (2-tailed)	.008	**.007**	.008	.000	
	N	51	**51**	51	51	51
**. Correlation is significant at the 0.01 level (2-tailed).						
*. Correlation is significant at the 0.05 level (2-tailed).						

17% of companies do not have even an intention to value of the IC even some of them have an idea to disclose it.

Academically and professionally educated staff is a common figure in the annual reports. Also some kind of disclosing part of experienced staff related to IC is also there. General trend is to disclose the details of talented staff and other variables given in the table.

They can suggest more than one place. Most of them suggested the financial statements or sustainability report to disclose the IC. Also some of them suggested that it is needed to disclose IC in a separate report atleast at the initial stage. Also they suggested that the real places to value of IC are financial statements. Because the monitory values cab be put in financial statements easily. Other parts are not much familiar among then related to value of IC.

Table 3. Summary of the correlations

Independent Variables	Dependent Variables	Correlation	
MPHC	ICDP	No	
MPOC	**ICDP**	**Yes**	
MPSC	ICDP	No	
MPHC	ICVP	No	
MPOC	**ICVP**	**Yes**	
MPSC	ICVP	No	
MPHC	Managerial Perception of Human Capital		
MPOC	Managerial Perception of Organizational Capital		
MPSC	Managerial Perception of Social Capital		
ICDP	Intellectual Capital Disclosure Practices		
ICVP	Intellectual Capital Value Practices		

Table 4. Availability of intellectual capital (disclosure)

	Previously had	Currently has	Intention to have	No even intention
- Academically educated staff	24	38	13	1
- Professionally qualified staff	29	50	1	0
- Experienced staff	30	51	0	0
- Talented staff	8	25	26	1
- Patents/Copy rights	3	4	28	18
- Trademarks	3	4	29	18
- Separate corporate culture	17	37	13	1
- Separate MIS system	12	32	19	1
- Loyal customers	25	44	7	0
- Business collaborations	3	10	36	6
- Distribution channels	11	27	24	0
- Favorable contracts	10	16	30	6
Average	**29%**	**55%**	**37%**	**8%**

Table 5. Availability of intellectual capital (value)

	Previously had	Currently has	Intention to have	No even intention
- Academically educated staff	25	40	10	0
- Professionally qualified staff	23	50	2	0
- Experienced staff	15	45	8	0
- Talented staff	7	10	40	0
- Patents/Copy rights	1	3	21	24
- Trademarks	2	2	22	24
- Separate corporate culture	0	1	43	6
- Separate MIS system	1	9	36	5
- Loyal customers	0	2	45	3
- Business collaborations	0	1	30	17
- Distribution channels	2	5	38	7
- Favorable contracts	3	5	28	16
Average	**13%**	**28%**	**53%**	**17%**

Table 6. Reporting place of intellectual capital in annual reports

	Disclosure	Value
- In the balance sheet	31	36
- In the notes	32	30
- Sustainability report	31	12
- Not in financial statements	0	0
- As a separate report	12	10

Findings on Human Capital

The researcher has found that there is a relationship between the managerial perception of human capital and intellectual capital disclosure practices. That means the mangers are thinking and more concerned about the disclosure practices of human capital as a part of the intellectual capital. Managers are more concerned about the leadership style, employee motivation, employee satisfaction, work related knowledge, entrepreneurial spirit and innovativeness of the company related to IC disclosure practices.

The secondary data analysis was based on the annual reports. Out of the samples only 22 (25%) companies have mentioned about human capital in their annual reports. Only one company has valued the human capital in rupee value and only one company has reported the human capital in a separate section by giving a considerable space in the annual report.

Findings on Organizational Capital

The researcher has found that there is a relationship between the managerial perception of organizational capital and intellectual capital disclosure practices. That means the mangers are thinking and more concerned about the disclosure practices of organizational capital as a part of the intellectual capital. Managers are more concerned about the quality of corporate strategy, quality of the processes, corporate culture, systems, financial relations and management credibility of the company related to IC disclosure practices.

Findings on Social Capital

The researcher has found that there is a relationship between the managerial perception of social capital and intellectual capital disclosure practices. That means the mangers are thinking and more concerned about the disclosure practices of social capital as a part of the intellectual capital. Managers are more concerned about the quality of the product, customer satisfaction, growth of the business, customer complains, new trends and favorable contacts of the company related to IC disclosure practices.

Findings on secondary data analysis were taken based on the annual reports. Out of the samples only 13 (15%) companies have mentioned about social capital in their annual reports. Only one company has valued the social capital has reported them in a separate section by giving a considerable space in the annual report.

Findings on Intellectual Capital

29% of the managers have mentioned that IC disclosure practices have been done previously in their companies. 55% said that they are practicing them currently. 37% of companies have an intention to disclose them. Only 8% of companies do not have even an intention to disclose. Generally 90% of managers are keener about the disclosure practice of IC.

13% of the managers have mentioned that IC value practices have been done previously in their companies. 28% said that they are practicing them currently. 53% of companies have an intention to value them. Only 17% of companies do not have even an intention to disclose. Generally 80% of managers are keener about the value practice of IC. Most of the managers are in an intention to value them. The reason for this is the lacking part of a common procedure to value them. Therefore they are reluctant to value them even they are in a good position to disclose them.

It is suggested to do a feasibility study and a cost benefit analysis before implementing the disclosure and value practices of IC. Also they have said that, to get the competitive advantage and financial wealth, it is good to record about IC. Apart from that some of them have suggested to do the disclosure and value practices of IC in annual reports. But they did not have suggested a procedure for that. The most common answer was that the introducing a common method for that.

There were some figures have been mentioned in the annual reports of intellectual capital. But there was no any common procedure and the researcher has found out the details of intellectual capital from the following areas of the annual reports. Those areas are as follows.

- Management Discussion and Analysis
- Company Profile
- Company Risk Management
- Human Resource Management / Organizational Structure
- Corporate Social Responsibility
- As a separate report named Intellectual Capital

SOLUTIONS AND RECOMMENDATIONS

Short Term

Short term recommendations mean that the recommendations which can be implemented within another one years. Those have been mentioned separately for the human, organizational and social capital.

Human Capital

Companies have to collect all the relevant data related to the human capital which have been mentioned in the previous chapters. Because the data related to the human is changing rapidly and cha behavior is unpredictable. Updating has to be done on time.

Human capital is appreciating daily due to the passage of time. They gather more experiences, skills and knowledge. Therefore the skill inventory has to be maintained by the companies.

There is a relationship between managerial perception and disclosure practices of human capital. Also value practices (Just mentioned the valued amounts and methods) have the relationship. Therefore the management has to decide to allocate a considerable time to discus about them and making decisions on them. Therefore the employee satisfaction and motivation factors have to be surveyed. Recruitment must me belated highly with the work related knowledge. Leadership style has to be evaluated and the giving the opportunity for the innovation is a must. Those have to be disclosed in the annual reports for the better understanding.

Organizational Capital

Companies have to collect all the relevant data related to the organizational capital which have been mentioned in the previous chapters. Because the data related to the organizational capital is highly competitive. Updating has to be done on time.

Organizational capital is changing with the rapid changing of the global business environment. To get the competitive advantages it is a must to investigate about the organizational capital of the companies and as well as of the other companied. It has to be disclosed in the annual report to show the prestige of the companies within the frame work. If not others can get the internal details of the companies and it will be d disadvantage.

There is a relationship between managerial perception and disclosure practices of organizational capital. Also value practices (Just mentioned the valued amounts and methods) have the relationship. Therefore the management has to decide to allocate a considerable time to discus about them and making decisions on them. Therefore the quality of the corporate strategy and processes has to be discussed and to be disclosed about them for showing the internal capacity of the company.

Corporate culture has to be unique and must be disclosed in the annual report to get the competitive advantages. Financial relations and management credibility is a must and those have to be maintained. Apart from the financial statements, it is needed to show the management credibility in the annual report in a strong way.

Social Capital

Companies have to collect all the relevant data related to the social capital which have been mentioned in the previous chapters. Because the data related to the organizational capital is highly competitive. Updating has to be done on time.

Socisl capital is changing with the changes of the behavior of the customers. To get the competitive advantages it is a must to investigate about the social capital of the companies and as well as of the other companies. It has to be disclosed in the annual report to show the prestige of the companies.

There is a relationship between managerial perception and disclosure practices of social capital. Also value practices (Just mentioned the valued amounts and methods) have the relationship. Therefore the management has to decide to allocate a considerable time to discus about them and making decisions on them. Therefore the, customer satisfaction on quality of the product, growth of the business/ market share and the favorable contracts have to be surveyed and must be disclosed for better representation of the company wealth.

Customer capital means the external capital. It is changing within very short period of time. Therefore companies have to be in alert and the details have to be disclosed to take the decision and to take the better understanding about the behavior of customers. Because the companies have some market research data. But the relevant data from them have to be disclosed.

Long Term

Long term recommendations mean that the recommendations which can be implemented within another five years. Those have been mentioned separately for the human, organizational and social capital.

Human Capital

It is a must to prepare a common disclosing and valuation procedure relevant to human capital of the companies. Due to the complexity of the behavior of humans it should be more practical and flexible. This can be done with the help of Chartered Institute and then can make a Sri Lanka Accounting Stranded also.

To disclose the human capital and value the human capital it is needed to make indicators separately. All the companies have to concern to make indicators for the following variables to disclose and value.

- Academically educated staff, professionally qualified staff, experienced staff, talented staff.
- Leadership style of the company.
- Employee motivation and satisfaction factors.
- Work related knowledge and competency of the workers of the company.
- Entrepreneurial spirit and the innovativeness among the employees.

Most of the companies are now tend to disclosure about their human capital. But as discussed still no any proper method for that. Therefore the above variables can be used to make a common procedure for disclosing and valuing of human capital.

Organizational Capital

Definitely have to make a common method to report and value the organizational capital. This is also can be counted to the balance sheet if there is a common procedure to value the organizational capital. Monitoring parts and preparation parts have to be done by the Chartered Institute under the guidance of the professionals.

To disclose the organizational capital and value the human capital it is needed to make indicators separately. All the companies have to concern to make indicators for the following variables to disclose and value.

- Patents/Copy rights, trademarks, separate corporate culture, separate MIS system
- Quality of corporate strategy
- Quality processes.
- Systems are totally using modern
- Financial relations are strong to maintain the liquidity and profitability.
- Management credibility

Some of the companies have disclosed the above things in the annual reports as their own way. Other companies have to follow them to at least disclose them. But in long run it is needed to produce a common method as a stated to disclose the organizational capital. Also it should be in monitory value to take them in to balance sheet. Now some of the companies as mentioned have disclosed the organizational capital with some of the values in a separate part of the annual report. But in long run it is needed to introduce a common model for that. Then only can be get the comparative idea and a real picture of the total asset and wealth of the business organizations.

Social Capital

Customer behavior is also changing within very short period of time. Therefore to face the competitors and challenges it is needed to use a common procedure to disclose and value the social capital also. Then the value can be counted to the balance sheet. All the preparation parts, valuing parts and monitoring parts have to be done by the Charted Institute for maintaining the consistency and validity.

To disclose the social capital and value the human capital it is needed to make indicators separately. All the companies have to concern to make indicators for the following variables to disclose and value.

- Loyal customers, business collaborations, distribution channels, favorable contracts
- Quality of the product/ service
- Customer satisfaction.
- Growth of the business
- Customer complaints
- Market share
- Favorable contracts and contacts

Some of the companies have disclosed the market share, customer details and some of the basic features of social capital in the annual reports. In short it is fair to mention about social capital in the annual report. But in long run it is a must to analyze the total details of the social capital to get the competitive advantages and sustainable development of the companies. Also it should be valued in monitory values.

FUTURE RESEARCH DIRECTIONS

According to this study it has no doubt that the Intellectual Capital is a modern day concept in the business organizations. It is a broad concept and the financial statement of the annual reports, actually a part of the intellectual capital in some point of view. Therefore it is needed to disclose and value the intellectual capital to get the clear picture of the organizations wealth and success. It is more close to the reality rather than the existing outputs of the companies which are presented through annual reports.

Here the researcher investigated only the disclosure practices of intellectual capital and check whether the valued amounts are disclosed or not. Most of the companies have disclosed them without values. The reason that the lacking of valuation model and methods. Therefore it is recommended to do further studies to fins a common valuation method or model for valuing the intellectual capital of the business organizations.

Intellectual Capital is a broad concept with an unlimited scope. Therefore the sections, areas are more to be investigated. According to the global competition and the advancements it is needed to make an Accounting Standard for Intellectual Capital. Therefore a common procedure is needed to disclosure and value the intellectual capital. At the initial stage it is fair to produce a common method to just disclose them. Then can introduce a model to value them. Therefore, before introducing an Accounting Standard immediately, it is a must to investigate the total field of Intellectual Capital further to identify the common features.

CONCLUSION

According to the literature survey there was no any considerable study has been done on intellectual capital in Sri Lankan context. The companies of Sri Lanka are lacking the disclosure practices on intellectual capital. In this research study the researcher tried to study the disclosure practices of the intellectual capital in Sri Lankan business organizations. For that the hypotheses have been created with two dependent and four independent variables. Especially the managerial perception and company characteristics have been linked with the intellectual capital disclosure practices and intellectual capital value practices. With testing the hypotheses by using the relevant statistical tests and analyzing the annual reports the researcher has found the considerable details on intellectual capital practiced by Sri Lankan business organization which are listed in Colombo Stock Exchange. The disclosure practice of intellectual capital is really important tool to get the best picture of the business organizations. There is a great impact on the figures available in the balance sheet especially to the capital and assets. Therefore the financial position has been understated. So, the recommendations spelt out above encompass a common procedure to improve the disclosure of intellectual capital. With proper design, development and implementation of these practices it should be possible to enhance the disclosure level of intellectual capital to the required levels in the annual reports of the organizations which are listed in the Colombo Stock Exchange.

REFERENCES

Abdolmohammadi, M. J. (2005). Intellectual capital: Disclosure and market capitalization. *Journal of Intellectual Capital*, *6*(3), 397–416. doi:10.1108/14691930510611139

Armstrong, M., & Baron, A. (2007). *Human capital management*. Academic Press.

Boedker, C., Guthrie, J., & Cuganesan, S. (2005). An integrated framework for visualizing intellectual capital. *Journal of Intellectual Capital*, *6*(4), 510–527. doi:10.1108/14691930510628799

Bradley, K. (1997). Intellectual capital and the new wealth of nations. *Business Strategy Review*, *8*(1), 53–62. doi:10.1111/1467-8616.00007

Brennan, N., & Connell, B. (2000). Intellectual capital: Current issues and policy implications. *Journal of Intellectual Capital*, *1*(3), 206–240. doi:10.1108/14691930010350792

Brooking, A. (1997). Management of intellectual capital. *Long Range Planning*, *30*(3), 364–365. doi:10.1016/S0024-6301(97)80911-9

Caddy, I. (2000). Intellectual capital: Recognizing both assets and liabilities. *Journal of Intellectual Capital*, *1*(2), 129–146. doi:10.1108/14691930010377469

Chaharbaghi, C., & Cripps, S. (2006). Intellectual capital: direction: not blind faith. *Journal of Intellectual Capital*, *7*(1), 29–42. doi:10.1108/14691930610639750

Edvinsson, L., & Malone, M. (1997). *Intellectual capital: realizing your rompany's true value by finding its hidden brainpower*. New York: HarperCollins.

Edvinsson, L., & Malone, M. (1997). *Intellectual capital: the proven way to establish your company's real value by measuring its hidden brain power*. London: Piatkus.

Gunawardana, K. D. (2009). *Quantitative Research Methodology*. Academic Press.

Guthrie, J. (2001). The management, measurement and the reporting of intellectual capital. *Journal of Intellectual Capital*, *2*(1), 27–41. doi:10.1108/14691930110380473

Guthrie, J., Steane, P., & Dunford, R. (2001). 'Stories from Australia on knowledge management and intellectual capital. *Journal of Intellectual Capital*, *2*(1).

Institute of Chartered Accountants of Sri Lanka. (2005). *SLAS 37 Intangible Assets*. Author.

International Accounting Standards Committee. (1998). *IAS 38 Intangible Assets*. London: International Accounting Standards Committee.

Jeewantha, G.K.C., Bandara, D., Hareendra, P., & Ajward, R.A. (2015). *Drivers of Corporate Voluntary Disclosures: Empirical Evidence from Sri Lankan Listed Companies*. Academic Press.

Johanson, U. (1999). *Mobilising change: characteristics of intangibles proposed by 11 Swedish firms*. Paper presented at the International Symposium Measuring and Reporting Intellectual Capital: Experiences, Issues and Prospects, Amsterdam, The Netherlands.

Kannan, G., & Aulbur, W. G. (2004). Intellectual capital: Measurement effectiveness. *Journal of Intellectual Capital*, *5*(3), 389–413. doi:10.1108/14691930410550363

Leon, M. V. T. (2002). Intellectual capital: Managerial perceptions of organizational knowledge resources. *Journal of Intellectual Capital*, *3*(2), 149–166. doi:10.1108/14691930210424743

Lim, L. L. K., & Dallimore, P. (2004). Intellectual capital: Management attitudes in service industries. *Journal of Intellectual Capital*, *5*(1), 182–194. doi:10.1108/14691930410512996

Nerdrum, L., & Erikson, T. (2001). Intellectual capital: A human capital perspective. *Journal of Intellectual Capital*, *2*(2), 127–135. doi:10.1108/14691930110385919

Petty, R., & Guthrie, J. (2000). Intellectual capital: Literature review. *Journal of Intellectual Capital*, *1*(2), 155–176. doi:10.1108/14691930010348731

Roslender, R., & Fincham, R. (2001). Thinking critically about intellectual capital accounting. *Accounting, Auditing & Accountability Journal*, *14*(4), 383–399. doi:10.1108/09513570110403425

Seetharaman, A., Low, K. L. T., & Saravanan, A. S. (2004). Comparative justification on intellectual capital. *Journal of Intellectual Capital*, *5*(4), 522–539. doi:10.1108/14691930410566997

Sri Lankan Archives Statistics. (n.d.). *Blue books reports.*

Sri Lankan Government. (1938). *Companies Act.*

Sri Lankan Government. (1982). *Companies Act.*

Sri Lankan Government. (2007). *Companies Act.*

Stewart, T. A. (1997). *Intellectual capital: the new wealth of organizations*. New York: Doubleday.

Sullivan, P. (2000). Value-driven intellectual capital: how to convert corporate assets into market value. Wiley/Arthur Andersen.

Sveiby, K. E. (1997). *The new organizational wealth: managing and measuring knowledge-based assets*. San Francisco, CA: Berrett-Koehler.

Sveiby, K.E. (1998, June). Intellectual capital: thinking ahead. *Australian CPA*, 18-22.

Sveiby, K. E. (1998b). *Measuring intangibles and intellectual capital ± an emerging first standard.* Retrieved from http://www.sveiby.com.au/EmergingStandard.html

Compilation of References

Abdolmohammadi, M. J. (2005). Intellectual capital: Disclosure and market capitalization. *Journal of Intellectual Capital, 6*(3), 397–416. doi:10.1108/14691930510611139

Abianga, E. U. (2010). Effective leadership and fellowship drives community development. *International Journal of Management and Enterprises, 7*(2).

Abosede, A. J., &Onakoya, A. B. (2013). Entrepreneurship, economic development and inclusive growth. *International Journal of Social Sciences and Entrepreneurship, 1*(3), 375-387.

Acemoglu, D., & Autor, D. (2011). Skills, tasks and technologies: Implications for employment and earnings. Handbook of Labour Economics, 4(4), 1043–1171

Acemoglu, D. (2003). Labour- and capital-augmenting technical change. *Journal of the European Economic Association, 1*(1), 1–37. doi:10.1162/154247603322256756

Acemoglu, D., & Jörn-Steffen, P. (1999). Beyond becker: Training in imperfect labour markets. *Economic Journal (London), 109*(453), 112–142. doi:10.1111/1468-0297.00405

Acemoglu, D., & Restrepo, P. (2015). The race between machine and man: Implications of technology for growth, factor shares and employment. *SSRN Electronic Journal, 9*(5). doi:10.2139srn.2781320

Acemoglu, D., & Restrepo, P. (2018). *Artificial intelligence, automation and work (No. w24196)*. National Bureau of Economic Research. doi:10.3386/w24196

Adair, J. (2005). Not Bosses But Leaders: How to lead the way to success. *MPG Book Limited*. Bodmin, Cornwall. *Administrative Science Quarterly, 30*, 78–102.

Adamu, P. A. (2003). Tariff policy and the development of Nigeria's Manufacturing sector. In *The Structure Growth and development of the Nigerian economy*. Essays in Honour of T.M. Yesufu. Iyoha.

Adawo, M. A. (2011). Has education (human capital) contributed to the economic growth of Nigeria? *Journal of Economics and International Finance, 3*(1), 46–58.

Addai, B. (2017). Women Empowerment through Microfinance: Empirical Evidence from Ghana. *Journal of Finance and Accounting, 5*, 1-11. . doi:10.11648/j.jfa.20170501.11

Adegbite, O. (2001). Business incubators and small enterprise development: The Nigerian experience. *Small Business Economics*, *17*(3), 157–166. doi:10.1023/A:1011801018398

Adelakun, O. J. (2011). Human capital development and economic growth in Nigeria. *European Journal of Business and Management*, *3*(9), 29–38.

Adelekan, S.A. (2017). Impact of financial crisis on entrepreneurial effort in developing SMES in Nigeria. *LASU Journal of Business Review, 4*(1).

Adelekan, S. A., Majekodunmi, S. A., & Omotayo, A. O. (2018). Impact of Entrepreneurship Development Programme on Economic Development of Lagos State, Nigeria. *IOSR Journal of Business and Management*, *20*(9), 74–81.

Adelekan, S. A., & Tijani, A. A. (2017). Effect of support for entrepreneurship development on economic growth and development in Nigeria. *European Scientific Journal*, *13*(13), 426–448. doi:10.19044/esj.2017.v13n13p426

Adelowo Caleb, M., Olaopa, R. O., & Siyanbola, W. O. (2012). Technology business incubation as strategy for SME development: How far and how well in Nigeria. *Science and Technology*, *2*(6), 172–181. doi:10.5923/j.scit.20120206.06

Adelowokan, O. A. (2012). Growth effect of Education and Health Expenditure in Nigeria (1970-2010). *African Journal of Science and Research*, *1*(1), 510–528.

Aghion, P., & Howitt, P. (1992). Capital, innovation, and growth accounting. *Oxford Review of Economic Policy*, *23*(1), 79–93. doi:10.1093/oxrep/grm007

Agnihotri, S., Palmer-Jones, R., & Parikh, A. (2012). Missing women in Indian Districts: A quantitative analysis. *Structural Change and Economic Dynamics*, *13*(3), 285–314. doi:10.1016/S0954-349X(02)00023-1

Agri, E. M., Kennedy, N. D., Bonmwa, G. O., &Acha, O. F. (2018). *Technology innovation and sustainable entrepreneurship development in Nigeria: Stakeholders' impact assessment in central Nigeria*. Academic Press.

Akanni, O.W. (2008). Entrepreneurship in Nigeria: Problem, challenges and prospects. *Nigeria Management Review, 14*(1&2).

Akhigbe, O. J. (2013). Human resource planning: A key factor in ensuring the effectiveness and efficiency of organization. *Journal of Emerging Trends in Economics and Management Science*, *4*(4), 388–397.

Akhtar, S. H., Renyong, H., Khaskheli, A., & Ali, A. (2015). Understanding the dynamics of human capital development in Pakistan: A socio economic obstacle framework. *Journal of Poverty, Investment and Development*, *13*(4), 44–53.

Akintayo, D. I. (2007). Access to education, manpower development and job performance effectiveness of workers: The relevance of distance education programmes in Oyo and Lagos State of Nigeria. *Trends in Educational Studies Journal*, *2*(1), 29–41.

Akintimile, M. (2012). Women empowerment and economic development. *Journal of Economic Literature*, *50*(4), 1051–1079. doi:10.1257/jel.50.4.1051

Al Wahshi, A. S., Omari, M., & Barrett, R. (2013). *Human resource planning: Sector specific considerations*. ECU Publications.

Allen, J. R. (2019). *Why we need to rethink education in the artificial intelligence age*. Retrieved May 9, 2019 from https://www.brookings.edu/research/why-we-need-to-rethink-education-in-the-artificial-intelligence-age/

Alnachef, T. H., & Alhajjar, A. (2015). Effect of Human Capital on Organizational Performance: A Literature Review. *International Journal of Science and Research*, 1154-1158.

Alter, A., Ghilardi, D., & Hakura, D. (2017). Public investment in a developing country facing resource depletion. *Journal of African Economies*, *26*(3), 295–321. doi:10.1093/jae/ejw031

Alvesson, M., Bridgman, T., & Willmott, H. (2009). *The Oxford Handbook of Critical Management Studies*. Oxford, UK: Oxford University Press. doi:10.1093/oxfordhb/9780199237715.001.0001

Alvesson, M., & Willmott, H. (2012). *Making sense of management: A critical introduction*. Los Angeles, CA: Sage.

Amit, R., & Schoemaker, P. (1993). Strategic Assets and Organisational Rent. *Strategic Management Journal*, *14*(1), 33–46. doi:10.1002mj.4250140105

Ananiadou, K., & Claro, M. (2009). *21st Century Skills and Competences for New Millennium Learners in OECD Countries.* OECD Education Working Papers, No. 41. OECD Publishing.

Anderson, P. Y. (1987). Informal sector or modern labour market? Towards a synthesis. *Social and Economic Studies*, *36*(3), 149–176.

Anya, C. J. P., Umoh, G. I., & Worlu, G. (2017). Human resource planning and organizational performance in oil and gas firms in Port Harcourt. *International Journal of Academic Research*, *3*(9), 110–129.

Anyim, F., Mba, S., & Ekwoaba, J. (2012). The imperative of integrating corporate business plan with manpower planning. *International Journal of Business and Management*, *7*(8), 56–62. doi:10.5539/ijbm.v7n8p56

Apea, E. (2019). *Are the Churches flying with One Wing? A New Look at Ordination of Women.* Emmanuel Apea.

Archan, S., & Tutschek, E. (2002). *Schlüsselqualifikationen: Wie vermittle ich sie Lehrlingen?* Vienna: Institut für Bildungsforschung der Wirtschaft.

Ariely, G. (2003). *Knowledge management as a methodology towards intellectual capital.* Presented at the 3rd European Knowledge Management Summer School, San Sebastian, Spain.

Armstrong, M., & Baron, A. (2007). *Human capital management.* Academic Press.

Armstrong, M. (2004). *Managing Performance: Performance Management in Action* (1st ed.). London: Chartered Institute of Personnel & Development.

Armstrong, M. (2011). *Handbook of human resource management practice* (8th ed.). Kogan Page.

Armstrong, M., & Taylor, S. (2014). *Armstrong's Handbook of Human Resource Management Practice*. London: Kogan Page Publishers.

Arntz, M., Gregory, T., & Zierahn, U. (2004). Benefit Coverage Rates and Household Typologies: Scope and Limitations of Tax-Benefit Indicators (OECD Social, Employment and Migration Working Papers No. 189). Paris: OECD. doi:10.1787/081036000058

Arsad, M. (2012). *Human resource management practices and organizational performance: A study on administrators in Universiti Teknologi Mara* (Unpublished MSc Dissertation). Universiti Utara Malaysia.

Arts Times. (n.d.). Available: https://arttimes.co.za/creativity-currency-4th-industrial-revolution/

Aslam, H. D., Aslam, M., Ali, N., Habib, B., & Jabeen, M. (2013). Human resource planning practice in managing human resource: A literature review. *Human Resource Planning*, *3*(1), 200–2012.

Aslam, H. D., Aslam, M., Ali, N., Habib, B., & Jabeen, M. (2014). Human resource planning practice in managing human resource: A literature review. *International Journal of Human Resource Studies*, *3*(1), 200–217. doi:10.5296/ijhrs.v3i1.6253

Atiku, S. O. (2018). Reshaping human capital formation through digitalization. In *Radical Reorganization of Existing Work Structures through Digitalization* (pp. 52–73). Hershey, PA: IGI Global. doi:10.4018/978-1-5225-3191-3.ch004

Autor, D. (2015). Why Are There Still So Many Jobs? The History and Future of Workplace Automation. *The Journal of Economic Perspectives*, *59*(3), 3–30. doi:10.1257/jep.29.3.3

Autor, D. H., & Dorn, D. (2013). The Growth of Low-Skill Service Jobs and the Polarization of the US Labor Market. *The American Economic Review*, *103*(5), 1553–1597. doi:10.1257/aer.103.5.1553

Autor, D. H., Levy, F., & Murnane, R. J. (2003). The Skill Content of Recent Technological Change: An Empirical Exploration. *The Quarterly Journal of Economics*, *118*(4), 1279–1333. doi:10.1162/003355303322552801

Avvisati, F., Jacotin, G., & Vincent-Lancrin, S. (2014). Educating Higher Education Students for Innovative Economies: What International Data Tell Us. *Tuning Journal for Higher Education*, *1*(1), 223. doi:10.18543/tjhe-1(1)-2013pp223-240

Awan, A. G. (2012). Diverging trends of human capital in BRIC countries. *International Journal of Asian Social Science*, *2*(12), 2195–2219.

Awopegba, P. O. (2009). *Human resources, high level manpower and the development of the Nigerian economy*. Lagos: Processed.

Aytac, A., & Deniz, V. (2005). Quality function deployment in education: A curriculum review. *Quality & Quantity*, *39*(4), 507–514. doi:10.100711135-004-6814-8

Azadeh, S. (2012). *Moral Leadership: Transformational Leadership*. Paper presented at the Southern African Management Conference, Windhoek, Namibia.

Babalola, J. (2015). Investment in human capital and personal income distribution. *Journal of Political Economy*, *66*(4), 281–302.

Babatunde, O., & Ikenga, E. (2015). The Impact of Leadership Style in Employee's Performance in an Organisation. Nigeria. *Public Policy and Administration Research.*, *5*(1), 194–204.

Baker, C. B. (2011). *Beginning to understand why New Hampshire's rural educators chose not to join New Hampshire's newly developed on-line professional learning communities: A quantitative and qualitative study (Order No. 3588428)*. Retrieved from ProQuest Dissertations & Theses Global.

Bakewell, O., & Jónsson, G. (2011). Migration, mobility and the African city. Oxford, UK: IMI: International Migration Institute.

Bakewell, O. (2008). Them in their place: The ambivalent relationship between development and migration in Africa. *Third World Quarterly*, *29*(7), 1341–1358. doi:10.1080/01436590802386492

Bandura, A. (1977). *Social learning theory*. New York, NY: General Learning Press.

Baradaran, M. S., Yadollahi Farsi, J., Hejazi, S. R., & Akbari, M. (2019). A Competency-based Typology of Technology Entrepreneurs: A Systematic Review of the Empirical Studies. *Iranian Journal of Management Studies*, *12*(2), 17–37.

Barnes, D. (2008). *Operations management, an international perspective*. Thompson Learning.

Barney, J. (1991). Firm Resources and Sustained Competitive Advantage. *Journal of Management*, *17*(1), 99–120. doi:10.1177/014920639101700108

Barney, J. B., Ketchen, D. J. Jr, & Wright, M. (2011). The future of resource-based theory: Revitalization or decline? *Journal of Management*, *37*(5), 1299–1315. doi:10.1177/0149206310391805

Barrett, G. V., & Depinet, R. L. (1991). A reconsideration of testing for competence rather than for intelligence. *The American Psychologist*, *46*(10), 1012–1024. doi:10.1037/0003-066X.46.10.1012 PMID:1746769

Barrett, K., & Richard, G. (2006). *Seven steps of effective workforce planning. When Boomers retire*. Governing Magazine.

Bart, C. K. (2001). Exploring the application of mission statements on the world wide web. *Internet Research, 11*(4), 360–369. doi:10.1108/10662240110402812

Bartlett, C. A., & Ghoshal, S. (2002). Building competitive advantage through people: Human, not financial, capital must be the starting point and ongoing foundation of a successful strategy. *MIT Sloan Management Review*, *43*(2), 34–42.

Bartodziej, C. J. (2017). The concept industry 4.0. In *The Concept Industry 4.0* (pp. 27–50). Wiesbaden: Springer Gabler. doi:10.1007/978-3-658-16502-4_3

Bartram, D. (2012). *The SHL universal competency framework*. SHL White Paper. Retrieved from http://assessmentanalytics.com/website/wp-content/uploads/2013/08/White-Paper-SHL-Universal-Competency-Framework.pdf

Bartram, D. (2005). The Great Eight competencies: A criterion-centric approach to validation. *The Journal of Applied Psychology*, *90*(6), 1185–1203. doi:10.1037/0021-9010.90.6.1185 PMID:16316273

Bartram, T., & Casimir, G. (2007). The relationship between leadership and follower in-role performance and satisfaction with the leaders: The mediating effects of empowerment and trust in the leader. *Leadership and Organization Development Journal*, *208*(1), 4–9. doi:10.1108/01437730710718218

BCG. (2015). *Embracing Industry 4.0 and Rediscovering Growth*. Retrieved from https://www.bcg.com/capabilities/operations/embracing-industry-4.0-rediscovering-growth.aspx

Bechet, T. P., & Maki, W. R. (1987). Modeling and forecasting focusing on people as a strategic resource. *Human Resource Planning*, *10*(4), 12–25.

Becker, G. S. (1994). Human capital (3rd ed.). Chicago: The University of Chicago Press.

Becker, G. S. (1964). *Human capital: A theoretical and empirical analysis with special reference to education*. New York: Columbia University Press.

Begley, T. M., & Boyd, D. P. (1987). Psychological characteristics associated with performance in entrepreneurial firms and smaller businesses. *Journal of Business Venturing*, *2*(1), 79–93. doi:10.1016/0883-9026(87)90020-6

Behery, M. (2008). Leadership, knowledge sharing and organizational benefits within UAE. *The Journal of American Academy of Business, Cambridge*, *12*, 227–236.

Belete, J. (2015). *Effects of leadership style on employees' performance in case of Kaffa Zone Higher Public Educational Institutions*. Jimma University.

Berger, T., & Frey, C. B. (2016). Structural Transformation in the OECD: Digitalisation, Deindustrialisation and the Future of Work (OECD Social, Employment and Migration Working Papers No. 193). OECD. doi:10.1787/5jlr068802f7-en

Bernardin, H. J. (2002). *Human resource management: An experiential approach*. Irwin Professional Pub.

Biagi, B., Faggian, A., Rajbhandari, I., & Venhorst, V.A. (2018). New frontiers in interregional migration research. *Advances in Spatial Science*. . doi:10.1007/978-3-319-75886-2-4

Bidgoli, H. (2018). Successful integration of information technology in healthcare: Guides for managers. *Journal of Strategic Innovation and Sustainability*, *13*(3), 22–37.

Black, D., Kolesnikova, N., & Taylor, L. (2014). Why do so few women work in New York (and so many in Minneapolis)? Labor supply of married women across U.S. cities. *Journal of Urban Economics*, *79*, 59–71. doi:10.1016/j.jue.2013.03.003

Blackden, M., & Wodon, Q. (2006). *Gender, time use, and poverty in sub-Saharan Africa*. World Bank Working Paper No. 73. Washington, DC: The World Bank.

Blackden, M., Canagarajah, S., Klasen, S., & Lawson, D. (2016). *Gender and growth in Sub-Saharan Africa*. UNU-WIDER Research Paper No. 2006/37. Accessed on 17th January, 2019 at http://www.rrojasdatabank.info/rp2006-37.pdf

Block, J. (1990). Family size, outcomes for children, and gender disparities. *Economic and Political Weekly*, *28*(1), 1811–1821.

Boedker, C., Guthrie, J., & Cuganesan, S. (2005). An integrated framework for visualizing intellectual capital. *Journal of Intellectual Capital*, *6*(4), 510–527. doi:10.1108/14691930510628799

Boon, J., & van der Klink, M. (2002). Competencies: The triumph of a fuzzy concept. *Academy of Human Resource Development Annual Conference Proceedings*, *1*, 327–334.

Borghans, L. A. D., Grip, H., & Heijke, H. (1996). Labour market information and the choice of vocational specialization. *Economics of Education Review*, *15*(1), 59–74. doi:10.1016/0272-7757(95)00041-0

Bose, M. S., & Goyal, D. (2019). Critical success factors of agri-business incubators and their impact on business. *CUSTOS E AGRONEGOCIO ON LINE*, *15*(1), 352–378.

Botha, D. (2015). *Free to Grow Report. Municipality of Swakopmund.*

Boyatzis, R. E. (1982). *The Competent Manager: A Model for Effective Performance*. New York: Wiley.

Boyatzis, R. E., & Sala, F. (2004). Assessing emotional intelligence competencies. In G. Geher (Ed.), *The Measurement of Emotional Intelligence* (pp. 147–180). Hauppauge, NY: Nova Science Publishers.

Bradley, K. (1997). Intellectual capital and the new wealth of nations. *Business Strategy Review*, *8*(1), 53–62. doi:10.1111/1467-8616.00007

Bradshaw, S; Castellino, J., & Diop, B (2013). *Women's Role in Economic Development: Overcoming the Constraints. Sustainable Development Solution Network.* A Global Imitative for the United Nations.

Branine, M. (2004). Job sharing and equal opportunities under the new public management in local authorities. *International Journal of Public Sector Management*, *17*(2), 136–152. doi:10.1108/09513550410523269

Brennan, N., & Connell, B. (2000). Intellectual capital: Current issues and policy implications. *Journal of Intellectual Capital*, *1*(3), 206–240. doi:10.1108/14691930010350792

Brockbank, W., Ulrich, D., & Yakonich, D. (2003). v. Ann Arbor, MI: University of Michigan Business School.

Brooking, A. (1997). Management of intellectual capital. *Long Range Planning*, *30*(3), 364–365. doi:10.1016/S0024-6301(97)80911-9

Brown, B. J., & Clow, J. E. (1997). *Introduction to business: Our business and economics world.* Westerville, OH: Glencoe Mc- Graw-Hill.

Bubou, G. M., & Okrigwe, F. (2012). Fostering technological entrepreneurship for socioeconomic development: A case for technology incubation in Bayelsa State, Nigeria. *Journal of Sustainable Development*, *4*(6), 138–149.

Bulla, D. N., & Scott, P. M. (1994). Manpower requirement forecasting: A case example. In Human Resource forecasting and modeling. The Human Resource Planning Society.

Buradum, T. F. (2017). Influence of human resource planning on organizational performance of fast food companies in Port Harcourt, Nigeria. *Imperial Journal of Interdisciplinary Research*, *3*(11), 1–10.

Burgoyne, J. (1988). *Competency Based Approaches to Management Development.* Lancaster: Centre for the Study of Management Learning.

Business News. (2019, April 10). *Google opens Africa's first AI Research Centre in Accra.* Retrieved May 9, 2019 from https://www.ghanaweb.com/GhanaHomePage/business/Google-opens-Africa-s-first-AI-Research-Centre-in-Accra-737336

Business-Higher Education Forum. (2013). *The National Higher Education and Workforce Initiative: Forging Strategic Partnerships for Undergraduate Innovation and Workforce Development.* Retrieved from http://www. bhef.com/publications/national-higher-education-andworkforce-initiative-forging-strategic-partnerships

Butler, J. E., Ferris, G. R., & Napier, N. K. (1991). *Strategy and human resource management.* Cincinnati, OH: South-Western Publishing Co.

Caddy, I. (2000). Intellectual capital: Recognizing both assets and liabilities. *Journal of Intellectual Capital*, *1*(2), 129–146. doi:10.1108/14691930010377469

Calderón, C., & Servén, L., S. (2010). Infrastructure and economic development in sub-Saharan Africa. *Journal of African Economies, 19*(3), 116–187.

Callaghan, P. (2017). *Exploring the Impact on Global Labour Markets*. Jobs and the Organisation of Work.

Calvès, A., & Schoumaker, B. (2004). Deteriorating economic context and changing patterns of youth employment in urban Burkina Faso: 1980–2000. *World Development, 32*(8), 1341–1354. doi:10.1016/j.worlddev.2004.03.002

Cameron, K. S., Freeman, S. J., & Mishra, A. K. (1993). Downsizing and redesigning organizations. In G. Huber & W. Glick (Eds.), *Organizational change and redesign* (pp. 19–63). New York: Oxford University Press.

Campbell, A., & Sommers Luchs, K. S. (1997). *Core Competency-Based Strategy*. London: Thomson.

Campos, F. M., Goldstein, L., McGorman, A. M., Boudet, M., & Pimhidzai, O. (2015). *Breaking the Metal Ceiling: Female Entrepreneurs Who Succeed in Male-dominated Sectors in Uganda. Africa Gender Innovations Lab*. Washington, DC: The World Bank. doi:10.1596/1813-9450-7503

Capuano, S., & Marfouk, A. (2013). African brain drain and its impact on source countries: What do we know and what do we need to know? *Journal of Comparative Policy Analysis, 15*(4), 297–314. doi:10.1080/13876988.2013.813122

Cardy, R. L., & Selvarajan, T. T. (2006). Competencies: Alternative Frameworks for Competitive Advantage. *Business Horizons, 49*(3), 235–245. doi:10.1016/j.bushor.2005.09.004

Carpenter, M., & Dunung, S. (2012). *Challenges and opportunities in international business*. Retrieved from http://2012books.lardbucket.org/pdfs/challenges-and-opportunities-in international-business.pdf

Cartwright, M. (2013). *Sappho of Lesbos, Palazzo Massimo. Ancient History Encyclopedia*. Retrieved June 10, 2019, from https://www.ancient.eu/image/2123/

Cascio, S. (2009). *Performance and staff freezes: how leading companies create sustained value*. New York: John Wiley & Sons.

Centre for Strategy and Evaluation Services (CSES). (2002). *Benchmarking of business incubator*. Brussels: European Commission Enterprise Directorate.

Chadwick, C., & Dabu, A. (2009). Human resources, human resource management, and the competitive advantage of firms: Toward a more comprehensive model of causal linkages. *Organization Science, 20*(1), 253–272. doi:10.1287/orsc.1080.0375

Chaharbaghi, C., & Cripps, S. (2006). Intellectual capital: direction: not blind faith. *Journal of Intellectual Capital, 7*(1), 29–42. doi:10.1108/14691930610639750

Chand, M., & Katou, A. A. (2007). The impact of HRM practices on performance in the Indian hotel industry. *Employee Relations*, *29*(6), 576–594. doi:10.1108/01425450710826096

Chandrasekar, K. (2011). Workplace environment and its impact on organisational behaviors in the Public Sector. *International Journal of Enterprise Computing and Business Systems.* Retrieved from http://www.ijecbs.com/January2011/N4Jan2011.pdf

Cheetham, G., & Chivers, G. (1996). Towards a holistic model of professional competence. *Journal of European Industrial Training*, *20*(5), 20–30. doi:10.1108/03090599610119692

Cheetham, G., & Chivers, G. (1998). The reflective (and competent) practitioner: A model of professional competence which seeks to harmonise the reflective practitioner and competence-based approaches. *Journal of European Industrial Training*, *22*(7), 267–276. doi:10.1108/03090599810230678

Chen, J., Cai, L., Bruton, G. D., & Sheng, N. (2019). Entrepreneurial ecosystems: What we know and where we move as we build an understanding of China. *Entrepreneurship and Regional Development*, 1–19.

Chen, K. J., & Chen, S. I. (2008). Personal traits and leadership styles of Taiwan' higher educational institution in innovative operations. *The Journal of American Academy of Business, Cambridge*, *12*(2), 145–150.

Chen, Y. F., & Tjosvold, D. (2006). Participative leadership by American and Chinese managers in China: The role of relationships. *Journal of Management Studies*, *43*(8), 1727–1752. doi:10.1111/j.1467-6486.2006.00657.x

Chidi, C. O., & Okpala, O. P. (2012). Theoretical approaches to employment and industrial relations: a comparison of subsisting orthodoxies. Theoretical and Methodological Approaches to Social Sciences and Knowledge Management, 2(1), 264-277

Chikwe, C. K., Ogidi, R. C., & Nwachukwu, K. (2015). Challenges of Research and Human Capital Development in Nigeria. *Journal of Education and Practice*, *6*(28), 44–47.

Choudhury, E. H. (2007). Workforce planning in small local governments. *Review of Public Personnel Administration*, *27*(3), 264–280. doi:10.1177/0734371X06297464

Chryssolouris, G., Mavrikios, D., & Mourtzis, D. (2013). Manufacturing Systems: Skills & Competencies for the Future. *Procedia CIRP*, *7*, 17–24. doi:10.1016/j.procir.2013.05.004

CIPD. (2009). *The cost to employer of redundancy*. Work Audit.

Clulow, V., Barry, C., & Gerstman, J. (2007). The resource-based view and value: The customer-based view of the firm. *Journal of European Industrial Training*, *31*(1), 19–35. doi:10.1108/03090590710721718

Cockerill, T. (1989, September). The kind of competence for rapid change. *Personnel Management*, 52-56.

Codagnone, C., Abadie, F. & Biagi, F. (2016). *The future of work in the 'Sharing Economy'. Market efficiency and equitable opportunities or unfair precarisation?* Institute for Prospective Technological Studies, JRC Science for Policy Report EUR 27913 EN. doi:10.2791/431485

Cole, G. A. (2002). *Personnel and Human Resource Management* (5th ed.). London: Continuum Publisher.

Colley, L., & Price, R. (2010). Where have all the workers gone? Exploring public sector workforce planning. *Australian Journal of Public Administration, 69*(2), 202–213. doi:10.1111/j.1467-8500.2010.00676.x

Corso, K. A., Dorrance, K. A., & LaRochelle, U. (2018). The physician shortage: A red herring in American health care reform. *Military Medicine, 183*(3), 220-224. doi:10.1093/milmed/usy211

Costley, K. C. (2012). *Why do we have theories?* Education Resources Information Centre.

Cotten, A. (2007). *Seven steps of effective workforce planning*. IBM Center for the Business of Government.

Cresswell, K., Cunningham-Burley, S., & Sheikh, A. (2018). Health care robotics: Qualitative exploration of key challenges and future directions. *Journal of Medical Internet Research, 20*(7), e10410. doi:10.2196/10410 PMID:29973336

Crook, C.K. (2007). Learning science and learning technology: A place for cultural psychology. *British Journal of Educational Psychology Monograph Series, 11*(5), 1–17.

Crook, T. R., Todd, S. Y., Combs, J. G., Woehr, D. J., & Ketchen, D. J. J. (2011). Does human capital matter? A meta-analysis of the relationship between human capital and firm performance. *The Journal of Applied Psychology, 96*(3), 443–456. doi:10.1037/a0022147 PMID:21244126

Cseh, M. (2003). Facilitating learning in multicultural teams. *Advances in Developing Human Resources, 5*(1), 26–40. doi:10.1177/1523422302239181

Cummings, T. G., & Worley, C. G. (2009). *Organizational development and change* (9th ed.). South Western College Publishing.

Curtis, D., & McKenzie, P. (2002). *Employability skills for Australian industry: literature review and framework development.* Canberra: Australian Chamber of Commerce and Industry.

D'Espallier, B., Guérin, I., & Mersland, R. (2013). Focus on Women in Microfinance Institutions. *Journal of Development Studies, 49.* doi:10.1080/00220388.2012.720364

Daniel, G. (2002). *The New leaders: Transforming the Art of Leadership into the Science of Results. Little brown.* London: Zancaster Press.

Dao, M. Q. (2004). Rural poverty in developing countries: An empirical analysis. *Journal of Economic Studies (Glasgow, Scotland), 31*(6), 500–508. doi:10.1108/01443580410569244

Das Gupta, M. (2007). Selective Discrimination against Female Children in Rural Punjab, India. *Population and Development Review*, *13*(1), 77–100. doi:10.2307/1972121

Das, P. N., & Nayak, B. (2015). Measuring the effectiveness of human resource planning: A case of Nilachal Ispat Nigam Limited. *IJST*, *8*(35), 1–9.

Davidson, P., & Honing, B. (2003). The role of social and human capital among nascent entrepreneurs. *Journal of Business Venturing*, *18*(3), 301–331. doi:10.1016/S0883-9026(02)00097-6

David, W. C., & Nigel, F. P. (2009). *Strategic Marketing* (9th ed.). McGraw-Hill.

De Castro, A. B., Shapleigh, E., Bruck, A., & Salazar, M. K. (2015). Developing blended online and classroom strategies to deliver an occupational health nursing overview course in a multi-state region in the United States. *Workplace Health & Safety*, *63*(3), 121–126. doi:10.1177/2165079915576919 PMID:25994977

Debashis, C. (2000). *Leading consciously: A pilgrimage toward self-mastery*. Butterworth.

Deist, F. D., & Winterton, J. (2005). What is Competence? *Human Resource Development International*, *8*(1), 27–46. doi:10.1080/1367886042000338227

Dejoux, C. (1999). *Organisation qualifiante et maturite´ en gestion des compe'tences*. Paris: Direction et Gestion des Entreprises.

Deloitte Australia. (2014). *Positioning for Prosperity: Catching the Next Wave. Building the Lucky Country Series*. Author.

Deming, D. J. (2015). The growing importance of social skills in the labor market. *National Bureau of Economic Research, 9*(3), 300-330. doi:10.3386/w21473

Denison, D. (1996). What is the difference between organizational culture and organizational climate? A native's point of view on a decade of paradigm wars. *Academy of Management Review*, *27*(3), 619–654. doi:10.5465/amr.1996.9702100310

Dessler, G. (2007). *Human Resource Management*. Pearson Prentice Hall.

Dorn, D., & Sousa-Poza, A. (2010). Voluntary and involuntary early retirement: An international analysis. *Applied Economics*, *42*(4), 427–438. doi:10.1080/00036840701663277

Dot Public Transport. (2006). Patterns of entry and exit in the U.S. manufacturing sector. *The Rand Journal of Economics*, *19*(4), 495–515.

Douglas, A. S., Robert, A. R., & Stephen, C. R. (2013). *On-Demand Supply Management, World-Class Strategies, Practices and Technology*. Ross Publishing.

Downes, S. (2007). Models for sustainable open educational resources. *Interdisciplinary Journal of E-Learning and Learning Objects*, *3*(1), 29–44. doi:10.28945/384

Draganidis, F., & Mentzas, G. (2006). Competency Based Management: A Review of Systems and Approaches. *Information Management & Computer Security, 14*(1), 51–64. doi:10.1108/09685220610648373

Drucker, P. (1995). *Managing in a time of great change. E.P.* New York, NY: Dutton.

Dubrin, A. J. (2007). *Leadership Research Findings, Practice and Skills* (5th ed.). Houghton Mifflin Company.

Dulewicz, V. (1989). Assessment centres as the route to competence. *Personnel Management, 21*(11), 56–59.

Duncan, T. D., Rahim, E., & Burrell, D. N. (2018). A panel on challenge in healthcare post-EMR adoption. Presented at Midwest Association for Information Systems, St. Louis, MO.

Dutta, C. (2018). The role of business incubators in entrepreneurship development: A brief review of literatures. *Research Bulletin, 44*(1), 105–120.

Dyer, S., Humphries, M., Fitzgibbons, D., & Hurd, F. (2014). *Understanding management critically.* Los Angeles, CA: Sage.

Eberhard, B., Podio, M., Alonso, A. P., Radovica, E., Avotina, L., Peiseniece, L., ... Solé-Pla, J. (2017). Smart work: The transformation of the labour market due to the fourth industrial revolution (I4. 0). *International Journal of Business & Economic Sciences Applied Research, 10*(3), 47–66.

Eckhardt, J. T., & Shane, S. A. (2003). Opportunities and entrepreneurship. *Journal of Management, 29*(3), 333–349. doi:10.1177/014920630302900304

Edgar, F., & Geare, A. (2004). Employee demographics in human resource management research, Research and practice in human resource management. *Human Resource Management, 12*(1), 61–91.

Edvinsson, L., & Malone, M. (1997). *Intellectual capital: realizing your rompany's true value by finding its hidden brainpower.* New York: HarperCollins.

Edvinsson, L., & Malone, M. (1997). *Intellectual capital: the proven way to establish your company's real value by measuring its hidden brain power.* London: Piatkus.

Edwards, R. (1979). *Contested Terrain: The Transformation of the Workplace in the Twentieth Century.* New York: Basic Books.

Eick, C. J. (2001). Job sharing their first year: A narrative of two partnered teachers' induction into middle school science teaching. *Teaching and Teacher Education, 18*(7), 887–904. doi:10.1016/S0742-051X(02)00049-5

Eigbiremolen, G. O., & Anaduaka, S. U. (2014). Human capital development and economic growth: The Nigeria experience. *International Journal of Academic Research in Business and Social Sciences, 4*(4), 25–35. doi:10.6007/IJARBSS/v4-i4/749

Ejere, S. I. (2011). Human capital formation as catalyst for national development: Nigeria in perspective. *International Business and Management*, *2*(2), 98–104.

Ellström, P. E. (1997). The many meanings of occupational competence and qualification. *Journal of European Industrial Training*, *21*(6/7), 266–274. doi:10.1108/03090599710171567

Endsley, M. R. (1996). Automation and situation awareness. In*Automation and human performance* (pp. 183–202). Routledge.

Enikanselu, S. A., & Oyende, A. I. (2010). *Introduction to Entrepreneurship*. Lagos, Nigeria: Enykon Consult.

Erasmus, B., Strydom, J., & Rudansky-Kloppers, S. (2016). *Introduction to Business Management* (10th ed.). Oxford University Press.

Erasmus, B. J., & Van Dyk, P. S. (2003). *Training management in South Africa*. Cape Town: Oxford University Press.

Erongo Regional Profile. (2013). *Swakopmund Local Economic Development Strategy*. Retrieved from www.swkmun.com.na

Estache, A., & Wodon, Q. (2014). *Infrastructure and Poverty in sub-Saharan Africa*. New York: Palgrave Macmillan. doi:10.1057/9781137348487

Esu, B. B. (2012). Linking human capital management with tourism development and management for economic survival: The Nigeria experience. *International Journal of Business and Social Science*, *3*(11), 1–12.

European Commission. (2016). *A New Skills Agenda for Europe*. Communication from the Commission to the European Parliament, the Council, the European Economic and Social Committee and the Committee of the Regions (COM). Retrieved from https://ec.europa.eu/transparency/regdoc/rep/1/2016/EN/1-2016-381-EN-F1-1.PDF

European Network of Education Councils. (2011). *Participation and stakeholder involvement in education policy making*. Retrieved May 10, 2019 from http://www.eunec.eu/sites/www.eunec.eu/files/event/attachments/report_brussels.pdf

Eze, B. U. (2018). Corporate entrepreneurship and manufacturing firms' performance. *Emerging Market Journal*, *8*(1), 12–17. doi:10.5195/EMAJ.2018.146

Fan, C. S., & Stark, O. (2007). International migration and 'educated unemployment. *Journal of Development Economics*, *83*(1), 76–87. doi:10.1016/j.jdeveco.2006.05.002

Fapohunda, T.M. (2017). An exploration of the effects of work life balance on productivity. *Journal of Human Resources Management and Labor Studies, 2*(2), 71-89.

Fayolle, A. (2013). Personal views on the future of entrepreneurship education. Entrepreneurship and regional development. *International Journal (Toronto, Ont.)*, *25*(7-8), 692–701.

Federal Office of Statistics. (2012). *Annual Abstract of Statistics* (2012 edition). Abuja: Author.

Feher, M. (2009). Self-appreciation; or, the aspirations of human capital. *Public Culture*, *21*(1), 21–41. doi:10.1215/08992363-2008-019

Felício, J. A., Couto, E., & Caiado, J. (2014). Human capital, social capital and organizational performance. *Management Decision*, *52*(2), 350–364. doi:10.1108/MD-04-2013-0260

Fennimore, M. (2013). *Introduction to Labour Relations in South Africa* (7th ed.). LexisNexis.

Ferguson, S. L., & Lloyd, J. (2017). Innovative information technology solutions: Addressing current and emerging nurse shortages and staffing challenges worldwide. *Nursing Economics*, *35*(4), 211.

Fitzsimons, H. O. (2006). *Gender inequality, income and growth: are good times for women?* Washington, DC: The World Bank.

Florida's Solar Progress. (2012). Available: https://ournewsynergy.wordpress.com/2012/01/06/the-5-pillars-of-the-third-industrial-revolution/

Foray, M., & Lundvall, Y. (2016). The gender gap, fertility, and growth. *The American Economic Review*, *126*(3), 374–387.

Foss, N. (1997). *Resources, firms and strategies: A reader in the resource-based perspective*. Oxford, UK: Oxford University Press.

Foss, N. J., & Knudsen, C. (Eds.). (1996). *Towards a Competence Theory of the Firm*. London: Routledge.

Foundations of Western Culture (FWC). (2018). *Industrial Revolution: Women's Roles in the Industrial Revolution*. Retrieved November, 19, 2018 from http://foundations.uwgb.org/womensroles/

Franck, R., & Galor, O. (2015). *The Complementarity between Technology and Human Capital in the Early Phase of Industrialization*. Retrieved August 27, 2018 from http://d.repec.org/n?u=RePEc:bro:econwp:2015-3&r=his

Freiling, J., & Schelhowe, C. (2014). The impact of entrepreneurial orientation on the performance of internationalisation. *Journal of Entrepreneurship. Management and Innovation*, *10*(4), 169–199.

Fu-Jin, W., Shieh, C., & Tang, M. (2011). Effect of Leadership Style on Organisational Performance as viewed from human resources management strategy. *African Journal of Business Management*, *4*(18), 3924–3936.

Ganesh, M., & Indradevi, R. (2015). Importance and effectiveness of training and development. *Mediterranean Journal of Social Sciences*, *6*(1), 334.

Gangani, N., McLean, G. N., & Braden, R. A. (2006). A Competency-Based Human Resource Development Strategy. *Performance Improvement Quarterly*, *19*(1), 127–140. doi:10.1111/j.1937-8327.2006.tb00361.x

Garikipati, S. (2008). The Impact of Lending to Women on Households Vulnerability and Women's Empowerment: Evidence from India. *World Development*, *36*(12), 2620–2642. doi:10.1016/j.worlddev.2007.11.008

Gartner, W. B. (1989). Who is an entrepreneur? Is the wrong question. *Entrepreneurship Theory and Practice*, *13*(4), 47–68. doi:10.1177/104225878901300406

Gattullo, M., Scurati, G. W., Fiorentino, M., Uva, A. E., Ferrise, F., & Bordegoni, M. (2019). Towards augmented reality manuals for industry 4.0: A methodology. *Robotics and Computer-integrated Manufacturing*, *56*, 276–286. doi:10.1016/j.rcim.2018.10.001

Gebhardt, J., Grimm, A., & Neugebauer, L. M. (2015). Developments 4.0 Prospects on future requirements and impacts on work and vocational education. *Journal of Teacher Education*, *3*(2), 117–133.

Giffords, E. D., & Dina, R. P. (2011). Strategic planning in non-profit organizations: Continuous quality performance improvement - a case study. *International Journal of Organization Theory and Behavior*, *7*(1), 66–80. doi:10.1108/IJOTB-07-01-2004-B004

Gittonga, T. R. (2012). *The impact of freezing recruitment on employee performance and productivity*. SENA.

Global, Ey. (2019). *Four things to know about fourth industrial revolution*. Available: https://www.ey.com/en_gl/digital/four-things-to-know-about-the-fourth-industrial-revolution

Gordon, R. (2012). *Is U.S. Economic Growth Over? Faltering Innovation Confronts the Six Headwinds (No. w18315)*. Cambridge, MA: National Bureau of Economic Research. doi:10.3386/w18315

Grangel-González, I., Halilaj, L., Coskun, G., Auer, S., Collarana, D., & Hoffmeister, M. (2016, February). Towards a semantic administrative shell for industry 4.0 components. *IEEE Tenth International Conference on Semantic Computing*, 230-237. 10.1109/ICSC.2016.58

Grant, R. (1996). Towards a knowledge-based view of the firm. *Strategic Management Journal*, *17*(S2), 109–122. doi:10.1002mj.4250171110

Grzybowska, K., & Łupicka, A. (2017). Key competencies for Industry 4.0. *Economics & Management Innovations*, *1*(1), 250–253. doi:10.26480/icemi.01.2017.250.253

Gudanowska, A. E., Alonso, J. P., & Törmänen, A. (2018). What competencies are needed in the production industry? The case of the Podlaskie Region. *Engineering Management in Production and Services*, *10*(1), 65–74. doi:10.1515/emj-2018-0006

Guerrero, M., &Urbano, D. (2019). A research agenda for entrepreneurship and innovation: the role of entrepreneurial universities. *A Research Agenda for Entrepreneurship and Innovation*, 107.

Guers, C., Martin, C., & Wybo, J. L. (2014, September). *The impact of the use of subcontracting on organizational reliability and safety. In 24th European Safety and Reliability Conference-ESREL 2014* (pp. 1027–1035). London: Taylor & Francis Group.

Guest, D. E. (1997). Human resources management and industrial relations. *Journal of Management Studies*, *24*(5), 503–521. doi:10.1111/j.1467-6486.1987.tb00460.x

Gunawardana, K. D. (2009). *Quantitative Research Methodology*. Academic Press.

Gürbüz, S. (2017). *Human Resources Management: Theory, Research, and Practice*. Ankara: Seçkin Yayınları.

Guthrie, J. (2001). The management, measurement and the reporting of intellectual capital. *Journal of Intellectual Capital*, *2*(1), 27–41. doi:10.1108/14691930110380473

Guthrie, J., Steane, P., & Dunford, R. (2001). 'Stories from Australia on knowledge management and intellectual capital. *Journal of Intellectual Capital*, *2*(1).

Haddadj, S., & Besson, D. (2000, January). Introduction a` la gestion des compe´tences. *Revue Franc¸ aise de Gestion*, 82-83.

Haeffner, M., & Panuwatwanich, K. (2018). Perceived Impacts of Industry 4.0 on Manufacturing Industry and Its Workforce: Case of Germany. In S. Şahin (Ed.), *8th International Conference on Engineering, Project, and Product Management (EPPM 2017)* (pp. 199–208). Cham: Springer International Publishing. 10.1007/978-3-319-74123-9_21

Hall, C. (2016). Does more general education reduce the risk of future unemployment? Evidence from an expansion of vocational upper secondary education. *Economics of Education Review*, *52*(9), 234–250.

Halley, A. A. (2001). *Downsizing*. Available: http://jobfunctions.bnet.com/thankyou.aspx?&docid=60722&view=60772&load=1

Hanushek, E. A. (2009). School policy: Implications of recent research for human capital investments in South Asia and other developing countries. *Education Economics*, *17*(3), 291–313. doi:10.1080/09645290903142585

Hanushek, E. A., & Woessmann, L. (2007). *The role of education quality for economic growth. Policy Research Working Paper, No.4122*. Washington, DC: World Bank. Retrieved from https://openknowledge.worldbank.org/handle/10986/

Harbison, F. H. (2004). *Education Manpower and Economic Growth.* Delhi: Oxford & IBH Publication Co.

Harbison, F. H. (1973). *Human Resources as the Wealth of Nations*. London: OxfordUniversity Press.

Harbison, F. H. (2014). Human resources development planning in modernization economics. *International Labour Review*.

Hargreaves, A. (2001). Emotional geographies of teaching. *Teachers College Record, 103*(6), 1056–1080. doi:10.1111/0161-4681.00142

Harky, Y. F. M. (2018). *The Significance of Recruitment and Selection on Organizational Performance: The Case of Private owned Organizations in Erbil, North of Iraq* (Doctoral dissertation). Istanbul Aydin University Institute of Social Sciences.

Harris, B., & Batty, M. (1993). Locational models, geographic information and planning support systems. *Journal of Planning Education and Research*, *12*(3), 184–198. doi:10.1177/0739456X9301200302

Harris, P. (2007). Flexible work policies- mean business. *Training and Development Journal*, 32–36.

Hartle, F. (1995). *How to Re-engineer your Performance Management Process*. London: Kogan Page.

Hassan, T. (2007). *Women and National Development: The Way Forward*. Ibadan: The Bama Mathal Lecture Radcliffe College.

Hayes, J. L. (1979). A new look at managerial competence: The AMA model of worthy performance. *Management Review*, *68*(11), 2–3.

Hecklau, F., Galeitzke, M., Flachs, S., & Kohl, H. (2016). Holistic Approach for Human Resource Management in Industry 4.0. *Procedia CIRP*, *54*, 1–6. doi:10.1016/j.procir.2016.05.102

Heinsman, H. (2008). *The Competency Concept Revealed: Its Nature, Relevance, and Practice* (PhD Dissertation). Vrije Universiteit, Kurt Lewin Institute.

Helfat, C., & Peteraf, M. (2003). The dynamic resource-based view: Capability lifecycles. *Strategic Management Journal*, *24*(10), 997–1010. doi:10.1002mj.332

Hellgren, J., Naswell, K., & Sverke, M. (2005). There is more to the picture than meets the eye: A comparison of downsizing survivors with changed and unchanged job content. *SA Journal of Industrial Psychology*, *31*(4), 87–93. doi:10.4102ajip.v31i4.216

Henderson, J. P., Dicken, M., Hess, M., Coe, N., & Yeung, H. W. C. (2002). Global production networks and the analysis of economic development. *Review of International Political Economy*, *9*(3), 436–464. doi:10.1080/09692290210150842

Heneman III, H. G., & Sandver, M. G. (1977). *Markov analysis in human resource administration, applications and limitations*. Management of Academy.

Henry, C., Hill, F., & Leitch, C. (2003). *Entrepreneurship education and training*. Aldershot, UK: Ashgate.

Hersey, P., Blanchard, K. H., & Johnson, D. E. (2000). *Management of organizational behaviour: Leading human resources* (8th ed.). Englewood Cliffs, NJ: Prentice Hall.

Hoskisson, R., Hitt, M., Wan, W., & Yiu, D. (1999). Theory and research in strategic management: Swings of a pendulum. *Journal of Management*, *25*(3), 417–456. doi:10.1177/014920639902500307

Houseman, S. N. (2001). Why employers use flexible staffing arrangements: Evidence from an establishment survey. *Industrial & Labor Relations Review*, *55*(1), 149–170. doi:10.1177/001979390105500109

House, R. J., & Aditya, R. N. (1971). The social scientific study of leadership: Quo Vadis. *Journal of Management*, *23*(3), 409–473. doi:10.1177/014920639702300306

HowkinsJ. (2013). Available: http://www.creativeeconomy.com/john.htm

Hozdić, E. (2015). Smart factory for industry 4.0: A review. *International Journal of Modern Manufacturing Technologies*, *7*(1), 28–35.

Hsueh, L., & Tu, Y. (2004). Innovation and the operational performance of newly established small and medium enterprises in Taiwan. *Small Business Economics*, *23*(2), 99–113. doi:10.1023/B:SBEJ.0000027663.84972.ac

Hughes, J. P., Guttorp, P., & Charles, S. P. (1999). A non-homogeneous hidden Markov model for precipitation occurrence. *Applied Statistics*, *48*(1), 15–30. doi:10.1111/1467-9876.00136

Huisman, C., Wissen, V., & Leo, J. (2004). Localization effects of firm start-ups and closures in the Netherland. *The Annals of Regional Science*, *38*(2), 291–310. doi:10.100700168-004-0196-7

IFAD. (2018). *IFAD competency framework: How we give our best*. International Fund for Agricultural Development. Retrieved from https://newunkampus.unssc.org/pluginfile.php/105615/mod_folder/content/0/Agency%20Leadership%20Frameworks/IFAD/IFAD%20Competency%20Framework.pdf?forcedownload=1

Igbokwe-Ibeto, C., Chukwuemeka, E., & Okechukwu, E. (2014). Enhancing human capital development and service delivery in Nigerian Tertiary institutions through effective academic staff. *Africa's Public Service Delivery & Performance Review*, *2*(3), 125–152. doi:10.4102/apsdpr.v2i3.62

Ikebuaku, K., & Dinbabo, M. (2018). Beyond entrepreneurship education: Business incubation and entrepreneurial capabilities. *Journal of Entrepreneurship in Emerging Economies*, *10*(1), 154–174. doi:10.1108/JEEE-03-2017-0022

Ikpe, D. (2013). *The world bank: development, poverty, and hegemony*. University of Kwazulu: National Press.

Inagaki, T., & Sheridan, T. B. (2018). A critique of the SAE conditional driving automation definition, and analyses of options for improvement. *Cognition Technology and Work*, 1–10.

INQAAHE. (n.d). *Mission and values*. Retrieved May 10, 2019 from https://www.inqaahe.org/presentation

Institute of Chartered Accountants of Sri Lanka. (2005). *SLAS 37 Intangible Assets*. Author.

International Accounting Standards Committee. (1998). *IAS 38 Intangible Assets*. London: International Accounting Standards Committee.

International Finance Corporation. (2017). *Tackling Childcare: The Business Case for Employer-supported Childcare*. Washington, DC: International Finance Corporation.

IPU. (2016). Women in Parliament in 2015 The year in review. Geneva: IPU.

Iqbal, N., Anwar, S., & Haider, N. (2015). Effect of leadership style on employee performance. *Arabic Journal of Business and Management Review.*, *5*(5), 1–6.

Ittner, C. D., & Larcker, D. F. (2002). Empirical managerial accounting research: Are we just describing management-consulting practice? *European Accounting Review*, *11*(4), 787–794. doi:10.1080/0963818022000047082

Jacobson, W. (2010). Preparing for tomorrow: A case study of workforce planning in North Carolina municipal governments. *Public Personnel Management*, *39*(4), 1–21. doi:10.1177/009102601003900404

Jaiyeoba, S. V. (2015). Human Capital Investment and Economic Growth in Nigeria, African Research Review. *An International Multidisciplinary Journal, Ethiopia*, *9*(1), 36–44.

Jalilian, H. M., & Weiss, J. (2000). *Industrial development and policy in Africa: Issues of de-industrialisation and development strategy*. Cheltenham, UK: Edward Elgar.

Jamal, W., & Saif, M. I. (2011). Impact of human capital management on organizational performance. *European Journal of Economics. Finance and Administrative Sciences*, *5*(34), 13309–13315.

Jeewantha, G.K.C., Bandara, D., Hareendra, P., & Ajward, R.A. (2015). *Drivers of Corporate Voluntary Disclosures: Empirical Evidence from Sri Lankan Listed Companies*. Academic Press.

Jerman, A., Pejić Bach, M., & Bertoncelj, A. (2018). A Bibliometric and Topic Analysis on Future Competences at Smart Factories. *Machines*, *6*(3), 41. doi:10.3390/machines6030041

Johanson, U. (1999). *Mobilising change: characteristics of intangibles proposed by 11 Swedish firms*. Paper presented at the International Symposium Measuring and Reporting Intellectual Capital: Experiences, Issues and Prospects, Amsterdam, The Netherlands.

Johanson, R. K., & Adams, A. V. (2004). *Skills development in sub-Saharan Africa*. Washington, DC: World Bank. doi:10.1596/0-8213-5680-1

Johne, A. (2009). Insurance product development: Managing the Changes. *International Journal of Bank Marketing*, *11*(3), 5–14. doi:10.1108/02652329310027693

Jon, M., & Randy, L. D. (2009). *Human Resources Development* (6th ed.). South Western.

Judge, T. A., Bono, J. E., Ilies, R., & Gerhardt, M. W. (2002). Personality and leadership: A qualitative and quantitative review. *The Journal of Applied Psychology*, *87*(4), 765–780. doi:10.1037/0021-9010.87.4.765 PMID:12184579

Kagermann, H., Helbig, J., Hellinger, A., & Wahlster, W. (2013). *Recommendations for implementing the strategic initiative INDUSTRIE 4.0: Securing the future of German manufacturing industry; final report of the Industrie 4.0 Working Group*. Forschungsunion.

Kane, R. L., & Stanton, S. (1991). Human resource planning: Where are we now? *Asia Pacific Journal of Human Resources*, *29*(2), 5–20. doi:10.1177/103841119102900202

Kannan, G., & Aulbur, W. G. (2004). Intellectual capital: Measurement effectiveness. *Journal of Intellectual Capital*, *5*(3), 389–413. doi:10.1108/14691930410550363

Kantane, I., Sloka, B., Buligina, I., Tora, G., Busevica, R., Buligina, A., ... Tora, P. (2015). Expectations by employers on skills, knowledge and attitudes of employees. *European Integration Studies*, *9*, 224–234.

Kapinga, A. F., Montero, C. S., Mwandosya, G. I., & Mbise, E. R. (2018). Exploring the contribution of business and technology incubators to women entrepreneurs' business development in Dar es Salaam, Tanzania. *Journal of Global Entrepreneurship Research*, *8*(1), 23. doi:10.118640497-018-0111-9

Kaplan, D., & Höppli, T. (2017). The South African brain drain: An empirical assessment. *Development Southern Africa*, *34*(5), 497–514. doi:10.1080/0376835X.2017.1351870

Karaca, Y., Moonis, M., Zhang, Y., & Gezgez, C. (2019). Mobile cloud computing based stroke healthcare system. *International Journal of Information Management*, *45*, 250–261. doi:10.1016/j.ijinfomgt.2018.09.012

Karia, A., Omari, S., Mwanaongoro, S., & Ondieki, A. (2016). The role of human resource planning on performance of public water utilities in Tanzania. *African Journal of Business Management*, *2*(1), 72–77.

Karthikeyan, C. (2015). Re-Skilling and Right-Skilling HR Component to Sustain in Turbulent Business Scenario: A Conceptual Study on Prevailing Strategies. *European Journal of Commerce and Management Research, SI*(1), 51-53.

Katua, T., Mukulu, E., & Gachunga, H. (2014). Effect of employee resourcing strategies on the performance of commercial banks in Kenya. *International Journal of Education and Research*, *2*(1), 1–20.

Katz, L. F., & Murphy, K. M. (1992). Changes in relative wages, 1963-1987: Supply and demand factors. *The Quarterly Journal of Economics*, *107*(1), 35–78. doi:10.2307/2118323

Kavanagh, M. J., Thite, M., & Johnson, R. D. (2012). *Human Resource Information Systems: Basics, Applications and future Directions* (2nd ed.). Sage Publishers.

Kazlauskaitė, R., & Bučiūnienė, I. (2008). The role of human resources and their management in the establishment of sustainable competitive advantage. *The Engineering Economist*, *5*(60), 78–84.

Keevy, J. (2011). *The recognition of qualifications across borders: the contribution of regional qualifications frameworks. Background paper commissioned by UNESCO*. Pretoria: South African Qualifications Authority.

Kennedy, A. (2014). Understanding continuing professional development: The need for theory to impact on policy and practice. *Professional Development in Education, 40*(5), 688–697.

Kerr, A. (2001). The effect of bias on the advancement of working mothers: Disentangling legitimate concerns from inaccurate stereotypes as predictors of advancement in academe. *Human Relations*, *61*, 1677–1711.

KianiMavi, R., Gheibdoust, H., Khanfar, A. A., & KianiMavi, N. (2019). Ranking factors influencing strategic management of university business incubators with ANP. *Management Decision*.

Kimani, S. M., & Waithaka, S. M. (2013). Factors affecting implementation of talent management in state corporations: A case study of Kenya Broadcasting Corporation. *International Journal of Business and Social Research*, *3*(4), 42–49.

Kim, D. O., & Bae, J. (2017). *Employment relations and HRM in South Korea*. Routledge. doi:10.4324/9781315256566

Kim, R. (2009). *Reassessing the ins and outs of unemployment mimeo*. University of Chicago.

King, E. M., Klasen, S., & Porter, M. (2008). *Gender and development challenge paper*. Paper Prepared for the 2008 Round of Copenhagen Consensus Project.

Kingsley, W. O. (2014). *Globalization and employment generation. Evaluating the impact of trade on aggregate employment in Nigeria in Industrial Sector*. NES 2014 Annual Conference Nigeria.

Kingsley, W. O. (2011). Work-life 'balance' in Nigeria. *Acta Sociologica*, *49*(4), 379–393.

Kinkel, S., Schemmann, B., & Lichtner, R. (2017). Critical Competencies for the Innovativeness of Value Creation Champions: Identifying Challenges and Work-integrated Solutions. *Procedia Manufacturing*, *9*, 323–330. doi:10.1016/j.promfg.2017.04.021

Kirch, D. G., & Petelle, K. (2017). Addressing the physician shortage: The peril of ignoring demography. *JAMA Network*, *317*(19), 1947–1948. doi:10.1001/jama.2017.2714 PMID:28319233

Kirega, V. P. G. (2006). *Kampala City Handbook*. Kampala, Uganda: Gava Associated Services.

Kishor, S. (2005). *Gender Differentials in Child Mortality in India: A Review of Evidence" in Women's Health in India*. Bombay: Oxford University Press.

Knopp, L. (2007). *2006 state of the business incubation industry*. Athens, OH: National Business Incubation Association.

Kogut, B., & Zander, U. (1992). Knowledge of the firm, combinative capabilities, and the replication of technology. *Organization Science*, *3*(3), 383–397. doi:10.1287/orsc.3.3.383

Kondola, R., & Fullerton, J. (1998). *Diversity in Action: Managing the Mosaic* (2nd ed.). IPD.

Kong, E. (2014). A qualitative analysis of social intelligence in nonprofit organizations: External knowledge acquisition for human capital development. *Knowledge Management Research and Practice*, *13*(4), 463–474. doi:10.1057/kmrp.2013.63

Kozík, T., & Handlovská, I. (2011b). The reduction of interest among elementary students in the field of technical education. *International Journal of Engineering Pedagogy*, *1*(3), 9–12. doi:10.3991/ijep.v1i3.1822

KPMG. (2019). *The future of HR 2019: In the Know or in the No.* Retrieved from https://home.kpmg/xx/en/home/insights/2018/11/the-future-of-human-resources.html

Krsticevic, V. (2015). *Gender Equality in International Tribunals and Bodies: A global campaign for gender parity in international representation an achievable step with global impact*. Academic Press.

Kurt, S. (2015). Government health expenditures and economic growth: A federal approach for the case of Turkey. *International Journal of Economics and Financial Issues*, *5*(2), 441–447.

Kusmin, K. L., Ley, T., & Normak, P. (2017) Towards a Data Driven Competency Management Platform for Industry 4.0. *Proceedings of the Workshop Papers of i-Know 2017.*

Kuznets, S. (1957). Quantitative aspects of the economic growth of nations. *Economic Development and Cultural Change*, *4*, 3–111.

Lajili, K. (2012). Towards building a human-capital based governance framework. *Journal of Management Policy and Practice*, *13*(3), 13–30.

Landherr, M., Schneider, U., & Bauernhansl, T. (2016). The Application Center Industrie 4.0-Industry-driven manufacturing, research and development. *Procedia CIRP*, *57*, 26–31. doi:10.1016/j.procir.2016.11.006

Lars, M. (2011). Work-life balance accounts, strategic human resource management and demographic change - the case of the German chemical industry. *International Journal of Employment Studies*, *19*(1), 99–125.

Lashley, S. (2001). *Workplace strategies and facilities management: Building in value*. Burlington, MA: Buttersworth-Heinemann.

Lasi, H., Fettke, P., Kemper, H. G., Feld, T., & Hoffmann, M. (2014). Industry 4.0. *Business & Information Systems Engineering*, *6*(4), 239–242. doi:10.100712599-014-0334-4

Lasi, H., Fettke, P., Kemper, H.-G., Feld, T., & Hoffmann, M. (2014). Industrie 4.0. *Wirtschaftsinformatik*, *56*(4), 261–264. doi:10.100711576-014-0424-4

Lave, J., & Wenger, E. (1991). *Situated learning: Legitimate peripheral participation*. New York, NY: Cambridge University Press. doi:10.1017/CBO9780511815355

Lee, A., Moy, L., Kruck, S. E., & Rabang, J. (2014). The Doctor is in, but is academia? Re-Tooling IT education for a new era in healthcare. *Journal of Information Systems Education*, *25*(4), 275–281.

Leon, M. V. T. (2002). Intellectual capital: Managerial perceptions of organizational knowledge resources. *Journal of Intellectual Capital*, *3*(2), 149–166. doi:10.1108/14691930210424743

Lerman, R. (2009). *Training tomorrow's workforce: Community college and apprenticeship as collaborative routes to rewarding careers*. Washington, DC: Centre for American Progress.

Leung, P. P. L., Wu, C. H., Ho, G. T. S., Ip, W. H., & Mou, W. L. (2015). Workforce modelling, analysis and planning: A feasibility study in a local nursing home. In *2015 IEEE International Conference on Industrial Engineering and Engineering Management (IEEM)* (pp. 1337–1341). IEEE.

Leung, K., Trevena, L., & Waters, D. (2016). Development of a competency framework for evidence-based practice in nursing. *Nurse Education Today*, *4*(39), 189–196. doi:10.1016/j.nedt.2016.01.026 PMID:27006055

Leuven, E., & Oosterbeek, H. (2004). Evaluating the effect of tax deduction on training. *Journal of Labor Economics*, *22*(2), 461–488. doi:10.1086/381257

Lewin, K. (1947). Frontiers in group dynamics: Concepts, methods and reality in social; Social equilibria and social change. *Human Relations*, *1*(1), 1787–1812. doi:10.1177/001872674700100103

Likert, R. (1967). *The human organization: Its management and value* (1st ed.). New York: McGraw-Hill.

Lim, L. L. K., & Dallimore, P. (2004). Intellectual capital: Management attitudes in service industries. *Journal of Intellectual Capital*, *5*(1), 182–194. doi:10.1108/14691930410512996

Lindahl, M., & Krueger, A. B. (2001). Education for growth: Why and for whom? *Journal of Economic Literature*, *39*(4), 1101–1136. doi:10.1257/jel.39.4.1101

Liu, H. (2014). Cloud computing in music theory: Using in universities. *Applied Mechanics & Materials,* (556-562), 6758.

London, M. (2001). *Leadership Development: Paths to Self-Insight and Professional Growth* (1st ed.). Lawrence Erlbaum Associates, Incorporated Publisher. doi:10.4324/9781410604514

Long, E. J. (1961). Economic basis of land reform in underdeveloped economies. *Land Economics*, *37*(2), 404–420. doi:10.2307/3159556

Longo, F., Nicoletti, L., & Padovano, A. (2017). Smart operators in industry 4.0: A human-centered approach to enhance operators' capabilities and competencies within the new smart factory context. *Computers & Industrial Engineering*, *113*, 144–159. doi:10.1016/j.cie.2017.09.016

Lucas, R. Jr. (1988). On the mechanics of economic development. *Journal of Monetary Economics*, *22*(1), 3–42. doi:10.1016/0304-3932(88)90168-7

Lucia, A. D., & Lepsinger, R. (1999). *The Art and Science of Competency Models: Pinpointing Critical Success Factors in an Organization.* San Francisco, CA: Jossey-Bass/Pfeiffer.

Lukac, D. (2015). The fourth ICT-based industrial revolution "Industry 4.0" — HMI and the case of CAE/CAD innovation with EPLAN P8. In *2015 23rd Telecommunications Forum Telfor (TELFOR)* (pp. 835–838). Belgrade: IEEE. 10.1109/TELFO;R.2015.7377595

Lumsden, C. J., Byrne-Davis, L., Mooney, J. S., & Sandars, J. (2015). Using mobile devices for teaching and learning in clinical medicine. *Archives of Disease in Childhood - Education and Practice*, *100*(5), 244–251. doi:10.1136/archdischild-2014-306620 PMID:26033788

Lunenburg, F. C. (2012). Human resource planning: Forecasting demand and supply. *International Journal of Management. Business Administration (London)*, *15*(1), 1–15.

MacGregor's XY Theory of Management. (1960). Available: https://www.businessballs.com/improving-workplace-performance/mcgregors-xy-theory-of-management/

Madrick, A. (1995). *Hiring freezes and employee performance.* London: Institute of Personnel Management.

Mafini, C., & Pooe, D. (2013). The relationship between employee satisfaction and organisational performance: Evidence from a South African government department. *SA Journal of Industrial Psychology*, *39*(1), 1–9. doi:10.4102ajip.v39i1.1090

Mainoma, M. A., & Aruwa, S. A. S. (2012). *Entrepreneurship: Principles, processes and development.* Kaduna, Nigeria: Felicity Publishing.

Makkonen, H., Pohjola, M., Olkkonen, R., & Koponen, A. (2014). Dynamic capabilities and firm performance. *DBA Africa Management Review.*, *2*(3), 614–626.

Makris, S., Karagiannis, P., Koukas, S., & Matthaiakis, A.-S. (2016). Augmented reality system for operator support in human–robot collaborative assembly. *CIRP Annals*, *65*(1), 61–64. doi:10.1016/j.cirp.2016.04.038

Mallela, C. S. R. (2012). Human resource planning: Then and now. *Prabandhan: Indian Journal of Management*, *5*(9), 27–31. doi:10.17010/pijom/2012/v5i9/60253

Mamedov, Z. F., Mineva, O. K., & Glinchevskiy, E. I. (2019). Innovative Approach To Human Capital Management Under Conditions Of Strong Turbulence of Fourth Industrial Revolution. Varazdin: Varazdin Development and Entrepreneurship Agency (VADEA).

Mansfield, R. S. (2000). Practical Questions for Building Competency Models. In *Proceedings of Competency-Based Management for the Federal Public Service Conference* (pp. 3-17). Ottawa, Canada: Academic Press.

Mansur, M. S., & Abuga, I. (2017). Incubator Based Activities and Technology Entrepreneurship Growth in North Western Nigeria. *KIU Journal of Humanities*, *2*(1), 157–168.

Markus, L., Thomas, H. C., & Allpress, K. (2005). Confounded by competencies? An evaluation of the evolution and use of competency models. *New Zealand Journal of Psychology*, *34*(2), 117–126.

Marshall, S. J. (2018). Internal and external stakeholders in higher education. In *Shaping the University of the Future* (pp. 77–102). Singapore: Springer. doi:10.1007/978-981-10-7620-6_4

Marsh, M. J. (2017). *Automation: Will The Fourth Industrial Revolution Lead to The Downfall of Human Labour?* Department of Finance, Texas Christian University.

MartinakD. (2017). *Povolanie robot.* Retrieved from https://www.minedu.sk/data/att/11077.pdf

Maslarić, M., Nikoličić, S., & Mirčetić, D. (2016). Logistics Response to the Industry 4.0: The Physical Internet. *Ocean Engineering*, *6*(1), 511–517. doi:10.1515/eng-2016-0073

Maslow, A. (1943). Theory of human motivation. *Psychological Review*, *80*, Pp3709–Pp396.

Mat, J. (2008). *The Influence of Leadership Style on Internal Marketing in Retailing* (PhD Thesis). University of Stirling.

Matley, H. (2005). *Business school graduates as nascent entrepreneurs: Some policy considerations*. NCGE Policy Paper 6. Retrieved from www.ncge.com

Maurik, J. V. (2001). Writers on Leadership. London: Penguin Books.

Mba, I. C., Mba, E. I., Ogbuabor, J. E., & Ikpegbu, C. H. (2013). Human Capital Development and Economic Growth in Nigeria. *Journal of Economics and Sustainable Development*, *4*, 18–25.

McClelland, D. (1973). Testing for competence rather than for 'intelligence'. *The American Psychologist*, *28*(1), 1–14. doi:10.1037/h0034092 PMID:4684069

McClelland, D. (1998). Identifying competencies with behavioural-event interviews. *Psychological Science*, *9*(5), 331–339. doi:10.1111/1467-9280.00065

McGrath, G. R., & MacMillan, I. C. (2000). *Entrepreneurial Mindset: Strategies for continuously creating opportunity in an age of uncertainty*. Harvard Business School Press Books.

McKee-Ryan, F., Song, Z., Wanberg, C. R., & Kinicki, A. J. (2005). Psychological and physical well-being during unemployment: A meta-analytic study. *The Journal of Applied Psychology*, *90*(5), 301–321. doi:10.1037/0021-9010.90.1.53 PMID:15641890

McKernan, J. (2013). *Curriculum action research: A handbook of methods and resources for the reflective practitioner*. Routledge.

McLean, S., Sheikh, A., Cresswell, K., Nurmatov, U., Mukherjee, M., Hemmi, A., & Pagliari, C. (2013). The impact of telehealthcare on the quality and safety of care: A systematic overview. *PLoS One*, *8*(8), 1–11. doi:10.1371/journal.pone.0071238 PMID:23977001

McMullan, W., Chrisman, J., & Vesper, K. (2001). Some problems in using subjective measures of effectiveness to evaluate entrepreneurial assistance programs. *Entrepreneurship Theory and Practice*, *26*(1), 37–54. doi:10.1177/104225870102600103

McNeese, G. (1997). Factors Contributing to Nurses Demotivation with Recognition Initiatives: A Review of the Research Literature. *International Journal of Nursing Studies*, *44*, 297–314.

Mehrara, M., & Musai, M. (2013). The relationship between Economic Growth and Human Capital in Developing Countries. *International Letters of Social and Humanistic Sciences*, *5*, 55–62. doi:10.18052/www.scipress.com/ILSHS.5.55

Meier, G. M. (1995). *Leading Issues in Economic Development* (2nd ed.). Oxford, UK: Oxford University Press.

Meindl, J. R., Ehrlich, S. B., & Dukerich, J. M. (1985). The romance of leadership. *Administrative Science Quarterly*, *30*(1), 78–102. doi:10.2307/2392813

Mendes, L., & Machado, J. (2015). Employees' Skills, Manufacturing Flexibility and Performance: A Structural Equation Modelling Applied to the Automotive Industry. *International Journal of Production Research*, *53*(13), 4087–4101. doi:10.1080/00207543.2014.993772

Mensah, N. P. W. (2010). *Nana Yaa Asantewaa, The Queen Mother of Ejisu: The Unsung Heroine of Feminism in Ghana* (An unpublished Master of Arts thesis). University of Toronto.

Meredith, G. G., Nelson, R. E., & Neck, P. A. (1991). *The practice of entrepreneurship*. University of Lagos Press.

Metilelu, O. O. (2016). Human capital development trends in the hospitality and tourism industry: A case of southwest Nigeria. *African Journal of Hospitality, Tourism and Leisure*, *5*(4), 1–9.

Meyer, J. P., & Herscovitch, L. (2001). Commitment in the workplace: Towards a general Model. *Human Resource Management Review*, *11*(3), 299–326. doi:10.1016/S1053-4822(00)00053-X

Michael, A. (2010). *Leadership style and organizational impact*. Retrieved from http://www.ala-apa.org

Milkovich, T. G., & Boudreau, J. W. (1993). *Human resource management*. Praha: Grada Publishing.

Mince, J. (2013). Occupational stress, work-home interference and burnout among Belgian veterinary practitioners. *Irish Veterinary Journal*, *61*(4), 233–241. PMID:21851711

Mingat, A. (1998). The strategy used by high-performing Asian economies in education: Some lessons for developing countries. *World Development*, *26*(4), 695–715. doi:10.1016/S0305-750X(98)00001-1

Mintzberg, H. (2010). Shifting the trajectory of civilisation. *Oxford Leadership Journal*, *1*(2), 1–10.

Monk, A. L. (2001). *The development of a competency model for auditors working in a professionalservices environment* (Unpublished master's thesis). University of South Africa, Pretoria, South Africa.

Moog, P. (2002). Human capital and its influence on entrepreneurial success. *Historical Social Research (Köln)*, *27*(4), 157–180.

Mosely, C. (2005). The value of professional teaching portfolios to prospective employers: School administrators' views. *Professional Educator*, *27*(3), 58–72.

Motyl, B., Baronio, G., Uberti, S., Speranza, D., & Filippi, S. (2017). How will Change the Future Engineers' Skills in the Industry 4.0 Framework? A Questionnaire Survey. *Procedia Manufacturing*, *11*, 1501–1509. doi:10.1016/j.promfg.2017.07.282

Mullins, L. J., & Dossor, P. (2013). *Hospitality management and organizational behavior. Firth Edition*. Pearson.

Mustaffa, Y. M. B. (2012). *Factors influencing organisational performance in Metro Specialist Hospital, Sungai Petani*. Universiti Utara.

Nadler, D. A., & Tushman, M. (1999). The organisation of the future: Strategic imperatives and core competencies for the 21st century. *Organizational Dynamics*, *27*(1), 45–58. doi:10.1016/S0090-2616(00)80006-6

Naile, I., & Selesho, J. (2014). The Role of Leadership in Employee Motivation. *Mediterranean Journal of Social Sciences*, *5*(3), 175–181.

Nath, H. (2017). The Information Society. *Space and Culture, 4*(3), 19-28.

Ndagi, A. (2017). Role of technology incubation on entrepreneurship development in Nigeria: A case of Minna technology incubation centre. *International Journal of Advanced Studies in Economics and Public Sector Management*, *5*(3), 131–138.

Neiman, B., & Karabarbounis, L. (2013). The global decline of the labour share. *The Quarterly Journal of Economics*, *129*(1), 61–103.

Nelen, A., De Grip, A., & Fouarge, D. (2011). *Is part-time employment beneficial for firm productivity?* IZA Discussion Paper No. 5423.

Nel, J., & De Beer, A. (2014). *Business Management: A contemporary approach* (2nd ed.). Juta.

Nelson, R., & Winter, S. (1982). *An evolutionary theory of economic change*. Cambridge, MA: Belknap Press.

Nerdrum, L., & Erikson, T. (2001). Intellectual capital: A human capital perspective. *Journal of Intellectual Capital, 2*(2), 127–135. doi:10.1108/14691930110385919

Ngambi, H. C., Cant, M. C., & Van Heerden, C. H. (2010). *Marketing Management: A South African perspective*. Cape Town, South Africa: Juta.

Ngui, T. K., Elegwa, K., & Hazel, G. G. (2014). Effect of employee resourcing on the performance of commercial banks in Kenya. *International Journal of Education and Research, 2*(1), 1–20.

Niehaus, R. J. (1995). Evolution of the strategy and structure of a human resource planning DSS application. *Decision Support Systems, 14*(3), 187–204. doi:10.1016/0167-9236(94)00016-L

Nieuwenhuizen, C., & Oosthuizen, T. F. J. (2017). *Business Management, a contemporary compilation* (3rd ed.). Future Vision Business Consultants.

Nkata, J.L. (2004). *Private higher education in Uganda: the case of its distribution, Contribution to access and costs*. Academic Press. doi:10.1177/1356389011411610

Noble, D. (2017). *Forces of production: A social history of industrial automation*. Routledge.

Norhidayah, D., Kasim, N., & Shamsudin, A. (2012). Framework of human resource planning (HRP) influencing factors for local workforce supply in Malaysian construction industry. *Journal of Technology Management in China, 7*(2), 177–197. doi:10.1108/17468771211242863

Norman-Major, K., & Gooden, S. (2012). *Cultural Competency for Public Administrators*. Armonk, NY: M.E. Sharpe Incorporated.

Northouse, P. G. (2010). *Leadership theory and practice* (5th ed.). Thousand Oaks, CA: SAGE Publication.

Northouse, P. G. (2013). *Leadership Theory and Practice* (6th ed.). London: SAGE Publication.

Obasan, K.A. (2005). *Entrepreneurship Theory and Practice*. Ogun: Gratia Associates International.

Odia, G. (2007). *Gender equality as development framework of women integration in economic development. African Journal of Social and Policy Studies, 12(1).*

OECD, PISA. (2015). Results Universal Basic Skills: What Countries Stand to Gain. Author.

OECD. (2015). *Skills for social progress: The power of social and emotional skills*. Retrieved May 10, 2019 from http://www.oecd.org/education/skills-for-social-progress-9789264226159-en.htm

OECD. (2017). *Concepts, measurement and trends. Is Informal Normal? Towards More and Better Jobs in Developing Countries*. Paris: Jutting and Laiglesia.

Ofori, D., & Aryeetey, M. (2011). Recruitment and selection practices in small and medium enterprises. *International Journal of Business Administration, 2*(3), 45–60. doi:10.5430/ijba.v2n3p45

Ojo, F. (2011). *Youth employment and youth employment programmes in Africa: The case of Nigeria, Addis Ababa, Jobs & Skills*. Presented at *UN Economic and Social Commission for Asia and the Pacific Conference*.

Ojokuku, R. M., Odetayo, T. A., & Sajuyigbe, A. S. (2012). Impact of Leadership Style on Organizational Performance: A case Study of Nigerian Banks. *American Journal of Business and Management*, *1*(4), 202–207.

Okojie, P. (2014). *Gender poverty and educational human capital investment in Nigeria*. Nigerian Economic and Financial Review.

Oladele-Emmanuel, B. D., Redlich, T., & Wulfsberg, J. (2018, June). Measuring Innovation: Insight from Nigeria's Innovation Incubators. In *2018 IEEE International Conference on Engineering, Technology and Innovation (ICE/ITMC)* (pp 1-9). IEEE. 10.1109/ICE.2018.8436304

Oladimeji, M. S., Abosede, A. J., & Eze, B. U. (2018). Innovation and internationalization of Nigeria deposit money banks. *Emerging Market Journal*, *8*(1), 1–11. doi:10.5195/EMAJ.2018.144

Oladoyin, R. D. (2010). *The role human capital development: an empirical study of Nigerian case, Oxford Business and Economics Conference Program*. Oxford, UK: St. Hugh's College, Oxford University.

Olaniyan, D. A., & Okemakinde, T. (2008). Human capital theory: Implications for educational development. *European Journal of Scientific Research*, *24*(2), 157–162.

Olaniyi, J. O. (2010). Implications of women's work for children's nutritional status in Sub Saharan Africa. *Social Science & Medicine*, *56*(10), 2109–2121.

Olaolu, D. (2018). An integrated framework for the critical success factors and incubator performance in Nigeria. Academy of Entrepreneurship Journal, 24(1).

Ollukkaran, B. A., & Gunaseelan, D. R. (2012). A study on the impact of work environment on employee performance. *International Journal of Management Research*, *2*(2), 71–85.

Oloko, R. (2015). Concept and measurement of Women's work in Nigeria and their implication for social change. In L. Olurode (Ed.), *Women and Social Change in Nigeria*. Lagos: Unity Publishing and Research Co.

Olomu, Y. (2014). The role of psychological well-being in job performance: A fresh look at an age-old quest. *Organizational Dynamics*, *33*(4), 338–351.

Oluwatobi, S. O., & Ogunrinola, O. I. (2011). Government expenditure on human capital development: Implications for economic growth in Nigeria. *Journal of Sustainable Development*, *4*(3), 72–80. doi:10.5539/jsd.v4n3p72

Onyina, P. A. (2014). The Impact of a Microfinance Programme on Clients: Evidence from Ghana. Scholar's Press.

Oosterbeek, H., & Webbink, D. (2007). Wage Effects of an Extra Year of Basic Vocational Education. *Economics of Education Review, 26*(4), 408–419. doi:10.1016/j.econedurev.2006.07.013

Oosthuizen, J. H. (2016). Entrepreneurial Intelligence: Expanding Scwab's Four-Type Intelligence Proposition to Meaningfully Address the Challenges of the Fourth Industrial Revolution. *Proceedings of the 28th Annual Conference of the Southern African Institute of Management Scientists.*

Opatha, H. H. D. N. P. (2010). *Human resource management.* Colombo: Author Published.

Osoba, A. M. (2017). Human capital variables and economic growth in Nigeria. *EuroEconomica, 6*(1), 7–18.

PAHRODF. (2017). *A Guidebook on Competency Modelling and Profiling.* Manila, Philippines: Author.

Paley, N. (2004). *Successful Business Planning: Energizing Your Company's Potential.* London Thorogood.

Parker, G. G., Van Alstyne, M. W., & Choudar, S. P. (2016). *Platform revolution: How networked markets are transforming the economy—And how to make them work for you.* New York: W.W. Norton & Company.

Penprase, B. E. (2018). The fourth industrial revolution and higher education. In *Higher education in the era of the fourth industrial revolution* (pp. 207–229). Palgrave Macmillan.

Penrose, E. (1959). *The Theory of the Growth of the firm.* Oxford, UK: Basil Blackwell Publisher.

Petersen, S. A., Heikurs, T., Cerinŝek, G., & Bedek, M. (2011). *Competence Portfolios.* European Commission.

Peterson, R. S., Smith, D. B., Martorana, P. V., & Owens, P. D. (2003). The Impact of Chief Executive Officer Personality on Top Management Team Dynamics: One Mechanism by Which Leadership Affects Organizational Performance. *The Journal of Applied Psychology, 88*(5), 795–808. doi:10.1037/0021-9010.88.5.795 PMID:14516245

Pettinger, T. (2014). *Women who changed the world.* Retrieved on April 21, 2018 from www.biographyonline.net

Petty, R., & Guthrie, J. (2000). Intellectual capital: Literature review. *Journal of Intellectual Capital, 1*(2), 155–176. doi:10.1108/14691930010348731

Phillips, D., & Thomas, G. (2017). *Within and between gender disparities in income and education: Benefits from Democracy.* IZA Discussion Paper Series, No. 3221. Institute for the Study of Labor (IZA). Retrieved from ftp:// repec.iz.org/RePEc/Discussionpaper/dp3221.pdf

Pitt, M. M. (2001). The Effect of Nonagricultural Self-Employment Credit on Contractual Relations and Employment in Agriculture: The Case of Microcredit Programs in Bangladesh. *Bangladesh Development Studies.*

Pitt, M. M., Khandker, S. R., & Cartwright, J. (2006). Empowering Women with Micro Finance: Evidence from Bangladesh. *Economic Development and Cultural Change*, *54*(4), 791–831.

Pitt, M. M., Khandker, S. R., Chowdhury, O. H., & Millimet, D. L. (2003). Credit Programs for the Poor and the Health Status of Children in Rural Bangladesh. *International Economic Review*, *44*(1), 87–118. doi:10.1111/1468-2354.t01-1-00063

Pitt, M. M., Khandker, S. R., McKeman, S.-M., & Latif, M. A. (1999). Credit Programs for the Poor and Reproductive Behavior in Low Income Countries: Are the Reported Causal Relationships the Result of Heterogeneity Bias? *Demography*, *36*(February), 1–21. doi:10.2307/2648131 PMID:10036590

Pitt, M., & Khandker, S. R. (1998). The Impact of Group-Based Credit Programs on Poor Households in Bangladesh: Does the Gender of the Participant Matter? *Journal of Political Economy*, *106*(5), 958–996. doi:10.1086/250037

Pradeesh, N. M. (2011). *Human resource planning and development: Study material VI semester*. School of Distance Learning, University of Calicut.

Pribanic, E. (2018). *What role does human capital play in an organisation?* Available: https://www.techfunnel.com/hr-tech/what-role-does-human-capital-management-play-in-an-organization/

Prifti, L., Knigge, M., Kienegger, H., & Krcmar, H. (2017). A Competency Model for "Industrie 4.0" Employees. *Proceedings der 13. Internationalen Tagung Wirtschaftsinformatik*, 46-60.

Prisecaru, P. (2016). Challenges of the fourth industrial revolution. *Knowledge Horizons. Economics*, *8*(1), 57.

Qian, N. (2013). Missing women and the price of tea in China: The effect of sex specific earnings on sex imbalance. *The Quarterly Journal of Economics*, *123*(3), 1251–1285. doi:10.1162/qjec.2008.123.3.1251

Quint, F., Sebastian, K., & Gorecky, D. (2015). A Mixed-reality Learning Environment. *Procedia Computer Science*, *75*, 43–48. doi:10.1016/j.procs.2015.12.199

Rahim, E., & Duncan, T. D. (2018). *Examining the evolution of sustainable leadership. In Contemporary Multicultural Orientations and Practices for Global Leadership*. IGI Global.

Rahman, S. (2007). *The Impact of Microcredit on Poverty and Women's Empowerment: A Case of Bangladesh* (Unpublished PhD Thesis). University of Western Sydney.

Rahmani, A. M., Gia, T. N., Negash, B., Anzanpour, A., Azimi, I., Jiang, M., & Liljeberg, P. (2018). Exploiting smart e-health gateways at the edge of healthcare internet-of-things: A fog computing approach. *Future Generation Computer Systems*, *78*, 641–658. doi:10.1016/j.future.2017.02.014

Raja, K. G., & Swapna, R. (2010). Evaluating the differences between Managerial and Executive Level Personal Competencies -A Critical analysis of Select IT Companies. *Bhavan's International. The Journal of Business*, *4*(2), 71–76.

Ras, E., Wild, F., Stahl, C., & Baudet, A. (2017). Bridging the skills gap of workers in Industry 4.0 by Human Performance Augmentation Tools: Challenges and Roadmap. *Proceedings of the 10th International Conference on Pervasive Technologies Related to Assistive Environments*, 428-432. 10.1145/3056540.3076192

Reed, K. K., Srinivasan, N., & Doty, D. H. (2009). Adapting human and social capital to impact performance: Some empirical findings from the US personal banking sector. *Journal of Managerial Issues*, 36–57.

Reid, W. M., & Taylor, R. G. (1989). An application of absorbing markov analysis to human resource issues in public administration. *Sage (Atlanta, Ga.)*, 76–74.

Reilly, P. (2003). Guide to workforce planning in local Authorities. Employer's Organization for Local Government.

Reimo, A. M., & Revenga, A. A. (2017). What works for women's work. Washington, DC: The World Bank.

Ricci, T. (2012). *Frank Bunker Gilbreth: Biography*. Available: https://www.asme.org/engineering-topics/articles/construction-and-building/frank-bunker-gilbreth

Richert, A., Shehadeh, M., Willicks, F., & Jeschke, S. (2016). Digital Transformation of Engineering Education - Empirical Insights from Virtual Worlds and Human-Robot-Collaboration. *International Journal of Engineering Pedagogy*, *6*(4), 23. doi:10.3991/ijep.v6i4.6023

Robbins, S. P., & Judge, T. A. (2011). *Organizational behavior* (14th ed.). Upper Saddle River, NJ: Prentice Hall.

Robbins, S., & Judge, T. (2007). *Essentials of organizational behavior*. Prentice Hal.

Robertson, I., Gibbons, P., Baron, H., MacIver, R., & Nyfield, G. (1999). Understanding Management Performance. *British Journal of Management*, *10*, 5-12.

Robert, T. (2014). The (perceived) returns to education and the demand for schooling. *The Quarterly Journal of Economics*, *25*(2), 515–548.

Roblek, V., Meško, M., & Krapež, A. (2016). A Complex View of Industry 4.0. *SAGE Open*, *6*(2), 215824401665398. doi:10.1177/2158244016653987

Romer, P. M. (1989). *Human capital and growth: theory and evidence (No. w3173)*. National Bureau of Economic Research. doi:10.3386/w3173

Roslender, R., & Fincham, R. (2001). Thinking critically about intellectual capital accounting. *Accounting, Auditing & Accountability Journal*, *14*(4), 383–399. doi:10.1108/09513570110403425

Rothwell, W. J., & Kazanas, H. C. (2011). *Mastering the instructional design process: A systematic approach*. San Francisco: John Wiley & Sons.

Rothwell, W. J., & Lindholm, J. E. (1999). Competency identification, modelling and assessment in the USA. *International Journal of Training and Development*, *3*(2), 90–105. doi:10.1111/1468-2419.00069

Rouse, M. (n.d.). Available: https://searchhrsoftware.techtarget.com/definition/human-capital-management-HCM

Rowold, J. (2011). Relationship between leadership behaviors and performance: The moderating role of a work team's level of age, gender and culture heterogeneity. *Leadership and Organization Development Journal*, *32*(6), 628–647. doi:10.1108/01437731111161094

Rubiano, M. E., & Viollaz, M. (2018). *Gender Differences in Time Use: Allocating Time between the Market and the Household.* Washington, DC: The World Bank.

Ruggeri, K., Farrington, C., & Brayne, C. (2013). A global model for effective use and evaluation of e-learning in health. *Telemedicine Journal and e-Health*, *19*(4), 312–321. doi:10.1089/tmj.2012.0175 PMID:23472702

Russell, C. J. (2000). A Longitudinal Study of Top Level Executive Performance. *Journal of Applied Psychology, Vol*, *86*(4), 560–573. doi:10.1037/0021-9010.86.4.560 PMID:11519641

Rüßmann, M., Lorenz, M., Gerbert, P., Waldner, M., Justus, J., Engel, P., & Harnisch, M. (2015). Industry 4.0: The future of productivity and growth in manufacturing industries. *Boston Consulting Group, 9*(1), 54-89.

Sandberg, J. (2000). Understanding human competence at work: An interpretative approach. *Academy of Management Journal*, *43*(1), 9–25.

Sanders, D. P., & Barth, S. P. (1968). Education and economic development. *Review of Educational Research*, *38*(3), 213–230.

Sandwell, C. (2011). A qualitative study exploring the challenges of humanitarian organisations. *Journal of Humanitarian Logistics and Supply Chain Management*, *1*(2), 132–150. doi:10.1108/20426741111158430

Saniuk, A., & Saniuk, S. (2017). Analysis of the Situation of Polish Enterprises in Industrial Networks in Industry 4.0. *Nauki O Zarządzaniu*, (31), 12–17. doi:10.15611/noz.2017.2.02

Sankay, O. J., Ismail, R., & Shaari, A. H. (2010). The impact of human capital development on the economic growth of Nigeria. *Prosiding Perkem*, *5*(1), 63–72.

Sanyal, S., & Hisam, M. W. (2018). The role of business incubators in creating an entrepreneurial ecosystem: A study of the sultanate of Oman. *Indian Journal of Commerce and Management Studies*, *9*(3), 9–16. doi:10.18843/ijcms/v9i3/02

Sariolghalam, N., Noruzi, M. R., & Rahimi, G. R. (2010). The enigma of Howard Gardner's multiple intelligences theory in the area of organizational effectiveness. *International Journal of Business and Management*, *5*(5), 161–173. doi:10.5539/ijbm.v5n5p161

Schallock, B., Rybski, C., Jochem, R., & Kohl, H. (2018). Learning Factory for Industry 4.0 to provide future skills beyond technical training. *Procedia Manufacturing*, *23*, 27–32. doi:10.1016/j.promfg.2018.03.156

Schiffeler, N., Stehling, V., Haberstroh, M., & Isenhardt, I. (2018). Fostering social construction of knowledge in hybrid teams by augmented reality. In *2018 IEEE Global Engineering Education Conference (EDUCON)* (pp. 1029–1034). Tenerife: IEEE. 10.1109/EDUCON.2018.8363343

Schuh, G., Gartzen, T., Rodenhauser, T., & Marks, A. (2015). Promoting Work-based Learning through INDUSTRY 4.0. *Procedia CIRP*, *32*, 82–87. doi:10.1016/j.procir.2015.02.213

Schultz, T. (2004). Investments in the schooling and health of women and men quantities and returns. *The Journal of Human Resources*, *28*(1).

Schultz, T. P. (1992). *Human Capital and Economic Development*. New Haven, CT: Economic Growth Center, Yale University.

Schultz, T. W. (1975). Investment in human capital. *The American Economic Review*, *51*(1), 1–17.

Schumpeter, J. (1934). *The theory of economic development*. Cambridge, MA: Harvard.

Schwab, K. & Samans, R. (2016). *The Future of Jobs: Employment, Skills, and Workfprce Strategy for the Fourth Industrial Revolution*. Global Challenge Insight Report.

Schwab, S. (2016). *The Fourth Industrial Revolution by Klaus Schwab*. Available: https://www.weforum.org/about/the-fourth-industrial-revolution-by-klaus-schwab

Scott, K. A., Fisher, G. G., Baron, A. E., Tompa, E., Stallones, L., & DiGuiseppi, C. (2017). Same-level fall injuries in U.S. workplaces by age, group, gender, and industry. *American Journal of Industrial Medicine*, *61*(2), 111–119. doi:10.1002/ajim.22796 PMID:29193187

Scullen, S. E., Mount, M. K., & Goff, M. (2000). Understanding the latent structure of job performance ratings. *The Journal of Applied Psychology*, *85*(6), 956–970. doi:10.1037/0021-9010.85.6.956 PMID:11125659

Seetharaman, A., Low, K. L. T., & Saravanan, A. S. (2004). Comparative justification on intellectual capital. *Journal of Intellectual Capital*, *5*(4), 522–539. doi:10.1108/14691930410566997

Seleim, A., Ashour, A., & Bontis, N. (2007). Human capital and organizational performance: A study of Egyptian software companies. *Management Decision*, *45*(4), 789–801. doi:10.1108/00251740710746033

Sen, A. (2018). More than 100 Million Women are Missing. *The New York Review of Books*, (December): 2018.

Sentryo. (2019). *The 4 Industrial Revolutions*. Retrieved on February 23, 2019 from https://www.sentro_net/the 4

Shimry, T. J., & Leohard, Y. (2012). *Schooling, Experience, and Earnings*. New York: NBER Press.

Shippmann, J. S., Ash, R. A., Battista, M. A., Carr, L., Eyde, L. D., Hesketh, B., ... Sanchez, J. I. (2000). The Practice of Competency Modelling. *Personnel Psychology*, *53*(3), 703–740. doi:10.1111/j.1744-6570.2000.tb00220.x

Shivam, N. (2019). *Work study: definition, role and objectives*. Available: http://www.economicsdiscussion.net/engineering-economics/work-study-definition-role-and-objectives/21681

Singer, H. L. (2018). Impact of education and health on employment. *European Journal of Administrative Sciences*, *13*(18).

Sivagandhi, S., & Dash, D. P. (2017). Microfinance and women Empowerment-Empirical evidence from the Indian states. *Regional and Sectoral Economic Studies*, *17*(2), 61–74.

Smith, A. (1776). *The Wealth of Nations*. Harmondsworth, UK: Penguin.

Snell, S., Bohlander, G. W., & Bohlander, G. (2010). *Principles of human resource management*. South-Western Cengage Learning.

Sparrow, P. (1995). Organisational Competencies: A Valid Approach for the Future? *International Journal of Selection and Assessment*, *3*(3), 168–177. doi:10.1111/j.1468-2389.1995.tb00024.x

Sri Lankan Archives Statistics. (n.d.). *Blue books reports*.

Sri Lankan Government. (1938). *Companies Act*.

Sri Lankan Government. (1982). *Companies Act*.

Sri Lankan Government. (2007). *Companies Act*.

Starr, J. (2004). The manager's role in coaching overcoming barriers to success. Development and Learning in Organisations. *International Journal (Toronto, Ont.)*, *18*(2), 9–12.

Stewart, T. A. (1997). *Intellectual capital: the new wealth of organizations*. New York: Doubleday.

Stock, T., & Seliger, G. (2016). Opportunities of sustainable manufacturing in industry 4.0. *Procedia Cirp*, *40*, 536–541. doi:10.1016/j.procir.2016.01.129

Stokes, P., & Oiry, E. (2012). An Evaluation of the Use of Competencies in Human Resource Development-a Historical and Contemporary Recontextualisation. *EuroMed Journal of Business*, *7*(1), 4–23. doi:10.1108/14502191211225356

Straka, G. A. (2004). *Measurement and evaluation of competence, in: 3rd European Research Report: Vocational Education and Training*. Thessaloniki: CEDEFOP.

Strange, R., & Zucchella, A. (2017). Industry 4.0, global value chains and international business. *Multinational Business Review*, *25*(3), 174–184. doi:10.1108/MBR-05-2017-0028

Sullivan, P. (2000). Value-driven intellectual capital: how to convert corporate assets into market value. Wiley/Arthur Andersen.

Sultan Qadri, F., & Abdul, W. (2011). Human capital and economic growth: Time series evidence from Pakistan. *Pakistan Business ReviK2ew*, *1*, 815-833.

Sun, R. Y. (2002). The relationship among the leadership style, organisational culture and organisational effectiveness based on competing value framework: An empirical study. Institute of Technology in Taiwan.

Sveiby, K. E. (1998b). *Measuring intangibles and intellectual capital ± an emerging first standard.* Retrieved from http://www.sveiby.com.au/EmergingStandard.html

Sveiby, K.E. (1998, June). Intellectual capital: thinking ahead. *Australian CPA*, 18-22.

Sveiby, K. E. (1997). *The new organizational wealth: managing and measuring knowledge-based assets*. San Francisco, CA: Berrett-Koehler.

Svennilson, I. (1972). A note on his scientific achievement and a bibliography of his contributions to economics. *The Swedish Journal of Economics*, *74*(3), 313–332. doi:10.2307/3439072

Swanepoel, B. J., Erasmus, B. J., Schenk, H. W., & Tshilongamulenzhe, M. C. (2014). *South African Human Resources Management: Theory and Practice* (5th ed.). Juta.

Swedberg, R. (2000). *Entrepreneurship. The Social Science View*. Oxford, UK: Oxford University Press.

Switzer, L. N., & Huang, Y. (2007). How does human capital affect the performance of small and mid-cap mutual funds? *Journal of Intellectual Capital*, *8*(4), 666–681. doi:10.1108/14691930710830828

Taiwo, O. (2013). *Leadership Style: Impact on Employees*. Lahti University of Applied Sciences.

Tann, J. (2015). Borrowing brilliance: Technology transfer across sectors in the early Industrial Revolution. *The International Journal for the History of Engineering & Technology*, *85*(1), 94–114. doi:10.1179/1758120614Z.00000000056

Teal, F. (2011). Higher education and economic development in Africa: A review of channels and interactions. *Journal of African Economies*, *20*(3), 50–79.

Thao, L. T., & Hwang, C. (2015). *Factors affecting employee performance*. PetroVietnam Engineering Consultancy J.S.C.

The Church of Pentecost. (2019). *General Headquarters 16th Extraordinary Council Meeting*. Accra: The Church of Pentecost.

The Economist. The Third Industrial Revolution. (n.d.). Available: https://www.economist.com/leaders/2012/04/21/the-third-industrial-revolution

The Fourth Industrial Revolution and sustainable development. (n.d.). Available: https://www.weforum.org/whitepapers/shaping-the-sustainability-of-production-systems-fourth-industrial-revolution-technologies-for-competitiveness-and-sustainable-growth

The Fourth Industrial Revolution. (n.d.). Available: https://www.weforum.org/agenda/2016/01/what-is-the-fourth-industrial-revolution/

The skills portal: skills for success. (2019). Available: https://www.skillsportal.co.za/content/10-essential-skills-4th-industrial-revolution

Thomas, D. (2013). Intra-household resource allocation: An inferential approach. *The Journal of Human Resources*, *25*(4), 635–646. doi:10.2307/145670

Timmons, J. A. (1978). Characteristics and role demands of entrepreneurship. *American Journal of Small Business*, *3*(1), 5–17. doi:10.1177/104225877800300102

Toit, A. D. (2007). Making sense through coaching. *Journal of Management Development*, *26*(3), 282–291. doi:10.1108/02621710710732164

Trace Project Report. (2005). *Overview of European Competency Frameworks*. TRACE Project number: 2005-2028/001 LE2-51OREF.

Trailhead: The four industrial revolutions. (n.d.). Available: https://trailhead.salesforce.com/en/content/learn/modules/learn-about-the-fourth-industrial-revolution/meet-the-three-industrial-revolutions

Troxler, P. (2013). *Making the 3rd industrial revolution. FabLabs: Of machines, makers and inventors*. Bielefeld: Transcript Publishers.

Turner, K. (1988). Natural attrition: The preferred option? *The Journal of Industrial Relations*, *30*(3), 363–380. doi:10.1177/002218568803000302

Ulewicz, R. (2017). The role of stakeholders in quality assurance in higher education. *Human Resources Management & Ergonomics*, *11*(1), 93–107.

Ulferts, G., Wirtz, P., & Peterson, E. (2009). Strategic human resource planning in academia. *American Journal of Business Education*, *2*(7), 1–10. doi:10.19030/ajbe.v2i7.4123

Understanding how customer service is changing. (n.d.). Available: https://trailhead.salesforce.com/en/content/learn/modules/customer-service-in-the-fourth-industrial-revolution/understand-how-customer-service-is-changing

UNDP Nigeria. (2018). Global Human Capital Report 2018. UNDP.

UNDP. (2012). *Human Development Report 2012*. New York: Oxford University Press.

UNDP. (2012). *Human Development Report 2012: Work for Human Development*. UNDP.

UNECA. (2014). *Africa Women's Report 2014*. UNECA.

UNIDO. (1999). *SMEs in Africa survive against all odds*. Retrieved from http://www.unido.org/doc/view?document_id=3927&language_code=en

United Nations Development Programme (UNDP). (2010). *Human development report 2010- 20th Anniversary Edition. The real wealth of Nations: Pathways to human development.* New York: University Press.

United Nations Population Division. (2018). *World Population Prospects*. Revision. Author.

Uwatt, M. (2003). Human Resource Development and Economic Growth in Nigeria, 1960-2000 Human Resource Development in Africa. In *Selected Papers for 2002 NES Annual Conference*. Nigerian Economic Society.

Vaidya, S., Ambad, P., & Bhosle, S. (2018). Industry 4.0–a glimpse. *Procedia Manufacturing, 20*, 233–238. doi:10.1016/j.promfg.2018.02.034

Vasconcelos, A. F. (2015). Older workers: Some critical societal and organizational challenges. *Journal of Management Development, 34*(3), 352–372. doi:10.1108/JMD-02-2013-0034

Velez, V. (2015). *Implementing child maltreatment prevention into the clinical setting: An on-line learning tutorial for advanced practice nurses (Order No. 3701612). Retrieved from ProQuest Central*. ProQuest Dissertations & Theses Global.

Vermeulen, L. P. (2002). A comparison of reasons and objectives for organisational downsizing in South Africa and Australia. *Management Dynamics, 11*(2), 28–39.

Vladikov, A. (2015). Human capital formation and use in Bulgaria. *Trakia Journal of Sciences, 13*(1Suppl.1), 8–15. doi:10.15547/tjs.2015.s.01.003

Volkmann, C. K., Tokarski, K. O., & Grunhagen, M. (2010). *Entrepreneurship in a European perspective*. Berlin: Gabler Verlag. doi:10.1007/978-3-8349-8752-5

Voon, M. L., Lo, M. C., Ngui, K. J., & Ayob, N. B. (2011). The influence of leadership styles on employees' job satisfaction in public sector organizations in Malaysia. International *Journal of Business. Management and Social Sciences, 2*(1), 24–32.

Vraniak, L., Mazánek, L., & Konečná, Z. (2017). Competence Approaches: Review of Current Concepts and Theories. *Ad Alta: Journal of Interdisciplinary Research, 7*(2), 134–137.

Vygotsky, L. S. (1978). *Mind in society: The development of higher psychological processes.* Cambridge, MA: Harvard University Press.

Wakabi, B. M. (2013). Leadership Style and Staff Retention in Organisations. *International Journal of Science and Research, 5*(1), 412–416.

Wallerstein, I. (1980). *The Modem World System II: mercantilism and the consolidation of the European world-economy 1600-1750.* New York: Academic Press.

WEA. (2018). *Competency Framework 2018*. Workers Educational Association. Retrieved from https://www.wea.org.uk/file/5290/download?token=pO4OeKgG

Webber, E. (2018). *Building Successful Communities of Practice*. San Francisco: Blurb Publishing.

Wernerfelt, B. (1984). A resource-based view of the firm. *Strategic Management Journal*, *5*(2), 171–180. doi:10.1002mj.4250050207

Werther, W. B. Jr, Ruch, W. A., & McClure, L. (1986). *Productivity through people*. St. Paul, MN: West Publishing.

What is ERP? Oracle South Africa. (2019). Available: https://www.oracle.com/za/applications/erp/what-is-erp.html

White, R. W. (1959). Motivation reconsidered: The concept of competence. *Psychological Review*, *66*(5), 297–333. doi:10.1037/h0040934 PMID:13844397

Wickramasinghe, V., & Zoyza, N. (2008). Gender, Age and Marital Status as Predictors of Managerial Competency Needs: Empirical Evidence from a Sri Lankan Telecommunication Service Provider. *Gender in Management*, *23*(5), 337–354. doi:10.1108/17542410810887365

Wilson, E. V., & Tulu, B. (2010). The rise of a Health-IT academic focus. *Communications of the ACM*, *53*(5), 147–150. doi:10.1145/1735223.1735259

Winkler, A. (2016). *Women's labor force participation. Family-friendly policies increase women's labor force participation, benefiting them, their families, and society at large*. IZA World of Labor, Paper 289.

Winthrop, R., & McGivney, E. (2016). *Rethinking education system in a changing world*. Retrieved May 10, 2019 from https://ssir.org/articles/entry/rethinking_education_in_a_changing_world#

Wisskirchen, G., Biacabe, B. T., Borman, U., Muntz, A., Niehaus, G., Soler, G. J., & von Brauchitsch, B. (2017). *Artificial Intelligence and Robotics and Their Impact on the Workplace*. IBA Global Employment Institute.

Witkowski, K. (2017). Internet of things, big data, industry 4.0–innovative solutions in logistics and supply chains management. *Procedia Engineering*, *182*, 763–769. doi:10.1016/j.proeng.2017.03.197

Wodon, Q. (2018). *What Is the Cost of Gender Inequality in Lost Earnings? Global Estimates Based on the Changing Wealth of Nations. Mimeo*. Washington, DC: The World Bank.

Wolf, M., Kleindienst, M., Ramsauer, C., Zierler, C., & Winter, E. (n.d.). Current and future industrial challenges: demographic change and measures for elderly workers in Industry D 4.0. *International Journal of Engineering*, 10.

Women, U. N. (2017). *Shaping the International Agenda: Raising Women's Voices in International in Intergovernmental Forums*. Geneva: International Gender Champions.

Woodruffe, C. (1991, September). Competent by any other name. *Personnel Management*, 30-33.

Woodruffe, C. (1990). *Assessment Centre: Identifying and developing competences*. London: IPM.

World Bank. (2003). *Operationalizing the 2003 World Development Report: Conflict, Security and Development*. Washington, DC: The World Bank.

World Bank. (2006a). *International migration, remittances and the brain drain*. Washington, DC: World Bank.

World Bank. (2006b). *Global economic prospects. Economic implications of remittances and migration*. Washington, DC: World Bank.

World Bank. (2016). *World Development Report 2016: Learning to Realize Education's Promise*. Washington, DC: The World Bank.

World Bank. (2018). *World Development Indicators*. Available at https://data.worldbank.org/indicator/SG.GEN.PARL.ZS

World Economic Forum. (2016). *The Future of Jobs: Employment, Skills and Workforce Strategy for the Fourth Industrial Revolution*. Retrieved August 27, 2018 from https://www.weforum.org/reports/the-future-of-jobs

World Economic Forum. (2016a). *The Future of Jobs: Employment, Skills and Workforce Strategy for the Fourth Industrial Revolution*. Retrieved August 27, 2018 from https://www.weforum.org/reports/the-future-of-jobs

World Economic Forum. (2016b). *What role will education play in the Fourth Industrial Revolution?* Retrieved May 9, 2019 from https://www.weforum.org/agenda/2016/01/what-role-will-education-play-in-the-fourth-industrial-revolution/

World Economic Forum. (2017). Available: http://www3.weforum.org/docs/WEF_Future_of_Jobs.pdf

World Economic Forum. (2017). *System Innovative on Shaping the Future of Education Gender and Work*. Retrieved August 27, 2018 from https://www.weforum.org/systeminitiatives/shaping-the-future-of-education-gender-and-work

World Economic Forum. (2018). *The Future of Jobs Report 2018*. Geneva: Centre for the New Economy and Society, World Economic Forum.

World Gender Development Report. (2012). *World Economic Forum*. The Global Gender Gap Report.

Worrall, J. (1989). Structural realism: The best of both worlds? *Dialectica*, *43*(1-2), 99–124. doi:10.1111/j.1746-8361.1989.tb00933.x

Wren, D. A., & Bedeian, A. G. (2009). *The evolution of management thought*. Hoboken, NJ: John Wiley & Sons.

Wright, D. (2005). *The Ultimate Guide to Competency Assessment in Healthcare* (3rd ed.). Minneapolis, MN: Creative Health Care Management.

Wright, P., & Geroy, D. G. (2001). Changing the mindset: The training myth and the need for word-class performance. *International Journal of Human Resource Management*, *12*(4), 586–600. doi:10.1080/09585190122342

Xie, A., & Huang, X. (2012). *Advances in computer science and education*. London: Springer. doi:10.1007/978-3-642-27945-4

Xue, Y., Greener, E., Kannan, V., Smith, J. A., Brewer, C., & Spetz, J. (2018). Federally qualified health centers reduce the primary care provider gap in health professional shortage counties. *Nursing Outlook*, *66*(3), 263–272. doi:10.1016/j.outlook.2018.02.003 PMID:29685322

Yang, B., & Wang, X. (2009). Successes and challenges of developing human capital in the People's Republic of China. *Human Resource Development International*, *12*(1), 3–14. doi:10.1080/13678860802638784

Yener, M. I., Gurbuz, F. G., & Acar, P. (2017). Development and validation of a talent management measurement instrument. *Journal of Business Economics and Finance*, *6*(3), 233–245.

Yusubova, A., Andries, P., & Clarysse, B. (2019). The role of incubators in overcoming technology ventures' resource gaps at different development stages. *R & D Management*, radm.12378. doi:10.1111/radm.12378

Zhang, X., Tai, D., Pforsich, H., & Lin, V. W. (2018). United States registered nurse's workforce report card and shortage forecast: A revisit. *American Journal of Medical Quality*, *33*(3), 229–236. doi:10.1177/1062860617738328 PMID:29183169

Zhu, W., Chew, I., & Spangler, W. (2005). CEO transformational leadership and organizational outcomes: The mediating role of human-capital-enhancing human resource management. *The Leadership Quarterly*, *16*(1), 39–52. doi:10.1016/j.leaqua.2004.06.001

About the Contributors

Sulaiman Olusegun Atiku is currently a Senior Lecturer (Human Resource Management) at Harold Pupkewitz Graduate School of Business (HP-GSB), Namibia University of Science and Technology, Namibia. He is a pragmatic researcher specializing in Human Capital Formation for the Fourth Industrial Revolution, and Green Human Resource Management. He has over 11 years' experience in Higher Education. A native of Lagos, Sulaiman graduated from the University of KwaZulu-Natal with a PhD degree in Human Resource Management. The author acquired his Masters of Science degree in Human Resource Management and Industrial Relations at the Lagos State University, Nigeria. His Bachelor of Science (Honours) degree was also awarded at the Lagos State University in the field of Industrial Relations and Personnel Management. He has lectured several courses in his field home/abroad and published many scholarly articles in international journals. He is a member of the International Labour and Employment Relations Association (ILERA), Nigerian Institute of Management (NIM), Certified Institute of Warehousing and Materials Management (CIWM), and Institute of People Management (IPM) South Africa.

* * *

Richard Afedzie is a senior lecturer at Pentecost University College in Accra, Ghana. He is a lecturer in Business Management, specifically in Human Resource Development. He has been teaching since 2012 and teaches courses in Change Management, Organisational Development and Introduction to Management at both the graduate level and undergraduate level.

Sulaiman Olusegun Atiku is currently a Senior Lecturer (Human Resource Management) at Harold Pupkewitz Graduate School of Business (HP-GSB), Namibia University of Science and Technology, Namibia. He is a pragmatic researcher specializing in Human Capital Formation for the Fourth Industrial Revolution, and Green Human Resource Management. He has over 11 years' experience in Higher Education. A native of Lagos, Sulaiman graduated from the University of KwaZulu-

Natal with a PhD degree in Human Resource Management. The author acquired his Masters of Science degree in Human Resource Management and Industrial Relations at the Lagos State University, Nigeria. His Bachelor of Science (Honours) degree was also awarded at the Lagos State University in the field of Industrial Relations and Personnel Management. He has lectured several courses in his field home/abroad and published many scholarly articles in international journals. He is a member of the International Labour and Employment Relations Association (ILERA), Nigerian Institute of Management (NIM), Certified Institute of Warehousing and Materials Management (CIWM), and Institute of People Management (IPM) South Africa.

Ayansola Ayandibu holds a B.Sc Hons in Accounting, Masters of Business Administration and also a Ph.D in Leadership Studies. He has worked in the co-operate environment for 8 years in Nigeria before relocating to South Africa. Dr. Ayandibu worked for Lieutanant Consulting, Midrand, Johannesburg in 2012 as an Accountant / Economist. He has been lecturing at University of KwaZulu Natal since February, 2013 till date in the Discipline of Management and Entrepreneurship. Ayansola has lectured Accounting, Management and Entrepreneurship modules in the University Of KwaZulu Natal. He has also published articles in accredited journals. Dr. Ayandibu has attended international conferences in the University of London, UK, Harvard University (USA) and Ryerson University, Totonto Canada. Dr. Ayandibu is presently a Post Doctoral Fellow in the Department of Business Management, University of Zululand. He also lectures in the same department He has supervised many Honours student. He is currently supervising Honours, Masters and Ph.D students. Dr. Ayansola Ayandibu is a member of South African Institute of Management (SAIM), South African Institute of Business Accountants (SAIBA) and Institute of Chartered Economist of Nigeria (ICEN).

Neeta Baporikar is currently Professor (Business Management) at Harold Pupkewitz Graduate School of Business (HP-GSB), Namibia University of Science and Technology, Namibia. Prior to this she was Head-Scientific Research, with Ministry of Higher Education CAS-Salalah, Sultanate of Oman, Professor (Strategic Management and Entrepreneurship) at IIIT Pune and BITS India. With more than a decade of experience in industry, consultancy and training, she made a lateral switch to research and academics in 1995. Dr. Baporikar holds D.Sc. (Management Studies) USA, PhD in Management, University of Pune INDIA with MBA (Distinction) and Law (Hons.) degrees. Apart from this, she is also an External Reviewer, Oman Academic Accreditation Authority, Accredited Management Teacher, Qualified Trainer, Doctoral Guide and Board Member of Academics and Advisory Committee in accredited B-Schools. Reviewer for international journals, she has to her credit several conferred doctorates, refereed research papers, and authored books in the area of Entrepreneurship, Strategy, Management and Higher Education.

Frank Boateng is a Chartered Manager and a Fellow of the Chartered Management Institute in the UK. He is a Chartered Public Administrator and a Chartered Management Consultant with the Chartered Institute of Administrators and Management Consultants of Ghana. He holds a Ph.D. in Management from Walden University in Minnesota USA and a Master of Philosophy in Business Consulting and Enterprise Risk Management from Kwame Nkrumah University of Science and Technology in Ghana, an MBA in Finance from the University of Leicester Business School in UK and a Bachelor of Science in Business Administration with Accounting option from the Central University Business School in Ghana. Dr Boateng has over eighteen years experience in the Mining Industry and has occupied positions from Assistant Accountant, Senior Accountant, Accounts Payables Manager, Senior Business Analyst, Financial Controller, Finance & Administration Manager, Commercial Manager, Country Managing Director and Group CEO. He serves as advisor and Board Member to Boards in Ghana and United States of America. Currently,Dr Boateng is a Faculty Member of the Faculty of Integrated Management Science at University of Mines and Technology, Tarkwa and a Director at Brickwater Associates, a firm of Chartered Accountants

Darrell Norman Burrell is a leadership coach with the Asian American Government Executive Network (AAGEN) and a guest lecturer with the Hispanic-Serving Health Professions Schools (HSHPS) organizations. He is a certified executive coach and a certified diversity professional. He is an alumnus of the prestigious Presidential Management Fellows Program www.pmf.gov. Dr. Burrell also has over 8 years of US federal government service with US Nuclear Regulatory Commission. In 2016, Dr. Burrell completed a Master of Arts in Interfaith Action at Claremont Lincoln University as a Global Peacemaker Fellow where he engaged in research on diversity and inclusion in the workplace as it relates to religion. Dr Burrell has a doctorate degree with majors in Education and Executive Leadership Coaching from A.T. Still University. Dr. Burrell has an Education Specialist (EdS) graduate degree in Higher Education Administration from The George Washington University. He has two graduate degrees one in Human Resources Management/Development and another Organizational Management from National Louis University. He also has a Master of Arts degree in Sales and Marketing Management from Prescott College.

Terrence Duncan is a Divisional Director of Safety and WC and provides quality enterprise risk management solutions to 40 skilled nursing facilities and assisted living communities in four states. Such duties include the management and direction of worker's compensation claims, litigation management, fleet safety management, consultation and recommendations regarding ADA and FMLA in conjunction with Human Resources, negotiation of worker's compensation claims, and OSHA loss control audits. Conducted over 300 loss control audits to provide guidance and recommendations to prepare for any potential OSHA audits and Life Safety Surveys. Provides education and leadership training at the field level, as well as provide guidance and recommendations to other Divisional and Regional leadership.

Benneth Eze lectures at the department of Business Administration, Hallmark University, Nigeria. Their research interests include Entrepreneurship and management.

Tinuke Fapohunda is an Associate Professor in the Department of Industrial Relations and Personnel Management at the Lagos State University, Ojo. She holds a Ph. D in Industrial Education. She has been an Associate Member, of the Institute of Personnel Management of Nigeria (2003), a Fellow of the Certified Institute of Shipping of Nigeria since 2005 and a member, Academy of Management Sciences since 2006. Prior to joining the services of the Lagos State University she worked as a Research Assistant with the Nigerian Institute of Social and Economic Research (NISER). She has taught many courses at university level since then. She has a rich experience in teaching, research and consulting.

Martin Fero, PhD. – senior lecturer, researcher and sociologist focused on sociology of organization and labour, work competences, youth and intergenerational differences in the workplace. Expert skills in quantitative research and IBM SPSS Statistics analytical software. Member of the Committee of the Slovak Sociological Association by the Slovak Academy of Sciences and chairman of the Department of Sociology of Organization and Labour of the Slovak Sociological Association by the Slovak Academy of Sciences. Involved in several international research projects: Work competencies in the context of Industry 4.0, Impact of coexistence of different generations on the organization's sustainable performance, Research-based analysis of the EU Programme Youth in Action, RAY study on learning in Youth in Action.

Helena Fidlerová, Ph.D., works as senior researcher at Faculty of Materials Science and Technology in Trnava, Institute of Industrial Engineering and Management in the field of Industrial Engineering. She graduated in field Management and Quality and finished her PhD. study in the field Industrial Management with PhD thesis Environmental Process Model of Logistics in Strategic Business. Units in 2006 and since her study has extensive experience in domestic research projects VEGA, KEGA and international projects (bilateral cooperation INTERREG

Austria –Slovakia- ALTECS, Visegradfund cooperation Her key competences are issues of sustainable development, competences, industrial engineering, sustainable logistics, integrated management systems and the application of statistical methods in practice. She has written several monographs and chapters of monographs, 12 publications indexed in Scopus and WOS. Overall, having more than 58 domestic and international responses, including 17 in WOS/Scopus.

Kennedy D. Gunawardena is a professor of Accounting Information Systems at the department of Accounting, University of Sri Jayewardenepura, Sri Lanka. In addition to being the professor of Accounting in his department, He is the chairman of the Board of studies and Coordinator of the PhD in management program of Management, faculty of Management studies and commerce in the same university. He teaches Cost and Management Accounting, Accounting Information Systems, Artificial Neural Networks for Accounting and Research Methodology in Accounting and finance for the undergraduates and Postgraduates students.

Gary Hanney is an Assistant Professor/Healthcare Manager with extensive experience achieving excellent results in training, mentoring, customer service, leadership and accountability, conflict resolution, qualitative and quantitative analysis, economic analysis and management theories, applications and practice. Has an excellent track record of outstanding employee relationship, budgeting, public relations and oral/written communication.

Irrshad Kaseeram is an Associate Professor and Deputy Dean of Research at the University of Zululand, South Africa. He is a senior member of the Department of Economics and has over a decade of teaching experience in undergraduate and postgraduate Economics. His research interests include Macroeconometrics and Microeconomics modelling in studying development issues, and he has published extensively in these areas.

Joseph Nketia, Ph.D., CPA, is an Assistant Professor of Accounting at the The Bill Munday School of Business. Prior to joining the faculty at St. Edward's University, Joe was an adjunct accounting instructor at the University of Texas at Dallas teaching business valuation. He has over 12 years corporate experience in fund reporting and business valuation. His corporate experiences have mainly been in the area of financial statement analysis, internal controls for small business, business valuation, financial statements preparation and reporting. He has previously worked for one of the top four accounting firms and one of the largest investment management firms in the United States. Professor Nketia's research interest includes quality financial reporting (earnings management), corporate governance, capital market, business valuation and small business operations.

Ivana Novotná is the senior assistant at the Centre of Languages, Humanities and Academic Sport at Slovak University of Technology in Bratislava, Faculty of Materials Science and Technology in Trnava, where she holds a position of a deputy head. She teaches Introduction to Cognitive Sciences. In the past she taught Sociology of Work, Industrial Sociology and Entrepreneur Studies. Her research focuses on Industry 4.0 and investigating the coexistence interactions between generations of employees. She has written research paper "Significance of Coaching in the Context of Emotion regulation" (with Jarmila Blahová and Sláva Šatanková), "Slovak related students at technical universities in the Czech Republic, 1918-1939" (with Milan Petráš et al.), "Fundamentals of Sociology" (with Andrej Rajský), "Mental Hygiene" (with Jarmila Blahová and Zuzana Porubčanová), "Intensity and the way of using on-line digital media within the context of off-line reality of the young" (with Jarmila Blahová and Martin Fero).

Paul Adjei Onyina is a Senior Lecturer and the Dean of Faculty of Business Administration of the Pentecost University College, Accra Ghana. He obtained his PhD in Economics from Macquarie University, Sydney Australia. He had earlier attended the University of Ghana, Legon and obtained his Master of Philosophy in Economics degrees and the Bachelor of Arts (Economic with Geography). He worked with Ghana Statistical Service before joining the pioneers in starting the Pentecost University College early 2005. As part of ensuring time tested faculty for the University College, he was granted a study leave to further his studies at where he obtained his PhD in Economics. He has been speaking at various conferences locally and internationally on development economics issues. His specialization is in microfinance, impact analysis on policies that target the poor and vulnerable in society. He is married to Lydia and is blessed with three children- Akosua, Kwadwo and Yaw.

Martina Porubčinová, PhD. is a sociologist. She finished her PhD. study in the field of prognostics at Institute for Forecasting of the Slovak Academy of Sciences in Bratislava. Since 2002 she works as a researcher at Slovak Academy of Sciences. Her research interest is focused on Information society, digital literacy, labor market and human capital development. She has participated in several research projects (VEGA, APVV, project FP7-SSH-2011-2). .

Adelekan Saidi is a Lecturer at Mountain Top University, Ogun State. He started his academic career from Tai Solarin College of Education (TASCE), and obtained his Nigeria Certificate in Education (NCE). He went further to continue his educational career at Lagos State University, Ojo, where he bagged B.Sc. Economics. Dr. Adedeji Adelekan did his first Master Degree, M.Sc. in Management at the University of Lagos, Akoka. In 2012 he added another feather to his cap when he got another Master degree, M.Sc. in Environmental Resources Management (ERM) at the Lagos State University, Ojo. In continuation of his quest for more knowledge, he enrolled for his Ph.D. in Management and Entrepreneurship at the University of KwaZulu-Natal, Durban, South Africa and successfully completed it in September, 2017. He has attended several conferences, workshops, and seminars both at national and international levels (e.g. 21st century academic Forum Conference at Harvard University, USA in 2016 and Annual South Africa Business Research Conference, at Cape Town, South Africa, 2017 and the 6th Academic International Conference on Business, Marketing and Management, at University of Cambridge, United Kingdom, May, 2018). He has over the years consulted for several organizations in the areas of entrepreneurship and business development. He has published about 20 academic article and 2 books in both local and international journals. He is a Fellow Institute of Managerial Economists of Nigeria, member Nigeria Institute of Training and Development (NITAD) and Member Institute of Business Strategy (MIBS).

Mustafa Kemal Topcu holds Ph.D. degree in defense management and MBA degree. His graduate is B.Sc. in system engineering. He studied moderating role of psychological contract in human capital productivity in his doctoral dissertation. He is currently strategic and technologic product development mentor for SMEs. He is also certified government audit professional (class A) and mentor accredited by European Mentoring & Coaching Council. He mentored Afghan Army and experienced joint and common operations, working with NATO, UN, ISAF, South Eastern Brigade, and US Army in addition to national positions in defense planning units of Turkish Armed Forces. He writes, trains, and consults on corporate governance, internal control, internal audit, defense management, corporate social responsibility, organizational development, project management, management and organizational studies, industrial psychology, strategic planning, human resources management, and change management. He lectures management and organization, human resources management courses at undergraduate and graduate levels. He is a member of international scientific committee of Conference on Defense Resources Management (National Defense University of Romania). He is fluent at English. He is married with Sibel Topcu and has two sons.

Index

E

F

G

H

I

J

K

L

M

N

O

P

R

S

T

V

W

www.ingramcontent.com/pod-product-compliance
Lightning Source LLC
LaVergne TN
LVHW080607300926
849162LV00005B/1072
9781522598107